ANARCHISM

Anarchism is by far the least broadly understood ideology and the least studied academically. Though highly influential, both historically and in terms of recent social movements, anarchism is regularly dismissed. *Anarchism: A Conceptual Approach* is a welcome addition to this growing field, which is widely debated but poorly understood.

Occupying a distinctive position in the study of anarchist ideology, this volume – authored by a handpicked group of established and rising scholars – investigates how anarchists often seek to sharpen their message and struggle to determine what ideas and actions are central to their identity. Moving beyond defining anarchism as simply an ideology or political theory, this book examines the meanings of its key concepts, which have been divided into three categories: Core, Adjacent, and Peripheral concepts. Each chapter focuses on one important concept, shows how anarchists have understood the concept, and highlights its relationships to other concepts.

Although anarchism is often thought of as a political topic, the interdisciplinary nature of *Anarchism: A Conceptual Approach* makes it of interest to students and scholars across the social sciences, liberal arts, and the humanities.

Benjamin Franks is Lecturer in Social and Political Philosophy at the University of Glasgow's Dumfries campus. He is the author of *Rebel Alliances* and co-editor of *Anarchism and Moral Philosophy*. His work has appeared in *The Journal of Political Ideologies*, *Capital and Class*, and *Anarchist Studies*.

Nathan Jun is Associate Professor and Coordinator of the Philosophy Program at Midwestern State University. He is the author of *Anarchism and Political Modernity*. He has published several edited volumes and journal articles on political theory, the history of political thought, and contemporary European philosophy.

Leonard Williams is Professor of Political Science at Manchester University in North Manchester, Indiana. He is the author of *American Liberalism and Ideological Change*. His writings on anarchism have appeared in *New Political Science*, the *Journal for the Study of Radicalism*, and *Anarchist Developments in Cultural Studies*.

'This path-breaking book, with its multiple yet integrated perspectives and insights, is by far the most sophisticated analysis to have been written on anarchism as an ideology. It sets a new standard for understanding and analyzing anarchism's complexities and nuances that all future scholarship on the subject will have to respect and incorporate.'

Michael Freeden, *Emeritus Professor of Politics, University of Oxford*

'Franks, Jun, and Williams' pioneering application of Michael Freeden's approach to ideology gives us a rigorous, sharp, and fresh account of anarchism. Showing how anarchists have interpreted key concepts, contributors to the volume explain the distinctiveness of anarchist analysis, exploding some entrenched myths about the inconsistencies of anarchist political thought in the process. The editors' arrangement of these contributions creates an invigorating picture of anarchist ideology. If it's possible to imagine alternative conceptual mappings, it is because they have demonstrated how anarchism can be constructed and re-constructed in its own terms.'

Ruth Kinna, *Professor of Political Theory, Loughborough University*

'This book provides both a vision of anarchism as a distinct political ideology as well as describing the current debates in anarchist thought and practice. On top of being useful to those engaged in anarchist studies and research it will be very useful for those interested in political ideologies and philosophy more widely.'

Jon Bigger, *anarchist activist, writer and researcher*

ANARCHISM

A Conceptual Approach

Edited by Benjamin Franks, Nathan Jun, and Leonard Williams

NEW YORK AND LONDON

First published 2018
by Routledge
711 Third Avenue, New York, NY 10017

and by Routledge
2 Park Square, Milton Park, Abingdon, Oxon OX14 4RN

Routledge is an imprint of the Taylor & Francis Group, an informa business

© 2018 Taylor & Francis

The right of Benjamin Franks, Nathan Jun, and Leonard Williams to be identified as the authors of the editorial material, and of the authors for their individual chapters, has been asserted in accordance with sections 77 and 78 of the Copyright, Designs and Patents Act 1988.

All rights reserved. No part of this book may be reprinted or reproduced or utilised in any form or by any electronic, mechanical, or other means, now known or hereafter invented, including photocopying and recording, or in any information storage or retrieval system, without permission in writing from the publishers.

Trademark notice: Product or corporate names may be trademarks or registered trademarks, and are used only for identification and explanation without intent to infringe.

Library of Congress Cataloging in Publication Data
Names: Franks, Benjamin, editor. | Jun, Nathan J., 1979- editor. | Williams, Leonard A., 1952- editor.
Title: Anarchism : a conceptual analysis / edited by Benjamin Franks, Nathan Jun, and Leonard Williams.
Description: New York, NY : Routledge, 2018. | Includes bibliographical references and index.
Identifiers: LCCN 2017044519 | ISBN 9781138925656 (hardback) | ISBN 9781138925663 (pbk.) | ISBN 9781317406815 (epub) | ISBN 9781317406808 (mobipocket/kindle)
Subjects: LCSH: Anarchism.
Classification: LCC HX833 .A5683 2018 | DDC 335/.83--dc23
LC record available at https://lccn.loc.gov/2017044519

ISBN: 978-1-138-92565-6 (hbk)
ISBN: 978-1-138-92566-3 (pbk)
ISBN: 978-1-315-68365-2 (ebk)

Typeset in Bembo
by Taylor & Francis Books
Printed and bound by CPI Group (UK) Ltd, Croydon, CR0 4YY

CONTENTS

List of tables vii
List of contributors viii
Acknowledgements xii

Introduction 1
Benjamin Franks, Nathan Jun, and Leonard Williams

PART 1
Core Concepts 13

1 Anti-Hierarchy 15
  Randall Amster

2 Prefiguration 28
  Benjamin Franks

3 Freedom 44
  Nathan Jun

4 Agency 60
  David Bates

5 Direct Action 74
  Vicente Ordóñez

6 Revolution 86
  Uri Gordon

PART 2
Adjacent Concepts   99

  7 Horizontalism   101
       Mark Bray

  8 Organisation   115
       Iain McKay

  9 Micropolitics   129
       Laura Portwood-Stacer

10 Economy   142
       Deric Shannon

PART 3
Peripheral Concepts   155

11 Intersectionality   157
       Hillary Lazar

12 Reform   175
       Leonard Williams

13 Work   188
       Ekaterina Chertkovskaya and Konstantin Stoborod

14 DIY   203
       Sandra Jeppesen

15 Ecocentrism   219
       Sean Parson

Index   *234*

TABLES

I.1 The Two Modes of Decontestation. 6

CONTRIBUTORS

Randall Amster is Director and Teaching Professor in the Program on Justice and Peace at Georgetown University, and serves as Editor-in-Chief of the *Contemporary Justice Review*. His books include *Peace Ecology* (Routledge, 2015), *Anarchism Today* (Praeger, 2012), and *Lost in Space: The Criminalization, Globalization, and Urban Ecology of Homelessness* (LFB, 2008).

David Bates is a Principal Lecturer and Director of Politics and International Relations at Canterbury Christ Church University. His research is concerned with two key areas: first, contemporary social and political theory, with specific reference to the Marxist and anarchist 'traditions'; second, the theoretical underpinnings of contemporary social movements.

Mark Bray is a historian of Modern Europe and a political organizer. He is the author *of Antifa: The Anti-Fascist Handbook* and *Translating Anarchy: The Anarchism of Occupy Wall Street* as well as the co-editor of *Anarchist Education and the Modern School: A Francisco Ferrer Reader*. Currently he is a lecturer at Dartmouth College.

Ekaterina Chertkovskaya is a researcher in degrowth and critical organization studies based at Lund University. Critiques of modern forms of work and consumption, as well as the possibilities of organising them in line with degrowth, are some of the central themes of her work. She is also a member of the editorial collective of *ephemera: theory & politics in organization* – an independent open access journal.

Benjamin Franks is the Lecturer in Social and Political Philosophy at the University of Glasgow's Dumfries campus. He is the author of *Rebel Alliances: The*

Means and Ends of Contemporary British Anarchisms (AK Press) and co-editor of *Anarchism and Moral Philosophy* (Palgrave Macmillan). His work has appeared in *The Journal of Political Ideologies*, *Capital and Class*, and *Anarchist Studies*. He has also contributed to *Black Flag* and *Class War*.

Uri Gordon is Assistant Professor in Political Theory at the University of Nottingham, and co-convener of the Anarchist Studies Network. He holds a DPhil from the University of Oxford and has previously taught at Loughborough University and the Arava Institute for Environmental Studies. He is the author of *Anarchy Alive! Anti-Authoritarian Politics from Practice to Theory* (Pluto Press, 2008) and has published in *Social Movement Studies*, *The Journal of Political Ideologies*, *Antipode*, and *Peace and Change*, among others. His research uses participatory methods to produce political theory with activists in radical environmental, social justice, and anti-militarist movements. Uri is also co-editor of the monograph series *Contemporary Anarchist Studies* (Manchester University Press) and the forthcoming *Routledge Handbook of Radical Politics*. His work has been translated into 13 languages.

Sandra Jeppesen researches with autonomous media and anti-authoritarian social movements from an intersectional queer, trans*, feminist, anti-racist, anti-capitalist, and anti-colonial perspective. She is co-founder of the Media Action Research Group (MARG, mediaactionresearch.org), and was a member of the former *Collectif de Recherche sur l'Autonomie Collective* (CRAC) in Montreal. Currently she is an Associate Professor in Interdisciplinary Studies/Media Studies at Lakehead University, Orillia, Canada, where she also holds the Lakehead University Research Chair in Transformative Media and Social Movements.

Nathan Jun is Associate Professor and Coordinator of the Philosophy Program at Midwestern State University. He is the author of *Anarchism and Political Modernity* (2012); the editor of *Brill's Companion to Anarchism and Philosophy* (2017) and *Proletarian Days: A Hippolyte Havel Reader* (forthcoming); and co-editor of *Revolutionary Hope: Essays in Honor of William L. McBride* (with Shane Wahl, 2013), *Without Borders or Limits: An Interdisciplinary Approach to Anarchist Studies* (with Jorell Meléndez Badillo, 2013), *Deleuze and Ethics* (with Daniel Smith, 2011), and *New Perspectives on Anarchism* (with Shane Wahl, 2010).

Hillary Lazar is a doctoral candidate in Sociology at the University of Pittsburgh, where she teaches about social movements, gender, and power and resistance. She also holds an MA in US and World History from San Francisco State University. She is currently researching personal transformation in prefigurative spaces and focuses on anarchism in contemporary mobilizations. Hillary has been published in *Perspectives on Anarchist Theory* and worked on several book projects including *Emma Goldman: A Documentary History of the American Years*. She is a collective member of the Big Idea Bookstore and a content editor for Agency: An Anarchist PR Project and is part of the efforts to organize graduate student workers.

Iain McKay is an independent anarchist writer and researcher. He has produced *An Anarchist FAQ*, *Mutual Aid: An Introduction and Evaluation* as well as editing and introducing *Property is Theft! A Pierre-Joseph Proudhon Anthology* and *Direct Struggle Against Capital: A Peter Kropotkin Anthology* (all published by AK Press). He has written for *Anarchist Studies*, *Black Flag*, *Freedom*, and *Anarcho-Syndicalist Review* as well as anarchist websites (primarily *Anarchist Writers*). He most recent project is making Kropotkin's 1913 book *Modern Science and Anarchy* available in English for the first time (forthcoming from AK Press in 2018).

Vicente Ordóñez completed his Ph.D. in Philosophy at the University of Valencia (Spain). He is currently Lecturer in Social and Political Philosophy at the Jaume I University and Visiting Fellow at the Centre for Applied Philosophy, Politics and Ethics of the University of Brighton. His book *El ridículo como instrumento político* [The political uses of ridicule] (2015) has been awarded with the first prize by the Complutense University of Madrid National Essay Prize. He is working on the research project "El potencial de las éticas aplicadas en las herramientas de participación del Gobierno Abierto y de la sociedad civil" – uji-a2016–04.

Sean Parson is an assistant professor in the departments of Politics and International Affairs and the MA program in Sustainable Communities at Northern Arizona University. He is finishing up a book manuscript *Cooking Up a Revolution: Food Not Bombs, Homes Not Jails, and Resistance to Gentrification* and has three edited volumes that should be released in early 2018. He is currently working on a book length project on horror, climate change, and nihilism on what he is calling the Cthulhuscene. When not writing and grading, he mostly spends time hiking the mountains with his four-legged best friend Diego.

Laura Portwood-Stacer is an independent scholar and developmental editor. She is the author of *Lifestyle Politics and Radical Activism* (Bloomsbury, 2013), an ethnographic study of subcultural practices within the US anarchist movement.

Deric Shannon is a former line cook, cashier, and fast food worker, now an associate professor of sociology at Emory University's Oxford College. His work largely focuses on political economy, food, social theory, and ecology. His peer-reviewed work has appeared in *Educational Studies*, *Qualitative Report*, *Critical Sociology*, *Sexualities*, *Peace Studies Journal*, and *Theory in Action*. He has edited, co-edited, and co-authored six books, and his work has been translated into Spanish, Turkish, and Polish. He is currently working on his first single-authored monograph, *Eating: Adventures in the Sociology of Being Human*, and a co-authored book with Davita Silfen Glasberg and Abbey S. Willis, *The State of State Theory: State Projects, Repression, and Multi-Sites of Power*.

Konstantin Stoborod is a research associate at University of Leicester. His research is in the areas of critical theory of organization, alternative organizing, and psychoanalysis. He is a member of the editorial collective of the open access journal *ephemera: theory & politics in organization*. Before joining the collective he co-edited *Ephemera*'s special issue 'Management, Business, Anarchism' on various aspects of intersection of anarchist thought and management theory.

Leonard Williams is Professor of Political Science at Manchester University in North Manchester, Indiana. He is the author of *American Liberalism and Ideological Change* and co-editor of *Political Theory: Classic and Contemporary Readings*. His writings on anarchism have appeared in *New Political Science*, the *Journal for the Study of Radicalism*, and *Anarchist Developments in Cultural Studies*.

ACKNOWLEDGEMENTS

The editors wish to express their gratitude to Natalja Mortensen, Maria Landschoot, and Lillian Rand of Routledge for their patience and helpfulness in bringing this volume to publication; to the co-ordinators of the 3rd Anarchist Studies Network Conference at Loughborough University for providing space for the stream of panels on conceptual approaches to anarchism, and in particular, to Elizabet Vasileva for her efficient and patient assistance; to the contributors for their hard work and dedication to the project; to various colleagues who provided helpful comments and peer review; and finally, to Michael Freeden for his inspiring and influential work.

INTRODUCTION

Benjamin Franks, Nathan Jun, and Leonard Williams

Michael Freeden's (1996) morphological approach to studying ideologies focuses on how major ideologies are based on the decontested meanings of political concepts. The approach builds on two basic assumptions – that people think about politics in patterned ways and that political thinking has a conceptual structure. Given that most political concepts are essentially contested, any given ideology develops from certain shared understandings of those concepts. Conceptual meaning is thus decontested – made fixed or stable, but only temporarily – within a given ideological context.

This approach to analyzing ideologies traces how decontested concepts exist in particular constellations or clusters within any given ideological family. The general morphological structure consists of three types of concepts – core, adjacent, and peripheral (Freeden 1996, 77–82; 2013, 124–126). Core concepts are the enduring and indispensable ones; they are the concepts that provide an ideology with its essential identity, with the views that separate it from other perspectives. Adjacent concepts provide additional nuance and anchoring for some of the core concepts; they help give a bit of specificity and context for core concepts. Peripheral concepts are those that provide an ideology with the flexibility it needs to adapt to changing circumstances; they are tied to particular times and places, to the concerns of the moment.

In the context of this structure of meaning, various kinds of relationships among an ideology's concepts are possible. Noteworthy relationships include what Freeden (2003, 60–66) calls "the four Ps": (1) *proximity* – the ability of concepts to define each other; (2) *priority* – core versus periphery; (3) *permeability* – the extent to which ideologies intersect and overlap; and (4) *proportionality* – the relative space or attention to particular issues given by the ideology. In the context of both structure and relationships, the morphological approach enables one to tell both synchronic and diachronic stories about the development of any given ideology.

Freeden's method differs from other approaches used by political philosophers and theorists interested in anarchism. Freeden distinguishes his conceptual approach from analytical philosophy, which, in some forms examines anarchism in terms of universal principles tested through logical analysis for consistency and defended through argumentative rigor. Robert P. Wolff's (1976) account develops a "philosophical anarchism" based on the single supreme value of rejecting all coercion. As such, it provides a very thin description of anarchism. Paul McLaughlin (2007, 29) by contrast identifies anarchism through two wider universal characteristics: a) a principled skepticism toward all forms of authority, especially, but not solely, state authority and b) a commitment to eradicating illegitimate forms of authority.

There are problems with this analytical approach to anarchism. First, in the case of Wolff – and those who follow him, like Dudley Knowles (2001; 2007) and A. John Simmons (1987; 1996) – the approach ignores the accounts of anarchism by actual anarchist movements and thus misrepresents the ideology in favor of an academic construction. Further, the analytic approach by concentrating on identifying universal characteristics overlooks the ways that ideologies develop historically and in distinctive locations. In addition, analytical philosophy's stress on logical consistency mischaracterizes ideologies, which often have contradictory – albeit constrained – features that are necessary for them to function. The tendency to overstress logical consistency occurs as the analytic approach tends to check each principle in abstract against the others and highlight areas of disagreement and conflict. The conceptual approach, by examining constituent concepts as mutual parts of an ideological cluster identifies how each concept is understood in relation to the others (proximity) and conflicts are diminished by their priority.[1] By utilizing Freeden's morphological approach, the authors in this volume describe the changing priority and proportionality of the concepts, highlight their proximity to each other with frequent cross-referencing to other pivotal concepts, and discuss the relative permeability of these concepts with other ideological clusters.

There are other, useful, theoretical approaches to developing the understanding of key ideologies or cultural phenomena. The canonical *Dictionary of Marxist Thought* produced by Tom Bottomore et al. (1983) provides often detailed, expert explanations of major terms and theoretical developments within Marxism. Despite its brevity and its Leninist leanings, the entry on anarchism by Geoffrey Ostergaard (1983) is largely supportive and knowledgeable, though largely concerned with anarchism's relationship to Marxism. However, because it covers hundreds of concepts and theorists, the book's breadth makes it hard to discern which takes greatest priority – even the length of entries is not a necessary mark of importance to political movements rather than to theoretical debates. In many cases, unlike in conceptual-morphological analysis, the

Dictionary's concentration is on exegetic analysis of Marx's true meaning, rather than how concepts, theories, and ideologies are interpreted by the movements that use them.

Raymond Williams' (1976) highly influential work in radical cultural studies, *Keywords* – which oddly is not referred to by Freeden in his main morphological works – identifies the social impacts of contested cultural terms.[2] Williams traces the changes in meanings of contested terms diachronically and synchronically, and notes how they are sites of conflict. Williams rightly identified the contested nature of core concepts, however, unlike the morphological approach, he underplays the ways in which ideologies attempt to decontest them. Similarly, there is little cross-referencing to other proximate terms that provide the means for temporarily fixing meanings in order to provide a guide for action. Williams' work, although highly political, nevertheless focuses on cultural developments rather than political movements per se. So, whilst major ideologies are covered, including anarchism, their accounts are short. Like Ostergaard in the *Dictionary*, Williams is not unsympathetic in his description of anarchism, but also largely locates it in relation to Marxism – which, in its later manifestations, Williams considers as having incorporated anarchism's main features.

Although the conceptual-morphological approach has been used by Freeden and other scholars to distinguish the familiar generic ideologies, anarchism has not yet been given a full-scale, book-length treatment. Certainly, the nature of anarchism as ideology or political theory makes such a treatment difficult. Insofar as particular anarchists resist being pigeonholed or having their views taken as representative of the whole, the varieties of anarchism are legion. Further, contemporary anarchists (theorists and activists alike) have regarded anarchism not as a settled point of view, a theory per se, but rather as a set of commonly used practices and actions. Because its approach to politics is not like the others, and because its adherents resist being saddled with the status of an ideology, anarchism has not been given the same treatment as liberalism or conservatism, say. Yet, despite the assertions of some activists, anarchism does indeed serve them as a guiding perspective, as a political theory, as an ideology. As such, it seems appropriate to analyze it morphologically.

One reason for doing so is to better understand the underlying values of anarchism. Many contemporary theorists of anarchism have suggested that it is fundamentally an ethical point of view, but the grounds of that ethic are often left unstated and unspecified. A morphological analysis of anarchism would provide the conceptual underpinnings for such ethical claims. A second reason for studying anarchism using Freeden's perspective is that conceptual analysis within the anarchist tradition is still rather underdeveloped. In other volumes in which anarchists engage in conceptual analysis, the only concept that ever seems to be under review is "anarchism" itself. Such an approach assumes what should be the result, namely, an understanding of the core ideas of anarchism. This brings us to the final reason for developing the morphology of anarchism. Doing so will help anarchists manage the boundary problem that currently confronts them. With anti-statist attitudes – attitudes that have long been central to the anarchist tradition – becoming prominent on the economic and political right, anarchists seeking to sharpen their message and identity are struggling to determine what is central and unique to their ideas and actions. As a result, we believe that a conceptual morphology, sensitive to both academic and practical concerns, would be of significant value to theorists and activists alike.

Two Modes of Decontestation

Disagreements over the meaning of basic political concepts such as freedom, equality, and justice result from the fact that such concepts are "essentially contested" – i.e., they lack a "clearly definable general … or correct use" and, as such, are subject to "inevitably endless disputes" over their meanings (Gallie 1956, 168–169). As Freeden (1994, 141–143; 2013, 119) points out, this is because the range of possible meanings for such concepts exceeds what "can be expressed in any single account or definition."

Consider the concept of "equality," for example. In order to use this concept, one must first assign a particular meaning to it. This, in turn, requires one to identify its referent – i.e., what it is a concept of. The problem, of course, is that equality "carries more than one meaning" and so is understood by different people in different ways (Freeden 2015, 124). Some claim that it refers to political equality, others to social equality, still others to economic equality, and so on. Indeed, even those who agree that "equality" has multiple referents may disagree over the individual meanings of these referents or their relative significance within the overall meaning of the concept itself. So whilst equality was a core concept in earlier forms of anarchism, appearing regularly in analyses and proposals by, for instance, Bakunin and Goldman in their writings on women, marriage and family, and demands for economic and social equality alongside political equality (Bakunin 1953, 326–327; Bakunin 1972, 86–87; Goldman 1969, 47–67, 195–212), they, like Freeden (1994, 143–144), were aware of its multiple meanings. Their claims for equality were therefore premised upon a recognition of difference and individualized self-development (Bakunin 1972, 87–88; Goldman 1969, 70–71, 78). As a result, whilst the discourse of equality has not disappeared from anarchism, it has largely been subsumed as a component of other core concepts like freedom, anti-hierarchy, and intersectionality.

As noted previously, Freeden's (2015, 124; 1996, 88) morphological approach defines ideologies as complex "clusters" or "composites" of decontested political concepts "with a variety of internal combinations." This definition involves two important claims: first, that ideologies are assemblages of particular political concepts "characterized by a morphology" – i.e., an inner structure that organizes and arranges those concepts in particular ways; and second, that they "decontest" political concepts – i.e., "remove [them] from contest by attempting to assign them a clear meaning" (Freeden 1996, 77; 2015, 59). The first of these features is a function of the second, and vice versa. On the one hand, an ideology's structure is determined by the ways it decontests the concepts it contains. On the other hand, the decontested meanings assigned to these concepts are determined by how they are organized and arranged within the ideology, as well as the historical, cultural, and linguistic contexts within which the ideology itself is situated (Freeden 2015, 54, 76–77).

According to Freeden, ideologies assign fixed meanings and degrees of relative significance to concepts by means of two basic operations. The first, which we will call "micro-decontestation," involves identifying, defining, and organizing their "micro-components" – i.e., the particular referents that specify what they are concepts *of* (Freeden 2013, 124–125). Every concept has several possible micro-components, each of which, in turn, has several possible meanings and degrees of relative significance within the overall concept. This allows for "diverse conceptions of any concept" and an "infinite variety" of "conceptual permutations" within "the ideational boundaries ... that anchor [them] and secure [their] components" (Freeden 2013, 124, 126, 128, 125.).

The second, which we will call "macro-decontestation," involves arranging concepts within a hierarchy of "core," "adjacent," and "peripheral" elements as well as determining their relative significance among other concepts of the same type (Freeden 2013, 125). The core concepts of a particular ideology, as we have noted, are distinguished by their "long-term durability" and are "present in all known cases of the ideology in question" (Freeden 2013, 125–126). As such, "they are indispensable to holding the ideology together, and are consequently accorded preponderance in shaping that ideology's ideational content" (Freeden 2013, 126). Adjacent concepts, in contrast, "are second-ranking in the pervasiveness and breadth of meanings they impart to the ideology in which they are located. They do not appear in all its instances, but are crucial to finessing the core and anchoring it ... into a more determinate and decontested semantic field" (Freeden 2013, 125). Lastly there are peripheral concepts, which are "more marginal and generally more ephemeral concepts that change at a faster pace diachronically and culturally" (Freeden 2013, 125). Each of these categories, moreover, has an internal hierarchy that accords different degrees of "proportional weight" to the concepts they comprise (Freeden 2013, 125). (See Table I.1.)

As an example of micro-decontestation, let us suppose that there are two ideologies, A and B, both of which recognize "the good life" as a core concept. Let us further suppose that A identifies "the good life" exclusively with happiness, whereas B identifies it exclusively with freedom. In this case, we would say that A and B identify "the good life" with different micro-components insofar as they have different understandings of what "the good life" is a concept of. On the other hand, even if A and B agree that "the good life" refers to both happiness and freedom, they may nonetheless assign these referents different meanings (as when, for example, A defines happiness in terms of the absence of pain and B

TABLE I.1 The Two Modes of Decontestation.

Micro-decontestation	Macro-decontestation
Meaning is assigned to a concept on the basis of its internal components. This involves: • Determining which individual micro-components are included in a concept and which are excluded • Assigning meanings to individual micro-components • Assigning varying degrees of relative significance to individual micro-components	Meaning is assigned to a concept on the basis of its relationship to other concepts. This involves: • Determining which individual concepts are included in an ideological morphology and which are excluded • Identifying individual concepts as core, adjacent, or peripheral • Assigning varying degrees of relative significance to all the individual concepts within a particular level of the conceptual hierarchy

defines it in terms of well-being or flourishing) and/or different degrees of significance (as when B regards freedom as more integral to the good life than happiness and A does the opposite). For Freeden (2013, 124), it is precisely conceptual permutations of this sort that account for variation within otherwise stable ideological families as well as their development and evolution "at variable speeds across time and space."

As an example of macro-decontestation, let us suppose that A recognizes both "individualism" and "the good life" as core concepts, whereas B recognizes "the good life" as a core concept but not "individualism." In A's case, the importance ascribed to individualism will necessarily be reflected in the particular meaning it assigns to the good life, and vice versa. The same is not true of B, since it doesn't recognize individualism as a core concept. Thus, although A and B both recognize the good life as a core concept, the particular meanings they assign to it will differ depending on the presence or absence of other concepts, as well as the way concepts are positioned within the ideological morphology. Even if A and B both recognize individualism and the good life as core concepts, they may nonetheless accord them different degrees of proportional weight – for example, B might regard the good life as more important than individualism and A might do the opposite – and, in so doing, assign them different meanings.

In short, there are many different ways to decontest concepts at both the micro- and the macro-level. Sometimes these differences are a function of the identification, definition, and organization of micro-components within the concepts themselves. At other times they are a function of the presence or absence of other concepts; of the relative position of concepts within the morphology; or of the different levels of proportional weight accorded to concepts that occupy the same relative position in the morphology. This means that even ideologies that recognize the same core concepts can be and often are quite different from one another. It also means that a single ideological tradition can include a variety of distinct tendencies. For instance, deeper green anarchisms include principles of anti-hierarchy and horizontalism but by giving greater priority to ecocentrism, the notions of agency, organization, and methods differ from more labor-orientated anarchisms that give greater priority to economic exploitation at the point of production (Williams 2009; Franks 2016). Similarly, insurrectionary anarchism is marked from more stable forms of social anarchism, but the former's shift in the proportionality of the core given to immediacy has now emerged as a microcomponent of prefiguration (Williams and Thomson 2011).

A Morphology of Anarchism

The scholarly literature on anarchism has grown significantly in the last couple of decades (Kinna 2012, 3). However, sustained efforts to explore aspects of the anarchist tradition from the standpoint of ideology or political culture have been relatively few in number (Gordon 2008). Freeden's projects like the *Journal of Political Ideologies* and the *Oxford Handbook of Political Ideologies* have given space to summaries and analyses of different aspects of anarchism that apply, assess, and refine his method (Adams and Jun 2015; Pauli 2015; Franks 2013, 2016) and it has also been adopted elsewhere (Kinna and Prichard 2012). More typical approaches tend to provide an overview of anarchist ideas and have gravitated either toward historical surveys (Woodcock 1983; Berry 2009; Marshall 2010) or toward primers for the curious (Ward 1996; Rooum 2001; Sheehan 2003; Milstein 2010). Rather than attempt to formulate a unitary definition of anarchism as an ideology or political theory, this book emerges out of our attempt to apply Freeden's conceptual-morphological analysis to anarchism as an ideology.

After identifying some core, adjacent, and peripheral concepts of anarchism, we enlisted the help of authors whose work on anarchism has been particularly noteworthy. Each of the chapters that follow explores a specific concept and discusses its significance within the anarchist tradition broadly construed – that is, the explorations are not necessarily tied to any given thinker, time period, or tendency within the anarchist movement. As ideological concepts are to be understood in their relations to other concepts, the chapters below will necessarily cross-refer and interrelate. Each chapter is sorted into one of three parts, corresponding to whether it addresses a core, an adjacent, or a peripheral concept.

Core Concepts

Part 1 contains chapters that explore the core concepts of anarchism as an ideology. These are the concepts that, for any ideology, "are both culturally and logically necessary to its survival" (Freeden 1996, 78). The ways in which their meanings are decontested and their relationships are set help us understand what separates anarchism from other ideological perspectives – whether compatible with or antagonistic to anarchist ideas.

In this first part of the book, we begin with basic values. Chapter 1 directs our attention to anarchism's opposition to hierarchy in human relations. As a fundamentally anti-authoritarian perspective, it seeks both to demolish the institutions that promote hierarchy and to construct viable alternative organizations. Chapter 2 highlights the role played by prefiguration in the organizations, intentions, and practices of anarchist activists. In Chapter 3, the focus is on freedom, which has often been identified as the anarchist value *sine qua non*. However, careful examination of the concept's use in the tradition reveals that there is no single conception of freedom that all anarchists share.

After reviewing core values, we turn to a set of concepts that shape what anarchists do. Chapter 4 begins at the most general level by examining the concept of agency. Within the anarchist tradition, how one conceives of the capacity for free choice and autonomous action – that is, for self-determination – shapes the direction that a radical politics may take. With Chapter 5, we explore another concept routinely employed as a synonym for anarchism, namely direct action. Engaging in (anti-)political practices in an unmediated way, acting as if one were already free, has long characterized the anarchist resistance to the state and other forces of domination. Finally, in Chapter 6, we conclude the first part of the book by examining the extent to which anarchism defines itself as a revolutionary doctrine, to which it embraces revolution as the vehicle for social and political transformation.

Adjacent Concepts

Part 2 contains chapters that explore the concepts that we regard as adjacent ones. Adjacent concepts, as we have noted, provide additional nuance and anchoring for some of the core concepts. They make the connections across concepts and ideologies that create "the meanings necessary to provide interpretations of political reality and plans for political action" (Freeden 1998, 752).

The chapters in the second part of the book extend our thinking about the core concepts. Chapter 7 examines how anarchists prefer social relations that are not only anti-hierarchical in aim, but also horizontalist in practice. Horizontalism in this sense connotes the anarchist preference for acting through leaderless, autonomous, and directly democratic mobilizations. Chapter 8 reveals that anarchists have spent much time discussing how to organize to meet social needs and achieve their political goals. Showing a marked preference for organizations that are free – voluntary and libertarian – anarchist ideology understands organization in ways that express and expand upon its core concepts. Similarly, the exploration of micropolitics in Chapter 9 moves beyond general values underlying large-scale political action to a recognition that anarchists seek to extend the struggle against domination into every sphere of life. Finally, with Chapter 10, we conclude our look at adjacent concepts by examining the prevalence of anti-capitalist views within the anarchist tradition.

Peripheral Concepts

Part 3 contains chapters that explore the concepts that we regard as important, but peripheral ones for anarchism. Peripheral concepts enable an ideology to further link its core concepts and basic ideas to concrete reality. They provide the flexibility an ideology needs not only to meet the challenges of time, place, and circumstance, but also to begin its evolution in response to social and political change. Peripheral concepts appear either on the margin or on the perimeter. On the margin, an ideology contains ideas and concepts "whose importance to the core, to the heart of the ideology, is intellectually and emotionally insubstantial" (Freeden 1996, 78). Ideas on the perimeter include a range of specific policy proposals or concrete applications of more general concepts (Freeden 1996, 80).

In this part, the chapters treat concepts and ideas that address any number of contemporary concerns to which anarchists must pay heed as they work out the implications of their ideology. Chapter 11's focus on intersectionality reminds us that, in the complex societies of the twenty-first century, anarchism must account for diverse instantiations of oppression, while recognizing the interdependence of various systems of domination. Though anarchism appears as a revolutionary ideology, Chapter 12 shows how a longstanding tension between reform and revolution, and the ambivalent attitudes such a tension fosters, characterize thinking about anarchist identity and anarchist practice.

In Chapter 13, the authors present an anarchist critique of work and discuss the possibilities for creating an anarchist work ethic – a study that returns us to thinking about anarchism as a theory of organization. Chapter 14 highlights the ways in which the quintessential anarchist ethos of DIY (Do It Yourself) yields a set of principles for translating key concepts and ideas into practice across various domains. Finally, in Chapter 15, we recognize that anarchism has considered ecological issues more often and more deeply than other radical ideologies – an important contribution to a world facing the potentially catastrophic effects of global climate change.

Conclusions

This book brings together contributions from prominent scholars of anarchism to identify, describe, and analyze key political concepts and their positions within anarchist ideological structures. The chapters are free-standing in that they provide clear, useful, and well-researched accounts of key concepts, but they also inter-relate as each concept is understood in relation to the others. As such, this volume provides a sophisticated and sustained application of Freeden's conceptual-morphological analysis to anarchism. Collectively these contributions describe and highlight the relative stability of anarchist core concepts, but also their adaptability as they draw in and interact with adjacent and peripheral concepts.

To be sure, the book resulting from this collaborative project to study anarchism in the manner of Freeden's morphological approach has its limitations. Certainly, we did not attempt to account for every conceivable concept that has entered the anarchist lexicon. Ideologies evolve to deal with new material challenges and to compete with the responses from rival ideologies. As a result, new concepts arise and the relative status of existing concepts changes. Any project such as this must necessarily have a finite scope. Choices have to be made in order to begin the project and see it through to realization. Indeed, this effort, like any other, has to come to an end somewhere and sometime. More significantly, conceptual analysis of any kind runs the risk of remaining abstract and idealistic. It is easy to regard our project as one that neglects the material contexts in which ideologies appear and are employed. Still, we believe that each author of the chapters that follow has tried to remain in touch, explicitly or implicitly, with important practical concerns.

Nevertheless, by concentrating on the patterns of concepts and their relative interactions, we believe that the book will be a resource for further studies into various hybrids and sub-categories of anarchism – new anarchisms, insurrectional anarchisms, and post-anarchisms, as well as more familiar eco-anarchisms, anarcha-feminisms, anarcho-syndicalisms, and libertarian Marxisms. It will also provide a basis for examining the permeability of anarchist concepts, sketching the possibilities for developing solidarities based on shared norms and practices, and identifying where apparently similar terminology belies a significantly different worldview.

Notes

1 For further discussion of analytical versus conceptual approaches, see Benjamin Franks (2011) and Nathan Jun (2016).
2 Some theorists like Dean Blackburn (2017) have drawn some parallels between shared features of Freeden and Williams, with respect to the critique of liberal and orthodox Marxist accounts of ideology.

References

Adams, Matthew S., and Nathan J. Jun. 2015. "Political Theory and History: The Case of Anarchism." *Journal of Political Ideologies* 20(3): 244–262.

Bakunin, Michael. 1953. *The Political Philosophy of Michael Bakunin*. Edited by G.P. Maximoff. New York: The Free Press.

Bakunin, Michael. 1972. *Bakunin on Anarchy*. Edited by Sam Dolgoff. New York: Vintage (Pirated edition).

Berry, David. 2009. *The History of the French Anarchist Movement 1917–1945*. Edinburgh: AK Press.

Blackburn, Dean. 2017. "Still the Stranger at the Feast? Ideology and the Study of Twentieth Century British Politics." *Journal of Political Ideologies* 22(2): 116–130.

Bottomore, Tom, Laurence Harris, V.G. Kieman, and Ralph Milliband, eds. 1983. *A Dictionary of Marxist Thought*. Oxford: Blackwell.

Franks, Benjamin. 2011. "Anarchism and Analytic Philosophy." In *The Continuum Companion to Anarchism*, edited by Ruth Kinna, 50–71. London: Continuum.
Franks, Benjamin. 2013. "Anarchism". In *The Oxford Handbook of Political Ideologies*, edited by Michael Freeden, Lyman Tower Sargent, and Marc Stears, 385–404. Oxford: Oxford University Press.
Franks, Benjamin. 2016. "Ideological Hybrids: The Contrary Case of Tory Anarchism." *Journal of Political Ideologies* 21(2): 160–180.
Freeden, Michael. 1994. "Political Concepts and Ideological Morphology." *The Journal of Political Philosophy* 2(2): 140–164.
Freeden, Michael. 1996. *Ideologies and Political Theory: A Conceptual Approach*. Oxford: Oxford University Press.
Freeden, Michael. 1998. "Is Nationalism a Distinct Ideology?" *Political Studies* 46(4): 748–765.
Freeden, Michael. 2003. *Ideology: A Very Short Introduction*. Oxford: Oxford University Press.
Freeden, Michael. 2013. "The Morphological Analysis of Ideology." In *The Oxford Handbook of Political Ideologies*, edited by Michael Freeden, Lyman Tower Sargent, and Marc Stears, 115–137. Oxford: Oxford University Press.
Freeden, Michael. 2015. *Liberalism: A Very Short Introduction*. Oxford: Oxford University Press.
Gallie, W.B. 1956. "Essentially Contested Concepts." *Proceedings of the Aristotelian Society* 56: 167–198.
Goldman, Emma. 1969 [1917]. *Anarchism and Other Essays*. New York: Dover.
Gordon, Uri. 2008. *Anarchy Alive! Anti-Authoritarian Politics from Practice to Theory*. London: Pluto Press.
Jun, Nathan. 2016. "On Philosophical Anarchism." *Radical Philosophy Review* 19(3): 551–567.
Kinna, Ruth, ed. 2012. *The Bloomsbury Companion to Anarchism*. London: Bloomsbury.
Kinna, Ruth, and Alex Prichard. 2012. "Introduction." In *Libertarian Socialism in Black and Red*, edited by Alex Prichard, Ruth Kinna, Saku Pinta, and David Berry, 1–16. Basingstoke: Palgrave Macmillan.
Knowles, Dudley. 2001. *Political Philosophy: An Introduction*. London: Routledge.
Knowles, Dudley. 2007. "The Domain of the Political." *Philosophy* 82(1): 23–43.
Marshall, Peter. 2010. *Demanding the Impossible: A History of Anarchism*. London: PM Press.
McLaughlin, Paul. 2007. *Anarchism and Authority*. Aldershot: Ashgate.
Milstein, Cindy. 2010. *Anarchism and Its Aspirations*. Oakland, CA: AK Press.
Ostergaard, Geoffrey. 1983. "Anarchism." In *A Dictionary of Marxist Thought*, edited by Tom Bottomore, Laurence Harris, V.G. Kiernan, and Ralph Milliband, 18–19. Oxford: Blackwell.
Pauli, Benjamin. 2015. "The New Anarchism in Britain and the US: Towards a Richer Understanding of Post-War Anarchist Thought." *Journal of Political Ideologies* 20(2): 134–155.
Rooum, Donald. 2001. *What is Anarchism? An Introduction*. London: Freedom.
Sheehan, Seán. 2003. *Anarchism*. London: Reaktion.
Simmons, Andrew John. 1987. "The Anarchist Position: A Reply to Kloso and Senor." *Philosophy and Public Affairs* 16(3): 206–268.
Simmons, Andrew John. 1996. "Philosophical Anarchism." In *For and Against the State*, edited by John Sanders and Jan Narveson, 19–40. Lanham, MD: Rowman and Littlefield.
Ward, Colin. 1996. *Anarchy in Action*. London: Freedom Press.
Williams, Dana. 2009. "Red vs. Green: Regional Variation of Anarchist Ideology in the United States." *Journal of Political Ideologies* 14(2): 189–210.

Williams, Leonard, and Brad Thomson. 2011. "The Allure of Insurrection." *Anarchist Developments in Cultural Studies* 1: 265–289.
Williams, Raymond. 1976. *Keywords: A Vocabulary of Culture and Society*. London: Fontana.
Wolff, Robert P. 1976. *In Defense of Anarchism*. London: Harper.
Woodcock, George. 1983. *Anarchism: A History of Libertarian Ideas and Movements*. Harmondsworth: Penguin.

PART 1
Core Concepts

1
ANTI-HIERARCHY

Randall Amster

The centrality of an anti-hierarchical perspective is evident in anarchist theory and action alike. Indeed, it might be said that a robust notion of anti-hierarchy is the *sine qua non* of anarchism, the core concept that differentiates it at root from other ideologies. In its thoroughgoing critique of hierarchy, anarchism establishes itself as a singular sociopolitical theory, one that sets a high bar of critical analysis for how deeply it is willing to inquire into quintessential hegemonies surrounding governance, economics, social relations, knowledge production – and even into the workings of anarchist organizing itself. While *anarchy* is often translated as "rejection of the state," it is this central penchant for challenging hierarchy in a more generalized sense that is a hallmark of the anarchist idea, and that further opens up not only its deconstructive potential but also its underappreciated constructive capacities to imagine and implement viable alternatives.

In the anarchist lexicon, there is a plethora of reflections on these concepts, often intermingling analyses of related phenomena such as liberty, authority, autonomy, and community. Familiar slogans of "No Gods, No Masters" pervade the field, as do invocations of being "against all authority." This baseline spirit of defiance and fierce independence is central to the anarchist tradition, and has enjoyed a resurgence in the contemporary landscape as anarchist principles and practices have begun to permeate a range of movement contexts. Anywhere one finds people struggling for equitable processes, just outcomes, or sustainable futures, there is likely to be at least a modicum of engagement with anarchist values involved on some level. And in some contexts – as when issues of privilege and power are put front and center in a group's internal processes, or when impacted communities rise up to challenge state violence – critical issues around hierarchy can be at the root of the inquiry. Thus, when we consider the notion of anti-hierarchy as a core anarchist tenet, it is important to recognize that an array of corollary concepts is connected to this foundational value as it impacts a wide spectrum of radical praxis:

> The intellectual framework of most of contemporary American anarchism rests on a critique of hierarchy .... Capitalism, organized religion, and the state are important forms of hierarchy, but the concept includes other relations of domination .... Hierarchy pervades our social relations and reaches into our psyche ...
>
> This analysis of hierarchy has broadened contemporary anarchism into a critique of all forms of oppression, including [not only] capitalism, the state, and organized religion but also patriarchy, heterosexism, anthropocentrism, racism, and more .... The political task according to contemporary anarchism is to attack all forms of oppression, not just a "main" one, because without an attack on hierarchy itself, other forms of oppression will not necessarily wither away after capitalism (or patriarchy, or colonialism) is destroyed.
>
> (Olson 2009, 36–37)

The depth of its critique of hierarchy is one of the principal points of distinction between anarchism and other radical theories. For instance, in the quote above, we see that concepts such as patriarchy and heterosexism are included in the anarchist critique, sometimes falling under the label of "anarcha-feminism." As Carol Ehrlich has observed, whereas radical feminists in general often engage with these issues – including related notions such as autonomy over one's body, challenging stereotypes, abolishing repressive laws, contesting male privilege, and providing women with tools for empowerment – "anarchist feminists are concerned with something more. Because they are anarchists, they work to end all power relationships, all situations in which people oppress each other .... For anarchists, ... the central issues are always power and social hierarchy" (Ehrlich 1996, 174). Anarcha-feminists accordingly have been critical of movements that seek to seize state power or that set up a leadership elite, instead emphasizing an approach centered on gaining autonomy "and insisting that everyone have it" (Ehrlich 1996, 174). Exploring the full implications of this critique across a range of issues, and understanding what it means for theorizing and organizing alike, are fundamental to anarchism's overall workings.

Despite its core attributes and sense of permeation, however, the anarchist inquiry is not ended simply by invoking "anti-hierarchy" as something approaching an *a priori* principle. As with most matters of consequence, there is a range of ways in which anti-hierarchical thinking is applied in the anarchist milieu. Thus, while anarchists may be agreed on the idea of the State as constituting a locus of unjust exercises of authority, and hence representing a form of hierarchical governance that is untenable at the outset, some might still at times participate in movements working within electoral or legal frameworks. Moreover, the question of how far anti-hierarchy extends is one that can illuminate some distinctions within the field – as with the widely held conception of capitalism as being based on exploitation and thus inconsistent with anarchism, despite some proponents advancing (problematically, as we shall see) the notion of "anarcho-capitalism." Likewise, invocations of individualism have pervaded anarchism, with community and/or society implicitly or explicitly seen as antagonistic – whereas varieties of communitarian anarchism are sometimes premised on a notion of non-coercive authority as a building block. Anarchists can be autonomists, syndicalists, egoists, communalists, atheists, spiritualists, and more; despite these varied viewpoints, however, endemic issues of power and responsibility can bring with them a common emphasis on hierarchy as a fundamental concept.

Anarchism thus admits a wide variety of perspectives under its rubric and, moreover, even encourages an openly critical stance toward its own workings and ostensible principles. This suggests that we might view anarchism more as a set of interrelated processes than as a settled goal, and hence as a perpetual means toward its own evolving ends. When we say that anti-hierarchy is a core anarchist concept, then, it is not so much in reference to a plank in an ideological foundation as it is describing a tool for engaging a wide range of issues and unpacking various intersecting forms of oppression. Anti-hierarchical analysis functions simultaneously as a means for deconstructing authoritarian structures in society and for building alternatives that do not replicate these structures in form or content. Anti-hierarchical processes thus serve to keep anarchism *anarchistic* – i.e., to not lapse into what it is struggling against. As such, the task involves opening space for being authoritative without becoming authoritarian.

Authority

This brief introduction serves to illustrate some of the complexities with anti-hierarchical thinking, and it also strengthens the case for it being an indispensable feature of anarchism. There are many contemporary treatments of such inquiries; one that is instructive to consider at the outset comes via a section from *An Anarchist FAQ* focusing specifically on the primary question, "Why are anarchists against authority and hierarchy?":

> First, it is necessary to indicate what kind of authority anarchism challenges. While it is customary for some opponents of anarchism to assert that anarchists oppose all kinds of authority, the reality of the situation is more complex. While anarchists have, on occasion, stated their opposition to "all authority" a closer reading quickly shows that anarchists reject only one specific form of authority, what we tend to call hierarchy ....
>
> Therefore, anarchists are opposed to *irrational* (e.g., illegitimate) authority, in other words, hierarchy – hierarchy being the institutionalization of authority within a society. Hierarchical social institutions include the state,

private property and the class systems it produces and, therefore, capitalism. Due to their hierarchical nature, anarchists oppose these with passion.

(Anarchist Writers 2008, original emphasis)

Of particular note here is the connection (and potential distinction) between hierarchy and authority, with the introduction of the concept of hierarchy as "institutionalized authority." The focus on "irrational" or "illegitimate" forms of authority, being highly subjective terms, further suggests places where anarchists may converge and (more to the point) where they may diverge.

For instance, consider the example of Voltairine de Cleyre (a contemporary of, and at times challenger to, Emma Goldman), who famously said that "we love liberty and hate authority" (Brigati 2004, ii). In her life and work, de Cleyre held to a radical conception of anti-authoritarianism, emphasizing the primacy of individual responsibility: "Anarchism, to me, means not only the denial of authority, not only a new economy, but a revision of the principles of morality. It means the development of the individual as well as the assertion of the individual. It means self-responsibility, and not leader worship" (Brigati 2004, 9). This serves as an effective summation of the spheres in which anti-hierarchical analysis will often be seen to apply: economics, morality, responsibility, governance, and the central questions of social organization. Grappling with these concepts straightforwardly and complexly illuminates some of anarchism's potential tensions, as various camps within the milieu are staked out and as different methodologies for inducing transformation are debated. Yet baseline critical inquiries into distributions of power and the reification of hierarchies in society remain widely held.

The annals of anarchism are replete with treatments of the question of authority, as fervently depicted by Michael Bakunin in addressing the rhetorical query, "Does it follow that I reject all authority?" Allowing for the expression of organic expertise, Bakunin (1970 [1916], 32) responds: "Far from me such a thought. In the matter of boots, I refer to the authority of the bootmaker; concerning houses, canals, or railroads, I consult that of the architect or engineer." Yet as Bakunin (1970 [1916], 32) explains, this deference must not lapse into institutionalized hierarchies: "But I allow neither the bootmaker nor the architect ... to impose his authority upon me .... I recognize no infallible authority." In the end, Bakunin (1970 [1916], 33) articulates how an anarchist conception of authority – as fluid, voluntaristic, mutualistic, and nonhierarchical – would function in practice: "Each directs and is directed in his turn. Therefore, there is no fixed and constant authority, but a continual exchange of mutual, temporary, and, above all, voluntary authority and subordination."

In this sense, we come to understand anti-hierarchical and anti-authoritarian patterns in anarchism not simply as expressions of aversion or rejection, but perhaps more so as proactive, ongoing checks against the emergence of reified, institutionalized forms of power in society. One can have temporary forms of authority so long as they do not harden or expand beyond particular moments in time and areas of training or expertise – but the creeping nature of centralization and institutionalization requires constant vigilance if we are to maintain social relations built upon a foundation of mutual, voluntary modes of association. In general, anarchists have proven adept at applying subtle distinctions in concrete contexts, and likewise at embracing diverse perspectives on processes and goals alike, and (perhaps uniquely among political theories) to unflinchingly inquire as to their own patterns in order to stand against those associated with the dominant structures in society. As Colin Ward (1973, 39) discerns, "if you look around … you will see everywhere in operation the opposite concept: that of hierarchical, authoritarian, privileged, and permanent leadership." The impetus of anarchism to explore, expose, and contest such arrangements leads directly to its rejection of the State (no matter its "representative" nature) – since when power coalesces behind a veneer of rigid hierarchy, coercion and violence inexorably ensue.

The State

The relationship between anarchists and the State (capitalized here to indicate state-power formations in general rather than a particular nation-state) seems straightforward at the outset: anarchism entails a clear rejection of the State. Yet this basic premise is complicated by the reality of anarchists overwhelmingly living within states and thus supporting them (either implicitly or explicitly) on myriad levels. Even those actively working to contest state power oftentimes find themselves constrained by the State in the tools they employ and battles they engage. The State, in this manner, presents itself as inevitable, nonnegotiable, necessary, and omnipresent. State power is said to rest upon a "social contract" in which people voluntarily give up their power to do whatever they please in favor of protection (from themselves and each other) and security – but anarchists have long observed that the power of the State is actually maintained through coercion, force, manipulation, punishment, and entrenched hierarchies.

The situation is further complicated by the realization that the State is not merely a physical manifestation of the "monopoly of violence," but is equally an agglomeration of social relations and concomitant forms of consciousness. Thus, the struggle is not simply over modes of governance, means of production, and patterns of distribution – it is perhaps even more so about whether the locus of our relationships and mindsets can be decoupled from the pervasive tentacles of state control, as Gustav Landauer's (2010) famous dictum indicates:

> A table can be overturned and a window can be smashed. However, those who believe that the state is also a thing or a fetish that can be overturned or smashed are sophists … The state is a social relationship; a certain way of people relating to one another. It can be destroyed by creating new social relationships; i.e., by people relating to one another differently.

> ... We, who have imprisoned ourselves in the absolute state, must realize the truth: *we* are the state. And we will be the state as long as we are nothing different; as long as we have not yet created the institutions necessary for a true community and a true society of human beings.
>
> *(214, original emphasis)*

In this sense, consider the range of hierarchical roles inherent to state power: the officer, the judge, the lawmaker, the general, the assessor, the warden, the decision-maker. All of these roles reflect not only tangible power arrangements but also implicit assumptions about what is necessary to maintain societal functions – and all rely on our willingness to accept their reality.

Landauer's formulation is potent yet not specific in how to accomplish the end of replacing state-bound relationships with new ones. Part of the challenge, as Landauer suggests, is that the State is not simply political or pecuniary, but represents a way of thinking as much as a way of being. To the extent that the State is a form of "imprisonment" (a point perhaps becoming increasingly evident in the age of mass incarceration and mass surveillance), it is a physical prison and a mental one all at once. In other words, the rigid hierarchies of state power are a function not only of political economy but of social psychology as well. Ultimately, it is this latter sense of internalized hierarchizing – "*we* are the state," as Landauer insists – that must be contested, and which lies at the root of what anarchism seeks to liberate us from. "It is especially clear to anarchists," as Seán M. Sheehan (2003, 122) concludes, "that the existing order is rooted in the control of social life and that the acceptance of certain attitudes, reinforced through structures of authority and obedience, makes up a state of intellectual imprisonment which in some of its aspects takes on forms of psychic repression – what Max Stirner called 'wheels in the head.'" Over time, many come to internalize dominant forms of organization, to rely upon them, to tacitly (if not overtly) consent to their hegemony, and even to replicate them.

Sheehan (2003, 122) goes on to observe that the anarchist project of developing alternatives includes an attempt "to understand why more people do not revolt and why so many submit to structures of authority that make them unhappy." Yet beyond questions of happiness – which are malleable, and thus subject to manipulation – there are more obvious forms of oppression that are part and parcel of the State and its penchant for uncontestable hierarchies: "The modern nation-state is an absolutely necessary condition for the wars and exterminations of the twentieth and the present century that have expended human beings as if they were inanimate .... It may well be, when all is said and done, that the nation-state is responsible for the extermination of our species or the extinction of our planet" (Sartwell 2008, 8–9). As anthropologist Douglas Fry (2012, 880) concludes, "hierarchical societies such as [states] are more likely to engage in war and practice more severe forms of warfare than are comparatively egalitarian [societies]." Or more colloquially, in the oft-quoted words of Randolph Bourne (2010): "War is the health of the State."

The anarchist penchant for breaking down rigid hierarchies and contesting forms of entrenched authority is therefore not primarily about seizing power or accomplishing revolutionary aims for their own sake; it is, rather, an attempt to free ourselves from political, economic, and psychic imprisonment, and ultimately to prevent the scourge of structural violence and perpetual war from decimating people and the planet alike. Anarchism thus rejects the closure of the future in favor of opening up a space for people together to determine the conditions of their existence in a direct rebuke to the inevitability of collapse. Put this way, the anti-hierarchical impulse in anarchism can be viewed as an existential proposition, in the recognition that rigidly hierarchical systems are socially and ecologically unsustainable. It is not simply a values-orientation at work, or an attempt to score points in some academic debate; anarchists take seriously the notion that a worldview premised on hierarchical structures is not viable, and moreover that one based on nonhierarchical relations is not only preferable but possible. Perhaps the clearest demonstration of this line of reasoning in a contemporary context comes through a critical examination of economic systems and the emergence of global capital.

Capital

With the rise of a globally integrated economic system, rendered possible by burgeoning technologies of communication and conveyance, there has been a corollary increase in global patterns of repression, surveillance, and militarism. Oftentimes these incipient forces of authoritarianism have been cloaked under the guise of "natural market forces" or "structural adjustment programs" – but increasingly they appear more starkly with the advent of open-ended warfare, escalating civil and ethnic tensions, widespread impoverishment, and mass refugeeism. At the same time, mounting evidence of environmental degradation, resource depletion, and a rapidly changing climate has paralleled this era of multinational corporate expansion. Despite these global crises, in many parts of the world it is simply "business as usual" set against a backdrop of creature comforts, palliatives and distractions, and a patina of plenty. And of course, this ascent of a hegemonic global capitalist system has presented acute problems for anarchists.

On the one hand, as noted above in the context of the State, anarchists exist within emergent networks of global capital and at times utilize these networks as tools for organizing – sometimes even arguing that the ostensibly decentralized nature of these networks can serve to enable egalitarian movements. However, as Jeffrey Juris (2009, 215, original emphasis) cautions, "there is nothing *inherently* anarchistic or even progressive about network forms or practices," and in fact, "distributed networks have expanded more generally as a strategy for enhancing coordination, scale, and efficiency in the context of post-Fordist capital accumulation." While such networks may appear decentralized, "they also involve varying degrees of hierarchy and can be used for divergent ends, including finance, production, policing, war, and terror" (Juris 2009, 215). Still, as Juris (2009, 215, original emphasis) concludes, "although they are not *necessarily* egalitarian, distributed networks suggest a *potential* affinity with egalitarian values," making them attractive tools for anarchist organizing. Notable examples in the anarchist milieu include CrimethInc. (a network of radical publishing collectives), the now-dormant Indymedia, and Infoshop (a longtime online platform).

On the other hand, despite being at times tempted (or even constrained) to utilize opportunities presented by a global capitalist system and its (literal and figurative) networks, anarchists remain staunchly anti-capitalist in their rhetoric and analysis alike. As Albert Meltzer (2000, 50) pointedly notes, "the philosophy of 'anarcho-capitalism' dreamed up by the 'libertarian' New Right, has nothing to do with Anarchism as known by the Anarchist movement proper." The logic is clear: capitalism is seen as inherently authoritarian, ruthlessly exploitative, insidiously hierarchical, and logically unsustainable – thus rendering it anathema to anarchism. As observed with the State, the development of reified roles within capitalism tells the story: the boss, the manager, the chief executive, the board, the security guard, the resource extractor; likewise, we can observe nearly everywhere patterns of imposed austerity, privatization of common wealth, and widening inequalities of access and opportunity. Disingenuous concepts of a "free market" apart from state control as equating with individual freedom run counter to anarchism's search for egalitarian, equitable forms of socioeconomic organization. Moreover, as Uri Gordon (2009, 252) opines, "capitalism can only go so far in delaying its confrontation with the objective limits to its growth," despite fervent attempts by corporations and the states that sponsor them aimed at "prolonging the period of manageable crisis so as to allow hierarchical institutions to adapt away from capitalism." In this light, it can be surmised that those profiting from the current system are invested not in ideologies but in the perpetuation of their domination.

Against this eventuality, anarchism envisions participatory and nonhierarchical economic forms based on "self-determination, room to act, voluntariness, and cooperation" (Buck 2009, 67). Such a vision is not prescriptive, even as exemplars such as cooperatives and collectives begin to appear as potential alternatives to depersonalized, hierarchized corporate structures. The premise is to cultivate a network of relationships – social, political, economic, and ecological – in which "the processes of social life educate *participants* toward an autonomous, cooperative ethic" that enables mutualistic and voluntary forms of exchange (Buck 2009, 67, original emphasis). In this active vision, the coercive methods of capitalism, achieved through force and artifice alike, will be supplanted by modes of production and distribution that emphasize collaboration and complementarity, in the belief that people living and working together in such a system will likewise reflect these egalitarian values. In order to accomplish this, it is necessary to explore not only how resources are allocated and exchanges are accomplished, but likewise how decisions are made and relationships are formed. We thus need to examine further how power functions, and whether its application in a given context is consistent with an anti-hierarchical impulse.

Domination and Power

As a starting point for deconstructing power relations, Cindy Milstein (2010, 12–13) has observed that anarchism is based on a premise "that people would be much more humane under nonhierarchical social relations and social arrangements," and thus entails "the absence of both domination (mastery or control over another) and hierarchy (ranked power relations of dominance and subordination)." In this sense, anarchism's essential project is to abolish dominator relations and hierarchical modes of organization in favor of egalitarian and horizontal forms – hence moving, as Milstein (2010, 13) characterizes it, from "power-over social relations" to ones based on "power-together and in common." Similarly, Starhawk (2002, 169–178) views hierarchical relations as "power-over," and counterposes nonhierarchical ones as being constructed upon a framework of "power-with" or "power-among." As Gordon (2008, 54) concludes, the intention is to conceive of "influence without force, coercion, manipulation or authority," once again yielding the idea of power-with, or "power as non-coercive influence."

It is precisely in this dualistic formulation that we come to understand negational constructions of being *anti-* something (of which the word *anarchy* itself is a prime example) as only telling part of the story. Being "anti-hierarchy" could be viewed as nonsensical or even perilous without offering something in its place. The challenge for anarchism is that it is expressly non-prescriptive, in the sense of not setting forth ironclad principles or immutable ideologies, instead favoring conceptual mechanisms which people can uniquely apply (or not) in their own contexts. So, the anarchist project of rejecting dominant forms of hierarchy and power necessarily includes a desire to offer alternatives and models of "new social relationships" (in Landauer's terms), without in the process creating new hierarchies of knowledge and practice in their place. The struggle to accomplish this is historically relevant, and represents an important contemporary evolution of anarchism's principles; as Todd May (1994, 65, 85) has discerned, "the suppressive assumption regarding power" was traditionally regarded as core to anarchism, yet steadily has been reformulated in recent times as a "new type of anarchism" that views power not merely as "a closed holism, a concentric field, or a hierarchy," but also in potentially horizontal terms as a network, an intersection of struggles, or a "field of social relationships."

The vision of an anarchist society, then, is based on a reformulation of relationships from ones based on domination and power-over (as typified, suborned, and inculcated by the State and capital) to ones that are fluid, complementary, mutual, and egalitarian in nature. There is no blueprint or prescription for achieving or maintaining such a society, yet this overarching ethos has been central to anarchism historically and remains so in a contemporary context. These patterns are epitomized by the anarchist penchant for cultivating autonomous collectives as an alternative to central control – with notable examples including the Anarchist Black Cross (prisoner support) and Food Not Bombs (food sharing), among others – in which coordination is maintained over time without reified power structures and as individual participants and roles rotate. In this sense, it might be said that "power in an anarchist society finds itself ebbing and flowing as various needs arise and are addressed, but at no time does it become centralized in a manner that allows it to be turned back on the very people in whom it inheres" (Amster 2012, 7). Attaining such a society, with its delicate balance of non-hierarchical power and authority, has been a driving concern for anarchists – and is one that necessitates innovative forms of organizing.

Organizing

As indicated by the foregoing, the connections between hierarchy, power, authority, and organizing are thus evident in anarchism, where a baseline rejection of rigid social forms leads to opportunities for cultivating egalitarian modes of coordinated action – ones that continually work to keep in check any nascent patterns of institutionalized power before they fully develop. This often means, paradoxically, that anarchism involves *more* rather than *less* organization (despite its caricature as being synonymous with chaos and disorganization), and entails a greater emphasis on methods of coordination since such cannot be taken for granted and must therefore be negotiated (by free equals) on a continual basis. As Nicolas Walter (2002) explains:

> Anarchists actually want much more organisation, though organisation without authority .... What anarchists do reject is the institutionalisation of organisation, the establishment of a special group of people whose function is to organise other people. Anarchist organisation would be fluid and open; as soon as organisation becomes hardened and closed, it falls into the hands of a bureaucracy, becomes the instrument of a particular class, and reverts to the expression of authority instead of the co-ordination of society.
>
> *(38–39)*

In an anarchist society, there would be no "outsourcing" of decision making or the provision of basic functions; instead, it would become incumbent upon people in the context of their cultures and environments to cultivate durable and equitable forms of exchange and coordination.

In a more contemporary context, David Graeber (2009, 105) has observed that "anarchist principles – autonomy, voluntary association, self-organization, direct democracy, mutual aid – have become the basis for organizing new social movements" around the world. In addition to developing and deploying methods for contesting unjust power arrangements – including affinity groups, convergences, decentralized networks, and direct actions – anarchists likewise have been vital to projects seeking to foster "independent, sustainable alternatives and community self-sufficiency," in the belief that the emergence of such nonhierarchical examples of social organization "can amount to a powerful form of propaganda by the deed, displaying attractive models that people can implement" (Gordon 2009, 257). Again, consistent with the dualistic anarchist vision, the intention is to both confront and supplant the State and capital by exposing their baseline hierarchical forms and supporting the creation of viable nonhierarchical alternatives. The stakes for this project are high, and the scope of its application is expansive.

As contemporary movements engage with an increasing spectrum of issues, we are reminded that "hierarchies sustain and reproduce oppression" across a range of spheres, from the social and political to the economic and environmental (DeLeon and Love 2009, 160). Nevertheless, and in a penultimate nod to anarchism's complexity and willingness to challenge even its own potential reifications, departed colleague and agitator *par excellence* Joel Olson (2009, 37, original emphasis) insists that we consider the argument that not all hierarchies are equally oppressive, and that we refrain from propounding a unitary analysis that "mistakenly blends a *moral* condemnation of all forms of oppression with a *political and strategic* analysis of how power functions." For Olson (2009, 37), the particular manifestation of racial hierarchies reinforces "nearly every other form of oppression" in the United States (and perhaps elsewhere). Olson's (2009, 41) cautionary insight counsels that a generic emphasis on hierarchies without deeper contextualization can yield amorphous, ineffective movements that do not adequately contest power through "sustained organizing based on a coherent strategy to win political space in a protracted struggle."

Further complexifying matters, as we have seen, is the realization that not all forms of authority or exercises of power are inherently antagonistic to anarchist praxis – and conversely, not all decentralized networks are necessarily anarchist in form or function. As Starhawk (2002, 169–170) has observed, hierarchies exist in nature as emblematized by a tree's "branching pattern" in which "the twigs connect to one branch, the branches to one larger limb, the limbs to the trunk." The problem arises when we fail to recognize the delicate balance and mutual exchange of component parts that render a tree possible and that belie its surface appearance as a hierarchy. Problematically, "in human societies, branching patterns are often used to collect wealth, resources, and labor from one group and to disperse them to another group," yielding a set of structural conditions in which "inequality and imbalance are justified by assigning a higher value to those who are the recipients of wealth and the makers of decisions" (Starhawk 2002, 170). Beyond autonomic biological functions, human individuals and societies possess the capacity to express intentions and values in our personal and collective affairs alike, meaning that we can learn to identify unjust exercises of authority and create societies without them. While this project has been historically challenging to sustain, notable exemplars of anarchistic societies and communities are evident, from collectivist initiatives in the Spanish Civil War and long-term occupations such as Christiania in Copenhagen, Denmark, to radical spaces such as ABC No Rio in New York City and Red Emma's Bookstore Coffeehouse (a worker-owned collective in Baltimore, MD).

As these and other similar efforts suggest – consonant with the theoretical framework advanced by myriad anarchist authors – what is being sought is an evolving social order that is infused with anti-hierarchical tendencies at every turn, that continually checks its own processes and principles for authoritarian incursions, and that structurally promotes more horizontal and equitable forms of governance and distribution at all points throughout the system(s). This is more than merely a set of hypothetical inquiries or analytical exercises; anarchists actively practice and strive to implement these concepts (albeit imperfectly at times) in the present as a means toward "prefiguring" a more just and sustainable future. In the end, perhaps the ultimate hierarchy to be dismantled is the one in which many (if not most) people accept as uncontestable the dominant forms of institutionalized authority that have infused structural violence and injustice throughout the web, and that have pushed the world to the brink of global cataclysm. Anti-hierarchy as a core anarchist tenet rejects such inevitabilities, instead encouraging an empowered perspective that provides conceptual tools for achieving its own realization.

References

Amster, Randall. 2012. *Anarchism Today*. Santa Barbara, CA: Praeger.
Anarchist Writers. 2008. "Why are anarchists against authority and hierarchy?" In *An Anarchist FAQ*. Accessed September 23, 2015. http://anarchism.pageabode.com/afaq/secB1.html.
Bakunin, Michael. 1970 [1916]. *God and the State*. New York: Dover Publications.
Bourne, Randolph. 2010 [1919]. "The State." *The Anarchist Library*. Last modified 18 November 2010. Accessed October 17, 2017. https://theanarchistlibrary.org/library/randolph-bourne-the-state.
Brigati, A.J., ed. 2004. *The Voltairine de Cleyre Reader*. Oakland, CA: AK Press.
Buck, Eric. 2009. "The Flow of Experiencing in Anarchic Economies." In *Contemporary Anarchist Studies: An Introductory Anthology of Anarchy in the Academy*, edited by Randall Amster, Abraham DeLeon, Luis A. Fernandez, Anthony J. Nocella II, and Deric Shannon, 57–69. Abingdon: Routledge.
DeLeon, Abraham, and Kurt Love. 2009. "Anarchist Theory as Radical Critique: Challenging Hierarchies and Domination in the Social and 'Hard' Sciences." In *Contemporary Anarchist Studies: An Introductory Anthology of Anarchy in the Academy*, edited by Randall Amster, Abraham DeLeon, Luis A. Fernandez, Anthony J. Nocella II, and Deric Shannon, 159–165. Abingdon: Routledge.
Ehrlich, Carol. 1996. "Socialism, Anarchism, and Feminism." In *Reinventing Anarchy, Again*, edited by Howard J. Ehrlich, 169–186. San Francisco, CA: AK Press.
Fry, Douglas P. 2012. "Life Without War." *Science* 336 (18 May): 879–884. doi: 10.1126/science.1217987.

Gordon, Uri. 2008. *Anarchy Alive! Anti-Authoritarian Politics from Theory to Practice*. London: Pluto Press.
Gordon, Uri. 2009. "Dark Tidings: Anarchist Politics in the Age of Collapse." In *Contemporary Anarchist Studies: An Introductory Anthology of Anarchy in the Academy*, edited by Randall Amster, Abraham DeLeon, Luis A. Fernandez, Anthony J. Nocella II, and Deric Shannon, 249–258. Abingdon: Routledge.
Graeber, David. 2009. "Anarchism, Academia, and the Avant-garde." In *Contemporary Anarchist Studies: An Introductory Anthology of Anarchy in the Academy*, edited by Randall Amster, Abraham DeLeon, Luis A. Fernandez, Anthony J. Nocella II, and Deric Shannon, 103–112. Abingdon: Routledge.
Juris, Jeffrey S. 2009. "Anarchism, or the Cultural Logic of Networking." In *Contemporary Anarchist Studies: An Introductory Anthology of Anarchy in the Academy*, edited by Randall Amster, Abraham DeLeon, Luis A. Fernandez, Anthony J. Nocella II, and Deric Shannon, 213–223. Abingdon: Routledge.
Landauer, Gustav. 2010. *Revolution and Other Writings: A Political Reader*, edited and translated by Gabriel Kuhn. Oakland, CA: PM Press.
May, Todd. 1994. *The Political Philosophy of Poststructuralist Anarchism*. University Park, PA: The Pennsylvania State University Press.
Meltzer, Albert. 2000. *Anarchism: Arguments for and Against* (7th ed.). San Francisco, CA: AK Press.
Milstein, Cindy. 2010. *Anarchism and Its Inspirations*. Oakland, CA: AK Press.
Olson, Joel. 2009. "The Problem with Infoshops and Insurrection: US Anarchism, Movement Building, and the Racial Order." In *Contemporary Anarchist Studies: An Introductory Anthology of Anarchy in the Academy*, edited by Randall Amster, Abraham DeLeon, Luis A. Fernandez, Anthony J. Nocella II, and Deric Shannon, 35–45. Abingdon: Routledge.
Sartwell, Crispin. 2008. *Against the State: An Introduction to Anarchist Political Theory*. Albany, NY: State University of New York Press.
Sheehan, Seán M. 2003. *Anarchism*. London: Reaktion Books.
Starhawk. 2002. *Webs of Power: Notes from the Global Uprising*. Gabriola Island, BC: New Society Publishers.
Walter, Nicolas. 2002 [1969]. *About Anarchism*. London: Freedom Press.
Ward, Colin. 1973. *Anarchy in Action*. New York: Harper & Row.

2
PREFIGURATION

Benjamin Franks

> "Anarchism, as I learned it from my comrades, was about taking democracy seriously and organizing prefiguratively"
>
> *Andrej Grubačić (2013, 186)*

Introduction

Prefiguration has been a core concept of anarchism since, at least, the 1880s. It has been pivotal in identifying and formulating forms of libertarian organisation. It plays a central analytic role in the generation of anarchist governance principles and assists in the identification of – and engagement with – particular agents of change. Prefiguration is also a central feature of anarchist evaluations of tactics and an important element in libertarian critiques of rival political movements.

This chapter is going to describe and clarify the term "prefiguration" and explore some criticisms raised in the works of contemporary theorists like Uri Gordon, Marianne Maeckelbergh, and Luke Yates. They variously propose that prefiguration is conceptually inadequate as it is vague enough as a guiding principle to allow for hierarchical and oppressive activity and it is unclear as to whether it applies to types of organisation or tactic or epistemology. Prefiguration will also be defended from orthodox Marxist and post-anarchist critics who argue that prefiguration is inadequate or detrimental to a genuinely revolutionary (anti-)politics.

This latter criticism comes in three forms. First, Leninists argue that prefiguration's attempts to foreshadow emancipatory, post-revolutionary social relations are ineffective against capitalism. It is, they argue, necessary to reproduce certain features of capitalist hierarchy in order to overcome it. The second criticism emerges from the economic determinist orthodox Marxist tradition, but is also associated with writings of Herbert Marcuse. This argument asserts that it is not possible to know the values and practices of a liberated society in circumstances where capitalist oppression and alienation are pervasive. Thus, one cannot prefigure liberatory values because the ideological weight of capitalism occludes these from our consciousness. The third set of criticisms come from post-anarchism and differ from the previous ones. Whilst Leninist and determinist readings argue that there are ultimate liberatory values, but we cannot know or realise them under capitalism, post-anarchist critics argue that there are no goals for anarchist actions to prefigure. Post-anarchism argues that, as prefiguration ties actions in the present to ultimate endpoints, it must be ultimately a form of *archē* (generative first principle for social domination), reducing multiple subjects to a singular, unitary goal and thus reasserting deterministic structures of governance.

Origins

The application of the term "prefiguration" to radical politics is of comparatively recent vintage,[1] with its initial use traced by John Hammond (2015, 293 n3) to Carl Boggs (1977a; 1977b) and Wini Breines (1980; 1989). However, although the expression "prefiguration" is barely mentioned prior to the 1970s, the underlying concept has been a stable and core feature of anarchism going back to its earliest origins in modern resistance to capitalism. Prefiguration, in its most general form, denotes an identity between (anti-)political methods and (anti-)political goals or ends. It can be found overtly in James Guillaume's criticisms of orthodox Marxist methods: "How could one want an equalitarian and free society to issue from an authoritarian organisation? It is impossible" (quoted in Kenafick 1984, 7). Later, Emma Goldman (1923, 429–430) affirms Guillaume's analysis, using her experience in Russia during the Leninist revolution:

> All human experience teaches that methods and means cannot be separated from the ultimate aim. The means employed become, through individual habit and social practice, part and parcel of the final purpose; they influence it, modify it, and presently the aims and means become identical. ... The great and inspiring aims of the Revolution became so clouded with and obscured by the methods used by the ruling political power that it was hard to distinguish what was temporary means and what was final purpose.

There are suggestions that prefigurative concepts can be identified in earlier works of classical anarchists (to use George Crowder's [1991] useful, albeit disputable, category)[2] such as Pierre-Joseph Proudhon (Vieta 2014, 785–786) and Mikhail Bakunin (van de Sande 2015). So central has prefiguration become to many contemporary anarchist theorists and activists, that sometimes this identification of the earlier canon might be a result of a *post hoc* reading of earlier writings. Knowing that prefigurative reasoning is important, it becomes identified even where it is not present. Alternatively, such readings might be recognising prefigurative ideas that are "in the gristle" (to use Peter Linebaugh's phrase) of early anarchism. This does not mean that the notion was peripheral to the main skeleton of anarchist thought, but that the concepts and the articulation were "not yet well-defined or full-blooded" (Linebaugh 2009, viii): the concept of prefiguration was still developing and evolving. It becomes most clearly expressed not just with particular forms of (anti-)political organisation and method, but in contrast to alternative political methods of another rival revolutionary tradition which was also evolving at this time, namely traditional Marxism (or Leninism). As Guillaume, Goldman, Boggs, and Breines articulate, prefiguration became one of the main ways in which anarchism and heterodox Marxisms, like autonomism, became distinguished from Marxist orthodoxy (Gautney 2009).

Prevalence

One indicator of a core concept is that it is a stable and central feature of an ideological structure (Freeden 2003, 72). Prefiguration is just such a concept: it is a dominant feature of anarchist analysis and practice in many different geographic and historical locations. Arif Dirlik (1991, 65–66, 83) notes that, although the early anarchists in China employed instrumental reasoning in their selection and justification of tactics, by the time anarchism differentiated itself from other revolutionary traditions prefigurative reasoning came increasingly to the fore. The methods for revolutionary change had to be consistent with humane, emancipatory objectives, identified as an ethical principle or "moral purpose" (Dirlik 1991, 89–90). Prefigurative considerations, for Chinese anarchists, did not rule out selective assassination. So too the reassertion of prefiguring future forms of social organisation, as well as aiding the evasion of state repression, lay behind the decentred network of Japanese anarchists in the 1930s, such as the *Nôson Seinan Sha* or Farming Villages Youth Association (Crump 1996, 31). Benedict Anderson (2005, 72) suggests that similar prefigurative forms of reasoning can be found in the preferences for self-generated, decentred anarchist organisation in Spain, Italy, and Cuba.

Such similarity in core concepts across geographies is not surprising. Anarchists were travelling between different countries, engaging with, and publishing in host as well as home country journals and magazines. Anarchist internationalism meant, for instance, that activists in the Philippines, Japan, and China were readily engaging with European fellow anarchist writers, translating European writers for domestic audiences, and similarly, publishing in American and French anarchist periodicals (Anderson 2005; Crump 1996, 15; Dirlik 1991, 13–14, 114, 155–160).

The principle of prefiguration, especially insofar as it distinguishes anarchism from social democracy and Leninism, remains an enduring theme into the current era. The contemporary South Africa-based anarchist Lucien van der Walt (2011, original emphasis), citing Bakunin and Peter Kropotkin in support, declares:

"Anarchist communism" must be created *from below*, through *self-managed* struggles, by participatory-democratic movements of the broad working class and peasantry. The movements must embody in the *present* the forms and values they seek – they must *prefigure* the future; to use hierarchy is to reproduce it.

For Heather Gautney (2009, 478), the commitment to the principle of prefiguration unites contemporary anti-state Marxism of the anti- (or non-) Leninist autonomist tradition and social anarchism. Prefiguration provides a clear division between standardly anarchist, tactical approaches and the consequentialism of orthodox Marxism. There are, however, occasions when there are theoretical weaknesses in the account of prefiguration, as it is not altogether clear what is being foreshadowed: is it primarily a pragmatic guide to organisation, an epistemology, or an ethic?

Clarifying Prefiguration

As mentioned in the introduction, some critics of prefiguration (Gordon 2015; Yates 2015) have pointed to an apparent vagueness in the concept that is potentially damaging politically. These critics suggest that concentrating on prefiguration is detrimental as the concept is insufficient to distinguish anarchism from other ideologies. According to Gordon (2015), any "political movement can coherently 'prefigure' any set of goals and social forms." Racist groups and liberal democrats can prefigure their goals in their methods and forms of organisation, as Gordon (2015) points out, "if any political group prefigures its desired society, then the concept seems to lose any elucidatory value."

If we draw upon Freeden's (2003, 60–61) conceptual approach to consider this problem, it is clear that the *priority* of prefiguration in the conceptual structure of anarchism is different from that in liberal constitutionalism and racist popularism. Whilst these statist movements may use prefigurative approaches, they are also much more willing than anarchism to engage in consequentialist political methods in order to gain control of the state. Thus, prefiguration is only a peripheral and local concern, whilst in anarchism it is conceptually core and more stable. The *proximity* of prefiguration to other anarchist principles is also relevant. As Freeden explains, political concepts only make sense in relation to the other key concepts within an ideology. As some authors (Breines 1989, 6; Gautney 2009, 480; Yates 2015, 3) have noted, prefiguration is linked to other anarchist principles such as "anti-authoritarianism," "anti-hierarchy," and "horizontalism." These principles are antipathetic to fascist or liberal forms of politics. Anarchist writings (Anarchist Federation 2015; van der Walt 2011) often explicitly describe their core principles in relation to antistatism and anti-capitalism, thereby distinguishing anarchism from any liberal or nationalist appropriations.

A further problem is the question of to what does the term "prefiguration" refer. Is it the "prefigurative activities [or] … the collective identity processes of the countercultures" (Yates 2015, 5)? With Maeckelbergh (2011, 4–5) also pointing to its uses in terms of anti-instrumentalist organisation and strategy as well as identity formation, another question emerges: should prefiguration be applied to forms of organisation, tactics, epistemology and ethic?

Examples of prefiguration are often given in relation to the first two. The Industrial Workers of the World's (IWW; 2015) slogan that "By organizing industrially we are forming the structure of the new society within the shell of the old" highlights the organisational and inter-personal focus of prefiguration. Similarly, anarchist tactics such as squatting or occupying workplaces, usually labelled "direct action" or "do it yourself culture," explicitly refer to concepts of prefiguration (Verson 2007, 171–186; Wall 1999, 156–157; Sparrow n.d.).

Maeckelbergh (2011), citing Nöel Sturgeon, identifies prefiguration as a form of epistemology:

> Prefiguration is not a theory of social change that first analyses the current global political landscape, develops an alternative model in the form of a predetermined goal, and then sets out a five-year plan for changing the existing landscape into that predetermined goal. Prefiguration is a different kind of theory, a "direct theory" … that theorizes through action, through doing. … [W]hat makes the alterglobalization movement different from previous movements is that the alternative "world" is not predetermined; it is developed through practice and it is different everywhere. This goal of pursuing "(an)other world(s)" in an open and explicitly not predetermined way requires practice over time, and that is what makes prefiguration the most strategic approach.
>
> *(3)*

Maeckelbergh's account identifies prefiguration with a specific form of (anti-) political knowledge production. It rejects standard universalist, rationalist, and naturalist versions, suggesting that knowledge is generated through practical activities, and it is through these that objectives are identified and realised in social practices. Her account rightly does not reject theoretical knowledge (*theoria*): the pursuance of "(an)other world(s)" is just such an abstract goal, but its derivation and the conceptual attributes become fleshed out through engaging in collective actions.

Thus, Maeckelbergh's version of prefiguration does not rest just on epistemology, but also includes the norms of goods-generating social activity. As such, it links the accounts of prefiguration found as far back as Goldman to contemporary groups such as the Anarchist Federation, who reassert the IWW slogan. They stress that a prefigurative practice is constituted by the radical integration of all elements – method, tactic, ethic, and epistemology.

> The most important part of the working class tradition that we call communism is the refusal to make a distinction between ends and means. The organisations that we build while fighting capitalism will be the basis of anything that comes after the revolution. If those organisations do not embody the principles of the society that we want to see then that society will not come about. If we want a future where everyone contributes to the decisions that affect them, then we have to build organisations now in which this happens. The Anarchist Federation is one such organisation.
>
> This is known as prefiguration and is one of the central ideas of anarchism. The idea is summed up by one important slogan: "building the new society in the shell of the old." What this means is that our struggle is not simply against capitalism. We also fight, as far as is possible, to live as we wish to right now, to build alternatives to capitalism right under its nose.
>
> *(Anarchist Federation 2013)*

Here the values of accessibility, co-operation, and anti-hierarchy are embodied in participatory (and adaptable) norm-governed practice to both contest existing forms of domination and to foreshadow its transformation. These practices develop internal goods (goods in themselves) – like social solidarity, comradeship, bravery, and wisdom – and external goods, things that assist in the production of benefits, but are not in-themselves desirable (Plato, 2007, 357c-d, 103; Aristotle 1976, 73–74).

Similarly, Grubačić's observation that opened this chapter ties prefiguration to particular forms of decision making and social organisation (not the democratic, representative state form). In the context of (dis-)organisation, for instance, prefiguration refers largely to efforts to prevent or minimise hierarchy and coercive structures in the here and now, as a means of contesting such repressive social structures. Grubačić (2013) goes on to identify prefiguration with "an ethics of practice," which emphasises anti-authoritarian means to augur emancipatory goals. Like Boggs and Gautney, Grubačić uses this feature of anarchism to distinguish this form of revolutionary socialism from traditional Marxism.

Unified Practice-based Prefiguration

Like Maeckelbergh and Yates, contemporary writers like David Graeber have tended to use the alterglobalisation and Occupy movements as their case studies for prefigurative organisation. These reports analyse not just the consensual, inclusive decision-making processes, but also the ways that these structures enable the generation of immanent goods – positive experiences in the here and now for participants – and external goods – tangible benefits to others not directly involved or to participants at some future date. "[B]y modelling the desired social relations, more fulfilling and less estranged than those typical of alienated capitalist society ... [the] outcome of the occupation was the creation of a vibrant community" (Hammond 2015, 298). Yates and Maeckelbergh give explicitly multi-dimensional accounts of prefiguration, which include developing political practices that have decision making, ethics, accounts of future goals, generation of immediate goods and social transformation.

Practices are rule-governed activities that generate internal and external goods, that persist to generate traditions, and that interact with other social activities (MacIntyre, 1984, 187–190, 221). The norms of each practice are stable and adaptable. Practices thus include principles of transformation and transcendence. Engagement in a social practice alters the identity of the subject, developing their social traits (virtues), such as compassion, integrity, and bravery. Different social practices develop different combinations of virtues, with none universally at the fore. In some instances, new virtues develop (for instance, resilience and environmental concern), which transform existing practices and re-interpret external goals.

Similarly, Andreas Reckwitz (2002) develops a sociological account of practices that is consistent with Alasdair MacIntyre's interpretation, but instead references Michel Foucault and Pierre Bourdieu. Reckwitz, like MacIntyre, views practices as stable combinations of resources (materials, technologies), competencies (knowledge, skills, techniques) and shared, but not necessarily identical meanings (including ideas and values). For MacIntyre (1984, 221), stable practices develop into traditions (the preferred term here); for Reckwitz (2002, 256), they constitute a "social structure." There are a number of advantages of practice-based approaches to analysing social activity: amongst them is that this methodology avoids the epistemological and ontological problems of viewing agents as either wholly autonomous or totally determined. It recognises how being involved in a practice limits choices and viewpoints, generates particular discourses and identities, but also offers options within that activity, which grow with greater expertise and make altering and transcending that practice possible.

Thus, there are a number of significant strengths in viewing prefiguration as being embodied in social practices. Most noticeably, it is consistent with the general approaches already adopted, even if this terminology is not employed. Boggs (1977a, 99), whose account initially concentrates on the organisational differences within radical political movements, develops a more unified account, taking into account norms, identities, goals (external goods), and immanent values in the material practice. "By 'prefigurative' I mean the embodiment, within the ongoing political practice of a movement, of those forms of social relations, decision making, culture and human experience that are the ultimate goal" (Boggs 1977a, 100).

Viewing prefiguration as being realised in and through a material practice also helps to answer Yates' and Maeckelbergh's insightful query as to what "prefiguration" refers to. They highlighted how it is unclear as to whether prefiguration refers to a form of decision making, the tactic, the social organisation, or its norms. A practice-based account, by contrast, answers that we only understand tactics in the context of how they are shaped by, and assist in the generation and maintenance of, social collectives, which have specific decision-making structures. The tactic of a strike or an industrial occupation only becomes a prefigurative form of anarchist direct action, as the nineteenth-century syndicalist Émile Pouget (1994) argues, if it is the agents themselves who are in control of the action. Thus, prefigurative challenge to hierarchical control of production is achieved through collaborative, free organisation that supports it. Syndicalism embodies, in part, the values of a new society. If the same activity was mandated by the state or the production of authoritarian and secretive manipulation, the meaning of the industrial action would be different. Organisational forms (whether participatory democracy or consensus) and distinctive organisational function, on their own, can be empty of practical activity; such is the complaint against "the talking shop" which does little but give a veneer of radicalism to its otherwise inactive members. Such organisations are prefigurative of social anarchism only when they generate particular types of (diverse) identities and values, produce further tactics, and interact with other radical traditions. As John P. Clark (2013, 37–38, 65) notes, recognising that anarchist values arise within and through material practices reasserts the materialist basis of anarchist theory (against accusation of idealism) and explains how these values develop and transform.

Conceptualising prefiguration as referring to the social practices it is embedded in, also provides a reply to the criticism that anarchism is "utopian" (meaning impossible).[3] Realising in the here-and-now actual social relationships based on anarchist principles, albeit in a temporary and marginal form, demonstrates the feasibility and desirability of anarchism and provides empirical examples to assess and inspire. Rather than being an indication of confusion or incoherence, the diversity of prefigurative forms indicates its strength and applicability to various different contexts. Finally, this unified practice-based perspective on prefiguration can assist in answering claims that prefiguration is either impossible or oppressive, that one cannot anticipate or evoke the values, social relationships, and productive activities of an emancipated future.

Further Criticisms of Prefigurative (Anti-)Politics

Concentrating on the evolving combination of norms, values, social relationships and resources that constitute anti-hierarchical social practices, rather than particular forms in isolation, can overcome some of the criticisms of prefiguration outlined in the introduction. From an orthodox Marxist perspective, there is the criticism that the types of revolutionary organisation structure required to efficiently and effectively overthrow capitalism are not necessarily the same as those required to maintain and support the generation of anti-hierarchical social goods in a post-revolutionary society. This is the justification which Lenin (1963, 151–154) and his later followers – like Paul Blackledge (2010), John Molyneux (2011, 77–81), and Chris Harman (1996, 33–34) – gave for having separate hierarchical institutions for waging the revolution and for social administration immediately after the revolution, in contrast to the free communist structures that would arise sometime later. The vanguard party with its separately maintained cadre is necessary in the run up to revolutionary change, but will wither away soon after the bourgeois state has been "put to an end" and been replaced initially by the "proletarian republic" and then with pluralistic, democratic bodies (Lenin 1976, 22–26, 73–74). For Leninists, prefiguration prevents the generation of the necessary organisation for the revolutionary overthrow of the dominant class and the need for centralised efficient structures in the immediate aftermath. Thus, it is either inappropriate for revolutionary activity or objectively counter-revolutionary.

From similar orthodox Marxist positions, there is a second criticism of prefiguration, which suggests that ethical values can only reflect the dominant economic interests and thus naturalise existing relations of production.[4] This criticism is shared by some readings of Marcuse, which challenge prefigurative (anti-)politics by asking how it is possible to know the values of a future post-revolutionary society, and how these post-capitalist values can be realised, in pre-revolutionary alienated circumstances, where our consciousnesses are determined by the prevailing technological conditions.

This criticism of identifying liberatory values to be foreshadowed is developed in a different direction by certain thinkers associated with post- and post-left anarchism, such as Jacques Rancière (2014), Saul Newman (2010, 12, 51–52), and Hakim Bey (1985, 3–4). They argue that anarchism is ontologically empty. It is defined in terms of absence of an *archē*.[5] "There is no becoming, no revolution, no struggle, no path; already you're monarch of your own skin" (Bey 1985, 4). This means that there is no guiding principle, no ontological foundation, and no ultimate goal. If prefiguration involves prefiguring goals into action, then, such critics claim, one is generating a *telos* (determining endpoint) which restricts individual freedom.

There are a number of replies to the first, Leninist criticism of prefiguration, that the practices and forms of organisation required to foment revolution are distinct from those required post-revolution. As Blackledge explains, the hierarchical revolutionary party is a necessary instrument for the successful development of revolution; it is justified consequentially, not because it prefigures desirable social relationships.

> For the party to succeed in this task is to create the conditions for its own dissolution! Because socialism will be achieved once the divisions within the working class and between it and other oppressed and exploited groups are overcome, there will be no need for revolutionary parties in a mature socialist society. By their nature therefore revolutionary parties, as opposed to other forms of solidarity, cannot prefigure socialism: they are rather a (necessary and transient) instrument in the struggle for socialism.
>
> *(Blackledge 2010)*

However, contemporary libertarian socialists versed in Hegel, like Clark (2013) and Lamb (1996), point out that in a dialectical process there is no fixed *telos*; thus there is no abstract universal goal which can act as the final justification for illegitimate actions.[6] Instrumental arguments justify all sorts of vicious, oppressive behaviours, including the torture of innocent people (Anderson 2010) and the mass bombings of civilians (Miller 2014). These arguments provide justification for efficient routes to an ultimate, desirable end. By contrast, anarchist Hegelians argue that goals are non-universal, and related to particular types of social practice, which can adapt and change over time. More importantly for the prefigurative critique of Leninist instrumentalism, means in a dialectical process themselves can become ends and ends can be reduced to means.

Referring to G.W.F. Hegel's *Phenomenology of Spirit*, Lamb (1996) points out how initially the *mediating term* – the instrument for an agent to achieve its goals – becomes dominant and becomes the end itself. Just as the master relies on the bondsman to achieve their desires, and grows ever more dependent on the slave to a point where the inferior becomes more powerful than the master, so too the revolutionary party (supposedly the means of achieving social and economic emancipation) becomes more important than the client class and the goal it is supposed to serve. By contrast, having an identity between means and ends prevents authoritarian methods from becoming authoritarian goals. Similarly, Clark (2013, 78), using Hegel's own method to criticise his statism, observes that the products of the "history of communal solidarity constitute the true ethical substantiality that is the primary material base, present here and now, for the emergence of the free, nonalienated, nondominating society of the future."

The second argument provides an important challenge. Anticipating a future world appears to be a form of arrogance, for it suggests the ability of prophecy: to know the values of a future society and thus how others should live. MacIntyre (1970, 62–73), in an uncharacteristically flawed book, interprets Marcuse in this way. MacIntyre picks up on Marcuse's description of how the developing technological infrastructure develops to secure and enhance capitalist economic interests. It intensifies the division of labour, reduces us to abstract labour, thus dictating our speed of movement and tracking our activities. Technology also offers to resolve our alienation, promising ever-better forms of distraction. It constantly satisfies needs and then creates new desires, further trapping individuals into this form of life. As a result, consciousness becomes "one-dimensional" and enquiry is geared towards finding ever-more efficient means of production, based on the measurable phenomena of the here-and-now. It becomes progressively harder to imagine alternative ways of living based on different values.

> The incessant dynamic of technical progress has become permeated with political content, and the Logos of technics has been made the Logos of continued servitude. The liberating force of technology – the

instrumentalization of things – turns into a fetter of liberation; the instrumentalization of man.

(Marcuse 1986, 159)

Advancing technology rather than acting as the means for revolutionising the economic base and thus the ideological superstructure, which includes political and ethical (philosophical) ideas, turns humanity simply into objects of production, incapable of critical thinking and thus unable to generate radical ideas and counter-capitalist practices (Marx 1981, 20–21). Thus, it leaves only Marcuse and the dialectically-informed tiny minority, able to identify true values (MacIntyre 1970, 64).

However, such an analysis is not only flawed but unfair to Marcuse. Marcuse does not argue that the critical universe has completely closed, but that technology rather than promoting new forms of radical consciousness, now increasingly limits the radical imagination, facilitating greater integration and control of traditional sources of opposition – but such closure is not complete (Kellner 1990, 245–246). There are continued and new sources of opposition. Like the autonomists who come after him, Marcuse (1987; 2013) is aware of gaps within capitalism, where other values are generated and sustained, either in free play or aesthetic practices, where non-instrumental values flourish. Whilst capitalism *appears* totalising, it is not actually all-encompassing and universal, nor can it be. It requires and generates oppositional forces, which it then attempts to reconfigure for the benefit of exchange value, setting up new antagonisms and forms of resistance (Cleaver 1979; Shortall 1994).

In addition, anarchists are making much more modest claims for their prefigurative approaches. They recognise that the values, activities, and identities that they presently foreshadow are only a *synecdoche* (a small fragment of the whole), which is necessarily incomplete and provisional. Further, practices are always evolving and can transform with new values arising that represent a radical transcendence of the existing activity. This revolutionary and transcendent potential within all practices is neatly identified by Goldman (1923):

> No revolution can ever succeed as a factor of liberation unless the *means* used to further it be identical in spirit and tendency with the *purposes* to be achieved. Revolution is the negation of the existing, a violent protest against man's inhumanity to man with all the thousand and one slaveries it involves. It is the destroyer of dominant values upon which a complex system of injustice, oppression, and wrong has been built up by ignorance and brutality. It is the herald of *new values*, ushering in a transformation of the basic relations of man to man, and of man to society. It is not a mere reformer, patching up some social evils; not a mere changer of forms and institutions; not only a re-distributor of social well-being. It is all that, yet more, much more. It is, first and foremost, the *transvaluator*, the bearer of new values. It is the great

teacher of the *new ethics,* inspiring man with a new concept of life and its manifestations in social relationships. It is the mental and spiritual regeneration.

Its first ethical precept is the identity of means used and aims sought. ... [Revolution] signifies not mere external change, but internal, basic, fundamental change. That internal change of concepts and ideas, permeating ever-larger social strata, finally culminates in the violent upheaval known as revolution. Shall that climax reverse the process of transvaluation, turn against it, betray it?

As Goldman indicates, in opposition to Leninist instrumentalism, prefigurative practice which embodies liberatory values is a core feature for successful emancipatory, revolutionary action. In doing so it contests oppressive, vicious activities, and transforms them, generating previously unheralded identities and values.

Goldman's argument, however, faces the final criticism from a branch of post-anarchism. It argues for an anarchism that is ontologically empty. This form of post-anarchism takes its cue from the original Ancient Greek interpretation of anarchism, as without (*an*) a primary cause for a social relationship (*archē*). This post- (and, perhaps paradoxically, pre-modern) anarchism is one without a guiding goal (*telos*) to shape the social world in a particular way. It rejects *archic* relationships, such as those of parents over children, or monarchs over subjects, which according to the Ancients (Pre-Socratic as well as Plato and Aristotle) are the products of natural differences. These natural causes compel relationships towards the true fulfilment (Plato 2007; Frantzanas forthcoming).

Using this account of *archē* and thus developing their version of *an-archē*, Rancière (2014), Newman (2010, 53–54), and others argue rightly, that claims to a single, fixed universal goal are limiting and ontologically and epistemologically suspect. Their solution, however, is to all *teleology*. As a result, such post-anarchisms cannot be prefigurative. If there is no *telos*, then there is nothing to prefigure, instead it is a matter of immediate, unconditional encounters between individuals (Newman 2010, 56).

However, there are problems with this post-anarchist position. It mistakes rejecting a single universal *telos* for rejecting also the multitude of guiding and evolving goals (*telē* or *teloi*). Such a position, seems difficult to sustain for an engaged (anti-)politics. Without an understanding of goals, most social practices would be unsustainable and incomprehensible. When engaging in football or cookery there are identifiable goals towards which these practices are geared (scoring most goals or producing an enjoyable meal).

A practice will tend to have a stable goal, although it might alter over the tradition, so the goal of cookery might now include creating an ecologically sustainable course. Post-anarchists engage in goal-orientated activities, such as dialogues with other practitioners and theorists, book-writing and teaching. These might not have universal or fixed *tele*, but they are a necessary feature of their social practices that help construct post-anarchism as a recognisable tradition.

Collegiality and solidarity, which Newman (2010, 118–119), following Emmanuel Levinas, believes are part of ethical engagement with others, are core, stable virtues that prefigure wider forms of anti-hierarchical social interaction.

Goals develop and are refined as the practitioner becomes more skilled and the tradition develops. As goods-rich practices intersect with other adjacent practices, new perspectives and lacunae in previous ambitions become apparent, and some are abandoned or transcended as material circumstances change. Identifying shared interests and ambitions provides the basis for solidarity between practitioners from apparently different traditions. Imposing single targets onto diverse activities and traditions, such as the profit motive of corporate neo-liberalism distorts, corrupts, and undermines these activities. Rejecting a single universal (*telos*) is thus epistemologically, ethically, and ontologically consistent with anarchism, however, rejecting all goals would undermine valuable social practices and make anti-hierarchical prefiguration impossible.

Conclusion

Prefiguration is a core feature of anarchist practices both historically and spatially. Whilst it can be a feature of other hierarchical and oppressive political ideologies, the priority it is given in anarchism (and its proximity to anti-capitalist and horizontal social relations) distinguishes it from the more peripheral role it plays in the conceptual constellations of, say, liberalism and fascism. Prefiguration is best understood as relating to material social practices, which unify norms, social organisation, and method in generating immediate, internal goods as well as shared, external goods.

Critics of prefiguration rightly identify something disconcerting, perhaps uncanny, about such *prolepsis*, which is why it is a theme in tragedy and horror films such as *Don't Look Now*.[7] It can suggest a limitation of autonomy, as the actions of the present are determined by the future and the upcoming is already foreseen and thus predestined by the present. However, this misunderstands the nature of anarchist teleology. So, whilst post-anarchists rightly argue there is no fixed or single *telos*, there are still multiple, developing goals, specific to the evolving traditions of prefigurative practice. The goals and values embodied in these practices include, by necessity, the possibility of evolution and transcendence. Without some stable (but not fixed or singular) goals most practices are inoperable and the journey – or links – between practices becomes incoherent. Prefiguration is, thus, core because it is a central norm that clarifies other anarchist principles that are important to the internal operation of practices and the ways these intersect with each other to develop into radical traditions.

Notes

1 Uri Gordon (2015) has traced the term's wider political meanings back to early Christian theology, but there is the risk of the *genetic fallacy* in concentrating on this feature of

prefiguration, as there is little indication that any anarchist activist or theorist looked to these sources as a guide. It would be mistaken to base its modern and contemporary meanings on a largely unconnected origin.
2 To see criticisms of the classification, consult Adams (2013).
3 See, for instance, Plekhanov (1895).
4 Alan Gilbert (1981, 173–174), for instance, identifies these approaches to reading Karl Marx's moral theory, but rejects them as inaccurate interpretations of Marx's theoretical position.
5 I am grateful to my colleague Sotiris Frantzanas who is completing a systematic analysis of *an-archē*.
6 In addition, you can see in Bakunin (2005, 133) a significant debt to Hegel, although he views Hegel as irredeemably idealist.
7 *Don't Look Now*, 1973, directed by Nicolas Roeg.

References

Adams, Matthew. 2013. "The Possibilities of Anarchist History: Rethinking the Canon and Writing History." *Anarchist Developments in Cultural Studies* 1: 33–63.
Anarchist Federation. 2013. "Introduction to Anarchist Communism." Anarchist Federation. Accessed 7 September 2015. https://afed.org.uk/introduction-to-anarchist-communism/.
Anarchist Federation. 2015. "Aims and Principles." Anarchist Federation. Accessed 7 September 2015. https://afed.org.uk/about/aims-principles/.
Anderson, Benedict. 2005. *Under Three Flags: Anarchism and the Anti-Colonial Imagination*. London: Verso.
Anderson, Bruce. 2010. "We Not Only Have a Right to Use Torture. We Have a Duty." *The Independent*, 15 February. Accessed 20 January 2015. www.independent.co.uk/voices/commentators/bruce-anderson/bruce-anderson-we-not-only-have-a-right-to-use-torture-we-have-a-duty-1899555.html.
Aristotle. 1976. *Ethics*. Harmondsworth: Penguin.
Bakunin, Mikhail. 2005. *Statism and Anarchy*. Cambridge: Cambridge University Press.
Bey, Hakim. 1985. *T.A.Z.: The Temporary Autonomous Zone, Ontological Anarchy, Poetic Terrorism*. New York: Autonomedia.
Blackledge, Paul. 2010. "Marxism and Anarchism." *International Socialist* 125 (5 January). Accessed 13 January 2016. http://isj.org.uk/marxism-and-anarchism/.
Boggs, Carl. 1977a. "Marxism, Prefigurative Communism, and the Problem of Workers' Control." *Radical America* 11 (November): 99–122.
Boggs, Carl. 1977b. "Revolutionary Process, Political Strategy and the Dilemma of Power." *Theory and Society* 4 (Autumn): 359–393.
Breines, Wini. 1980. "Community and Organization: The New Left and Michels' 'Iron Law.'" *Social Problems* 27 (April): 419–429.
Breines, Wini. 1989. *Community and Organization in the New Left 1962–68: The Great Refusal*. New Brunswick, NJ: Rutgers University Press.
Clark, John. 2013. *The Impossible Community: Realizing Communitarian Anarchism*. London: Bloomsbury.
Cleaver, Harry. 1979. *Reading "Capital" Politically*. Brighton: Harvester.
Crowder, George. 1991. *Classical Anarchism: The Political Thought of Godwin, Proudhon, Bakunin, and Kropotkin*. Oxford: Clarendon.
Crump, John. 1996. *The Anarchist Movement in Japan*. London: Anarchist Communist Editions.
Dirlik, Arif. 1991. *Anarchism in the Chinese Revolution*. Berkeley: University of California.

Frantzanas, Sotiris. Forthcoming. *Redefining Anarchy: From Metaphysics to Politics*.
Freeden, Michael. 2003. *Ideology: A Very Short Introduction*. Oxford: Oxford University Press.
Gautney, Heather. 2009. "Between Anarchism and Autonomist Marxism." *WorkingUSA* 12(3): 467–487.
Gilbert, Alan. 1981. "Historical Theory and the Structure of Moral Argument in Marx." *Political Theory* 9(2): 173–205.
Goldman, Emma. 1923. *My Disillusionment with Russia*. New York: Doubleday, Page & Company. Libcom.org. Accessed 19 January 2016. https://libcom.org/files/Emma%20Goldman-%20My%20Disillusionment%20in%20Russia.pdf.
Gordon, Uri. 2015. "Prefigurative Politics and Anarchism." Recently published as 'Prefigurative politics between ethical practice and absent promise.' "Political Studies" (2017) <www.journals.sagepub.com/doi/pdf/10.1177/0032321717722363>.
Grubačić, Andrej. 2013. "The Anarchist Moment." In *The Anarchist Turn*, edited by Jacob Blumenfeld, Chirar Bottici, and Simon Critchley, 186–201. London: Pluto Press.
Hammond, John. 2015. "The Anarchism of Occupy Wall Street." *Science and Society* 79 (April): 288–313.
Harman, Chris. 1996. "Party and Class." In *Party and Class*, edited by Tony Cliff, Duncan Hallas, Chris Harman, and Leon Trotsky. London: Bookmarks.
Industrial Workers of the World. "Preamble to the IWW Constitution." Industrial Workers of the World. Accessed 20 October 2015. www.iww.org/culture/official/preamble.shtml.
Kellner, Douglas. 1990. "From 1984 to One-Dimensional Man: Critical Reflections on Orwell and Marcuse." *Current Perspectives in Social Theory* 10: 223–252.
Kenafick, K.J. 1984. "Foreword" to Mikhail Bakunin, *Marxism, Freedom and the State*. London: Freedom Press.
Lamb, Dave. 1996. "Libertarian Socialism." Accessed 20 March 2017. http://libcom.org/library/libertarian-socialism-dave-lamb.
Lenin, Vladimir. 1963. *What Is to Be Done?* Oxford: Clarendon.
Lenin, Vladimir. 1976. *The State and Revolution*. Peking: Foreign Languages Press.
Linebaugh, Peter. 2009. "Introduction." In Thomas Paine, *Rights of Man and Common Sense*. London: Verso.
MacIntyre, Alasdair. 1970. *Marcuse*. London: Fontana/Collins.
MacIntyre, Alasdair. 1984. *After Virtue*, 2nd ed. London: Duckworth.
Maeckelbergh, Marianne. 2011. "Doing is Believing: Prefiguration as Strategic Practice in the Alterglobalization Movement." *Social Movement Studies: Journal of Social, Cultural and Political Protest* 10: 1–20.
Marcuse, Herbert. 1986. *One-Dimensional Man*. London: Ark.
Marcuse, Herbert. 1987. *Eros and Civilisation*. London: Ark.
Marcuse, Herbert. 2013. *The Aesthetic Dimension*, London: Beacon.
Marx, Karl. 1981. *A Contribution to the Critique of Political Economy*. London: Lawrence & Wishart.
Marx, Karl, and Friedrich Engels. 1976. *The German Ideology*. Moscow: Progress.
Miller, Henry I. 2014 "The Nuking of Japan Was Tactically and Morally Justified." *Forbes*, 5 August. Accessed 20 January 2016. www.forbes.com/sites/henrymiller/2014/08/05/the-nuking-of-japan-was-a-military-and-moral-imperative/#2715e4857a0b28e 46cb3553b.
Molyneux, John. 2011. *Anarchism: A Marxist Criticism*. London: Bookmarks.
Newman, Saul. 2010. *The Politics of Postanarchism*. Edinburgh: Edinburgh University Press.
Plato. 2007. *Republic*. Harmondsworth: Penguin.

Plekhanov, Georgi. V. 1895. *Anarchism and Socialism*. Marxist Internet Archive. Accessed 20 March 2017. www.marxists.org/archive/plekhanov/1895/anarch/index.htm.

Pouget, Émile. 1994. "Direct Action." Libcom.org. Accessed 13 January 2016. http://libcom.org/library/direct-action-emile-pouget.

Rancière, Jacques. 2014. "Anarchism, Para-Academia, Pure Politics, and the Non-Human." *Anarchist Directions in Cultural Studies*. www.anarchist-developments.org/index.php/adcs_journal/article/view/92/100.

Reckwitz, Andreas. 2002. "Toward a Theory of Social Practices: A Development in Culturalist Theorizing." *European Journal of Social Theory* 5(2): 243–263.

Shortall, Felton. 1994. *The Incomplete Marx*. Aldershot: Avebury.

Sparrow, Rob. n.d. "Anarchist Politics & Direct Action." Spunk Library. Accessed 12 January 2016. http://spunk.org/texts/intro/sp001641.html.

van de Sande, Mathijs. 2015. "Fighting with Tools: Prefiguration and Radical Politics in the Twenty-First Century." *Rethinking Marxism* 27(2): 177–194.

van der Walt, Lucien. 2011. "What Anarchism and Syndicalism offer the South African Left." Zabalaza.net, 12 July. Accessed 6 September 2015. http://zabalaza.net/2011/07/12/what-anarchism-and-syndicalism-offer-the-south-african-left/.

Verson, Jennifer. 2007. "Why We Need Cultural Activism." In *Do it Yourself: A Handbook for Changing the World*, edited by Trapese Collective, 171–186. London: Pluto Press.

Vieta, Marcelo. 2014. "The Stream of Self-Determination and Autogestión: Prefiguring Alternative Economic Realities." *Ephemera* 14(4): 781–809.

Wall, Derek. 1999. *Earth First! and the Anti-Roads Movement*. London: Routledge.

Yates, Luke. 2015. "Rethinking Prefiguration: Alternatives, Micropolitics and Goals in Social Movements." *Social Movement Studies: Journal of Social, Cultural and Political Protest* 14: 1–21.

3
FREEDOM

Nathan Jun

Whereas earlier forms of political thought emphasized "the idea of a natural order discernible by reason to which human beings ought to conform," modern political thought "begins, ends, and is animated throughout by the idea of freedom" (Franco 1999, 2) – a fact that is aptly demonstrated by the sheer number and variety of political ideologies that acknowledge it as a core concept. Notwithstanding this "near unanimity on … the centrality of freedom in understanding political life" (ibid.), political ideologies disagree sharply over the meaning of the concept as well as "its measurement, distribution, and institutional requirements" (Kukathas 2012, 685). At particular issue are the following questions:

First, what is the ontological status of freedom? In other words, what kind of thing is the concept of freedom a conception *of*?
Second, who or what is free? In other words, to whom or what does the concept of freedom apply?
And third, is freedom valuable as an end in itself or merely as a means to achieving other valuable ends?

Liberalism – the ideology most commonly associated with the concept – typically defines freedom as a state, condition, or capacity (of some kind or another) that is morally valuable (in some sense or other) and which applies solely or chiefly to individual persons rather than collective entities. Beyond these general points of agreement, liberals have ascribed a wide range of more or less plausible meanings to freedom, and "different streams within liberalism express preference for some … of those meanings" over others (Freeden 2015, 59). As Michael Freeden (2015) notes:

Broadly speaking, the meaning of liberty [within liberal ideologies] will stretch between securing an area of harmless activity, or even passive existence, unimpeded by physical or state initiated intrusion ... and enabling the exercise of human potential through actively removing any hindrances that could seriously dehumanize human beings.

(59)

This observation highlights the extent to which liberalism and other broad ideological traditions can and do express themselves as distinct orientations that differ over the meaning and scope of core concepts – in which case political disagreement is just as often *intra-ideological* as it is *inter-ideological*.

The tendency of conventional discussions of ideology to underemphasize or altogether overlook this fact is vividly illustrated in the case of anarchism. From its origins in the nineteenth century to the present, anarchism has been routinely identified with the rejection of the state – so much so, in fact, that the term "anarchist" is often treated as a synonym for "anti-statist."[1] This identification follows from a more general but no less ubiquitous habit of characterizing anarchists as "extreme libertarians" (Ritter 1980, 9) who value "unlimited and absolute freedom" (Zenker 1897, 9), make a "holy dogma of the abstract freedom or autonomy of the individual" (Belfort Bax 1891, 145), and demand "the right of every person to do as he or she pleases always and under all circumstances" (Morris 1996, 88) – all of which suggests that their most fundamental and distinctive political value is a hyperbolized form of negative liberty that is otherwise "virtually the same as that of many of the classical liberals" (Vincent 2009, 125).[2]

It is certainly true that anarchists hold freedom in especially high esteem and that this makes it "more plausible than any other value as their overriding aim" (Ritter 1980, 9). William Godwin (1798, 331), for example, identified freedom as "the most valuable of all human possessions." Pierre-Joseph Proudhon, a self-described "partisan ... of all liberties" (Proudhon 2011, 702), referred to it as his "banner and rule" (Proudhon 1875, 375). And Mikhail Bakunin, who called himself a "fanatic lover of liberty" (Bakunin 1972, 261), defined it as "the absolute source and condition of all good that is truly worthy of that name" (Bakunin 1953, 155). That said, it is a grave mistake to portray anarchists as "single-minded devotees of freedom" who seek liberty "above all else" (Ritter 1980, 9, 39), and this for at least two reasons. First, doing so neglects their commitment to other values and, by extension, fails to provide a clear distinction between anarchism and other ideologies that value freedom, including liberalism. Second, and more importantly, it ignores the considerable extent to which anarchists have disagreed amongst themselves regarding "what freedom *is* ... what relationships exist *between* freedom and other concepts ... [and] how *central* freedom is in [anarchism's] arrangement of concepts and values" (Gordon 2008, 20).

Although there is no question that freedom is a core concept of anarchism – "one that is both central to, and constitutive of [it]" and, by extension, to "the particular ideological community to which it gives inspiration and identity" (Ball 1999, 391–392) – this does not mean that freedom is the only or even the most important element "in [anarchists'] model of a good society" (Ritter 1980, 38), nor that anarchism understands freedom in the same way as other ideologies like liberalism. Because anarchism has long been and continues to be a global political movement whose ideas evolve from and are disseminated through a complex array of decentralized transnational networks (Altena and Bantman 2014, 12), the ideas in question are constantly being "reimagined in fresh national contexts … adapted and modified to meet the specific challenges facing activists and thinkers in these countries, and translated – both literally and figuratively – into prevailing cultural scripts" (Adams and Jun 2015, 259).[3] In practice, this has led to the proliferation of diverse conceptions of freedom within and across multiple contexts and, as a result, it is extremely difficult to adumbrate a single conception of freedom that all anarchists share in common.

One of the principal merits of Freeden's morphological approach is that it avoids reducing complex ideologies like anarchism to a "series of simplified generalizations" and "distances itself from [simpler] accounts of ideological distinctiveness and diversity by dismissing identification of … ideologies with one central concept" (Freeden 2013, 117, 125). Instead, Freeden treats ideologies as complex, dynamic, and variable conceptual assemblages that are distinguished by their *morphologies* – that is, the various ways they organize and arrange concepts so as to accord them specific meanings and degrees of significance. Although this approach recognizes that ideologies have core elements that are "indispensable to holding [them] together, and are consequently accorded preponderance in shaping [their] ideational content" (126), it avoids defining them strictly in terms of these (or any other) concepts. Its goal as such is not only to identify the core concepts of ideological morphologies but also, and more importantly, to investigate the various "conceptual permutations" these morphologies contain. Because these are virtually unlimited, ideologies have "the potential for infinite variety and alteration" and so are capable of expressing themselves in a wide and diverse range of manifestations (128, 126). This is true even of core concepts, the meanings of which can vary enormously from one particular "manifestation" of a given ideology to the next (125).

In this chapter, I draw upon Freeden's morphological approach to examine the various ways freedom has been conceptualized within the anarchist tradition. My principal aims in doing so are two-fold: first, to determine how and to what extent these conceptions serve to differentiate anarchism from liberalism and other ideologies that claim freedom as a core concept; and second, to explore the role they play in the formulation of diverse anarchist tendencies. As I shall argue, prevailing anarchist conceptions of freedom uniformly obviate the "assumed tension between the freedom of the individual and the good of society" as well as "between negative and positive definitions of the concept" (Honeywell 2014, 118). Indeed, the rejection of such dichotomies is a unifying theme in anarchism more generally and a key aspect of its ideological distinctiveness.

The Concept of Freedom

As noted previously, intra- and inter-ideological disagreements over the meaning of freedom often concern its ontological status, scope, and value. This suggests that standard conceptualizations of freedom contain at least three kinds of micro-components – one that specifies what freedom is a concept *of*, a second that specifies to whom or what freedom applies, and a third that specifies how and why freedom is valuable. As Chandran Kukathas (2012, 534) notes, contemporary understandings of the ontological status and scope of freedom have been "most profoundly shaped by the analysis of Isaiah Berlin … [who] … argues that, in the history of ideas, liberty has had two quite different meanings or senses." In Berlin's (1969, 121) classic formulation, negative liberty (or "freedom from") is the absence of external interference, coercion, or constraint – the freedom to "be left to do or be what [one] is able to do or be, without interference by other persons." A person is free in this sense "to the degree that no man or body of men interferes with his activity," which means that negative liberty is "simply the area within which a man can act unobstructed by others" (122). Positive liberty ("freedom to"), in contrast, is the freedom "to be [one's] own master …" such that one's "life and decisions depend on [oneself], not on external forces of whatever kind …" (131). To be free in this sense is to be autonomous or self-determining, i.e., "a thinking, willing, active being, bearing responsibility for one's own ideas and able to explain them by reference to one's own ideas and purposes" (133).

Although negative and positive freedom both apply to individuals, the former designates a state or condition that individuals occupy, whereas the latter designates a capacity that they possess. This raises the question of whether negative and positive freedom are "two different interpretations of a single concept" (Berlin 1969, 166) or whether they are altogether separate concepts, as Berlin himself believed. The latter, if true, has important ramifications for the ontological status of freedom, as it would imply that negative and positive freedom do not have any possible referents in common and, by extension, that they pertain to entirely different sorts of things. (Some liberals who take this view recognize *both* as core concepts – albeit with varying degrees of relative significance – while others will only recognize one or the other as a core concept.) The former, in contrast, would suggest that negative and positive freedom are simply two different ways of (micro-)decontesting the same concept – i.e., of defining and arranging that concept's micro-components, determining its position in relation to other concepts within a given liberal morphology, or both.

At first glance, the fact that negative freedom refers to a state or condition and positive freedom refers to a capacity would appear to support the notion that they are altogether separate concepts referring to altogether different kinds of things. Whether it truly does so, however, depends on how we define the term "capacity," and here there are at least two possibilities. The first, which I call an *actionable capacity*, refers to an actual power or ability to act in a particular way under existing conditions. The second, which I call a *potentiality*, refers to a hypothetical capacity to act in a particular way that is only realizable under certain conditions. For example, to say that Jones has the (actionable) *capacity* to speak Japanese means that she has the actual power or ability to speak Japanese right now, whereas to say that Jones has the *potential* to speak Japanese means that she has the power to speak Japanese only under certain conditions (say, the condition of knowing how to speak Japanese, of having functioning cognitive and linguistic faculties, of having a functioning larynx, and so on). In other words, if the conditions necessary for Jones to speak Japanese do not obtain, then Jones does not have the potential to speak Japanese unless and until they are.

According to this view, X has the potential to ϕ if and only if there is a range of possible conditions under which X has an actionable capacity to ϕ. If such conditions do not exist, then X does not have the potential to ϕ. For example, if Jones has suffered irreparable damage to the parts of her brain that are responsible for language usage or acquisition, then there are no possible conditions under which she will have an actionable capacity to speak Japanese – in which case we would say Jones lacks the potential to do so. On the other hand, if Jones has the power or ability to speak Japanese under actually existing conditions, it follows trivially that these are possible conditions under which Jones has an actionable capacity to speak Japanese – in which case the fact that Jones has an actionable capacity to speak Japanese implies that she has the potential to do so prior to those conditions obtaining.

In many cases, X is prevented from ϕ-ing by external impediments that are a direct or indirect consequence of deliberate human intervention (Kukathas 2012, 535). For example, if Smith binds Jones to a chair and gags her, Jones will obviously lack an actionable capacity to speak Japanese because Smith is forcibly inhibiting her ability to do so. This doesn't mean that there are no possible conditions under which Jones has the actionable capacity to speak Japanese – only that Smith is preventing those conditions from obtaining right now. As long as such conditions remain possible, Jones retains the potential to speak Japanese even if she lacks the actionable capacity to do so.

The same is true in cases where lack of actionable capacity is the result of external factors that have nothing to do with human intervention (as when Jones suffers severe head trauma in the midst of an extreme weather event) or, indeed, of factors that are entirely internal to the agent him/herself (as when Jones refrains from speaking Japanese because she has an irrational fear of doing so). X's lack of actionable capacity to ϕ does not imply that X lacks the potential to ϕ unless there are no possible conditions under which X has the ability to ϕ. If it is possible for Jones to recover from her head injury or overcome her irrational phobia, then Jones retains the potential to speak Japanese because there are possible conditions under which she has an actionable capacity to do so. If no such conditions exist, then Jones lacks both the potential as well as the actionable capacity to speak Japanese.

In the strict sense, X is negatively unfree if and only if X lacks an actionable capacity to ϕ on account of human interference. If positive freedom means an actual ability or power to act autonomously under existing conditions, then one cannot be positively free without also being (at least mostly) free from anything that hinders or obstructs his or her ability to act autonomously – in which case negative freedom is a necessary but not sufficient condition for positive freedom in the sense of having an actionable capacity to act autonomously. This suggests, in turn, that negative freedom is a component of the concept of positive freedom rather than an altogether separate concept. If, on the other hand, positive freedom merely refers to the *potential* to act autonomously, then negative freedom is neither a necessary *nor* a sufficient condition for positive freedom, since it is possible for one to be positively free even if s/he lacks negative freedom, and vice versa. In this case it would make more sense to regard negative freedom and positive freedom as altogether separate concepts.

Questions concerning the scope and ontological status of "freedom" have important axiological ramifications as well. If negative and positive freedom are regarded as components of the same concept, how much and what kind of proportional weight are these components assigned within the internal structure of that concept? Does each have equal intrinsic value, or, as some liberals contend, is negative freedom only valuable insofar as it serves as a means to achieving or realizing positive freedom? And if this is so, *how* valuable is negative freedom in comparison to other conceptual micro-components that are regarded as instrumentally valuable? On the other hand, if negative and positive freedom are regarded as separate concepts, where does each stand in relation to the ideological core of liberalism? If only one of them is a core concept, which one qualifies as such, and why? If both are core concepts, are they equally valuable, or does one have greater proportional weight than the other?

Given the sheer number and variety of possible definitions of freedom, it comes as no surprise that liberalism lacks uniform answers to these questions. The same is true, as it turns out, of every ideology that recognizes freedom as a core concept – a fact which, unfortunately, has seldom been acknowledged in the case of anarchism. As we shall see, this is because the predominant conception of freedom in the anarchist tradition is largely incompatible with Berlin's paradigm.

Freedom as an Anarchist Concept

As was noted in the introduction, there is a longstanding tendency to associate anarchism with an essentially liberal conception of negative freedom predicated on the total rejection of "coercion or compulsion" (Vincent 2009, 125). According to Paul Thomas (1980), for example:

> Many of [anarchism's] doctrinal features point ... back ... through the Enlightenment of the eighteenth century into the liberal tradition ...

> Anarchist convictions and doctrines are with rare exceptions based upon a negative view of liberty — a view according to which freedom is to be understood in the first instance as freedom *from* some obstacle or impediment to its exercise, in this case the state and its auxiliaries. All anarchist convictions can be summed up under the rubric not of the hindering of hindrances to but of the *removal of obstacles* from some vision of the good life. It is this imperative that links anarchism to the liberal tradition ....
>
> *(8, emphasis in original)*

Likewise, R.B. Fowler (1972):

> Does our exploration of nineteenth-century anarchist thinking about individualism and coercion direct us to a single, defining pattern? The answer must be that what emerges is a mood permeated by the desire to make every person as free to do as he truly wished, within the constraints of social life and the requirements of nature. This mood suggests that anarchism might be best understood in relation to nineteenth-century laissez-faire liberalism. The enthusiasm of both outlooks for maximum negative liberty and individual development is unmistakable. Perhaps laissez-faire liberal theorists differed only in advocating the preservation of a little "government" because they were a shade less confident of humanity.
>
> *(745)*

Accounts of this sort, it must be admitted, are not altogether inaccurate. There is no question that "anarchist sympathy for negative freedom [is] enormous" and that "their writings resonate with their demand for it" (Fowler 1972, 746), as is made clear by the following representative quotations[4]:

> The character of the revolution must at first be negative, destructive. Instead of modifying certain institutions of the past, or adapting them to a new order, it will do away with them altogether. Therefore, the government will be uprooted, along with the Church, the army, the courts, the schools, the banks, and all their subservient institutions ...
>
> *(James Guillaume, quoted in Bakunin 1972, 357).*

> Anarchy is anti-government, anti-rulers, anti-dictators, anti-bosses. ... Anarchy is the negation of force; the elimination of all authority in social affairs; it is the denial of the right of domination of one man over another ...
>
> *(Albert Parsons, quoted in Parsons 1886, 12).*

> Anarchism, contrary to authority, is the name given to a principle or theory of life and conduct under which society is conceived without government ...
>
> *(Kropotkin 1968, 284)*

Anarchism ... teaches that the present unjust organization of the production and distribution of wealth must finally be completely destroyed ...
(de Cleyre 2005, 301).

The same is true of the notion that there is a significant historical and ideological affinity between anarchism and classical liberalism, at least in this respect. Anarchists themselves have frequently argued as much, as when Rudolf Rocker (2004, 11) asserts that anarchism "has in common with Liberalism the idea that the happiness and prosperity of the individual must be the standard of all social matters ... [as well as] ... the idea of limiting the functions of government to a minimum ...."

Nevertheless, there are several problems with the position described above. In the first place, anarchism "has never been, nor ever aspired to be, a fixed, comprehensive, self-contained, and internally consistent system of ideas, set of doctrines, or body of theory" (Jun 2012, 49) and so is not "necessarily linked to any [one] philosophical system" (Malatesta 1965, 19). As Freeden (1996, 311) notes, on the contrary, anarchism "straddles more than one ideological family" and has "carved out a niche related to and intersecting with [all of] them." This accounts for the multifarious array of tendencies, orientations, and schools of thought through which anarchism has been expressed. In the second place, the fact that all forms of anarchism emphasize negative freedom scarcely entails that they understand this concept in the same way as classical liberalism, nor that their conception of freedom is principally negative in character.

Of particular relevance to the first point is the well-known distinction between "individualist anarchism" and "social anarchism." Like classical liberals, virtually all of the major theorists associated with the former are committed to three broad claims: first, that "the solitary individual – the agent who is and always has been isolated from others – is nevertheless capable, in principle, of displaying all distinctive human capacities"; second, that "any property that can serve as an ultimate political value ... [is] capable of being instantiated by the socially isolated person, by the solitary individual"; and third, "that the ultimate criteria of political judgment ... are provided by non-social as distinct from social values" (Pettit 2005, 23, 26, 28). For individualist anarchists, the notion that society is or could be anything more than a mere collection of individuals is a "scientific abstraction" (Yarros 1994, 35). But if there is no society apart from individuals, this means there is no such thing as "social well-being" apart from aggregate individual well-being, the essential condition of which is "individual sovereignty" (Yarros 1994, 34), i.e., the absolute and inviolable right to do as one pleases to the extent compatible with the freedom of others (Armand 1907). Such a right belongs to human beings by nature; it is not "bestowed" upon them by society. As Benjamin Tucker writes, on the contrary, "the individual is the gainer by society exactly in proportion as society is free, and ... the condition of a permanent and harmonious society is the greatest amount of individual liberty compatible with equality of liberty ..." (quoted in Martin 1970, 25).

The fact that individuals have "inalienable moral jurisdiction" (McElroy 2004, 4) over their own property – including their bodies – implies a negative right to not be subjected to "imposition, constraint, violence, [and] governmental oppression, whether these are a product of all, a group, or of one person" (Armand 1907). Because justice is coextensive with honoring this right, and because the latter is only possible under the "condition of absolute liberty," it follows that any political, social, or economic institution that limits negative freedom is unjust by definition (Martin 1970, 55). This applies not only to the State but also to the various laws, customs, and traditions that govern individual behavior. For many individualist anarchists, it also applies to capitalism and other forms of economic exchange that deny workers the fruits of their labor.

Social anarchism, in contrast, has consistently emphasized "community, mutuality, free cooperation, and … social arrangements of a reciprocal character" (Egoumenides 2014, 2–3) as indispensable components of freedom and "demand[ed] the abolition of all economic monopolies and the common ownership of the soil and all other means of production, the use of which must be available for all without distinction …" (Rocker 2004, 11). To this extent it is better understood as a "confluence" of liberalism and socialism than as an extreme form of liberal individualism (ibid.). Although I do not share the view that social anarchism is "the only anarchism" (Schmidt and van der Walt 2009, 19), the preponderance of historical evidence makes clear that it has long been and continues to be the predominant anarchist tendency and, to this extent, is arguably the most representative of the anarchist tradition as a whole. This suggests, in turn, that we are within our rights to treat its conception of freedom as normative.

The social anarchist conception of freedom rests on three fundamental claims. First, "true liberty" for social anarchists is not a "*negative* thing" that involves "being free *from* something" but rather "the freedom *to* something … the liberty to be, to do; in short the liberty of actual and active opportunity" (Goldman 1998, 98). Positive freedom in this sense corresponds to an individual's capacity to "grow to [his or her] full stature … [to] learn to think and move, to give the very best of [himself or herself] … [to] realize the true force of the social bonds that tie men [sic] together, and which are the true foundations of a normal social life" (Goldman 1910, 67). In this way, it serves as the primary vehicle through which "all the latent powers of individual …" are expressed and the principal means of satisfying her "desire to create and act freely" (Goldman 1910, 61).

Second, because the actualization of "the material, intellectual, and moral powers that are latent in each person" (Bakunin 1972, 261) and "the all-around development and full enjoyment of all physical, intellectual, and moral faculties" (Bakunin 1992, 46) is not possible "outside of human society or without its cooperation …" (46), individual freedom is a "collective product" (46), born of "collective and social labor" (Bakunin 1972, 236). For social anarchists, the fact that human beings "share the same fundamental human qualities … share the same basic fate … [and] … have the same inalienable claim on freedom and happiness" (Fromm 2001, 228) implies that human nature itself – which is "immanent and inherent, forming the very basis of our material, intellectual and moral being" (Bakunin 1972, 262) – is inexorably social. This suggests, in turn, that "the isolated individual cannot possibly become conscious of his [sic] freedom" and, by extension, that "the freedom of other men [sic], far from negating or limiting [individual] freedom, is, on the contrary, its necessary premise and confirmation" (237). A similar point is made by Errico Malatesta, who argues that solidarity "is the only environment in which Man [sic] can express his personality and achieve his optimum development and enjoy the greatest possible wellbeing" (Malatesta 1974, 29), as well as by Emma Goldman, who contends that individual freedom is "strengthened by cooperation with other individualities" and that "only mutual aid and voluntary cooperation can create the basis for a free individual ... life" (Goldman 1998, 118).

Third, the fact that "the freedom of each" finds its "necessary *raison d'etre* in ... the freedom of others" (Malatesta 1974, 29) implies that "equality is an absolutely necessary condition for freedom" (Bakunin 1992, 48). Equality in this context refers not to the "forced equality of the convict camp" (Berkman 2003, 164) but to the equal opportunity of "each human being to bring to full development the powers, capacities, and talents with which nature has endowed him [sic]" (Guérin 1998, 57). As Alexander Berkman (2003) writes:

> True anarchist equality implies freedom, not quantity. It does not mean that every one must eat, drink, or wear the same things, do the same work, or live in the same manner. Far from it: the very reverse in fact ... Individual needs and tastes differ, as appetites differ. It is equal opportunity to satisfy them that constitutes true equality. Far from leveling, such equality opens the door for the greatest possible variety of activity and development. For human character is diverse ... Free opportunity of expressing and acting out your individuality means development of natural dissimilarities and variations.
>
> *(164)*

For social anarchists, "equality [is not] secondary to liberty, as usually happens under the liberal reading ... [and] the demand for it goes beyond the formal equality of rights" (Egoumenides 2014, 90). The converse is also true: because equality of the sort described above is not possible in the absence of freedom, it follows that freedom itself is a necessary condition for equality and, by extension, that the two are "mutually dependent values" (Ritter 1980, 3).

In the last section, we noted that the meaning of freedom is a partial function of the meanings and degrees of relative significance assigned to at least three micro-components – one that specifies what freedom is a concept *of*, a second that specifies to whom or what freedom applies, and a third that specifies how and why freedom is valuable. In the social anarchist conception, the first of these micro-components identifies freedom as a *state* or *condition* marked by the achievement of maximal human development or flourishing, which means that freedom is a *teleological* as well as *eudaimonistic* concept; the third identifies maximal human development or flourishing as an end in itself, which means that freedom is a concept of *intrinsic value*; and the second identifies freedom as fundamentally social in character, which means that freedom is a *non-monistic* or *non-individualist* concept.

While the first micro-component is clearly the most significant with regard to the overall meaning of freedom, its meaning depends on its relationship to the other two. If freedom is a *non-individualist* concept, for example, this implies that individuals are free only to the extent that the societies to which they belong are free, and, by extension, that societies are free only to the extent that they realize, or are capable of realizing, the end of maximal human development or flourishing. Similarly, the notion that freedom is a concept of *intrinsic value* implies that freedom itself is distinct from the various background conditions necessary for its realization, which conditions themselves are merely instrumentally valuable. Although some of these conditions are roughly analogous to "negative" and "positive" freedom in Berlin's sense of these terms, freedom itself cannot be reduced to either of them and, as such, is neither wholly negative nor wholly positive.

Unlike individualist anarchists and classical liberals, social anarchists do not regard the removal of external coercion or constraint as an intrinsically valuable or desirable end. In the absence of egalitarian social conditions, negative freedom of this sort is little more than untrammeled license to do as one pleases, even if this means exploiting, oppressing or commanding others (Malatesta 1965, 53) or seeking "well-being, prosperity, and good fortune to the disadvantage of everyone else, despite them and on their backs" (Bakunin 1992, 57). As such, it does nothing on its own to promote the maximal development of individuals and, in many cases, actually serves to hinder it. This suggests that negative freedom is only valuable to the extent that it serves as a necessary condition for positive freedom – i.e., autonomy or self-determination.

For social anarchists, the fact that human beings have "a consciousness of self, of being different from others" instills a "craving for liberty and self-expression …" (Goldman 1998, 439) that is only satisfied when they are "left to act for themselves, to feel responsibility for their own actions in the good or bad that comes from them" (Malatesta 1981, 26). In this sense, the positive capacity for autonomy – no less than the desire to act autonomously – is an essential characteristic of humanness, the actualization of which is only possible in the absence of externally imposed restrictions that "inhibit or prevent people from participating in determining their actions or the conditions of their actions" (Young 1990, 15). Such restrictions destroy human beings' instinctive "spirit of revolt" and replace it with a spirit of servility and submission, thereby transforming them into "will-less automatons without independence or individuality" (Berkman 2003, 65). To this extent, their eradication is absolutely crucial for the development of autonomous "self-thinking individuals" (Berkman 2003,

65) who are "educated to freedom and the management of their own interests" (Malatesta 1981, 26).

Although negative freedom is a necessary condition for positive freedom in this sense, it is not sufficient. Because the capacity for actionable autonomy requires access to "education, scientific instruction ... material prosperity" (Bakunin, quoted in Clark 2013, 178) and other means of developing "private judgment and independence" (Honeywell 2014, 119), it follows trivially that those who lack such access are not positively free. In some cases, this is the result of external interference, coercion, or restraint – as, for example, when members of marginalized groups are prevented by law from attending school or entering certain occupations – but it is just as often a consequence of unequal social or economic conditions. For example, although the United States guarantees formal equality of opportunity to all its citizens regardless of race, gender, socio-economic status, this doesn't mean that poor people of color have the same opportunities as wealthy whites in practice. Even in the absence of laws that deliberately discriminate against them, the mere fact that the former are socially and/or economically unequal severely limits the range of opportunities available to them and, by extension, their capacity for actionable autonomy.

While all of this might seem to imply that individual autonomy is itself an intrinsically valuable end, we have already seen that this is not the case for social anarchists. On the contrary, just as negative freedom is a necessary but insufficient condition for individual autonomy, individual autonomy is a necessary but insufficient condition for individual development. Because individual autonomy is nothing more than a capacity (whether actionable or merely potential) for self-determined action, and because this capacity is solely a function of the conditions under which actions are performed rather than the particular end or set of ends toward which they are directed, the mere fact that actions are autonomous scarcely guarantees that they are maximally conducive to the growth or development of the individuals performing them, nor even increases the likelihood of their doing so. For example: although political, social, and economic elites enjoy a virtually unlimited capacity for self-determined activity, this is largely because they monopolize the means of developing such a capacity in the first place. Because "self-determination" of this sort comes at the expense of others' autonomy, however, it is profoundly at odds with "the full development and the full enjoyment by each person of all human faculties and capacities," as this "can only be provided to each through collective labor ... of the whole society" (Bakunin, quoted in Clark 2013, 178).

The fact that the social anarchist conception of freedom includes a negative dimension ("concern with coercive impositions on the individual") *as well as a* positive dimension ("concern with the development of the 'critical, original, imaginative, independent, non-conforming' character") (Honeywell 2014, 119) – both of which depend on robust conditions of solidarity and equality – serves to distinguish it from the "individualistic, egoistic liberty extolled by ... the schools of bourgeois liberalism" (Bakunin 1972, 261) no less than from the individualist anarchist conceptions described above. For this reason, it is exceedingly difficult "to construct a collective family profile" that would justify lumping social anarchism and individualist anarchism together "under one roof" (Freeden 1996, 311).

The matter is further complicated by the fact that social anarchism itself encompasses an array of divergent tendencies. Although all such tendencies agree that freedom is coextensive with maximal human development, they nonetheless have different understandings of what the latter entails. This, in turn, has led to disagreements over the precise form of political, social, and economic organization that freedom requires as well as the revolutionary strategies necessary to bring about a genuinely free society. That said, these disagreements have invariably had less to do with the definition of freedom itself than the meanings and degrees of relative significance assigned to various conceptual micro-components. Though they have played an important role in fostering political diversity and intellectual fluidity, they are nonetheless in keeping with the consistent patterns of conceptual decontestation that have defined social anarchism from its origins to the present day.

Conclusion

When anarchism is defined solely in terms of what it opposes, the underlying motivations for that opposition tend to be obscured. For social anarchists, any concept of freedom that lacks an explicitly teleological dimension is an abstraction devoid of concrete moral significance. The problem with institutions like the State accordingly, is not that they are antithetical to freedom so much as to the substantive moral end toward which freedom is directed – that is, human growth, development, and improvement. Far from demonstrating that anarchism is "amorphous and full of paradoxes and contradictions" (Miller 1985, 2), the inability of standard accounts to accommodate this understanding of freedom is a consequence of their own shortcomings, not least their tendency to define freedom as a generic condition of agency decoupled from particular ends.

Although institutions like the State actively obstruct – if not altogether sabotage – our individual and collective efforts to maximize happiness and wellbeing, this doesn't mean that abolishing such institutions will automatically usher in a heaven on earth. On the contrary, just as the absence of disease is insufficient by itself to guarantee health, freedom requires much more than the absence of oppressive institutions; it requires the *presence* of new forms of political, social, and economic organization, new ways of thinking, feeling, acting, living, being, and so forth. In striving to achieve this presence, anarchism's foremost aspiration is not (or not just) the destruction of the actual but the creation of the possible. To this extent, it is the very opposite of a purely negative politics.

Notes

1 This is largely owing to the influence of Paul Eltzbacher (1960).
2 This is more or less how contemporary politics textbooks tend to portray anarchism as well. See, for example, Kenneth Janda, Jeffrey Berry, and Jerry Goldman (2013, 22), and Andrew Heywood (2012, 143).
3 For more on the history of anarchism as a transnational movement, see Steven Hirsch and Lucien van der Walt (2010); Andrew Hoyt (2013); Travis Tomchuk (2015); Davide Turcato (2007); and Kenyon Zimmer (2015).
4 For additional examples, see Goldman (1910, 68); Berkman (2003, 145); Hippolyte Havel (1932, 5); David Weick (1979, 139); and Stuart Christie (2004, 162).

References

Adams, Matthew and Nathan Jun. 2015. "Political Theory and History: The Case of Anarchism." *The Journal of Political Ideology* 20(3): 244–262.
Altena, Bert and Constance Bantman, eds. 2014. *Scales of Analysis in Anarchist Studies: Reassessing the Transnational Turn.* London: Routledge.
Armand, Émile. 1907. "Anarchist Individualism as Life and Activity." The Anarchist Library. https://theanarchistlibrary.org/library/emile-armand-the-anarchism-of-emile-armand.
Bakunin, Mikhail. 1953. *The Political Philosophy of Bakunin.* Edited by G.P. Maximoff. Glencoe, IL: Free Press.
Bakunin, Mikhail. 1972. *Bakunin on Anarchy: Selected Works by the Activist-Founder of World Anarchism.* Edited and translated by Sam Dolgoff. New York: Knopf, 1972.
Bakunin, Mikhail. 1992. *The Basic Bakunin.* Edited by Robert Cutler. Buffalo, NY: Prometheus.
Ball, Terence. 1999. "From 'Core' to 'Sore' Concepts: Ideological Innovation and Conceptual Change." *The Journal of Political Ideologies* 4(3): 391–396.
Belfort Bax, Ernest. 1891. *Outlooks from the New Standpoint.* London: Swan Sonnenschein & Co.
Berkman, Alexander. 2003 [1928]. *What is Anarchism?* Oakland, CA: AK Press.
Berlin, Isaiah. 1969. *Four Essays on Liberty.* Oxford: Oxford University Press.
Christie, Stuart. 2004. *My Granny Made Me An Anarchist.* Oakland, CA: AK Press.
Clark, John. 2013. *The Impossible Community: Realizing Communitarian Anarchism.* London: Bloomsbury.
de Cleyre, Voltairine. 2005. "McKinley's Assassination from the Anarchist Standpoint" [1907]. In *Exquisite Rebel: The Essays of Voltairine de Cleyre,* edited by Sharon Presley and Crispin Sartwell, 299–306. Albany, NY: SUNY Press.
Egoumenides, Magda. 2014. *Philosophical Anarchism and Political Obligation.* London: Bloomsbury.
Eltzbacher, Paul. 1960 [1900]. *Anarchism: Exponents of the Anarchist Philosophy.* London: Freedom Press.
Fowler, R.B. 1972. "The Anarchist Tradition of Political Thought." *The Western Political Quarterly* 25(4): 738–752.
Franco, Paul. 1999. *Hegel's Philosophy of Freedom.* New Haven, CT: Yale University Press. 1999.
Freeden, Michael. 1996. *Ideologies and Political Theory.* Oxford: Clarendon Press.
Freeden, Michael 2013. "The Morphological Analysis of Ideology." In *The Oxford Handbook of Political Ideologies,* edited by Michael Freeden, Lyman Tower Sargent, and Marc Stears, 115–137. Oxford: Oxford University Press.

Freeden, Michael 2015. *Liberalism: A Very Short Introduction*. Oxford: Oxford University Press.
Fromm, Erich. 2001 [1942]. *The Fear of Freedom*. New York: Routledge.
Godwin, William. 1798. *An Enquiry Concerning Political Justice*. London: G.G. and J. Robinson.
Goldman, Emma. 1910. *Anarchism and Other Essays*. New York: Mother Earth.
Goldman, Emma 1998. *Red Emma Speaks*. Edited by A.K. Shulman. Amherst, NY: Humanity Books.
Gordon, Uri. 2008. *Anarchy Alive!: Anti-Authoritarian Politics from Practice to Theory*. London: Pluto Press.
Guérin, Daniel. 1998. *No Gods, No Masters*. Edited by P. Sharkey. Oakland, CA: AK Press.
Havel, Hippolyte. 1932. *What's Anarchism?* Stelton, NJ: The Modern School.
Heywood, Andrew, ed. 2012. *Political Ideologies: An Introduction*. 5th edition. Basingstoke: Palgrave Macmillan.
Hirsch, Steven, and Lucien van der Walt, eds. 2010. *Anarchism and Syndicalism in the Colonial and Postcolonial World, 1870–1940: The Praxis of National Liberation, Internationalism, and Social Revolution*. Leiden: Brill.
Honeywell, Carissa. 2014. "Bridging the Gaps: Twentieth-Century Anglo-American Anarchist Thought." In *The Bloomsbury Companion to Anarchism*, edited by Ruth Kinna, 111–139. London: Bloomsbury.
Hoyt, Andrew. 2013. "Methods for Tracing Radical Networks: Mapping the Print Culture and Propagandists of the Sovversivi." In *Without Borders or Limits: An Interdisciplinary Approach to Anarchist Studies*, edited by Nathan Jun and Jorell Meléndez-Badillo, 75–106. Newcastle-upon-Tyne: Cambridge Scholars Publishing.
Janda, Kenneth, Jeffrey Berry, and Jerry Goldman, eds. 2013. *The Challenge of Democracy: American Government in Global Politics*. 12th edition. Boston: Cengage.
Jun, Nathan. 2012. *Anarchism and Political Modernity*. New York: Continuum.
Kropotkin, Peter. 1968. *Kropotkin's Revolutionary Pamphlets*. Edited by Roger Baldwin. New York: Benjamin Blom.
Kukathas, Chandran. 2012. "Liberty." In *A Companion to Contemporary Political Philosophy*, edited by Robert Goodin, Philip Petit, and Thomas Pogge, 685–698. London: John Wiley & Sons.
Malatesta, Errico. 1965. *Life and Ideas*. Edited by Vernon Richards. London: Freedom Press.
Malatesta, Errico. 1974 [1891]. *Anarchy*. Edited by Vernon Richards. London: Freedom Press.
Malatesta, Errico. 1981 [1898]. *Fra Contadini: A Dialogue on Anarchy*. Translated by J. Weir. London: Bratach Dubh Editions.
Martin, James. 1970. *Men Against the State*. Colorado Springs, CO: Ralph Myles.
McElroy, Wendy. 2004. *The Debates of Liberty: An Overview of Individualist Anarchism, 1881–1908*. Lanham, MD: Lexington Books.
Miller, David. 1985. *Anarchism*. London: J.M. Dent and Sons.
Morris, William. 1996. *The Collected Letters of William Morris*, vol. 3, edited by N. Kelvin. Princeton, NJ: Princeton University Press.
Parsons, Lucy. 1886. *The Famous Speeches of the Eight Chicago Anarchists in Court*. Chicago.
Pettit, Philip. 2005. "The Contribution of Analytical Philosophy." In *A Companion to Contemporary Political Philosophy*, edited by Robert Goodin and Philip Pettit, 5–35. Oxford: Blackwell.
Proudhon, Pierre-Joseph. 1875. *Correspondance de P.-J. Proudhon*, vol. 4. Paris: Lacroix & Co.

Proudhon, Pierre-Joseph. 2011. "The Federative Principle" [1863]. In *Property is Theft!: A Pierre-Joseph Proudhon Anthology*, edited by I. McKay, 689–720. Oakland, CA: AK Press.
Ritter, Alan. 1980. *Anarchism: A Theoretical Analysis*. Cambridge: Cambridge University Press.
Rocker, Rudolf. 2004 [1938]. *Anarcho-syndicalism*. Oakland, CA: AK Press.
Schmidt, Michael and Lucien van der Walt. 2009. *Black Flame: The Revolutionary Class Politics of Anarchism and Syndicalism*. Oakland, CA: AK Press.
Thomas, Paul. 1980. *Karl Marx and the Anarchists*. London: Routledge and Kegan Paul.
Tomchuk, Travis. 2015. *Transnational Radicals: Italian Anarchists in Canada and the U.S. 1915–1940*. Winnipeg: University of Manitoba Press.
Turcato, Davide. 2007. "Italian Anarchism as a Transnational Movement, 1885–1915." *International Review of Social History* 52(3): 407–444.
Vincent, Andrew. 2009. *Modern Political Ideologies*. London: John Wiley & Sons.
Weick, David. 1979. "The Negativity of Anarchism." In *Reinventing Anarchy*, edited by Howard Ehrlich, Carol Ehrlich, Daniel De Leon, and Glenda Morris, 138–155. London: Routledge & Kegan Paul.
Yarros, Victor. 1994. "Anarchy or Government" [1896]. In *The Individualist Anarchists: An Anthology of Liberty (1881–1908)*, edited by Frank H. Brooks, 29–38. New Brunswick, NJ: Transaction.
Young, Iris Marion. 1990. *Justice and the Politics of Difference*. Princeton, NJ: Princeton University Press.
Zenker, E.V. 1897. *Anarchism: A Criticism and History of the Anarchist Theory*. London: G.P. Putnam's Sons.
Zimmer, Kenyon. 2015. *Immigrants Against the State: Yiddish and Italian Anarchism in America*. Champaign-Urbana, IL: University of Illinois Press.

4

AGENCY

David Bates

Michael Freeden (1996; 2003) has argued that ideologies consist of core and peripheral concepts. For Marxists, class conflict would be a core concept; the Marxist who rejects all formulations of this idea ceases to be a Marxist. For anarchists, it is more of a challenge to identify such core concepts (Bates 2017). Anarchism as an ideology is necessarily difficult to characterise. We might argue that there is not so much an ideological identity called "anarchism" as there are many "anarchisms." Moreover, the various expressions of anarchism have emerged in contexts of opposition. One such context is the historical opposition between anarchism and Marxist communism. Another is the opposition between the various historical formations of anarchism itself – considered practically and philosophically. Consequently, anarchist ideas of agency – to use a term of Quentin Skinner (1968) – have always had an illocutionary dimension; that is, they were developed (not always intentionally) as a performative political response to their contexts of articulation. This makes it exceptionally difficult to provide a positive definition of agency from an anarchist point of view. The latter part of this chapter will suggest that we can start to rethink agency beyond its anarchist (and Marxist) horizons by drawing on the work of thinkers such as Michael Hardt and Antonio Negri.

Political Agency

Agency normally refers to an entity's capacity for action in its environment. Agency in the sociological sense is a term usually located alongside that of structure. Structure refers to those social arrangements that constrain or enable our opportunities and actions. Agency pertains to the capacity individuals have for free choice and autonomous action. Agency in the political sense may be used in at least two senses, both specifically connected to the idea of freedom. First, we may be said to have agency to the extent that we are not subjected to external forms of coercion. Second, we are free to the extent that we can exercise our capacities; thus, political agency is concerned with self-determination.

Let us begin with a minimal statement of the anarchist view of agency. First, anarchists tend to consider agency as intimately connected to a radical idea of freedom as self-determination. Human freedom and arbitrary power cannot be reconciled. For classical anarchists, the structure of the state form is the mechanism for the exercise of arbitrary power *par excellence*. In short, human freedom — hence, the exercise of agency — is not possible where state rule is hegemonic.

Second, most anarchists understand self-determination in a radically social sense. The anarchists discussed in this chapter were all "fanatics of freedom" — yet most considered that the free exercise of human agency had necessary social determinants. In short, the classical anarchist idea of agency is a positive one.

Third, and consequently, this understanding of radical social freedom is but an application of a theory of political agency, one grounded in the social dimension. Many classical anarchists were concerned not simply to criticise arbitrary state power, but also to locate the group best situated to bring about the overthrow of such power. Agency in the political sense is to this extent not a peripheral concept; rather, it is a necessary condition for freedom.

The focus of this chapter will be to unpack key anarchist arguments pertaining to the third theme, as they emerged in the context of the historical debate between anarchism and Marxism. My reasons for this focus are not arbitrary. The historical conflict between anarchism and Marxism can be regarded as the means by which anarchism is constituted as the complex series of ideologies to which I have referred.

Anarchism, Agency, and the Encounter with Marx(ism)

Pierre-Joseph Proudhon and Mikhail Bakunin were contemporaries and associates of Karl Marx, yet both came to detect in Marx's work an authoritarianism of philosophy and of personality.

Marx eventually characterised his work as a "science" of history and of political economy. Such a move troubled Proudhon. Indeed, Proudhon (1846) wrote to Marx pleading with him not to seek to impose a new ideological dogma, a new theology of communism on the revolutionary movement. Marx, unsurprisingly, did not respond; however, he later referred with derision to the so-called dialectical "sophistication" of Proudhon's work (Marx 1865). Indeed, from then on, he started a polemic against Proudhon — whose 1846 work, *The Philosophy of Poverty*, Marx critiqued in *The Poverty of Philosophy* (1847). In it, Marx wrote of Proudhon that "He wants to be the synthesis — he is a composite error" and that "He wants to soar as the man of science above the bourgeois and proletarians; he is merely the petty bourgeois, continually tossed back and forth between capital and labour, political economy and communism."

On a simple level, we might remark that Marx seemed to assume that Proudhon was an undereducated fool, a man not versed adequately in the finer points of German philosophy. Proudhon in turn considered Marx an incurable elitist who pretended to wish for the emancipation of the working classes, but in reality would prefer nothing other than becoming a philosopher king.

More relevant to our argument are some key political and philosophical issues. Marx is critical of what he considers Proudhon's inadequate understanding of dialectics. From Marx's (1847) perspective, Proudhon's "dialectic" was one of simple compromise, in which "[t]he problem to be solved" is "to keep the good side, while eliminating the bad." Proudhon's approach led him to advocate a synthesis of small-scale property with human labour. For Marx, however, this was little more than a derisory "petty-bourgeois" class location.

Yet Proudhon's position is more sophisticated than Marx's polemical characterisation suggests. Proudhon had a more positive view of the middle classes than one would find in Marxian discourse. Key aspects of the middle classes are regarded by Proudhon as the "labouring bourgeoisie," as "entrepreneurs, masters of principals of an enterprise [*patrons*], shopkeepers, manufacturers of fabricators [*fabricants*], farmers or agriculturalists [*cultivateurs*], scholars, artists, etc…" (quoted in Knowles 2013, 70, original emphasis). Where for Marx such "petty bourgeois" class locations would embody a living contradiction, for Proudhon their positive aspects meant that they would provide important elements of any future synthesis of property and labour.

In a letter to Marx, Proudhon (1846, original emphasis) wrote of a wish

> to bring about the return to society, by an economic combination, of the wealth which was withdrawn from society by another economic combination. In other words, through Political Economy to turn the theory of Property against Property in such a way as to engender what you German socialists call *community* and what I will limit myself for the moment to calling *liberty* or *equality*.

Turning "Property against Property" implied – as Proudhon would state in correspondence of 1850 – "the conciliation of classes, symbol of the synthesis of doctrines" (quoted in Knowles 2013, 70). Calling up the spirit of Rousseau, Proudhon expanded the horizon of his discourse beyond the middle classes as such to "the people." For Proudhon, the people were the "organic union of wills that are individually free, that can and should voluntarily work together, but abdicate never. Such a union must be sought in the harmony of their interests, not in an artificial centralisation, which, far from expressing the collective will, expresses only the antagonisms of individual wills …" (quoted in Knowles 2013, 70).[1] Therefore, we can see that Proudhon addresses questions of agency through engaging with issues of class, but that the conclusions he reached are quite different to those of Marx.

If you turn to Proudhon's work looking for an intersectional account of political agency, you will be sorely disappointed. Indeed, you will be disgusted, for

Proudhon has some quite appalling views. We might be tempted to use contextual arguments as a form of apology for Proudhon's views. However, to do so is itself to be guilty of racism and sexism. Proudhon's "synthesis" is also premised on some violent exclusions. Proudhon was anti-Semitic. For example, in an excerpt from his private *Notebooks*, Proudhon (1847) wrote: "The Jew is the enemy of humankind. They must be sent back to Asia or be exterminated. By steel or by fire or by expulsion the Jew must disappear." So too, Proudhon's view towards women was abhorrent. Just as Marxists must address openly Marx's deeply problematic personal views and practices, so must the anarchist tradition account for the words of Proudhon (and Bakunin, et al.) which fit less well with the progressive narrative.[2]

If the so-called synthesis in Proudhon's dialectic was indeed a compromise, in Bakunin's dialectic there is no synthesis – only negation and destruction. Interestingly, however, Bakunin stares into the void and finds himself at home. His anarchist "politics" is a politics of negation, in which "The passion for destruction is a creative passion, too!" (Bakunin 1842). How does this understanding of dialectics inform Bakunin's understanding of the relationship between class and political agency? Where Proudhon sought transformative agency in key sectors of the middle classes, Bakunin finds it among the "lumpenproletariat." Although Bakunin's views do shift in accordance with the polemical context, he attempts to distinguish his account of revolutionary class agency from that of Marx. In "On the International Workingmen's Association and Karl Marx," Bakunin's more extreme understanding of negation leads him to embrace the "lumpenproletariat" as the "flower" of the proletariat (Bakunin 1990 [1872], 48).

Three years earlier – in a series of articles in *L'Égalité* in 1869 (a publication of the Romance Federation of the International) – he had adopted a type of illocutionary force which seems more "proletarian" in orientation. In an article of August 7, for instance, Bakunin (1869) wrote: "Do you understand that there is an irreconcilable antagonism between the proletariat and the bourgeoisie which is the necessary consequence of their respective economic positions?" Yet Bakunin's 1872 position is foreshadowed here, because in same article, he also wrote: "Until now [with the founding of the International] there has never been a true politics of the people, and by the 'people' we mean the lowly classes, the 'rabble,' the poorest workers whose toil sustains the world."

The discursive choice made by Bakunin is interesting. The "people" come to be equated with the poorest sections of the workers – not the unemployed "rabble" of which Marx was so critical, but rather the most precariously located (those closest to the threat of unemployment). Freeden (1996) has maintained that so-called "orthodox Marxism" adopts a restricted view of the proletariat which can be contrasted to the wider understanding of the working class found in anarchism. Freeden is correct to a point. However, the difference between Marx's and Bakunin's ideas of the proletariat is one of focus. For Marx, the most "advanced" workers were also the most exploited, yielding the greatest amount of surplus value. This was the fundamental basis of their revolutionary location.

For Bakunin, the poorest workers – the lumpenproletariat – were people who could not be "bought" in the way that privileged industrial workers could. They were not interested in bargaining up their wage levels to a position of relative comfort. Far removed from the labour aristocracy, they had nothing in common with the finance aristocracy! Bakunin did not merely ground his argument in rhetoric. He also thought his position could be justified through social and historical analysis. For Marx, the advanced revolutionary classes were in Britain and Germany, and the lumpenproletariat were little more than counter-revolutionary "scum" (Marx and Engels 2015[1848], 254; Cowling 2002). Bakunin (1873) believed that the "extremely poor" workers (e.g., those in Italy) would instead be the key agents of the "coming social revolution."

Is there not a "third way" between Bakunin's and Marx's views on class and agency? In exploring this issue, we need to provide a richer and intersectional account of transformative political agency. To achieve this would be beyond the scope of this chapter. However, we can suggest an opening for this account in the space where anarchism and Marxism come together – specifically, though not exclusively, in the work of Hardt and Negri. I will – somewhat controversially – characterise their work as close enough to post-anarchism to refer to it as such. There is undoubtedly a significant degree of overlap between anarchism and autonomist Marxism. Elsewhere, I have speculated on why Hardt and Negri refuse the label "anarchism," which is a result of the role played by Leninism in Italian revolutionary politics and of the discursive – and real – violence that Leninism has demonstrated to anarchism.

Indeed, the critical tone Lenin adopted towards anarchism has an illocutionary force similar to that of the polemical tone adopted by Marx. Discursively, in characterising himself as a Marxist, Lenin gained resources that could be mobilised to attack his anarchist opponents, along with their fellow travellers. For example, in a 1905 essay, Lenin accused Russian anarchists of acting in ways that discredited the proletarian struggle. Consequently, he argued, "we shall therefore resort to every means of ideological struggle to keep the influence of the anarchists over the Russian workers just as negligible as it has been so far" (Lenin 1905; see also Lenin 1901).

Of specific Russian anarchists, we might note Lenin's remarks about Leo Tolstoy. Anarchists usually consider Tolstoy's value to be his non-violent pacifism (Christoyannopoulos 2010). For Lenin (1908), Tolstoy's value was that his work embodied the class contradictions inherent in Russian society at the time; yet, Tolstoy's views amounted to little more than a philosophy of "peasant revolt." In short, Tolstoy failed to adopt the class position of the revolutionary proletariat. Lenin provides little in the way of evidence for such claims. It is hardly surprising that his account of Tolstoy is a polemical one, given that Tolstoy's politics were quite different from Lenin's own. It should also be no surprise that it is often challenging to find a positive account of political agency in Tolstoy's work. If anything, we tend to find displayed there a view that the wealthy should take a paternalistic attitude to the poor – a view which sits rather at odds with his anarchism.

In an 1899 text, "What is to be Done?" – appearing three years before Lenin's 1902 text of that name – we see Tolstoy's worries about the growth of class conflict in Russia. Tolstoy (1899, 262) wrote: "The hatred and contempt of the oppressed people are increasing, and the physical and moral strength of the richer classes are decreasing: the deceit which supports all this is wearing out, and the rich classes have nothing wherewith to comfort themselves." In such texts as *The Kingdom of God is Within You*, Tolstoy (1893) argued for a pacifist conception of Christian morality. This was a conception which it could be argued undermined revolutionary political agency and activity. Imagine that anarchists should take Christ's Sermon on the Mount – where we are asked to "turn the other cheek" – as the watchword of morality. Are the poor really to turn the other cheek, and allow their oppressors to carry on with business as usual? Tolstoy is not clear. Indeed, Tolstoy, who opposed all forms of violent political action, challenged the idea that anarchists should seek revolutionary transformation of the status quo.

The Russian anarchist Kropotkin also had an interesting relationship with Lenin. Initially, Lenin held Kropotkin in great respect. Kropotkin hoped to be of use to the revolution when he returned from exile in 1919, going first to St. Petersburg and then to Moscow. Yet after a tense meeting with Lenin, it became clear that the views of the two men differed substantially. Kropotkin was disgusted by Lenin's apparent contempt for human rights and freedom (Bonc-Brujevic 1919; Kropotkin 1920).[3]

In some ways, there is a close proximity between Marxist accounts of political agency and those of Kropotkin. That is, Kropotkin was keen to draw attention to issues of class contradiction in a way that one does not see in Tolstoy. Kropotkin (1880) departs from any simple idea of a class polarisation thesis; instead, there is an interesting focus on the multiplicity of class conflict. Kropotkin (1886) also presents a narrative of proletarian class struggle:

> The worker perceives that he has been disinherited, and that disinherited he will remain, unless he has recourse to strikes or revolts to tear from his masters the smallest part of riches built up by his own efforts; that is to say, in order to get that little, he already must impose on himself the pangs of hunger and face imprisonment, if not exposure to Imperial, Royal, or Republican fusillades.

Elsewhere – and this is the essence of Kropotkin's critique of Leninism – Kropotkin (1920) cautions directly against an authoritarian statist alternative to capitalist relations of production; although in his early work, there are suggestions that he regarded the peasantry as a sacrificial object for revolutionary goals (Kropotkin 1993, 67), a level of instrumentality which he was later to criticise Lenin for.

If Kropotkin's anarchism was a particular response to the immediate politics of Lenin's Leninism, then Hardt and Negri's post-anarchism is in part a response to the wider politics of Leninism – particularly as it functioned in Italy from the 1970s onwards.

Beyond Marxism and Anarchism

I want in this section to address the issue of agency through engaging with post-anarchism. Post-anarchism is a label typically associated with contemporary thinkers such as Todd May (1994) and Saul Newman (2010). It aims to bring together the insights of anarchist thinking with recent developments in post-structuralism. To this extent, post-anarchists do for classical anarchism what post-Marxists (such as Ernesto Laclau and Chantal Mouffe) did for classical Marxism.

In this chapter, I characterise the work of Hardt and Negri as post-anarchist. Like other post-anarchist thinkers, Hardt and Negri use post-structuralist modes of thinking, explicitly critique hegemonic and statist forms of thinking, and focus on intersectionality when understanding political agency. My characterisation of Hardt and Negri's thought as post-anarchist (Bates 2012) is controversial, though, not least because they reject the label: "No, we are not anarchists but communists who have seen how much repression and destruction of humanity have been wrought by liberal and socialist big governments" (Hardt and Negri 2000, 350, emphasis deleted). I have speculated (Bates 2012) that Hardt and Negri refuse the anarchist label because of the importance of Leninism in Italian revolutionary politics, yet they integrate the themes of anarchism into their work in subversive ways.

Indeed, it can be suggested that Hardt and Negri are post-modern Bakuninists – that is, they integrate many of the explicit themes of Bakunin's work into a post-modern or post-structuralist ontology. Bakunin had rejected the Marxist idea of dialectics; and I would contend that a dialectics without synthesis is no dialectics at all. Lenin (1914–16), it should be pointed out, had articulated a form of dialectics that explicitly referred to Hegel's *Logic*, the most "dialectical" text imaginable.

Post-anarchist thinkers such as Newman and May are influenced by a range of post-structuralist thinkers that we would typically regard as anti-dialectical (e.g., Michel Foucault, Friedrich Nietzsche, and Gilles Deleuze). Significantly, Hardt and Negri's own rejection of dialectical thinking is undoubtedly influenced by Deleuze. As they put it, "Reality and history, however, are not dialectical, and no idealist rhetorical gymnastics can make them conform to the dialect" (Hardt and Negri 2000, 131). History is not moving towards a teleological unity; rather, history is nothing but the production of difference, of multiplicity.

It can also be maintained that Bakunin's politics involves an implicit refusal of strategy, a theme that continues into the work of post-anarchists such as May and Newman. This refusal of strategy is adopted by Hardt and Negri as well. Indeed, Leninists and post-Marxists alike (Callinicos 2001; Laclau 2004, 24) have criticised Hardt and Negri for being anti-strategic, and hence anti-hegemonic, thinkers.

To return to the issue of political agency, we might note the following. First, Hardt and Negri do not adopt a type of "conciliatory" dialectics, which we find in the work of Proudhon. Hardt and Negri's anti-dialectics grounds a politics of refusal (Bates 2011) which leads them to the lumpenproletariat – the poor – as the group best situated to refuse the rule of capital (Hardt and Negri 2005, 130). For Hardt and Negri, "the poor" can be genuinely revolutionary; as they (2005, 129) put it: "the poor are not merely victims but powerful agents ... they are part of the circuits of social and biopolitical production." The "lumpenproletariat" are not a reactionary "other" to the proletariat, but rather a constituent element of it. This theoretical move clearly situates Hardt and Negri closer to the anarchism of Bakunin than to the classical Marxist position (or the Leninist approach).

It is possible to question the relative cogency of this argument. It could be maintained that Hardt and Negri's account – as with Bakunin and other anarchists before them – loses sight of the fact that the poor frequently come to embody forms of politics that are less than progressive (Žižek 2011). The politics of the poor can often appear as blind destruction with little in the way of creativity (Bates 2011). But the openness brought into play by the category of "the poor" and the "multitude" creates the space for a discussion of intersectionality not present in classical anarchist views of agency.

Second, for Hardt and Negri, exploitation in late capitalism is an expression of bio-power – a term which they appropriate from Foucault. Power – in the form of "Empire" – is increasingly all encompassing, if not totalising. Hardt and Negri (2000, xii) write that Empire "is a decentred and de-territorialising apparatus of rule that progressively incorporates the entire global realm within its open, expanding frontiers." Classical anarchist thinking – so the argument goes – had typically held to a mono-vocal conception of power. The power of the state was the "evil" to be refused. Foucault, as is well known, argued that, because power was all encompassing and multi-vocal, we had reached the point whereby we must "cut the head off the sovereign." In a similar fashion, invoking Deleuze and Félix Guattari, May (1994, 71) writes: "The picture here is of a network of forces of power that interact to yield the world (especially the political world) in which we live – or more accurately, which we are."

May, as well as Hardt and Negri, addresses the way in which contemporary neo-liberal capitalism exploits our emotional and affective lives, along with our materially productive ones. May focuses on the exploitation of desire, and indeed, on how we come to desire our own subjugation. Hardt and Negri are concerned with a broader political economy of exploitation; that is, with how the rule of measure comes to subjugate all aspects of our lives, and therefore to close down – though only partially – sites of refusal. Hardt and Negri understand exploitation as the rule of measure that extends beyond the "factory" to the "social factory." Society itself becomes the site of exploitation. As exploitation is everywhere, it is simultaneously nowhere. Power, so this argument goes, must be understood as multiplicity. Power is constitutive, but it can be constituted in new directions. A tactical politics therefore needs to refuse power and exploitation in all its manifestations as Empire. We must refuse how we are commanded to think, to act, and to feel. A tactical politics must refuse the machine, refuse government, and refuse "service with a smile." Accordingly, this expansion of exploitation simultaneously opens up key loci of "bio-political" refusal.

Third, Hardt and Negri come to replace the idea of the working class with the idea of the multitude. They (Hardt and Negri 2005, 107) insist that "the multitude gives the concept of the proletariat its fullest definition as all those who labour and produce under the rule of capital." Accordingly, the multitude embodies those who perform affective, linguistic, and material forms of labour. The multitude are all those who are subject to the rule of capital. The multitude here is also viewed as a category of becoming. As Hardt and Negri (2005, 105) write: "The question to ask … is not 'What is the multitude?' but rather 'What can the multitude become?'"

This focus on irreducible multiplicity is a decentring that comprises a crucial challenge to modernist ideas of agency and intentionality typical of classical Marxism and anarchism. Collective agency in these traditions is a process of unity of individuals and groups as a result of their realisation of objective economic interests. The common recognition of collective interests is, after all, the basis of Kropotkin's "mutual aid."

Writers such as Newman consider all so-called political interests as discursive constructs – a line of argument they share with Laclau and Mouffe. Hardt and Negri, in contrast, have taken an "immanentist" view. Post-anarchists such as Newman (2010, 123–124) have been critical of the "immanentism" and "essentialism" of Hardt and Negri's concept of the multitude. Accordingly, I do not want to over-stress the similarities between the work of Newman and May on the one hand, and Hardt and Negri on the other. However, I do consider that these differences do not negate the family resemblances of these approaches. Moreover, Newman overstates the essentialism of this approach – and hence overstates the differences of his work with that of Hardt and Negri. For the multitude's existence in a process of "becoming" is a networked "existence"; it is "rhizomatic."

If refusal is constitutive, still it does not have direction in a strategic sense. This raises another important issue. Whereas most Marxists consider social scientific knowledge as a necessary condition for the exercise of political agency, it is difficult to see the role that such knowledge could play in the performance of a rhizomatic bio-politics. Rhizomatic politics is driven not so much by a rationally underpinned agency, but by an affective politics of desire.

The concept of the multitude also poses another fundamental challenge to the key assumptions of classical anarchism and Marxism. We might note that a common concern that sets classical Marxists and anarchists against post-Marxists and post-anarchists is a concern with intersectionality. Newman and May are undoubtedly influenced by feminist and post-colonialist theory and practice, and so, acutely aware of the issues of intersectionality. Such influences are explicit in the work of Hardt and Negri.

Hardt and Negri draw on Judith Butler's theory of "performativity" in order to challenge essentialised relations of sex and gender. Hardt and Negri (2005) write:

> The natural conception of sex or the social and political body of "woman" ... subordinates the differences among women in terms of race and sexuality. In particular, the natural conception of sex brings with it heteronormativity, subordinating the position of the homosexual. Sex is not natural and neither is the sexed body of "woman" ...
>
> *(199–200)*

The analysis of "affective labour" – so central to Hardt and Negri's thought – is influenced by feminist discussions of the exploitation of love, labour and "desire" (a concept which plays a crucial role in May's post-structuralist anarchism). Hardt and Negri tackle directly in their work the differential exploitation of women in the labour process and at home (Del Rae 2000). Indeed, Hardt and Negri (2005, 111) characterise "affective labour" as the production and reproduction of life, itself embedded directly in capitalist, patriarchal, and racialised relationships. Accordingly, working class women – for example – have a substantially different experience of exploitation than working class men; black women a different experience of exploitation than white women, lesbian women than straight women, etc. Such forms of exploitation reproduce themselves across public and private spheres. Hardt and Negri, for example, address the way in which the "private" domain of the "family" is an important site of repression, exploitation and subjugation.

It is also important to note that Hardt and Negri's work provides a detailed discussion of so-called service-sector occupations, occupations with precise gendered and racialised configurations of exploitation. (To an extent, the acute awareness of the political economies of such relations distinguishes and differentiates their work from that of Newman and May – despite numerous commonalities.)

Hardt and Negri address the way in which a multiplicity of experiences leads to a more open view of politics. They write:

> the members of the multitude do not have to become the same or renounce their creativity in order to communicate and cooperate with each other. They remain different in terms of race, sex, sexuality and so forth. What we need to understand, then, is the collective intelligence that can emerge from the communication and cooperation of such varied multiplicity.
>
> *(Hardt and Negri 2005, 92, emphasis deleted)*

The post-colonial shift in Hardt and Negri's work also leads them to address the global aspects of exploitation – that is how the exploitation of the so-called developing world comes to function in the context of Empire. How debt relations serve to subjugate the global poor. How the global poor is itself a racialised category.

Of course, the fact of intersectionality presents key theoretical and practical problems for Marxists and anarchists alike. This is acutely the case with the central concern of this chapter – political agency. How, for example, can a common struggle against capitalist exploitation come about if political agency is not unified and hegemonic? What are the possibilities of different ethnic groups, genders, sexualities, etc. coming together with the aim of overthrowing neo-liberal capitalism? Hardt and Negri have maintained that Empire is totalising (though not total) – but what then of the biopolitics of resistance to this Empire? Interestingly, post-structuralists and post-anarchists have displaced "macro politics" with "micro politics." "Grand narratives" are dead – as is the industrial working class as an agent charged with overthrowing capitalism. Radical politics therefore can at best comprise a series of disruptions and subversions of hegemonic narratives. May (1994, 95) has written that post-anarchist politics struggles on many diffuse levels "not because multiple struggles will create a society without the centralisation of power, but because power is not centralised, because across the surface of those levels are the sites at which power arises."

Accordingly, disruption is only ever partial or temporary. What is interesting is that disruption in this context can take many new and unexpected forms. For Hardt and Negri, the politics of trade unionism may be on the wane, but the politics of "cross dressing" may comprise a direct assault on traditional gender relations. Indeed, if Empire is to be effectively refused, Hardt and Negri (2000) write:

> The will to be against really needs a body that is completely incapable of submitting to command. It needs a body that is incapable of adapting to family life, to factory discipline, to the regulations of traditional sex life, and so forth. (If you find your body refusing these "normal" modes of life, don't despair – realize your gift.)
>
> *(216)*

Concluding Remarks

I started this chapter with three points pertaining to most anarchist understandings of agency: First, anarchists regard freedom as self-determination, but self-determination is not possible where the state form is hegemonic. Second, self-determination has social preconditions. Third, self-determination necessitates radical political transformation. Consequently, the realisation of self-determination is premised on ideas concerning political agency. Anarchists – like Marxists – have been concerned to locate those individuals, groups and classes who might be best situated to contribute to bringing about such transformation. For Marxists, agency has a definite class location – the industrial proletariat were the group who could best usher in the future society. By contrast, it is difficult to discern one anarchist view regarding transformative agency.

Classical anarchists such as Proudhon, Bakunin, Tolstoy, and Kropotkin have quite different views regarding who are the agents best situated to bring about significant social transformation – from the lumpenproletariat in Bakunin, the labouring middle classes in Proudhon, the peasantry in Tolstoy, and the multiple class subject in Kropotkin. Classical anarchists tend to view such agency through a particular class lens, which gives little account of important forms of intersectionality (an exclusion they share with classical Marxists). None of these authors gives an adequate account of the relationship of gender and ethnicity to radical social transformation (though it should be noted Bakunin was an anti-German Pan-Slavist). Indeed, classical anarchists such as Proudhon and Bakunin were racist and sexist men who were not only blind, but also hostile, to such inclusions. Anarchist contemporaries of Kropotkin (and Lenin), such as Emma Goldman, did address questions of gender in their work, though a full re-appreciation of this fact is beyond the scope of this chapter.

The post-anarchist thought of Hardt and Negri comprises a way of looking at contemporary questions of political agency which brings together some of the best aspects of post-anarchist and Marxist thinking. In so doing, Hardt and Negri take us beyond a view of "agency" grounded in a pre-constituted essential subject. The "multitude" is "open," decentred, a network of becoming, an interplay of differences of gender, race, and class. This said, Hardt and Negri's arguments remain problematic. Perhaps in the end they present us not with answers, but with further questions. The non-hierarchical journey of answering these questions will undoubtedly enable us to problematise political agency anew, and to rethink radical politics beyond anarchism (and Marxism).

Notes

1 For a discussion of the influences of Rousseau's work on the writings of Proudhon, see Noland 1967.
2 The conflict between Marx and Bakunin was every bit as brutal as that between Marx and Proudhon. (And Bakunin was not fearful of deploying anti-Semitic tropes in this confrontation! Marx's communism was considered by Bakunin to be part of a world Jewish conspiracy, headed up by the Rothschilds!) Politically and philosophically, Bakunin adopted a quite distinct view of dialectics to that evident in Marx's work. Importantly for the concerns of this chapter, there is an interesting comparison we might make between Proudhon's dialectics and Bakunin's.
3 Lenin supposedly said: "How old he has become ... Now he is living in a country that is bursting with revolution, where everything has been completely turned upside down, and he cannot think of anything else but to talk about the cooperative movement ... But of course he is very old and we must surround him with care and help him with everything he needs as far as possible, but that needs to be dealt with very delicately and very carefully. He is very useful and precious for us because of his whole terrific past and because of everything he has done" (quoted in Bonc-Brujevic 1919). Of Lenin,

Kropotkin wrote: "Vladimir Ilyich (Lenin), your concrete actions are completely unworthy of the ideas you pretend to hold. Is it possible that you do not know what a hostage really is – a man imprisoned not because of a crime he has committed, but only because it suits his enemies to exert blackmail on his companions? ... If you admit such methods, one can foresee that one day you will use torture, as was done in the Middle Ages" (Kropotkin 1920).

References

Bakunin, Mikhail. 1842. *The Reaction in Germany.* www.marxists.org/reference/archive/bakunin/works/1842/reaction-germany.htm.

Bakunin, Mikhail. 1869. *On the Policy of the International Workingmen's Association.* www.marxists.org/reference/archive/bakunin/works/1869/policy-iwma.htm.

Bakunin, Mikhail. 1872. *Marxism, Freedom and the State.* www.marxists.org/reference/archive/bakunin/works/mf-state/ch03.htm.

Bakunin, Mikhail. 1873. *Statism and Anarchy.* www.marxists.org/reference/archive/bakunin/works/1873/statism-anarchy.htm.

Bakunin, Mikhail. 1990 (1872). *Marxism, Freedom and the State,* edited and translated by K.J. Kenafick. London: Freedom Press.

Bates, David. 2011. "Immaterial Labour and the Retreat from Class: Reflections on Hardt and Negri." *Studies in Marxism*, 12: 51–78.

Bates, David. 2012. "Situating Hardt and Negri." In *Libertarian Socialism: Politics in Black and Red,* edited by Alex Prichard, Ruth Kinna, Saku Pinta, and David Berry, 275–293. London: Palgrave.

Bates, David. 2017. "Anarchism." In *Political Ideologies,* edited by Paul Wetherly, 128–159. Oxford: Oxford University Press.

Bonc-Brujevic, V.D. 1919. "A meeting between V.I. Lenin and P.A. Kropotkin." www.marxist.com/meeting-lenin-kropotkin-bonc-brujevic1919.htm.

Callinicos, Alex. 2001. "Toni Negri in Perspective." *Socialist Review.* http://pubs.socialistreviewindex.org.uk/isj92/callinicos.htm.

Christoyannopoulos, Alexandre. 2010. *Christian Anarchism.* Cambridge: Imprint Academic.

Cowling, Mark. 2002. "Marx's Lumpenproletariat and Murray's Underclass: Concepts Best Abandoned?" In *Marx's Eighteenth Brumaire: (Post)Modern Interpretations,* edited by Mark Cowling and James Martin. London: Pluto Press.

Del Rae, Alisa. 2000. "Feminism and Autonomy: Itinerary of a Struggle." In *The Philosophy of Antonio Negri,* vol. 1, edited by Timothy S. Murphy and Abdul-Karim Mustapha, 48–72. London: Pluto Press.

Freeden, Michael. 1996. *Ideologies and Political Theory: A Conceptual Approach.* Oxford: Oxford University Press.

Freeden, Michael. 2003. *Ideology: A Very Short Introduction.* Oxford: Oxford University Press.

Hardt, Michael, and Antonio Negri. 2000. *Empire.* Cambridge: Cambridge University Press.

Hardt, Michael, and Antonio Negri. 2005. *Multitude.* London: Penguin.

Knowles, Rob. 2013. *Political Economy from Below: Economic Thought in Communitarian Anarchism.* London: Routledge.

Kropotkin, Peter. 1880. *The Spirit of Revolt.* http://dwardmac.pitzer.edu/Anarchist_archives/kropotkin/spiritofrevolt.html.

Kropotkin, Peter. 1886. *Anarchism: Its Philosophy and Ideal.* www.marxists.org/reference/archive/kropotkin-peter/1890s/x01.htm.

Kropotkin, Peter. 1920. Letter to Lenin 4 March 1920. http://dwardmac.pitzer.edu/Anarchist_Archives/kropotkin/kropotlenindec203.html.

Kropotkin, Peter. 1993. "Must We Occupy Ourselves with an Examination of the Ideal of a Future System?" In *Peter Kropotkin: Fugitive Writings*, edited by George Woodcock, 13–68. London: Black Rose.

Laclau, Ernesto. 2004. "Can Immanence Explain Social Struggles?" In *Empire's New Clothes: Reading Hardt and Negri*, edited by Paul A. Passavant and Jodi Dean, 21–30. London: Routledge.

Lenin, V.I. 1901. *Anarchism and Socialism*. www.marxists.org/archive/lenin/works/1901/dec/31.htm.

Lenin, V.I. 1902. *What is to be Done?* Moscow: Progress.

Lenin, V.I. 1905. *Socialism and Anarchism*. www.marxists.org/archive/lenin/works/1905/nov/24.htm.

Lenin, V.I. 1908. *Leo Tolstoy as the Mirror of the Russian Revolution*. www.marxists.org/archive/lenin/works/1908/sep/11.htm.

Lenin, V.I. 1914–1916. *Philosophical Notebooks*. www.marxists.org/archive/lenin/works/cw/volume38.htm.

Marx, Karl. 1847. *The Poverty of Philosophy*. www.marxists.org/archive/marx/works/1847/poverty-philosophy/ch02.htm.

Marx, Karl. 1865. "Letter to J B Schweizer: 'On Proudhon'." www.marxists.org/archive/marx/works/1865/letters/65_01_24.htm.

Marx, Karl, and Friedrich Engels. 2015 (1848). *The Communist Manifesto*. London: Penguin.

May, Todd. 1994. *The Political Philosophy of Post-Structuralist Anarchism*. University Park, PA: Pennsylvania State University Press.

Newman, Saul. 2010. *The Politics of Post-Anarchism*. https://theanarchistlibrary.org/library/saul-newman-the-politics-of-postanarchism.

Noland, Aaron. 1967. "Proudhon and Rousseau." *Journal of the History of Ideas*, 28(1): 33–54.

Proudhon, Pierre-Joseph. 1846. "Letter to Marx, Lyon, 17 May." www.marxists.org/reference/subject/economics/proudhon/letters/46_05_17.htm.

Proudhon, Pierre-Joseph. 1847. "On the Jews." www.marxists.org/reference/subject/economics/proudhon/1847/jews.htm.

Skinner, Quentin. 1968. "Meaning and Understanding in the History of Ideas." In *Meaning and Context: Quentin Skinner and His Critics*, edited by James Tully, 29–67. Ambridge: Polity.

Tolstoy, Leo. 1893. *The Kingdom of God is Within You*. https://theanarchistlibrary.org/library/leo-tolstoy-the-kingdom-of-god-is-within-you.pdf.

Tolstoy, Leo. 1899. "What is to be Done?" www.nonresistance.org/docs_pdf/Tolstoy/Whats_to_be_Done.pdf.

Žižek, Slavoj. 2011. "Shoplifters of the World Unite." *London Review of Books*. www.lrb.co.uk/2011/08/19/slavoj-zizek/shoplifters-of-the-world-unite.

5

DIRECT ACTION

Vicente Ordóñez[1]

> For nothing is more rousing than thought. Far from representing a gloomy resignation, it is the very quintessence of action. There is no more subversive activity than thinking, none more feared, more slandered, and this is not due to chance, nor is it innocuous. Thinking is political. And not only political thinking is, far from it. The mere *fact* of thinking is political. Hence the insidious battle led more efficiently than ever today against the *ability to think*, which, however, represents and will increasingly represent our only recourse.
>
> Viviane Forrester, The Economic Horror

Introduction

Power appears in many guises, not just as political authority – state, law and police: power is also immanent and transcendental. It is not just the law, which is imposed on citizens' heads and gestures by requiring them to obey the dictates of the state: wherever one goes, all kinds of rules state what it is *normal* to do. Resisting this power takes on a polyhedral appearance, standing against the law and rules, against regulations and models. Therefore, much liberating discourse stems from *bricolages*, but never from a single theory that is a fossil from the past.

The following fact should be emphasised from the start: anarchism has been defined throughout history as a denial of specific systems that exploit and dispossess. Precisely in this respect, anarchism is like philosophical scepticism: its doubts and denials are closely linked to the past doctrines that one wishes to judge and refute (McLaughlin 2007, 29). There are many forms of anarchism, just as there are many forms of scepticism. The form or forms in which the aforementioned systems have appeared will thus determine the specific way in which anarchism has displayed its action and its rejection.

Over the last forty years, the anarchist movement has taken on many different forms, depending on its arena of action and its central concerns. Where resistance to patriarchy was a significant feature of its struggle, anti-hierarchical prefigurative action took on a distinctly anarcho-feminist orientation. Where resistance to ecological destruction was most important, strains of green anarchism such as social ecology and Primitivism came to the fore. Indeed, anarchist tactics are extremely complex and fluid. Because it rejects any determining fixed principle that legitimates forms of control that seek to achieve a single predetermined goal, anarchism is a more experimental and transitory form of human organisation than some of its rigid, highly-structured target driven competitors. It would, however, be mistaken to see it as lacking an ideological structure of core, stable, mutually defining features (Freeden 1996). Anarchism can be defined in terms of a rejection of hierarchies, such as capitalism, racism or sexism, a social view of freedom in which access to material resources and the liberty of others are prerequisites to personal freedom and a prefigurative commitment to embodying goals in one's methods (Colson 2001; Franks 2006).

Direct action is a relatively stable feature of anarchism, although it is not a sufficient descriptor, since there have been other hierarchical groups, such as fascists and the professional revolutionaries of Marxist-Leninist urban terrorist groups – Red Army Faction, GRAPO or 17N – who have also claimed to support it (Alexander and Pluchinsky 1992, 132; Santiáñez 2013, 185). Because these direct action strategies connive with hierarchical power and reject prefigurative (anti-) politics, they received significant criticism from more consistent anarchist theorists and groups (Kinna 2005; Carr 2010; Amorós 2012). Anarchist direct action is infinitely multiform and unbounded; it encompasses different actors and situations and goes beyond an elitist revolutionary vanguard. Its praxis provokes disorder and invention, hierarchy is destroyed, verticality disappears because everything is circulating horizontally, and what is collective also becomes connective. Direct action is therefore not just a concept that is core to anarchism, but is a priority form of revolutionary action and of critical and extreme intervention: it favours the emergence of that which has hitherto been unknown – of forms of subjectivity far removed from the consumerist and gregarious ego, and confronts political and economic powers and their predatory dynamics.

Conceptualising Direct Action

A theoretical and practical notion that appears in revolutionary trade unionism and in libertarian communism in the nineteenth century, direct action is one of the most relevant contributions that anarchism offers to (anti-)political science and social practice (Colson 1997). Through unmediated action, oppressed individuals and groups attempt to overturn or destroy that which subjects them. This distinguishes direct action from mediated political strategies such as voting, lobbying, or rallying – which are activities that pursue certain results through one or more intermediaries. Hence these are vicarious forms of political participation because it is tacitly admitted that one cannot influence directly those areas of the public space but requires the assistance of intermediaries (Welp and Ordóñez 2017). Conversely, however, when direct action is put into practice, it suggests that all those who make up any given society have not only the right, but also, and above all, the capacity to permeate the public space. What specific means are available to achieve this? Blockades, picketing, wildcat strikes, demonstrations, sit-ins, occupations, sabotage or civil disobedience. The (anti-)political repertoire of direct action forms part of the *dissensual habitus* to which Simon Critchley (2008, 112) referred, among the wide variety of tactics employed by anarchism. Therefore, while some of these actions can take on violent forms of (anti-)political resistance, others are essentially non-violent, although they can be illegal.

Thus, here is a dialectical tension in the conceptualisation of direct action, as shown in one of the first attempts to clearly define what direct action is. In *L'action directe*, anarchist and revolutionary syndicalist Émile Pouget (1904) emphasised that direct action is a transparent and self-evident notion, but added that it could be either anodyne or very violent: there is no specific form of direct action. From propaganda by the deed to DiY protest groups, from anarcho-feminist activities against pornographic boutiques to Tolstoyan passive resistance, from The Weathermen to Action Directe Non Violente, the direct-action ethos is multifaceted and polyhedral. Despite difficulties, those contemporary authors who have tried to conceptualise "direct action" agree on one point: direct action must be framed within a prefigurative (anti-)political framework; namely, it is a kind of ideal action in which ends and means are indistinguishable because there should always be a correspondence between goals and praxis (Jordan 2002, 153; Franks 2006, 115; Gordon 2008, 4; Graeber 2009, 210).

Contemporary anarchists also stress that they do not take direct action to be a theory *per se*, but rather as a series of practices and actions in common use: direct action is employed as a guide for sabotage, occupation or guerrilla warfare tactics, as a set of ethical precepts or as a prefigurative action developed by oppressed individuals and groups in order to strengthen their revolutionary struggle (Colson 2001; Franks 2003; Taibo 2013; Ibáñez 2014). Nonetheless, direct action has been the subject of critical debate both inside and outside anarchism. Some anarchists see direct action as ineffective, contradictory or insufficient. Recently, Joseph Todd has argued that direct action needs to be complemented by effective disruptions to capital (Todd 2016). Joel Olson has underlined that the anarchist direct action methodology is separate from the struggles of the oppressed themselves: "the strategy of building autonomous zones or engaging in direct action with small affinity groups assumes that radicals can start the revolution. But revolutionaries don't make revolutions" (Olson 2009, 41). In this sense The Invisible Committee, a non-strictly anarchist collective that is very popular in anarchist circles, has emphasised that "no form of action is revolutionary in itself" (The Invisible Committee 2015, 142). Tiqqun, The Invisible Committee matrix, has also predicted the insufficiency of direct action tactics: "you can't take the global order for an enemy. Not/ directly./ For the global order has no place" (Tiqqun 2010, 213). For the members of the Tiqqun group, every initiative that tries to counteract power in physical and spatial terms is doomed to failure. When radical activities against oppression collide with power structures the results depend on the mass and the inertia of the combatants and on the place where politics are disputed. The disproportion between the driving force of the power apparatus and direct action is all too evident. But it is even more devastating when all traces of confrontation have been removed by the machinery of power. I believe, however, that critics assume that direct action is a strategic tool projected towards the future. However, direct action is not necessarily carried out in order to favour future generations, but rather with and for the beings involved in courageous ways of life. The people's *today* has annulled and replaced the bureaucracy's *tomorrow*. So what is against the system is not a future Utopia, but the day-to-day life of those who resist and confront authority (Urdanibia 2008).

An Examination of What Is Human

As dispossession archaeology teaches us, it is vital to pay special attention to structures and authorities that try to subjugate free citizens by imposing some external dominant *logos* upon them (Foucault 2002). Tools for developing skills of resistance, autonomy, initiative and criticism are key political elements of anarchism. Direct action represents one of the instruments anarchists use to implement their anti-hierarchy emancipatory struggle and to counteract the global network of power relations. Direct action is an (anti-)political tactic of confrontation that involves an exercise of freedom, social self-determination and responsibility by individuals or collectives who want to build alternatives to a society based on competition, consumerism, inequality, dispossession and the unlimited production of waste and pollution (Ward 1996). There are two requirements for an action to be considered "direct." First, there should be neither regulatory nor corrective actors between those who conceive some kind of direct action and the completion of the action itself. That means *spontaneity*, a concept that has nothing to do with uncontrolled and thoughtless action. Second, practical engagement in political struggles, its means, immediate and mediate objectives, voluntary mutual aid, etc., should be defined and decided by those who freely choose to take action. From the action's conception, right up until the various stages of its development, through to its culmination, no one – be it administrators, committees or activists – should interfere with or hinder the decisions taken. Hence, *autonomy* is the second main feature of direct action.

Different approaches to achieving anarchist goals have been tested. Sometimes anarchists have justified the use of violent action against the arbitrary excesses of existing powers while others have turned away from violent struggle to embrace non-violent action. Manuals of political theory tend to point to the text *Die*

Reaktion in Deutschland: Ein Fragment von einem Franzosen (1842) by Michael Bakunin as the spark that links direct action and violence; the sentence that ends this text is stressed: "the passion for destruction is a creative passion, too" (Bakunin 1973, 58). However, they tend to ignore its deeper content and theoretical context.[2] When carefully read, one finds that Bakunin does not hoist the flag of violence, but reflects on those who do not believe in freedom. This text – which was written against dilettantes, aristocrats and the bourgeois, and especially against the *reactionary fanatics* who accused Bakunin of heresy – states: "they see in us nothing other than embodied Antichrists, against whom every means is permitted. Shall we repay them with the same coin? No" (Bakunin 1973, 42). It is true that Bakunin admits one can be partial and unfair while fighting for freedom. Nevertheless, as Mark Leier (2009, 114) points out, for Bakunin this is a temptation that must be overcome, rather than defended.

Bakunin (1972, 204), like Kropotkin (2002, 25), did justify the violence of actions carried out against violent state institutions – nonetheless, Marshall (2008, 636) was right when he stated that the defenders of a minimal use of violence have probably predominated in anarchist thought. Colson (1997) has also pointed to the communication channels between *chemistry* and anarchism – the "cataclysmic cosmic dimension" of revolutionary anarchism. Not surprisingly, after 1968 several armed direct action groups which aimed to transform society came into being and proliferated in Europe. In the Spanish and French context, the Iberian Liberation Movement – Autonomous Combat Groups (MIL-GAC) and the Internationalist Revolutionary Action Groups (GARI) were well-known examples of armed anti-fascist groups that professed a non-Leninist revolutionary theory that openly fought all legislation dictated by capital and transgressed the law (Schmidt 2013, 102).

The theoretical assumptions of MIL-GAC were based on the pressing need for the working class to self-organise. Even expropriations or holdups were done with working class and revolutionary objectives in mind. Their creed was basically spontaneity of action and organisation in workplaces – that is, their "anti-trade" unionism. MIL-GAC was therefore a support group for the working class movement of the time, while fighting against permanent organisations. Any reference to MIL-GAC as a "group" should therefore be understood in the sense that they were more of an "affinity group" than a group understood as the embryo of a political organisation or union.[3] Its confrontations with the CNT were logical, as was the short-lived attraction it felt to the initial Comisiones Obreras (CCOO, Workers Commissions), which a number of the founders of the MIL-GAC were members of – until the absolute control of the CCOO by the Communist Party became obvious (Tajuelo 1977; Rosés 2002).

GARI, the groups considered to be the continuation of the MIL, were at some point less interesting because of their lack of theoretical production. GARI activity was more or less limited to sharing the views of those MIL-GAC members who had been imprisoned in Spain. By resorting to dynamite in its escalation of violence, GARI had the French police on tenterhooks. Yet politically speaking they were always isolated, and lacked the means to accomplish their objectives in military terms (Dartnell 1995, 78). The existence of both groups, and in particular their activity, was the tangible effect of the abuse of capital. Thus their direct action tactics were the result of class struggle. The eventual suppression of both groups, which certainly involved tragedy, did not represent the failure of the ideas that they defended, but only the serious inadequacy of the *means* used to defend them.

Ultimately, direct action is not an attack on the enemy: above all, it is an examination of what is human, a commitment to individual and collective possibilities. It is also an antidote to passivity and submission, regardless of whether the acting group is victorious or not. All direct action has to avoid restraining subjectivity because its objective must be to apply it. Tellingly, direct action and mutual aid coincide.

Worker's Councils, Unions, and Revolutionary Action Models

Direct action tactics must not only protect people's individual tendencies, but alter and transform social reality. The main reason for this is that today's States, transnational corporations and class-divided societies attempt to abolish all rights acquired through conflicts and workers' struggles, thus making exploitation without limits possible – the elimination of both the minimum wage and unemployment benefits, an increased ease of firing workers and the implementation of policies of social deterioration. I argue that a collective and international workers' instrument for organised struggle is urgently needed in order to stop the greed of capital and the irresponsibility of the exploiters.

In recent years, however, there has been increasing criticism of the union's emancipatory force: bureaucratisation, the professionalisation of their leaders, plus a consequent separation from their worker base have been identified as key points in the stagnation of trade unions and their outright deterioration. When a conflict breaks out, trade unions are not only incapable of struggling against capital, but they also cannot channel the energy of the rebellion into a revolutionary assault on the status quo: tools to generate confrontation have been replaced by programmed acts negotiated with the State and the Employers' Association (Adams 2011, 130; Fernández de Rota 2011, 140). The subsumption of unions to institutional machinery has consolidated the vertical structure of unions' federations and has eliminated any spark of spontaneity. All these facts lead to one question: is it possible to reintroduce direct action tactics – as advocated by anarcho-syndicalists and theorists of workers' councils – into trade union structures? As alternative institutions outside the structures of traditional unions, parties and government, workers' councils and almost all anarcho-syndicalist unions have rejected bureaucratic unionism and have stressed awareness of the goals of the struggle and the self-direction of workers. Alongside the self-action and self-reliance of the workers, anarcho-syndicalism and theorists of workers' councils have developed action models for the expropriation of the expropriators and forms of self-government that could reinvigorate class struggles (Guérin 1965, 126–131; Rocker 1989, 90; Pannekoek 2003, 65).

Nevertheless, entrenched unions oppose worker control as well as any self-activity that transfers the capacity of acting from union headquarters to the workplace (Ness 2011, 319). Furthermore, the vulnerability of unions results from – inter alia – capital's implementation of practices that destabilise workers (Orero 1979, 165). This scenario has rapidly created tension and frustration among workers. In Spain, disputes over the methods and aims of the anarcho-syndicalist movement led to a division of contemporary Spanish anarcho-syndicalism into two different unions, the CNT (National Labour Confederation) and the CGT (General Labour Confederation). After the death of the dictator Franco in 1975, the CNT was refounded and it re-emerged with new strength. However, it was not long before this impetus faded away because of police harassment and internal difficulties of all kinds, leading to an unfortunate split that continues today. The division of contemporary Spanish anarcho-syndicalism into two different unions was due mainly to the CNT's constant refusal to cooperate with the post-Francoist trade union bureaucracy, which refused to develop a plan for struggle based on direct action and autonomous experience (Calero 2006, 367).

The CNT and CGT's different ways of understanding anarcho-syndicalism underpin one of the episodes of the class struggle of our times, and have led to a controversy between the pre-eminence of subjectivity or of collectivity – or, more specifically, between anarcho-individualism on the one hand and libertarian communism or anarcho-syndicalism on the other hand. Yet the anarcho-syndicalism of the confederations of revolutionary trade unions can not only ensure the imposition of collective contracts, the defence of those affected by occupational injuries, the protection of migrants, and the internationalisation of the personnel of today's high-mobility societies but can also fight to encourage an environmentally-friendly mode of resource management through direct action tactics.

Green Anarchy or the Science of the Whole

The capitalist social order is based on greed, fantasy and fear, and its sacrament is the hypnotic and ridiculous commodity. It supposedly protects citizens but ultimately extorts and blackmails ordinary people. Gigantic anonymous multinational corporations are defined by a bulimia-like appetite for possession and annihilation, which impoverishes human and animal life and poisons water, the air and our very blood. This monstrous model – alienation as a planetary framework – is offered to citizens as an archetype so they can model their egos in the image and likeness of the catastrophe that disguises private economic profit as wealth. Violence and toxicity (material and ideological) are the true attributes of society, and dominate and crush us. Nowadays, ecology is the science of the whole, and it must be cultivated intensely, both theoretically and practically, by individuals and organisations.

Due to its critical frame and its integrative-reconstructive approach to reality, ecology "leads directly into anarchic areas of social thought. For, in the final analysis, it is impossible to achieve a harmonisation of man and nature without creating a human community that lives in a lasting balance with its natural environment" (Bookchin 1986, 80). Anarchism is the political tradition closest to ecology and, conversely, anarchism is moulded by ecological concerns (Carter 2003, 70). In this sense, radical environmental direct action groups like the Earth Liberation Front and the Earth Liberation Army, animal rights movements like the Animal Liberation Front, anti-technology cells like Círculo de Ataque-Punta de Obsidiana, and anonymous eco-vandals have developed social and ecological methods of struggle in order to effect pro-environmental policy changes (Anderson 2004; Green Anarchy 2008). Acts of sabotage against industrial plants or animal exploiters by means of damage to and destruction of property, arson attacks against oil and steel plants and high voltage power stations, or explosive attacks against high-pressure gas pipelines form part of the (anti-)political direct action repertoire of contemporary eco-activism.

Again, direct action plays a lead role in the struggle for a better world to live in. Our planet must no longer be treated as a storehouse of resources that, if appropriately subjugated to manufacture, merely satisfy demand. In the face of this dispossession, there is no choice but to develop the means and channels of international resistance and ecological consciousness. Revolutionary direct action must also avoid the limitations of any "enlightened" euro-ethnocentrism, for in today's mobile and changing societies, activists must pay attention to internationalism and to the dispossession of migrants.

Poetry as a Space of Direct Action

When the First Workers' International was founded, reports on the living conditions that capitalism imposed upon workers did not come from the working class alone, but also from artists like Rimbaud and Baudelaire, to name just two remarkable cases. Initially, however, the paths available for social criticism were all completely independent from one another. This was a terrible blow for revolutionary expectations and for the emancipation of workers, not only because the forces that emerged in parallel did not work together, but also because they regarded each other with much suspicion. This favoured the rule of capital and the conversion of workers' complaints into mere reiterative rhetoric.

Anarchism was the movement that put most emphasis on the role that culture could play in the emancipation of the human being.[4] However, anarchists formulated their works and their aesthetic theories as instruments of social revolution, and they never lost sight of the necessity of making their works into ideological weapons (Litvak 1981, 287). Gustav Landauer, for instance, believed quite literally that poets and poetry should form the basis of the revolution – "we need again, and again and again, the revolution, we need the poets" (Landauer 1997, 293).

This meant that social revolution should not be limited to economic, political and material demands, but should also include revolutionary art. In this regard, Kropotkin wrote that artists "will be an integral part of a living whole that would not be completed without them" (Kropotkin 2002, 105).

My interest here is to highlight the fact that, for anarchists, poetry has been understood as a means of agitation through the word and, therefore, as a form of direct action: "the people, the thinkers, the poets are a powder keg, loaded with spirit and the power of creative destruction" (Landauer 2010, 170). The poetic word thus becomes a tool for combat that has a revolutionary and propagandistic function on the one hand and an ethical-aesthetic dimension on the other – "I want my verses to be bombs that explode at the feet of the idol, such as Religion, Fatherland or Money," wrote the anarchist poet Alberto Ghiraldo (Glöckner 1995, 133). When half a century later Leo Ferré sang *at poetry school one does not learn at all: one fights!*, he was proclaiming the same core principle: revolutionary direct action poetry can electrify the masses, strengthen the methods of struggle, and inject fresh ideas through the influence of thought and pen.

In addition, anarchist poetry has been able not only to question the logic of the sign in general, but also the grammatical and syntactic conventions of individual languages. Poetry understood as a rhythmic expression linked to improvisation and lack of constraints bears a resemblance to free jazz, and stretches the boundaries of the anarchistic anti-hierarchical model to breaking point.[5] Words spontaneously created under the pressure of feeling, the political context, and the pulse of music rebel against any form of hierarchy and prevent the *despot's* speech from becoming a paralysing force imposed on the collectivity. When anarchist poets are able to establish systems of distribution and correspondence – in a Baudelairean sense – constant translations between two or more systems are required and confrontation with institutionalised language rules is stressed. In this regard, I would like to note Herbert Read's (1938, 15) efforts to join the two shores, poetry and anarchism, which are only separated in appearance: "I believe that the poet is necessarily an anarchist, and that he must oppose all organized conceptions of the State, not only those which we inherit from the past, but equally those which are imposed on people in the name of the future." Poetry, as a space with qualitative meaning, creates new myths that generate significance and effective ways of acting which enrich our life on this Earth, and help end the cycle of dissatisfaction and submission through the endless exercise of direct action.

Notes

1 The author would like to thank Javier Urdanibia for his time and help. Some of the ideas outlined in this work came to fruition through a fruitful process of collaboration with Javier.
2 McLaughlin (2002, 69) claims that *Die Reaktion in Deutschland* is inspired mainly by the work of Bruno Bauer, *Die Posaune des jüngsten Gerichts über Hegel den Atheisten und Antichristen: ein Ultimatum*. Nonetheless, I believe that *Die Reaktion* is one of the best

examples of the influence that Hegel's philosophy had on Bakunin. In fact, Bakunin's text seems to take the Hegelian programme, which so influenced him, to its ultimate consequences. As Hegel writes in *Phänomenologie des Geistes* (*Phenomenology of Spirit*) (Hegel 1952, 144), "*Durch den Kampf auf Leben und Tod*": it is through a struggle for life or death that one manages to maintain freedom.

3 The affinity group is a cellular structure linked with other groups for the purpose of collective direct action. Contrary to what one might think, libertarian "affinity" is not ideological but essentially sympathetic: it involves different temperaments, different forms of sensitivity, different traits and the different ways [of being] of those who support it (Colson 2001, 20). For more than fifty years in Spain, affinity groups were the most efficient organ for propaganda, human relationships and anarchist praxis (Peirats 1971, 324; Christie 2000, 28). They consisted of approximately ten members who shared a common social, political and ethical vision. The direct action tactics of affinity groups are well documented (Gómez Casas 1977; Bookchin 1986; Termes 2011). An attempt to reintroduce the affinity groups' (anti-)political repertoire was driven in North America by Up Against the Wall Motherfuckers in the 1960s (Neumann 2008, 60).

4 During the Spanish Civil War, for example, approximately 8,500 poems were published on the Republican side, most of which were written by anarchists (Salaün 1985, 304).

5 Consider, for example, the work of anarchist poet Π O: "'Howw yoo speling/ 'Pichka maa'tra'?!/ 'Guess! i say./...............Make it up! I...do./ What's tha use/ of 'learning' (then)?, he sez'" (Π O 1996: 488).

References

Adams, Jason. 2011. "The Constellation of Opposition." In *Post-Anarchism: A Reader*, edited by Duane Rousselle and Süreyyya Evren, 117–138. New York: Pluto Press.
Alexander, Yonah, and Pluchinsky, Dennis. 1992. *Europe's Red Terrorists: The Fighting Communist Organizations*. New York: Frank Cass.
Amorós, Miguel. 2012. *Salida de emergencia*. Logroño: Pepitas de Calabaza.
Anderson, Jon. 2004. "Spatial Politics in Practice: The Style and Substance of Environmental Direct Action." *Antipode: A Radical Journal of Geography* 36(1): 106–125.
Bakunin, Michael. 1972. *Bakunin on Anarchy*. Edited by Sam Dolgoff. New York: Vintage Books.
Bakunin, Michael. 1973. *Selected Writings*. Edited by Arthur Lehning. London: Jonathan Cape.
Bookchin, Murray. 1986. *Post-Scarcity Anarchism*. Montreal: Black Rose Books.
Calero, Juan Pablo. 2006. "Reconstruir un sueño." In *Historia del anarcosindicalismo español*, edited by Juan Gómez Casas. Madrid: La Malatesta.
Carr, Gordon. 2010. *The Angry Brigade: A History of Britain's First Urban Guerrilla Group*. Oakland: PM Press.
Carter, Neil. 2003. *The Politics of the Environment: Ideas, Activism, Policy*. New York: Cambridge University Press.
Christie, Stuart. 2000. *We, the Anarchists! A Study of the Iberian Anarchist Federation (FAI) 1927–1937*. Hastings: The Meltzer Press.
Colson, Daniel. 1997. "La science anarchiste." *Réfractions* no. 1 (Winter). https://refractions.plusloin.org/spip.php?article262.
Colson, Daniel. 2001. *Petit lexique philosophique de l'anarchisme: De Proudhon à Deleuze*. Paris: Le Livre de Poche.
Critchley, Simon. 2008. *Infinitely Demanding: Ethics of Commitment, Politics of Resistance*. London: Verso.

Dartnell, Michael Y. 1995. *Action Directe: Ultra Left Terrorism in France 1979–1987*. London: Frank Cass.
Fernández de Rota, Antón. 2011. "Acracy_Reloaded@post1968/1989: Reflections on Postmodern Revolutions." In *Post-Anarchism: A Reader*, edited by Duane Rousselle and Süreyyya Evren, 139–150. New York: Pluto Press.
Forrester, Viviane. 1999. *The Economic Horror*. Cambridge: Polity Press.
Foucault, Michel. 2002. *Archaeology of Knowledge*. London: Routledge.
Franks, Benjamin. 2003. "Direct Action Ethic." *Anarchist Studies Volume* 11(1): 13–41.
Franks, Benjamin. 2006. *Rebel Alliances: The Means and Ends of Contemporary British Anarchisms*. Edinburgh: AK Press and Dark Star.
Freeden, Michael. 1996. *Ideologies and Political Theory: A Conceptual Approach*. Oxford: Clarendon Press.
Glöckner, Wolfgang K. 1995. "Sean mis versos bombas que estallen a los pies del ídolo. La poesía como forma de 'acción directa'." In *El anarquismo español y sus tradiciones culturales*, edited by Bert Hofmann, Pere Joan i Tous, and Manfred Tietz, 129–138. Frankfurt am Main: Vervuert-Iberoamericana.
Gómez Casas, Juan. 1977. *Historia de la FAI*. Bilbao: Zero.
Gordon, Uri. 2008. *Anarchy Live! Anti-Authoritarian Politics from Practice to Theory*. London: Pluto Press.
Graeber, David. 2009. *Direct Action. An Ethnography*. Oakland: AK Press.
Green Anarchy. 2008. *Green Anarchy: An Anti-Civilization Journal of Theory and Action*, no. 25. http://greenanarchy.anarchyplanet.org/files/2012/05/greenanarchy25.pdf.
Guérin, Daniel. 1965. *L'anarchisme*. Paris: Gallimard.
Hegel, Georg Wilhelm Friedrich. 1952. *Phänomenologie des Geistes*, edited by Johannes Hoffmeister. Hamburg: Felix Meiner.
Ibáñez, Tomás. 2014. *Anarquismo es movimiento*. Barcelona: Editorial Virus.
Jordan, Tim. 2002. *Activism! Direct Action, Hacktivism and the Future of Society*. London: Reaktion Books.
Kinna, Ruth. 2005. *Anarchism: A Beginner's Guide*. Oxford: Oneworld.
Kropotkin, Peter. 2002. *The Conquest of Bread and Other Writings*, edited by Marshall Shatz. Cambridge: Cambridge University Press.
Landauer, Gustav. 1997. "Eine Sprache an die Dichter." In *Zeit und Geist: Kulturkritische Schriften 1890–1919*, edited by Rolf Kauffeldt and Michael Matzigkeit. Munich: Klaus Boer Verlag.
Landauer, Gustav. 2010. "Revolution." In *Revolution and Other Writings: A Political Reader*, edited by Gabriel Kuhn, 110–188. Oakland: PM Press.
Leier, Mark. 2009. *Bakunin: The Creative Passion – a Biography*. New York: Seven Stories.
Litvak, Lily. 1981. *Musa libertaria: Arte, literatura y vida cultural del anarquismo español (1880–1913)*. Barcelona: Antoni Bosch.
Marshall, Peter. 2008. *Demanding the Impossible: A History of Anarchism*. London: Harper Perennial.
McLaughlin, Paul. 2002. *Mikhail Bakunin: The Philosophical Basis of His Anarchism*. New York: Algora Publishing.
McLaughlin, Paul. 2007. *Anarchism and Authority: A Philosophical Introduction to Classical Anarchism*. Hampshire: Ashgate.
Ness, Immanuel. 2011. "Workers' Direct Action and Factory Control in the United States." In *Ours to Master and to Own: Workers' Councils from the Commune to the Present*, edited by Immanuel Ness and Dario Azzellini, 302–321. Chicago: Haymarket Books.

Neumann, Osha. 2008. *Up Against the Wall Motherfucker: A Memoir of the 60's with Notes for the Next Time*. New York: Seven Stories.
Olson, Joel. 2009. "The Problem with Infoshops and Insurrection: US Anarchism, Movement Building, and the Racial Order." In *Contemporary Anarchist Studies: An Introductory Anthology of Anarchy in the Academy*, edited by Randall Amster, Abraham DeLeon, Luis A. Fernandez, Anthony J. Nocella II, and Deric Shannon, 35–45. New York: Routledge.
Orero, Felipe. 1979. "CNT: ser o no ser." In *CNT, ser o no ser: La crisis de 1976–1979*, 43–212. Barcelona: Ruedo Ibérico.
Pannekoek, Anton. 2003. *Workers' Councils*. Oakland: AK Press.
Peirats, José. 1971. *La CNT en la revolución española* II. Paris: Ruedo Ibérico.
Π O. 1996. *24 Hours: The Day the Language Stood Still*. Melbourne: Collective Effort Press.
Pouget, Émile. 1904. *L'action directe*. Nancy: Réveil ouvrier. http://gallica.bnf.fr/ark:/12148/bpt6k84028z.
Read, Herbert. 1938. *Poetry and Anarchism*. London: Faber and Faber.
Rocker, Rudolf. 1989. *Anarcho-syndicalism*. London: Pluto Press.
Rosés, Sergi. 2002. *El MIL: una història política*. Barcelona: aliKornio ediciones.
Salaün, Serge. 1985. *La poesía de la guerra de España*. Madrid: Castalia.
Santiáñez, Nil. 2013. *Topographies of Fascism: Habitus, Space and Writing in Twentieth-Century Spain*. Toronto: University of Toronto Press.
Schmidt, Michael. 2013. *Cartography of Revolutionary Anarchism*. Oakland: AK Press.
Taibo, Carlos. 2013. *Repensar la anarquía. Acción directa, autogestión, autonomía*. Madrid: Catarata.
Tajuelo, Telesforo. 1977. *El MIL, Puig Antich y los GARI. Teoría y práctica 1969–1976*. Paris: Ruedo Ibérico.
Termes, Josep. 2011. *Història del moviment anarquista a Espanya (1870–1980)*. Barcelona: L'Avenç.
The Invisible Committee. 2015. *To Our Friends*. South Pasadena, CA: Semiotext(e).
Tiqqun. 2010. *Introduction to Civil War*. Los Angeles: Semiotext(e).
Todd, Joseph. 2016. "Occupations, Assemblies and Direct Action – A Critique of 'Body Politics'." *Red Pepper*. www.redpepper.org.uk/occupations-assemblies-and-direct-action-a-critique-of-body-politics/.
Urdanibia, Javier. 2008. *De si la servidumbre es voluntaria*. Denia: Los Cuadernos de los Solsticios.
Ward, Colin. 1996. *Anarchy in Action*. London: Freedom Press.
Welp, Yanina and Vicente Ordóñez. 2017. "La democracia directa a debate: procesos y mecanismos de participación ciudadana". *Recerca: Revista de Pensament i Anàlisi* 21: 9–14.

6

REVOLUTION

Uri Gordon

Unlike axial core concepts such as freedom or direct action, revolution does not name a value or a principle. In all its different decontestations by anarchists, Marxists, feminists and fascists, it is a descriptive concept applying to the manner of social change. The term thus occupies a location in these ideologies' conceptual arrangements equivalent to that of reform in social democracy and stability in conservatism. Although not by itself axial, revolution nevertheless retains the value-orientation characteristic of ideological language, since its decontestation depends on co-interpretation with the other concepts which make up the host ideology. As we shall see throughout this chapter, anarchists' visions of revolution have indeed been expressed in explicit engagement with other core concepts such as direct action, prefiguration, freedom and equality, as well as with adjacent and peripheral ones such as power, reform and attack.

Revolution clearly fits the description of an essentially contested concept. The endless and irresolvable struggle over its meaning is integral to real-world political contention, as competing ideologies shape and place it coherently within their own conceptual arrangements. This happens whether these ideologies are proponents of revolution (and thus employ it as a core concept) or ones that employ the term peripherally as a foil to their own programmes. Despite such struggles, however, essentially contested concepts do contain an ineliminable component, not in the sense of a philosophically sound definition but "in the sense that an empirically ascertainable cultural commonality ascribes to [it] some minimal element ... a generally shared and therefore *de facto* conventionally constant or stable feature" (Freeden 1996, 63). This ineliminable component cannot, however, by itself sustain the concept in the richness and specificity necessary for its deployment in an ideological structure. To this end, concepts rely on the specification of quasi-contingent meanings, generated in the concept's contextualisation among other logically and culturally adjacent ones, also decontested in ways specific to the ideology.

I would like to argue that one ineliminable component of the concept of revolution, captured in the metaphor of revolving motion, is that of deep social and/or political change – a thing replaced by its opposite. One military junta taking over from another amid street-fighting between their loyalist forces is not normally considered a revolution; the term indicates significant change in the nature of power arrangements, not only in the positions occupied within them. Another ineliminable component, at least in terms of political ideology, is that of rapid change. While the agricultural and industrial revolutions are commonly (and thus "legitimately") referred to as such, the term as it concerns us here clearly refers to a much briefer period of more or less violent mass mobilisation. The archetypical revolutions informing common usage remain the English, American, and various French and Russian revolutions, each of which peaked over a decade or two. Both of these ineliminable components appear to extend beyond political usage to revolutions in science and art.

What the ineliminable component cannot account for, however, is (a) the nature of the change achieved; and (b) the circumstances of revolution itself – its participants, undertakings, duration and aftermath. This is where the above-mentioned co-interpretation comes into play, as strategies for social change are articulated within conceptual configurations that are mostly made up of values and principles. These attach revolution to particular goals, as well as informing every ideology's account of what revolution should involve as an undertaking. Anarchist accounts are distinctive in rejecting mediation between mass grassroots action and revolutionary goals through vertical institutions, and thus the seizure of state power – whether by elections or a coup d'état. Articulated during mass uprisings and through transnational political agitation and mutual aid projects, such accounts have instead called for abolishing the state along with social classes and all regimes of domination and inequality.

Note that binding the concept of revolution to a wider conceptual configuration does not mean that competing accounts become alien to the ideology's vocabulary. Neither anarchists nor proponents of any other ideology featuring revolution as a core concept are likely to think that the Cuban or Iranian revolutions simply do not merit the designation. Decontestation here does not function in the same way as with axial concepts such as equality, whose meanings are fixed to the exclusion of other ideologies' accounts. Instead, what is decontested is the concept of *successful* revolution in terms of achieving the ideology's aims. Each revolutionary ideology thus contains, not an exclusive concept of revolution, but a nomenclature, in which the preferred account is placed in the core while others continue to be employed peripherally, often for the purpose of distinction and demarcation.

This is especially pronounced with anarchist ideology, where the core concept of revolution developed from the start in explicit opposition to statist forms of socialism. In this context, two distinctions have been perennial: between revolution and reform, and between political revolution and social revolution. The first distinction decontests revolution in terms of the circumstances of social change (rapid rather than gradual), its location (outside and as-against dominant institutions, rather than from within them), and its radical depth (abolition rather than amelioration of systemic inequalities). The second distinction continues to regard the depth of social change – a transformation of social structures (with abolition of the state, class, race, gender etc. as its asymptote) rather than a revolution merely in the political structures of the state. Furthermore, the distinction between political and social revolution orients anarchism towards certain accounts of revolutionary agency, specifically to the exclusion of vanguardist programmes for the seizure of state power. The archetypical "political revolution" in anarchist discourse remains the October Revolution. The term thus hyperlinks to the entire substance of opposition between anarchism and authoritarian Marxism, and stands at the background of intra-anarchist tensions around the role of the anarchist minority ahead of and during revolutions.

While these distinctions, explored in the following two sections, mark anarchism off from its competitors on the left, the concept of revolution has also been significantly "re-contested" within anarchist ideology in past decades. The rising influence of post-structuralist, intersectional, and queer analyses, with their emphasis on the dislocation of oppressive power, has moved the concept away from associations with finality and beyond circumscription within the abolition of formal institutions. These themes, and some of the debates they have raised, are discussed in the final section.

Revolution vs. Reform

First-order anarchist decontestations of revolution emerge most sharply in juxtaposition to reform: revolution is radical rather than moderate, rapid rather than gradual, and emerges from without and as-against dominant social arrangements rather than from within and in cooperation with them. In this context reform tends to be decontested as incremental change brought about through the provisions of existing power structures, typically the state. It involves anything from constitutional to regulatory change driven by one or more branches of government. In modern capitalist democracies, reformist measures can include petitions for legislation or court action, the promotion of electoral candidates, and engagement between organised labour and employers.

If the metaphor of revolving motion points to the extent of social change, then revolution signals the undoing of a social order rather than its incremental alteration. Pyotr Kropotkin (1886, 2) thus decontests revolution as "a rapid modification of outgrown economic and political institutions, an overthrow of the injustices accumulated by centuries past, a displacement of wealth and political power." For anarchists, the radical depth of social revolution points beyond an amelioration of classed, racialised, gendered and other hierarchies – typically through the state – and towards their abolition along with it.

The rapid rather than gradual nature of revolution is also taken for granted in most anarchist political language. Mikhail Bakunin (1866) wrote of "a universal, worldwide revolution" involving "the simultaneous revolutionary alliance and action of all the people of the civilized world;" whereas Kropotkin (1886, 2), while warning that revolution "is not the work of one day," also clearly has a limited time-frame in mind:

> It means a whole period, mostly lasting for several years, during which the country is in a state of effervescence; when thousands of formerly indifferent spectators take a lively part in public affairs; when the public mind, throwing off the bonds that restrained it, freely discusses, criticises and repudiates the institutions which are a hindrance to free development; when it boldly enters upon problems which formerly seemed insoluble.
>
> *(2)*

We will return to the question of revolution-as-event later on. For now, note that in addition to circumscribing revolution within a discrete period, Kropotkin's formulation also locates social change outside of dominant institutions. This can again be placed in opposition to reform, which moves to change such institutions from within through participation rather than repudiation. In this context, two distinct rationales for the rejection of reform are at work. The first is a strategical logic, which maintains that reform is impossible because the ruling classes will never assent to basic changes in the social structure, and will thus inevitably subvert, absorb and/or suppress any effort to alter them through gradual and legal means. As Alexander Berkman (1929, ch. 24) put it, no "great social evil" was ever "eliminated without a bitter struggle with the powers that be. … There is no record of any government or authority, of any group or class in power having given up its mastery voluntarily. In every instance it required the use of force, or at least the threat of it." Errico Malatesta similarly argued that reforms "tend to distract the masses from the struggle against authority and capitalism; they serve to paralyse their actions and make them hope that something can be attained through the kindness of the exploiters and governments" (Malatesta 1899). Instead, anarchists expect revolutionary social change to involve the actualisation of alternatives outside of hierarchical institutions, and conflict between the two.

The second rationale for rejecting reform is ethical: reform involves mediation of social change by vertical institutions – that is, the same means that anarchists reject as a matter of principle. On an early formulation by Bellegarrigue (1850, §VIII), "to fight politics with politics, to fight government with government, is to do politics and government, it is to confirm guardianship rather than abolishing it and to stop the revolution instead of accomplishing it." This ties closely to the anarchist ethos of identity between means and ends, and points to direct action and prefiguration as alternative core concepts defining the site and circumstances of revolution as anarchists desire it.

Direct action in its anarchist decontestation refers to the widest sense of action without intermediaries, whereby an individual or a group uses their own power and resources to change reality, by intervening directly in a situation rather than appealing to an external agent (Gordon 2008, 34–40). While more often used today in reference to disruptive tactics, the logic of direct action extends to constructive projects to realise alternative economies and social relations, as well as, importantly, to acts of expropriation during mass uprisings. By taking over productive resources and infrastructures, and placing them under the same alternative relations, revolutionary goals are directly realised.

Kropotkin (1988, 32–33) thus called upon the workers to "avail themselves of the first opportunity of taking possession of land and mines, of railways and factories ... expropriation on a vast scale, carried out by the workmen themselves, can be the first step towards a reorganisation of our production on Socialist principles." Expropriation is viewed here as the primary material dimension of revolution, an "*immediate solution* ... as soon as [the social movement] applies its crowbar to the first stones of the capitalist edifice ... the satisfaction of the wants of all must be *the first consideration of the revolutionist*" (Kropotkin 1988, 59, original emphasis). Workers' seizure of the means of production wins space for alternative economic relationships, constructed in tandem with the destruction of the dominant institutions – not afterwards.

Taken together, the disruptive, constructive, and expropriative aspects of direct action go beyond tactics to inform a strategic approach, in which material and organisational alternatives develop in the process of ongoing political confrontation. These can be expanded through expropriation during social uprisings to become a base for sustained revolution.

Social vs. Political Revolution

While the juxtaposition to reform is helpful in identifying the ineliminable components of revolution, the one between political and social revolution most strongly brings out its distinctively anarchist inflection. Berkman (1929, ch. 24) famously defines a social revolution as one that "seeks to alter the whole character of society," specifically the abolition of wage slavery and class oppression, as opposed to a political revolution which involves a mere change of rulers or of "governmental form." While Kropotkin's (1988) formulation also distinguishes between (social) revolution and "a violent change of government [which] may be the result of a simple insurrection," his concept of revolution is historical and modelled on the French and English revolutions. It thus offers a broader notion of social revolution than Berkman's, which is already decontested in terms of a desired anarchist one. The distinction, in any event, continues to point to the radical depth of revolution as anarchists desire it, with contemporary activists likely to emphasise the abolition of manifold intersecting systems of domination as its object.

The terminology of this distinction appears to date back very early in anarchist expression. Pierre-Joseph Proudhon (2004 [1845], 98), in an entry in his first notebook probably written between March and May 1845, remarks that "the social revolution is seriously compromised if it comes through political revolution." The remark is isolated, and may or may not have drawn on wider parlance. The distinction may have been driven by confrontation which ensued following the 1848 revolution in France, between bourgeois Republicans who viewed universal suffrage and the election of the Assembly as the final word of the revolution, and Parisian workers who expected it to result in universal access to the means of production (Hayat 2015). The terminology does seem well established by the aftermath of the Paris Commune, with Bakunin making plain use of these two "diametrically opposite" ideas of revolution to distinguish between centralist socialist programmes for the seizure of state power, and decentralist ones for the abolition of the state power and social reorganisation "from the bottom up, by the free association or federation of workers":

> Contrary to the belief of authoritarian communists – which I deem completely wrong – that a social revolution must be decreed and organized either by a dictatorship or by a constituent assembly emerging from a political revolution, our friends, the Paris socialists, believed that revolution could neither be made nor brought to its full development except by the spontaneous and continued action of the masses, the groups and the associations of the people … the Social Revolution should end … by destroying once and for all the historic cause of all violence, which is the power and indeed the mere existence of the State.
>
> *(Bakunin 1871)*

By "spontaneous" Bakunin does not mean impulsive, improvised and undirected activity, but instead activity that is self-directed, voluntary, and therefore antagonistic to the imposition of artificial, pre-ordained structures. Elsewhere Bakunin writes that only bourgeois impostors propose a socialist revolution that is merely political, and leaves "economic transformation" to a later stage. Instead, a revolution worthy of its name should be "nothing but the immediate and direct actuation of full and complete social liquidation" – that is, the replacement of the entire system of society with federated associations (Bakunin 1869). Using similar language, Kropotkin (1886) reasons for an understanding of social revolution as inevitably "the result of the numberless spontaneous actions of millions of individuals" rather than second-stage governmental decree:

> A revolution is not a mere change of government, because a government, however powerful, cannot overthrow institutions by mere decrees. Its decrees

would remain dead letters if in each part of the territory a demolition of decaying decaying institutions ... were not going on spontaneously.

(2)

This conception retains the notion of revolution as a rapid affair, but its emphasis on spontaneity also rejects mediation between mass action and revolutionary goals. This involves a notion of path-dependence. Choices made about the organisation of the revolutionary movement (top-down or bottom-up) effectively determine the form of the revolution (seizure of state power or abolition of the state) as well as its end result – free communism or new forms of oppression. In other words, a revolutionary movement that models an authoritarian and bureaucratic state will inevitably create one, hindering rather than promoting the liquidation of social domination. Diachronically, anarchists would see the experiences of numerous revolutions in which this scenario actually transpired as reaffirming their decontestations of social revolution in its oppositional relationship to strategies for winning or seizing state power. Above all, the lethal suppression of anarchism during and after the October Revolution has hardwired this opposition into its central place in the anarchist imaginary, as a tragic monument to vindicated foresight (Volin 1954).

The rejection of vanguardism raises the question of how anarchists can act as a minority without imposing their ideas on the rest of society. Malatesta attempts to work through this problem in two articles in *Umanità Nova*, published in 1922 – ironically, on the eve of the Fascists' March on Rome. He concludes that since the masses' exploitation works to prevent them from embracing anarchist communism, a revolution to end it would have to be the work of a conscious minority. However, since anarchy cannot be imposed, this could at best "create the conditions that make a rapid evolution towards anarchy possible" (Malatesta 1922b). Anarchists' role in a revolutionary context remains therefore to resist imposition itself – and thus all top-down political and class power – while "claiming and requiring, even by force if possible, the right to organize and live as we like, and experiment [with] the forms of society that seem best to us" (Malatesta 1922a). Malatesta avoids decontesting revolution as anarchist or not at all, and instead assumes that anarchists will remain a minority, not only in society at large, but also among the revolutionary forces that might successfully topple a government. Anarchists are therefore unlikely to prevent a new government from arising, in which case,

> at least we must struggle to prevent the new government from being exclusive and concentrating all social power in its hands; it must remain weak and unsteady ... we anarchist [sic] should never take part in it, never acknowledge it, and always fight against it ...
>
> We must stay with the masses, encourage them to act directly, to take possession of the production means ... to occupy housing, to perform public

services without waiting for resolutions or commands from higher-ranking authorities.

(Malatesta 1922b)

Malatesta's sober minoritarian strategy combines resistance and constructive direct action, seeking to bring the latter's lived experience of free association and mutual aid into conflict with social logics of command at every feasible opportunity. Its attachment to indefinite struggle and a "politics without promises" even in revolutionary circumstances may resonate with anarchists who couple prefigurative practice with utopian orientations (Gordon 2009, 2017), informing their projection of revolutionary strategies onto scenarios of industrial and ecological collapse.

Two further approaches to minoritarian action have been ascendant in recent decades. One approach emerges from groups inspired by Nestor Makhno's *Organisational Platform of the Libertarian Communists*, which emphasises the role of the specific anarchist organisation – hence the term *especifismo* used to describe this tendency in Latin America (Common Struggle 2003). While the Platform does call for anarchists to spread their ideas as participants in mass workers' organisations and social movements, it also states that they should form their own groups based on theoretical unity, tactical unity, collective responsibility, and federalism. On one account (FdCA 1985), the role of the specific organisation prior to any revolutionary transitional period is to create the full possible extent of communistic alternatives (cooperatives, schools, cultural activities, etc.) and to fight to keep self-management at the centre of every political struggle, while clearly identifying allies, adversaries, and enemies. In the transitional period, the specific organisation's "first task is to foresee and organise a retreat and defeat" and it should participate in armed resistance to any new state. As long as revolutionary forces are successful, however, it should "act as a centre of debate … and clearly indicate and propagate the tactic it recommends, and also denounce and combat errors" (FdCA 1985). Platformist advocates stress the need for a coherent anarchist response to volatile social circumstances, and the need to move beyond single-issue campaigns and local struggles, if anarchists are to find a common voice and coordinate their actions.

An almost polar opposite of *especifismo*, at least organisationally, is the minoritarian approach expressed by insurrectionary anarchist cells. Inspired by writers such as Alfredo Bonanno and The Invisible Committee, insurrectionary anarchists argue that hyper-technological capitalism has rendered federations and syndicalism obsolete, and that meaningful intervention in the ubiquitous "social war" requires a strategy of informal and temporary organisation in affinity groups and base nuclei for "immediate, destructive attack on the structures, individuals and organizations of Capital and the State" (Bonanno 1998). This approach, typically found in communiques that follow attacks on police stations, banks, and similar targets, abandons specialised activism and counter-hegemonic movement-building, views "civil" and legal means with contempt, and allies itself with urban riots and clandestine action. Some insurrectionary discourses also draw on anarcho-primitivist critiques of domestication and technology, articulating their motivations for action in terms of a wild egoist individualism (Loadenthal 2017).

Recontesting Revolution

In this final section, I would like to briefly examine some re-contestations of revolution in contemporary anarchist discourse. While much of early anarchist expression did unmistakably point to revolution as a discrete period of social upheaval potentially leading to a stateless and classless society, newer ideological constructs within anarchism point away from this conception. One context in which revolution is thus re-contested is anarchists' growing affinity with intersectional, queer, and post-structuralist analyses, which eschew essentialist foundations and view regimes of domination as decentralised and dislocated. From this point of view "there is no centre within which power is to be located" and no "central problematic within the purview of which all injustices can be accounted for" (May 1994, 11). While this approach is mainly articulated in opposition to orthodox Marxist notions of revolution as a final confrontation between two classes, it also destabilises the status of revolution as an event, since the abolition of formal institutions does not alone revolutionise social relations. As Tadzio Mueller (2003) puts it,

> One cannot continue to think revolution as a one-off event, since that implies the existence of one or only a small number of centres of power. If power is also embedded in value structures as the example of patriarchy on [a protest] site demonstrates, then "revolution" must be seen as a process, since it is clearly impossible to "revolutionise" values and attitudes from one day to the next.
>
> *(130)*

In similar terms, *Tiqqun* authors argue that since "Empire ... has expanded its colonization over the whole of existence ... it is on this total terrain, the ethical terrain of forms-of-life, that the war against empire [should be] played out" (Tiqqun 2011, 67). Such an analysis leads Simon Springer (2014, 264) to endorse a micropolitical approach to anarchism which rejects "end-state politics," opposes "permanent insurrection" to "final revolution," and "abandons any pretext of achieving a completely free and harmonious society in the future and instead focuses on the immediacies of anarchist praxis and a prefigurative politics of direct action in the present."

Tied to this turning away from finality are expressions that seek to entirely absorb revolution into the present tense, asserting e.g. that it is "not a grand apocalyptic moment" but "exists in every moment of our lives .... in the present, not in some mythic possible future" (Monkey n.d.). The term "revolutionary" is mobilised here to characterise anarchist politics as intrinsically valuable, rather than premised on self-sacrifice for a distant cause. For Torrance Hodgson (n.d.):

> The revolution is now, and we must let the desires we have about the future manifest themselves in the here and now as best as we can. When we start doing that, we stop fighting for some abstract condition for the future and instead start fighting to see those desires realized in the present ... as a part of the life one is striving to create, as a flowering of one's self-determined existence.

These approaches hold, with Gustav Landauer (1978 [1911], 107), that anarchism is "not a thing of the future, but the present, not a matter of demands, but of living," and echo Colin Ward's (1982, 14) emphasis on the ubiquity of self-determining, co-operative and non-hierarchical forms of organisation in everyday life, operating "side by side with, and in spite of the dominant trends of our society." This move to normalise forms of social organisation underpinned by co-operation, reciprocity, mutual aid, and inclusion turns against their instrumental subordination to an anticipated revolutionary moment. Direct action, communisation, and the cultivation of non-hierarchical relations are endorsed not only because they are instrumentally useful to revolutionary strategy, but also because they are sites of personal and collective liberation and lived ethical practice.

The turn to immediacy and lived practice has raised concerns that experimental efforts at a "revolution in everyday life" may become depoliticised, inward-looking and detached from any project for wider social transformation. Thus Joel Olson's (2009, 41) critique of the American anarchist movement as one in which "building free spaces and/or creating disorder are regarded as the movement itself" and "the necessary, difficult, slow, and inspiring process of building movements falls through the cracks between sabotage and the autonomous zone." Proponents argue, however, that the emphasis on present-tense liberation does not mean that political contention is abandoned, or that it cannot be attached to support for social movements' struggles; indeed, alternative social relations emerge more sharply and develop more rapidly in periods of political mobilisation and during popular uprisings. In recent years, American anarchists have proven far from inward-looking in their solidarity with grassroots movements of African- and Native Americans, without losing their ability to maintain and spread their political culture, as have their European counterparts in their support of self-organising refugees from Calais to Lesbos. This terrain of solidarity may remain on the social periphery, but it is far from an inward-looking lifestylism.

Revolution, to conclude, remains a core concept in anarchist ideology, and continues to play an essential role in differentiating its accounts of social change from those of both social democracy and authoritarian Marxism. While the rejection of vanguardism has led anarchists to articulate diverse alternative accounts of minoritarian intervention, there has been of late less clarity on the precise role of moments of mass confrontation and social effervescence within a project to abolish both hierarchical institutions and regimes of domination in everyday life. The recent cycle of contention has proven all too bitterly that the channelling of movements' energies into electoral politics is a lost cause. While the present period of reaction may force anarchists into retreating battles, the question of revolution must remain at the centre of attention if more advanced perspectives are to accompany the inevitable resurgence of global struggles that will follow.

References

Bakunin, Mikhail. 1866. "The Revolutionary Catechism." The Anarchist Library. https://theanarchistlibrary.org/library/michail-bakunin-revolutionary-catechism.

Bakunin, Mikhail. 1869. "Politique de l'Internationale." *L'Égalité* nos. 29–32 (7–28 August). http://kropot.free.fr/Bakounine-PolInter.htm.

Bakunin, Mikhail. 1871. "The Paris Commune and the Idea of the State." Anarchy Archives. http://dwardmac.pitzer.edu/Anarchist_Archives/bakunin/pariscommune.html.

Bellegarrigue, Anselm. 1850. *L'Anarchie, journal de l'ordre* no. 2. http://kropot.free.fr/Bellegarrigue-A02.htm.

Berkman, Alexander. 1929. "What Is Communist Anarchism?" The Anarchist Library. https://theanarchistlibrary.org/library/alexander-berkman-what-is-communist-anarchism.

Bonanno, Alfredo Maria. 1998. *The Insurrectional Project*, translated by Jean Weir. The Anarchist Library. http://theanarchistlibrary.org/library/alfredo-m-bonanno-the-insurrectional-project.

Common Struggle. 2003. "Anarchism and the Platformist Tradition." *Common Struggle*. http://nefac.net/platform/.

FdCA – Federazione dei Comunisti Anarchici. 1985. "Basic Strategy Document: On the Transitional Period." FdCA. www.fdca.it/fdcaen/organization/sdf/sdf_tp.htm.

Freeden, Michael. 1996. *Ideologies and Political Theory: A Conceptual Approach*. Oxford: Clarendon.

Gordon, Uri. 2008. *Anarchy Alive! Anti-Authoritarian Politics from Practice to Theory*. London: Pluto Press.

Gordon, Uri. 2009. "Utopia in Contemporary Anarchism." In *Anarchism and Utopianism*, edited by Laurence Davis and Ruth Kinna, 260–275. Manchester: Manchester University Press.

Gordon, Uri. 2017. "Prefigurative Politics between Ethical Practice and Absent Promise". *Political Studies* (2 October)

Hayat, Samuel. 2015. "Rendre visible la révolution sociale." *Libération* (22 October). www.liberation.fr/debats/2015/10/22/rendre-visible-la-revolution-sociale_1408141.

Hodgson, Torrance. n.d. "Towards Anarchy." Anarchynz. https://web-beta.archive.org/web/20131011195634/http://flag.blackened.net/anarchynz/therevolutionisnow.htm.

Kropotkin, Pyotr. 1886. "What Revolution Means." *Freedom* 1 (2): 1–2. http://dwardmac.pitzer.edu/journals/freedom/freedom1_2.html.

Kropotkin, Pyotr. 1988. *Act for Yourselves: Articles from Freedom, 1886–1907*, edited by Nicolas Walter and Heiner Becker. London: Freedom Press.

Landauer, Gustav. 1978 [1911]. *For Socialism*. St. Louis: Telos Press.

Loadenthal, Michael. 2017. *The Politics of Attack: Communiques and Insurrectionary Violence*. Manchester: Manchester University Press.

Malatesta, Errico. 1899. "Towards Anarchism." The Anarchist Library. http://theanarchis tlibrary.org/library/errico-malatesta-towards-anarchism.
Malatesta, Errico. 1922a. "Revolution in Practice." *Umanità Nova* no. 191 (7 October). http://dwardmac.pitzer.edu/Anarchist_Archives/malatesta/revpra.html.
Malatesta, Errico. 1922b. "Further Thoughts on Revolution in Practice." *Umanità Nova* no. 192 (14 October). http://dwardmac.pitzer.edu/Anarchist_Archives/malatesta/fur.html.
May, Todd. 1994. *The Political Philosophy of Poststructuralist Anarchism*. University Park, PA: The Pennsylvania State University Press.
Monkey. n.d. "Forest Life." Eco-action.org. www.eco-action.org/go/monkey.html.
Mueller, Tadzio. 2003. "Empowering Anarchy: Power, Hegemony, and Anarchist Strategy." *Anarchist Studies* 11(2): 122–149.
Olson, Joel. 2009. "Between Infoshops and Insurrection: US Anarchism, Movement Building, and the Racial Order." Libcom.org. http://libcom.org/library/between-info shops-insurrection-us-anarchism-movement-building-racial-order.
Proudhon, Pierre-Joseph. 2004 [1845]. *Carnets* I: 91. Dijon: Les Presses du Réel.
Springer, Simon. 2014. "Why a Radical Geography Must Be Anarchist." *Dialogues in Human Geography* 4(3): 249–270.
Tiqqun. 2011. *This Is Not a Program*. Los Angeles, CA: Semiotext(e).
Volin (Vsevolod Mikhailovich Eichenbaum). 1954. *The Unknown Revolution, 1917–1921*. London: Freedom Press. https://libcom.org/files/Volin%20The%20unknown%20revo lution.pdf.
Ward, Colin. 1982. *Anarchy in Action*. London: Freedom Press.

PART 2
Adjacent Concepts

7
HORIZONTALISM

Mark Bray[1]

The decades that have followed the fall of the Berlin Wall in 1989 have witnessed a historic resurgence of directly democratic, federalist politics among global social movements on a scale unheard of since the first decades of the twentieth century. From the Zapatistas and Magonistas of southern Mexico, to the global justice movement, to the squares movements of Tahrir Square, 15M (15th of May), Occupy, Gezi Park, and many more around the world, to Black Lives Matter, we can see the powerful impact of the style of leaderless (or leader*ful*),[2] autonomous, direct action-oriented organizing that has characterized resistance from below during this era. Some of the groups and individuals that composed these movements were directly, or indirectly, influenced by the enduring anti-authoritarian legacy of anarchism, whose international popularity has surged over recent decades in conjunction with a heightened interest in federalist, anti-capitalist politics. Many more, however, came to reject the hierarchical party politics of authoritarian communism not as the result of an explicitly ideological influence, but rather because occupations, popular assemblies, and consensus decision making were widely considered to be the most ethically and strategically appropriate forms of struggle given existing conditions. Such was the case for most of the Argentines who rose up to occupy their workplaces and organize neighborhood assemblies in the wake of the financial crisis of 2001. Out of this popular rebellion against neo-liberalism came the term "horizontalism" (*horizontalidad*). While this slippery term has meant slightly different things for different people, it generally connotes a form of "leaderless," autonomous, directly democratic movement building whose adherents consider it to be non-ideological. Since the Argentine uprising, the term "horizontalism" has established itself as the overarching label for this amorphous form of directly democratic organizing that has swept the globe.

Certainly horizontalism and anarchism overlap in their advocacy of federal, directly democratic, direct action-oriented, autonomous organizing. Long before the collapse of the Soviet Bloc, anarchists railed against the inherently deleterious effects of hierarchy and authoritarian leadership while building large-scale federal models of workers' self-management in the form of anarcho-syndicalist unions with memberships in the hundreds of thousands, or even above a million in the case of the Spanish CNT in the 1930s. In some cases, such as the French CGT in the early twentieth century, anarchist unionists even endorsed creating non-sectarian revolutionary syndicalist unions that could group the working class beyond political divides (Maitron 1992, 326; Maura 1975, 495). It is unsurprising that many anarchists have thrown their lot in with the horizontalist mass movements of the past decades in order to safeguard and promote their anti-authoritarian tendencies. The intense proximity that exists between these two currents raises some important questions: is horizontalism merely a new name for anarchism? Are they basically the same idea masquerading behind different histories? Given such a high level of overlap, are we simply quibbling about semantics if we insist on a distinction between the two?

To answer this question, I will draw a distinction between "horizontalism," which I use as a historically specific term to demarcate the wave of directly democratic popular mobilization that has emerged over the past few decades, and "horizontal," which I use as an analytical descriptor to describe any form of non-hierarchical activity, regardless of context. Once this distinction is drawn, it is apparent that although anarchism is inherently horizontal, the historical horizontalism of recent years is a fluid entity that occasionally promotes values and ideas that are at odds with anarchism as a result of its minimalist, "anti-ideological" ideology. Although some anarchists and others have characterized anarchism as "anti-ideological" as well, the history of the movement shows that most of its militants and theorists have viewed it as a solid, though flexible, doctrine anchored in a set of anti-authoritarian tenets. This stands in sharp contrast with the prevalent post-modern tendency of proponents of horizontalism to view it as a malleable set of practices disconnected from any specific political center. This "anti-ideological" focus on form over content, which is to say, its emphasis on how decisions are made over what is decided, has created significant tensions in the context of more or less spontaneous popular horizontalism for anarchists who are supportive of mass organizing and hopeful about the political openings provided by such movements. Because horizontalism attempts to divorce itself from ideology, its structures and practices are susceptible to resignification in decidedly non-horizontal directions, such as participation in representative government.

It is important to clarify that this critique of the "anti-ideology" of horizontalism applies to essentially spontaneous popular movements where thousands of random people suddenly engage in direct democracy with each other for the first time, not to examples like the Zapatistas of southern Mexico whose horizontal practices developed slowly over generations and were inextricably bound to widely shared values. When assemblies emerge without the opportunity for such steady growth and development, their lack of formal ideology greatly reduces the barriers to entry for a mass of disaggregated, disaffected people, yet it also makes the movement's content and trajectory capricious. The implicit horizontalist assumption that horizontal decision-making mechanisms are sufficient to yield egalitarian results stands in sharp contrast with the avowed anarchist commitment to both horizontal practices and anti-oppressive outcomes. This demonstrates that although anarchism is horizontal (in the analytical rather than the historically specific sense of the term), and horizontalism is anarchistic (meaning it bears many of the traits of anarchism), horizontalism and anarchism are not identical.

Horizontalism

In late 2001, a spontaneous rebellion erupted in Argentina when the government decided to freeze bank accounts to forestall a mounting financial crisis precipitated by the IMF-mandated privatization and austerity measures of the 1990s. In under two weeks, popular mobilizations ousted four governments. Against the hierarchical machinations of the political elite, social movements organized democratic neighborhood assemblies and workplace occupations around principles that were increasingly encapsulated in the concept of horizontalism. Occupied workplaces forged networks of mutual aid and assemblies formed locally before establishing inter-neighborhood organisms of direct democracy guided by both the sentiment and the practice of consensus decision making. This uprising was eminently prefigurative as it sought to embody the society it desired in its everyday practices. As Marina Sitrin (2006, 4) argues in her influential *Horizontalism: Voices of Power in Argentina*, horizontalism "is desired and is a goal, but it is also the means – the tool – for achieving this end." For many, it was "more than an organizational form," it was "a culture" that promoted new affective relationships and communal solidarity (Sitrin 2006, 49). This culture of openness and rejection of dogma could even impinge upon the consolidation of horizontalism as a fixed entity since, as the Argentine Colectivo Situaciones argued, "*horizontalidad* should [not] be thought of as a new model, but rather *horizontalidad* implies that there are no models.... *Horizontalidad* is the normalization of the multiplicity ... The risk is that *horizontalidad* can silence us, stop our questions, and become an ideology" (Sitrin 2006, 55).

The accounts Sitrin gathered from the direct participants in the Argentine uprising demonstrate that for many, horizontalism was perhaps an anti-ideological ideology composed of a fluid mixture of flexible, participatory, non-dogmatic values and practices oriented around consensus, federalism, and self-management. However, these attitudes and outlooks emerged in a number of different groups and movements long before they were associated with the term "horizontalism." In *Unruly Equality: U.S. Anarchism in the 20th Century*, Andrew Cornell (2016) demonstrates how the diffuse remnants of early twentieth-century anarchism that were increasingly inclined toward pacifism and the avant-garde in the 1940s and 1950s

> provided theories, values, tactics, and organizational forms, which activists in the antiwar, countercultural, and feminist movements took up [over the following decades]; in turn, these mass movements radicalized hundreds of thousands of people, a portion of whom adopted anarchism as their ideological outlook.
>
> *(245)*

The destruction of the American anarchist movement in the middle of the century and the polarization of the Cold War led many American anarchists to experiment with new tactics and strategies. This included consensus, which was first used by American anarchists in the radical anti-war organization Peacemakers in the late 1940s (Cornell 2016, 180–181). More than a decade later, consensus was introduced into the civil rights organization Student Nonviolent Coordinating Committee (SNCC) by Peacemakers organizer James Lawson (Cornell 2016, 229; Carmichael 2003, 300). This influence carried through Students for a Democratic Society (SDS) and other groups into the 1970s and 1980s where the New Hampshire Clamshell Alliance pioneered the use of spokescouncils and affinity groups in the anti-nuclear movement, feminist consciousness-raising circles experimented with non-hierarchical organization, and the Movement for a New Society (MNS) incorporated Quaker consensus methods (Farrell 1997, 241; Anarcho-Feminism 1977; Cornell 2011). During the same decades, similar tendencies were at play in Europe with elements of the feminist, anti-nuclear, and autonomous movements (Katsiaficas 1997). The tradition that these groups forged was adopted by subsequent groups such as the direct action AIDS group ACT UP, the radical environmentalist Earth First!, Food Not Bombs, and others feeding into the global justice movement at the turn of the twenty-first century (Gould 2009; Wall 2002; McHenry 2012). The squares movements of the Arab Spring, 15M, Occupy, Gezi Park, Nuit Debout, and others were in part a reboot of the assemblies, spokescouncils, affinity groups and direct actions of the global justice movement oriented around a specific geographic space in the form of the plaza. Others have been influenced by the concept of rhizomatic organizing put forth by Gilles Deleuze and Félix Guattari (1987; Chalcraft 2012; Anderson 2013). While the specific practices of these groups and movements varied,

> their investment in deliberation, consensus-building, individual participation, diversity, novel technologies, and creative engagement stands as a self-conscious counterpoint to doctrinaire and hierarchical models of mobilization, political, and religious sectarianisms, polarizing debates over national identity, and even representative forms of democracy.
>
> *(Anderson 2013, 154)*

Horizontalist opposition to representative democracy usually comes in the form of consensus decision making. Rather than formulating a proposal and simply concerning oneself with accumulating enough votes to push it through, consensus requires participants to take the concerns of the minority seriously and cater proposals to their outlooks. The idea is not that everyone has to agree all the time (the strawman portrayal of consensus), but rather that the majority is forced to make concessions to the minority and, for the group to function, the minority must grow accustomed to tolerating decisions that it finds less than ideal. Consensus seeks to promote not only the formal practice of assuring that proposals will satisfy the minority, but more deeply, a sense of unity within the group and a culture of care that can all too easily get trampled in the pursuit of a voting majority.

This form of decision making works best when all members of a group have a shared sense of purpose. When they don't, the process grinds to a halt. For example, Occupy Wall Street implemented modified consensus, only requiring 90% rather than 100% agreement, to provide a little breathing room for such occasions. Nevertheless, when members of a body are working at cross purposes it only takes 11% to shut down the objectives of the other 89%. Occupy Wall Street and many of the other squares movements encountered such problems when spontaneously incorporating thousands of random individuals into their decision-making bodies. Even when consensus is practiced by a cohesive group with a shared purpose it carries an inherent bias toward the status quo by making it more difficult to pass a proposal or resolution. As George Lakey of Movement for a New Society remarked, "consensus can be a conservative influence, stifling the prospects of organizational change" (Cornell 2011, 47). Clearly consensus carries a number of pitfalls, but so does majority voting. Ultimately it is very difficult to navigate conflict which is why anarchists place such a great emphasis on voluntary association (and, therefore, voluntary disassociation). Sometimes the only solution is for two groups to go their separate ways rather than forcing them to coexist.

Many of horizontalism's most energetic advocates view it as means and ends wrapped together into a unified set of practices and values. From this perspective, values inform practices which shift as they encounter varied circumstances. In turn, the horizontalist hostility to "dogma" allows values to adjust to the needs of the people as movement contexts twist and turn. Horizontalism's "non-ideological," "apolitical" focus on form, practice, and immediate problem-solving over large-scale "sectarian" conflicts has endowed this historically specific tendency with a portability and adaptability that has allowed it to flourish in contexts as different as rural Greece and lower Manhattan, Istanbul and Hong Kong. Unsurprisingly, the politics undergirding horizontalism have varied drastically. This is unproblematic if one has no predetermined goal; if one adheres to the liberal notion I have referred to elsewhere as "outcome neutrality" (Bray 2014). Yet, anarchism has always been about much more than direct democracy; it is a revolutionary socialist ideology grounded in anti-domination politics as well as non-hierarchical practice.

Anarchism and Horizontalism

Anarchist responses to the growth of popular horizontalism have ranged from elation to disgust, with many in between. Those who have been more enthusiastic have viewed horizontalist movements as opportunities for the mass promotion of non-hierarchical politics while critics have seen them as betrayals of truly horizontal principles especially as they have ventured into electoralism. There are a range of anarchist responses to horizontalism, as the examples below from Spain, the United States, and Turkey will demonstrate.

The shared federalism[3] of anarchism and horizontalism can be traced back to the eighteenth century. While one can also trace it back even further, in terms of the history of socialism it makes sense to start with the influence of the dictatorial Jacobin "republic of virtue" during the French Revolution, which pioneered elements of central planning and modern conscription. Over the following decades, the European republican movement was split between Jacobins and their sympathizers who longed for a renewed "reign of terror" and federal republicans who were aghast at the bloody consequences of centralized authority, even in the hands of republicans, and instead advocated local and regional autonomy. Unsurprisingly, many of the first disciples of the anti-authoritarian works of Proudhon and Bakunin began their political lives as federal republicans while many Marxists have hailed the Jacobin dictatorship as a preview of their desired dictatorship of the proletariat (Zimmer 2015, 73; Esenwein 1989, 16–17; Maura 1975, 68; Toledo and Biondi 2010, 365; Lenin 1975; Mayer 1999).

Anarchists advanced the federal republican opposition to centralization by forming a critique of the state, whether federal or centralized, and developing modes of struggle and methods of self-organizing that reflected the world they sought to create. Most Marxists reject the notion that anything approximating communism could be enacted in a capitalist society and therefore conclude that the form that an organization or party takes is only of instrumental value. For Marxist-Leninists, for example, this essentially amounts to the position that it is acceptable for a vanguard party to act in the best interest of the proletariat – to act as the proletariat would allegedly act if it had already achieved full class consciousness – as long as the same end result of communism is eventually achieved (though, of course, it never was). For most anarchists, however, the society of the future will inevitably reflect the values, principles, and practices that went into making it.

To understand how anarchists have attempted to put this idea into prefigurative practice, it's important to distinguish between what David Graeber (2002) and others have come to refer to as "capital-A" and "small-a" anarchism. Although the gap that separates the two tendencies is often vastly overstated, the distinction can help us identify the connection between consensus and majority decision making and the areas of overlap that exist between anarchism and horizontalism. The anarchists that Graeber referred to as "capital-A" anarchists are much more self-consciously influenced by the legacy of "classical" anarchism (from roughly the 1860s to 1940). They tend to focus on the construction of large federal organizations, such as anarcho-syndicalist unions or anarchist communist federations, that operate by majority voting with a strong focus on class struggle and mass resistance. Historically such organizations have operated by federating local unions or political groups into regional, national, and even international bodies that operate by majority voting as carried out by recallable mandated delegates. As opposed to parliamentary democracy where elected representatives decide on behalf of their constituents, anarchist delegates are only empowered to express the perspective of their union or locality. Legislative power remains at the base level while allowing collective self-management to scale up. This does not mean that such systems become hierarchical, rather they allow locally-grounded decision-making bodies to coordinate across large regions. Lately consensus has become so ubiquitous in certain horizontalist/anarchist circles that some don't realize that the majority of anarchists throughout history have implemented majoritarian voting.

The anarchists that Graeber referred to as "small-a" anarchists are generally those whose anarchism has grown out of the anti-authoritarian and countercultural currents of the Cold War era rather than "classical" anarchism. They tend to create smaller, less formally structured groups and collectives that operate by consensus, associate with more countercultural *milieux*, and focus on non-class politics such as environmentalism or feminism. "Small-a" anarchist collectives are essentially examples of small-scale horizontalism infused with anarchist politics. This is unsurprising considering the fact that horizontalism and "small-a" anarchism grew out of the same post-war constellation of non-hierarchical, consensus-oriented groups discussed above, and "small-a" anarchists were among the original organizers of many recent manifestations of popular horizontalism. This demonstrates that, to some extent, horizontalism grew out of certain strains of anarchism. They part ways, however, when horizontal practice is divorced from anti-authoritarian politics. Certainly some anarchists eventually disowned the horizontalist movements they helped create because they allegedly strayed too far in a popular and/ or reformist direction away from the more intentional and explicitly radical designs some of their early organizers had envisioned. Yet, pro-mass-movement anarchists (whether of a "smaller" orientation or not) have continued to play important roles in horizontalist movements because they see them as opportunities to promote elements of anarchist politics on a large scale.

I was certainly among those who joined Occupy Wall Street in order to advance the movement's non-hierarchical agenda and infuse it with more anarchist content while maintaining its popular appeal. I made a case for such an approach in my book *Translating Anarchy: The Anarchism of Occupy Wall Street* where I documented how 72% of OWS organizers in New York City had explicitly anarchist or implicitly anarchistic politics (Bray 2013). For these anarchist(ic) organizers, and their counterparts in other movements, the horizontalist movement is a broad, dynamic space where popular struggles can interact with revolutionary politics, ideally shifting through such comingling. Such struggles are opportunities for anarchists to reclaim the mantle of democracy and attack what they consider to be the fraud of hierarchical, capitalist, representative government. In the United States, for example, anarchists have had some of their greatest successes winning liberals and centrists over to their ideas by arguing that non-hierarchical direct democracy is the only *true* democracy. In a country where the ideal, if not the actual practice, of democracy is universally revered, such arguments can strike a popular chord.

Yet not all anarchists have been equally enamored with the squares movements. Some anarchists rejected Occupy either because their local encampment truly was reformist (the politics of the many Occupy encampments ranged widely) or because they were hostile to popular politics that was not explicitly anarchist (Bray 2013, 168). In Spain, for instance, many anarchists supported and participated in their 15M movement for similar reasons as the anarchists of Occupy, but a significant number withheld their full support because they considered the movement to be reformist (Taibo 2011; 2014). Even when some of the anarchist unions wanted to support a 15M march, for example, they were frustrated by the movement's refusal to have unions and parties march with their flags which stemmed from the 15M's desire to remain "non-sectarian."

Another interesting element of the relationship between the 15M and Spanish anarchists is that they generally don't attempt to reclaim the mantle of "democracy" from the political parties and government. For example, a popular 15M chant goes "They call it democracy, and it isn't." Once, however, I was marching near a group of anarchists who sarcastically chanted "They call it democracy, *and it is!*" Here, the intent of the chant is to convince listeners that the corruption and disregard for the masses that epitomized the government is inherent to its very nature. From an anarchist perspective, that is what governmental "democracy" is and will always be. In part this stems from the popular association between the post-Franco parliamentary regime and the term "democracy." For many Spaniards, the government that has been in power since the 1970s is "*la democracia*," and therefore the term has more of a specific meaning than in the United States, where it is understood more as an egalitarian decision-making method that the government allegedly happens to embody.

In 2013, the Spanish Grupos Anarquistas Coordinados (Coordinated Anarchist Groups) published a little book called *Contra la democracia* (Against Democracy). This book created quite a stir in Spain in December 2014 when it was cited as evidence to support the arrest in Catalonia and Madrid of eleven people from Spain, Italy, Uruguay, and Austria accused of being members of what the state claimed was "a terrorist organization of an anarchist nature" responsible for "several bomb attacks" ("Catalan Police" 2014). In what came to be known as Operation Pandora, seven of the original eleven were held on terrorist charges because they had "Riseup" e-mail accounts, owned copies of *Contra la democracia*, and were found with a canister of camping gas. Later, the Chilean anarchist Francisco Javier Solar, who was ultimately convicted with fellow Chilean Mónica Caballero of bombing the Pilar Basilica in Zaragoza in 2013, denied accusations of being one of the text's main authors (Pérez 2016).

Given the importance that the authorities placed on this text, one might assume that it's a bloodthirsty bomb-making manual, but in fact, it's simply a historical analysis and critique of democracy. The book's introduction concludes by arguing that "If we believe that democracy is liberty we will never stop being slaves. We will unmask this great lie! We will construct anarchy" (Grupos Anarquistas Coordinados 2013, 8). Later, in its only reference to the 15M, the text attacks the movement, because it "asks for electoral reforms that benefit the small political parties … it propagates citizenism (*ciudadanismo*) as ideology; a 'democratization' of the police … [and] the total pacification of conflicts through mediation and delegation by a corps of social services professionals" (Grupos Anarquistas Coordinados 2013, 68). Yet, despite these critiques of "*democracia*" and the 15M, the authors of this text are not against all directly democratic organizing. They advocate the creation of networks of social centers, free schools, and other bodies "to build a new society capable of freely self-managing (the only real sense that the term 'democracy' could have) …" (Grupos Anarquistas Coordinados 2013, 66). That, of course, is exactly what anarchists who call for true direct democracy have in mind. *Contra la democracia* shows us that although many anarchists in Spain and elsewhere may have a very similar vision of the future self-management of a post-capitalist society, some find it strategically useful to fight to reclaim "democracy" while others seek to permanently discard it.

Much of the reluctance that anarchists have had in getting involved in the Spanish 15M and other movements has had to do with the prevalent tendency of horizontalist mass movements to be siphoned into non-horizontal, electoral politics. The allure of representative government is so powerful that although early on movements may proclaim "*¡Que se vayan todos!*" ("Get rid of them all!") in Argentina or "*¡Que no nos representan!*" ("They don't represent us!") in Spain, frequently such cries are transformed into calls for horizontalism to be extended into office through the ballot box. Often such arguments are couched in terms of the perspective that after the initial wave of protest has raised awareness about an issue, what is necessary is to transition into the "serious work of making concrete change" through governing. In Spain, the most significant party that grew out of the 15M was *Podemos* (We can) which has formed electoral coalitions with other similar parties and platforms like *Barcelona en Comú* (Barcelona in Common) and *Ganemos Madrid* (Let's win Madrid) which calls for the promotion of "democratic municipalism" and the creation of political structures that are "democratic, horizontal, inclusive, and participatory …" (Ganemos Madrid 2016). Their rhetoric is rife with horizontalist references to "autonomy" and "*autogestión*" (self-management). They essentially claim to be merging the spirit and ideals of horizontalist assembly with the lamentable "necessity" of taking office. Moreover, they fully embrace horizontalism's antagonism toward formal ideology by rejecting the left/right binary and eschewing the usual trappings of leftism. Yet, within a year *Podemos* had already drastically moderated its platform to cater to the electoral center, thereby alienating a number of the party's more leftist leaders who later resigned ("Spain's Poll-Topping" 2014; Hedgecoe 2016). After the June 2016 elections *Podemos* leader Pablo Iglesias announced that it was time for his unconventional horizontalist party to become "normalized," and enter a phase "of much more conventional politics." He even went so far as to argue that "this idiocy that we used to say when we were of the extreme left that things change in the street and not in the institutions is a lie" (Ríos 2016).

Turkish anarchists also formulated critiques of horizontalism. As the Gezi Park occupation movement of 2013 in Istanbul's Taksim Square developed, the Turkish anarchist organization *Devrimci Anarşist Faaliyet* (Revolutionary Anarchist Action, DAF) distributed hundreds of copies of a pamphlet it had written called "An anarchist criticism to 'Occupy' as an activity of '99%.'" The pamphlet sought to diagnose what the group perceived to be the reformism and depoliticization of Occupy. It argued that the tactics of Occupy have "worn a libertarian discourse but [are] far far away from practicing it ..." and instead the movement tended, in their eyes, "to consume concepts such as occupy, direct democracy, freedom, action etc." While the pamphlet contains many insightful critiques of Occupy, certain elements of the authors' analysis suffered from the extreme distance separating them from events on the ground. At a meeting with several of the pamphlet's authors years later at the DAF office in Istanbul, I had the opportunity to answer their questions and clarify some misconceptions that they and many others had developed about Occupy Wall Street through the press and speak about the centrality of anarchist organizers. Nevertheless, the heart of their critique about the misapplication of libertarian principles applied to many (if not most) Occupy encampments and horizontalist movements in general. Despite the presence of DAF and their pamphlet, the Gezi Park movement also experienced electoral spinoffs such as the Gezi Party. Seeking to remain true to the movement's horizontalism, the party claimed that its leaders would only act as "spokespersons" ("Official Gezi Party" 2013).

Similar developments would have unfolded during the Occupy movement in the United States if it weren't for the narrowness of the two party system. Yet, several years later, many former Occupiers campaigned for Bernie Sanders in his failed bid for the Democratic Party's presidential nomination. Certainly many who participated in Occupy before supporting Sanders were simply leftists who travel from one manifestation of left populism to the next without any allegiance to (or often direct knowledge of) horizontalism. Others, however, attempted to argue that the Sanders campaign was an extension of Occupy. This was manifest in an article titled "Occupy the Party" from the Not An Alternative collective that appealed to former Occupiers to treat the campaign "like any street or park and occupy it" (Not An Alternative 2016). In the name of pragmatic populism, this article sought to drain the term "occupy" of its associations with direct action, direct democracy, "leaderlessness," and revolutionary politics to convince readers that it can be used as a catchy shorthand for buying into the cult of personality developing around a moderate social democrat attempting to burrow into a stratified, capitalist political party. From an anarchist perspective, parks and streets are terrain of struggle that can be occupied because non-hierarchical, direct action politics can be transplanted onto them. Working within political parties, especially those like the Democratic Party, requires jettisoning those practices and incorporating oneself into the party structure. As the Irish Workers Solidarity Movement organizer Andrew Flood (2014) argued in his essay "An anarchist critique of horizontalism," "horizontalism without a vision and method for revolution simply provides protest fodder behind which one government can be replaced with another." Indeed, many anti-horizontal organizers, have been perfectly willing to humor the directly democratic "quirks" of horizontalist movements while biding their time waiting for opportunities to convert popular upheavals into "protest fodder" for reformist objectives cloaked in the imagery of rebellion.

Conclusion

Debates over electoral participation within horizontalist movements are merely the latest rounds of a conflict that has challenged the broader socialist movement since the nineteenth century. Although his position changed several times, ever since Proudhon advocated electoral abstention in 1857 in response to the authoritarianism of Napoleon III, conflicts over electoralism have raged (Graham 2015, 62). Historically anarchists have opposed parliamentary participation for a variety of reasons, including their opposition to the hierarchical nature of representation, their rejection of the social democratic notion that it is possible to vote away capitalism (a goal that social democrats eventually discarded), and their argument that, as Mikhail Bakunin phrased it, "worker-deputies, transplanted into a bourgeois environment … will in fact cease to be workers and, becoming Statesmen, they will become … perhaps even more bourgeois than the Bourgeois themselves" (quoted in Graham 2015, 116).

In 1979 a group of German radicals attempted to bypass the dichotomy of socialist workers' parties and anarchist abstentionism to create a non-hierarchical "anti-party" that would operate based on consensus and rotate their representatives to preserve their commitment to direct democracy. This attempt to stuff horizontalism into the ballot box was called the Green Party. Despite the best of intentions, internal conflicts and "realist" calls for "pragmatism" doomed the party once it entered parliament. Within less than a decade it had become simply another left party (Katsiaficas 1997, 205–208).

In the wake of the sectarian strife of the twentieth century, many radicals have found refuge in the anti-ideological ideology of horizontalism. Yet, as we can see, it is often insufficient to guarantee truly horizontal and non-hierarchical outcomes. Even apart from electoralism, horizontalist movements have at times struggled to counteract the encroachment of patriarchal, homophobic, transphobic, white supremacist, and ableist tendencies that inevitably come when broad swaths of society are suddenly brought together. I can still hear the common refrain of many white men in Occupy Wall Street that we had "lost sight of Wall Street" as our main focus when we addressed race or gender. Horizontalist movements spread notions of direct democracy, direct action, mutual aid, and autonomy far and wide. This is incredibly important insofar as they influence broader cultures of resistance and extend beyond the standard reach of most radicalism. Since political ideologies are digested whole only by their most committed militants, shifting political sentiments and practices in mass contexts is essential. Yet, the horizontalist reliance on form over content runs the risk of producing a muddled populism that is easily redirected away from its non-hierarchical origins. As the work of Michael Freeden (1996) suggests, the meaning of horizontalism shifts depending on its political content. From an anarchist perspective, this illustrates the value of anarchism's holistic analysis of the interrelatedness of all forms of domination and the interconnectedness of forms of self-management and their political outcomes. While they differed on the details, anarchists from Mikhail Bakunin to Errico Malatesta, from Nestor Makhno to the creators of the *Federación Anarquista Ibérica* (FAI) in Spain have agreed on the need for anarchists to collectively engage with mass movements to disseminate their truly horizontal political visions.

Notes

1 I would like to thank Stephen Roblin, Deric Shannon, Miguel Pérez, Özgür Oktay, and Yesenia Barragan for their insightful feedback and helpful information.
2 By "leaderless," Occupy and others really referred to the absence of institutional leadership, not the absence of those who lead. Hence the shift some made toward the term "leaderful" which implied that in a horizontalist movement anyone could become a leader by getting involved.
3 I use the terms "federal" and "federalism" to refer to broadly decentralized forms of organization. Certainly the anarchist use of the terms "federation" or "confederation" to describe their organizations, such as the *Fédération Anarchiste* in France and Belgium or the *Confederación Nacional del Trabajo* in Spain, entails a greater level of decentralization than the federal state advocated by federalist republicans. Nevertheless, there is a shared tendency toward decentralization, even if different tendencies have taken it to greater lengths.

References

Anarcho-Feminism from Siren and Black Rose: Two Statements. 1977. London: Black Bear.
Anderson, Charles W. 2013. "Youth, the 'Arab Spring,' and Social Movements." *Review of Middle East Studies* 47(2): 150–156.
Bray, Mark. 2013. *Translating Anarchy: The Anarchism of Occupy Wall Street*. Winchester, UK: Zero Books.

Bray, Mark. 2014. "Five Liberal Tendencies that Plagued Occupy." *Roar Magazine*, May 14. https://roarmag.org/essays/occupy-resisting-liberal-tendencies/.
Carmichael, Stokely, with Ekwueme Michael Thelwell. 2003. *Ready for Revolution: The Life and Struggles of Stokely Carmichael (Kwame Ture)*. New York: Scribner.
"Catalan Police Take Down Anarchist Terror Group in Barcelona and 1,000 Supporters March in Protest." 2014. *The Spain Report*, December 16. www.thespainreport.com/articles/91-141216201022-catalan-police-take-down-anarchist-terror-group-in-barcelona-and-1-000-supporters-march-in-protest.
Chalcraft, John. 2012. "Horizontalism in the Egyptian Revolutionary Process." *Middle East Report* 262: 7.
Cornell, Andrew. 2011. *Oppose and Propose!: Lessons from Movement for a New Society*. Oakland, CA: AK Press.
Cornell, Andrew. 2016. *Unruly Equality: U.S. Anarchism in the 20th Century*. Oakland, CA: University of California Press.
Deleuze, Gilles, and Félix Guattari. 1987. *A Thousand Plateaus: Capitalism and Schizophrenia*. Minneapolis: University of Minnesota Press.
Esenwein, George R. 1989. *Anarchist Ideology and the Working-Class Movement in Spain, 1868–1898*. Berkeley: University of California Press.
Farrell, James J. 1997. *The Spirit of the Sixties: The Making of Postwar Radicalism*. New York: Routledge.
Flood, Andrew. 2014. "An Anarchist Critique of Horizontalism." Anarchist Writers, May 2. http://anarchism.pageabode.com/andrewnflood/anarchist-critique-horizontalism-occupy.
Freeden, Michael. 1996. *Ideologies and Political Theory: A Conceptual Approach*. Oxford: Clarendon.
Ganemos Madrid. 2016. "Organización." http://ganemosmadrid.info/organigrama-y-cronograma/.
Gould, Deborah B. 2009. *Moving Politics: Emotion and Act Up's Fight Against AIDS*. Chicago: University of Chicago Press.
Graeber, David. 2002. "The New Anarchists." *New Left Review* 13 (January-February): 61–73.
Graham, Robert. 2015. *We Do Not Fear Anarchy, We Invoke It: The First International and the Origins of the Anarchist Movement*. Oakland, CA: AK Press.
Grupos Anarquistas Coordinados. 2013. "Contra la democracia." https://es-contrainfo.espivblogs.net/files/2014/07/contra-la-democracia.pdf.
Hedgecoe, Guy. 2016. "Podemos Leaders Under Pressure Over Resignations." *The Irish Times*, March 19. www.irishtimes.com/news/world/europe/podemos-leaders-under-pressure-over-resignations-1.2579053.
Katsiaficas, George. 1997. *The Subversion of Politics: European Autonomous Social Movements and the Decolonization of Everyday Life*. Atlantic Highlands, NJ: Humanities Press.
Lenin, V. I. 1975. "Enemies of the People." In *The Lenin Anthology*, edited by Robert C. Tucker, 305–306. New York: W.W. Norton & Company.
Maitron, Jean. 1992. *Le mouvement anarchiste en France: Des origines à 1914*. Paris: Gallimard.
Maura, Joaquin Romero. 1975. *La rosa de fuego: el obrerismo barcelonés de 1899 a 1909*. Barcelona: Ediciones Grijalbo.
Mayer, Robert. 1999. "Lenin and the Jacobin Identity in Russia." *Studies in East European Thought* 51(2): 127–154.
McHenry, Keith. 2012. *Hungry for Peace: How You Can Help End Poverty and War with Food Not Bombs*. Tucson: See Sharp Press.

Not An Alternative. 2016. "Occupy the Party: The Sanders Campaign as a Site of Struggle." *Roar Magazine*, February 16. https://roarmag.org/essays/occupy-democratic-party-sanders-campaign/.

"Official Gezi Party Founded After Summer Protests." 2013. *Hurriyet Daily News*, October 24. www.hurriyetdailynews.com/official-gezi-party-founded-after-summer-protests.aspx?PageID=238&NID=56754&NewsCatID=338.

Pérez, Fernando J. 2016. "Los anarquistas chilenos se desligan de la bomba en el Pilar de Zaragoza." *El País*, March 8. http://politica.elpais.com/politica/2016/03/08/actualidad/1457428132_007140.html.

Ríos, Daniel. 2016. "Iglesias anuncia el fin del 'asalto' y el intento…" infolibre, July 6. http://www.infolibre.es/noticias/politica/2016/07/04/iglesias_anuncia_fin_del_quot_asalto_quot_busca_convertir_podemos_una_fuerza_politica_quot_normalizada_quot_52046_1012.html.

Sitrin, Marina, ed. 2006. *Horizontalism: Voices of Popular Power in Argentina*. Oakland, CA: AK Press.

"Spain's Poll-Topping Podemos Tones Down Radical Plans in Manifesto." 2014. Reuters, November 28. www.reuters.com/article/us-spain-podemos-idUSKCN0JC1OC20141128.

Taibo, Carlos. 2011. *El 15-M en sesenta preguntas*. Madrid: Catarata.

Taibo, Carlos. 2014. *El 15-M. Una brevísima introducción*. Madrid: Catarata.

Toledo, Edilene, and Luigi Biondi. 2010. "Constructing Syndicalism and Anarchism Globally: The Transnational Making of the Syndicalist Movement in São Paulo, Brazil, 1895–1935." In *Anarchism and Syndicalism in the Colonial and Postcolonial World, 1870–1940: The Praxis of National Liberation, Internationalism, and Social Revolution*, edited by Steven Hirsch and Lucien van der Walt, 363–393. Leiden: Brill.

Wall, Derek. 2002. *Earth First! and the Anti-Roads Movement: Radical Environmentalism and Comparative Social Movements*. London: Routledge.

Zimmer, Kenyon. 2015. *Immigrants Against the State: Yiddish and Italian Anarchism in America*. Urbana: University of Illinois Press.

8
ORGANISATION[1]

Iain McKay

"[O]rganisation, that is to say, association for a specific purpose and with the structure and means required to attain it, is a necessary aspect of social life. A man in isolation cannot even live the life of a beast ... Having therefore to join with other humans ... he must submit to the will of others (be enslaved) or subject others to his will (be in authority) or live with others in fraternal agreement in the interests of the greatest good of all (be an associate). Nobody can escape from this necessity." –

Errico Malatesta (1993, 84–85)

Introduction

Organisation is fundamentally a core aspect of any ideology as it is "the point where concepts lose their abstraction" and "are interwoven with the concrete practices sanctioned or condemned by an ideology" (Freeden 2003, 62). The organisational forms promoted by an ideology are stronger indicators of its *actual* core values than the words it uses.

The anarchist historian George Woodcock (1986, 226–227) proclaimed that "it seems evident that logically pure anarchism goes against its own nature when it attempts to create elaborate international or even national organisations, which need a measure of rigidity and centralisation to survive." A syndicalist union, in contrast, needs "relatively stable organisations and succeeds in creating them precisely because it moves in a world that is only partly governed by anarchist ideals." He reflected the opinions of a large band of more hostile commentators on anarchism who inflict a fundamental irrationality on anarchists. If "pure" anarchism is against any form of organisation beyond its "natural unit" of the "loose and flexible affinity group" then few sensible people would embrace it for neither a rail network nor a hospital could be reliably run by such a unit.

However, if we accept that anarchists are no different from other social activists, as fundamentally rational and realistic people – as Davide Turcato (2015) correctly argues – then we need to admit that anarchist theoreticians and activists would not be advocating an ideal that by "its own nature" precludes practical alternatives to the social ills they protest against. Theory needs to be reflected in practice and, as will be shown, anarchists have always addressed the need for social organisation.

The Ideological and Social Context: Locke and Rousseau

Anarchist thinkers and activists are not isolated individuals, but rather very much part of their society and its popular movements, seeking to gain influence for the ideas they have produced to solve the problems of their society. They are embedded in the world they were seeking to transform, aware of the intellectual and social context in which they live and critically engaged with both.

At the birth of anarchism, the ideological context was liberalism (as personified by John Locke) and democracy (as personified by Jean-Jacques Rousseau). The social context was the failure of the French Revolution and the rise of industrial capitalism as well as the oppositional movements each produced: radical republicanism and the labour and socialist movements, respectively.

Locke's liberalism rested on a defence of property, initiated by a commitment to individual self-ownership and ownership of one's own labour and the products it produces (Locke 2013, 289). Consensual exchange between individuals becomes the basis for just social relationships, and for the existence of the legitimate state, arising out of a myth of an initial social contact. As the myth justifies the appropriation of land and wealth by the few, Lockean consent becomes the means to deny the worker the full product of her labour as they need to exchange it to receive life's necessities (Macpherson 1964, 214–215). This theory justifies the liberal state which replaces the absolute Monarch and "stands over and above, and external to, the world of everyday life" (Pateman 1985, 67–72). It is the ultimate organisation for securing the power of the property owners.

Jean-Jacques Rousseau, by contrast, "denounces the liberal social contract as an illegitimate fraud" (Pateman 1988, 142). If Locke (2013, 308) proclaimed "we are *born Free*," then Rousseau (1996, 181, 99) replied that we are "everywhere in chains" and sought to explain why liberalism produced and justified the subjugation of "all mankind to perpetual labour, slavery, and wretchedness." In contrast to Lockean liberalism, Rousseau (1996, 225) recognised that the "greatest good of all" reduces down to "two main objects, liberty and equality" for the former "cannot exist without" the latter. He rightly argued that contracts between the wealthy few and the many poor will always benefit the former and, for the latter, become little more than the freedom to pick a master (Rousseau 1996, 162). The ideal society was one where "no citizen shall be rich enough to buy another and none so poor as to be forced to sell himself" (Rousseau 1996,

199). Liberal contractualism forces the property-less to obey the propertied. This "voluntary establishment of tyranny" undermines the very basis of liberty. The "moment a master exists, there is no longer a Sovereign" and to "renounce liberty is to renounce being a man, to surrender the rights of humanity and even its duties" (Rousseau 1996, 269, 104, 200).

Instead, argued Rousseau, political association had to be participatory. The "people of England regards itself as free; but it is grossly mistaken; it is free only during the election of members of parliament. As soon as they are elected, slavery overtakes it, and it is nothing" (Rousseau 1996, 266). The "people, being subject to the laws, ought to be their author" and so the "problem is to find a form of association which will defend and protect with the whole common force the person and goods of each associate, and in which each, while uniting himself with all, may still obey himself alone, and remain as free as before" (201, 203–204). However, sovereignty, "for the same reason as makes it inalienable, is indivisible" and so it was "essential, if the general will is to be able to express itself, that there should be no partial society within the State" (230, 212). Any government "is simply and solely a commission, an employment" and "mere officials of the Sovereign" (191).

The democratic critique of liberalism produced both the idea of popular sovereignty and the importance of equality. Rousseau's ideas were never implemented during his lifetime and so it is to his followers during the French Revolution we need to turn. This revolution was a conflict between both the people and the monarchy but also between the rising bourgeoisie and the toiling masses (Kropotkin 1971). Power under the Jacobins was centralised into fewer and fewer hands – from the electorate into representatives, from representatives into the government, from the government, finally, into the hands of Robespierre. The sections of Paris, unions and strikes were repressed as being "states within the state" for the Republic "called itself one and *indivisible*" for a reason while the centralisation of more and more decisions produced a bureaucracy of "thousands of officials ... to read, classify, and form an opinion" on them all (Kropotkin 1987, 51–54).

Like Locke, Rousseau's ideas had produced a situation where the few again ruled the many and class society continued.

Associationism: Fraternity Does Not Stop at the Workplace Door

Rousseau presented a critique of inequality but did not fundamentally criticise property. As he lived before the rise of industrial capitalism, with peasant farming and artisan workshops predominating, wage-labour was not widespread nor of prime importance in continental Europe. The solution for inequality was clear and did not need to question property (land reform) while the small scale of technology meant that most could become artisans working with their own tools in their own workshop.

The French Revolution, however, raised the issue of guilds and journeymen societies while one building employer reported that the:

> workers, by an absurd parody of the government, regard their work as their property, the building site as a Republic of which they are jointly citizens, and believe in consequence that it belongs to them to name their own bosses, their inspectors and arbitrarily to share out the work amongst themselves.
>
> *(Magraw 1992, 24–25)*

These perspectives only increased when the industrial revolution transformed France. Faced with the obvious authoritarianism within the factory, ex-artisans sought a solution appropriate to the changed circumstances they faced.

The workplace could not be broken up without destroying machines and the advantages they produced alongside master-servant relations. This created a new perspective in the working class. "Associationism was born during the waves of strikes and organised protests provoked by the Revolution of 1830" when "there appeared a workers' newspaper" which "suggested cooperative associations as the only way to end capitalist exploitation." This paper, *L'artisan, journal de la class ouvrière*, was produced by printers and "laid the basis for trade socialism" (Moss 1980, 32–33). While some intellectuals – the utopian socialists like Saint-Simon and Fourier – had raised various schemes for improving society, this was the first example of workers themselves making practical suggestions for their own liberation.

Across France, workers started to combine their existing organisations for mutual support with trade union activity as well as visions of a world without masters. This process intertwined with existing political Republican ideas. Radical neo-Jacobins recruited amongst workers which resulted in a "two-way interchange of ideas" with them taking up "the ideology of producer associationism which was becoming central" to artisanal socialism. Louis Blanc was the most public expression of this process and his "distinctive contribution was to fuse the associationist idea with the Jacobin-Republican political tradition" (Magraw 1992, 55, 71), but there were many others who expressed the associational idea in different forms (Vincent 1984, 127–140).

Anarchist Organisation: Laying the Foundations

By 1840 there was not only a wide appreciation of the need for some kind of association to replace capitalism but also extensive workers' organisations across France which aimed to do so. It was in this context that a working man, a printer by trade, would transform socialist politics forever by proclaiming himself an anarchist.

While Pierre-Joseph Proudhon will forever be linked with "property is theft," this was just one part of his answer to the question, *What is Property?* The other was "property is despotism" for property "violates equality by the rights of exclusion and increase, and freedom by despotism." Anarchy was "the absence of a master, of a sovereign," while proprietor was "synonymous" with "sovereign," for he "imposes his will as law, and suffers neither contradiction nor control" and "each proprietor is sovereign lord within the sphere of his property" (Proudhon 2011, 132–135). He echoed Rousseau:

> Liberty is inviolable. I can neither sell nor alienate my liberty; every contract, every condition of a contract, which has in view the alienation or suspension of liberty, is null ... Liberty is the original condition of man; to renounce liberty is to renounce the nature of man.
>
> *(Proudhon 2011, 92)*

This brings him into conflict with Locke. Rejecting the notion that master-servant contracts were valid, he dismisses its basis of property in the person: "To tell a poor man that he has property because he has arms and legs, – that the hunger from which he suffers, and his power to sleep in the open air are his property, – is to play with words, and add insult to injury." Property, then, is solely material things – land, workplaces, etc. – and their monopolisation results in authoritarian relationships. To "recognise the right of territorial property is to give up labour, since it is to relinquish the means of labour." Property results in the worker having "sold and surrendered his liberty" to the proprietor so ensuring exploitation. Whoever "labours becomes a proprietor" of his product but by that Proudhon did "not mean simply (as do our hypocritical economists)" – and Locke – the "proprietor of his allowance, his salary, his wages" but "proprietor of the value which he creates, and by which the master alone profits." Locke is also the target for Proudhon's comment that "the horse ... and ox ... produce with us, but are not associated with us; we take their product, but do not share it with them. The animals and workers whom we employ hold the same relation to us" (Proudhon 2011, 95, 106, 117, 114, 129).[2]

Yet if Locke was rejected, Rousseau did not provide a genuine solution (Noland 1967). While Proudhon favourably quotes Rousseau on "the conditions of the social pact" (Proudhon 2011, 565), he also shows how democracy failed to achieve its goals.

First, Rousseau's "programme speaks of political rights only; it does not mention economic rights." By ignoring the economic sphere, he ends up creating a class state in which the Republic "is nothing but the offensive and defensive alliance of those who possess, against those who do not possess," a "coalition of the barons of property, commerce and industry against the disinherited lower class" (Proudhon 2011, 566).

Second, Rousseau's political solution – a centralised, unitarian, indivisible republic – recreates the division between rulers and ruled which it claims to end. Thus, "having laid down as a principle that the people are the only sovereign,"

Rousseau "quietly abandons and discards this principle" and so "the citizen has nothing left but the power of choosing his rulers by a plurality vote." Echoing Rousseau's own words about England, Proudhon proclaimed that France was "a quasi-democratic Republic" in which citizens "are permitted, every third or fourth year, to elect, first, the Legislative Power, second, the Executive Power. The duration of this participation in the Government for the popular collectivity is brief … The President and the Representatives, once elected, are the masters; all the rest obey. They are *subjects*, to be *governed* and to be taxed, without surcease" (Proudhon 2011, 566, 573).

Democracy was simply not democratic enough. It "is the negation of the People's sovereignty" as it "says that *the People reigns and does not govern*, which is to deny the Revolution" and concludes "the People cannot govern itself and is forced to hand itself over to representatives." Instead of a democracy understood in the manner of the Jacobin left, Proudhon suggested in anarchy "all citizens … reign and govern" for they "directly participate in the legislation and the government as they participate in the production and circulation of wealth." While the state "is the external constitution of the social power" in which others "are charged with governing [the People], with managing its affairs," anarchists affirm that "the people, that society … can and ought to govern itself by itself … without masters and servants." When anarchists "deny the State" they "affirm in the same breath the autonomy of the people" for "the only way to organise democratic government is to abolish government" (Proudhon 2011, 261, 267, 280, 482–485).

This meant a real democracy requires decentralisation and federation otherwise "democracy is a fraud, and the sovereignty of the People a joke." The communes that "comprise the confederation" would be "self-governing, self-judging and self-administering in complete sovereignty," "universal suffrage form [their] basis," and each "enjoys a right of secession." Delegates would replace representatives for we "can follow" those we elect "step-by-step in their legislative acts and their votes" and "make them transmit our arguments" and when "we are discontented, we will recall and dismiss them." The electoral principle needed "the imperative mandate, and permanent revocability" as its "most immediate and incontestable consequences." In "a mutualist confederation, the citizen gives up none of his freedom, as Rousseau requires him to do for the governance of his republic!" (Proudhon 2011, 595, 716, 763, 273, 762).

These democratic principles must also be extended to the economy in order to challenge property relations that sustain relationships of dependency and mastery. Property "degrades us, by making us servants and tyrants to one another." Hence, freedom and property were incompatible and to secure the former we must seek the "entire abolition" of the latter – for "all accumulated capital being social property, no one can be its exclusive proprietor" and "the land [is] common property." While the *use* of property "may be divided" its ownership is "collective and undivided" for while "the right to product is exclusive," the "right to means is common." Anarchy required "industrial democracy" as "leaders, instructors, superintendents" must be "chosen from the workers by the workers themselves" and so everyone "participates ... as an active factor" with "a deliberative voice in the council ... in accordance with equality." Workplaces must become "worker republics" within an "*agricultural-industrial federation*" (Proudhon 2011, 248, 118, 153, 137, 112, 610, 119, 215, 780, 711).

Proudhon, then, stressed the "*abolition of man's exploitation of his fellow-man and abolition of man's government of his fellow-man*" were "one and the same proposition" for "what, in politics, goes under the name of *Authority* is analogous to and synonymous with what is termed, in political economy, *Property*." The "principle of AUTHORITY" was "articulated through" both and an "attack upon one is an attack upon the other" (Proudhon 2011, 503–506, original emphasis).

Yet while denouncing both the state and the capitalist workplace as authoritarian, and seeking to replace both by associations, Proudhon refused to apply his ideas within the family and advocated patriarchy. This contradiction saw Joseph Déjacque (2017 [1857], 25) applying Proudhon's own ideas to the family. It was a case of placing the "question of the emancipation of woman in line with the question of the emancipation of the proletarian" so that both enter "the anarchic-community." Proudhon did "cry out against the high barons of capital" but would "rebuild the high barony of the male upon the female vassal" and so, in Déjacque's view, was "a liberal, and not a LIBERTARIAN."

Patriarchy was another *archy* and subsequent anarchists recognised the need for consistency. The fundamental commonality between organisations anarchists oppose – the state, capitalist firms, marriage, etc. – is that they are authoritarian and "power and authority corrupt those who exercise them as much as those who are compelled to submit to them" (Bakunin 1953, 249). Anarchists, then, "deny every form of hierarchical organisation" (Kropotkin 2014, 385).

Anarchist Organisation: Principles and Practice

The first self-proclaimed anarchist text provided a response to Engels' challenge for anarchists to tell how they "propose to operate a factory, run a railway, or steer a ship without one will that decides in the last resort, without unified direction" (Marx and Engels 1989, 307). Indeed, anarchism was born precisely to do so and did so with a single word: *association*.

Anarchists recognise that freedom is a product of interaction between people and it is *how* we associate which determines whether we are free or not. While anarchism's perspective is social, Engels' is fundamentally liberal as it sees isolation as true freedom and so confuses agreement with authority, co-operation with coercion (McKay 2012, §H.4).

The *real* question is simple: is an association based on self-government of its members, or do a few decide for all? So, to qualify as libertarian, an organisation must be based on certain core principles that ensure that liberty is not reduced to simply picking masters.

An organisation that is not *voluntary* would hardly be free. So, free association requires that individuals decide for themselves which groups to join. Yet it is more than that for:

> to promise to obey is to deny or to limit, to a greater or lesser degree, individuals' freedom and equality … To promise to obey is to state, that in certain areas, the person making the promise is no longer free to exercise her capacities and decide upon her own actions, and is no longer equal, but subordinate.
>
> *(Pateman 1985, 19)*

Being free to join a group that is internally hierarchical is simply voluntary *archy* and so groups have to be *democratic* so that those subject to decisions make them. So, *how* we organise was what mattered as Michael Bakunin (1973, 147) explained: "man in isolation can have no awareness of his liberty. Being free for man means being acknowledged, considered and treated as such by another man, … Liberty is therefore a feature not of isolation but of interaction, not of exclusion but rather of connection …"

This means freedom does not end at the workplace door or with a marriage ceremony. The capitalist workplace is not consistent with anarchism for, lest we forget, "a corporation, factory or business is the economic equivalent of fascism: decisions and control are strictly top-down" (Chomsky 1993, 127). This means that "staying *free* is, for the working man who *has to sell* his labour, an impossibility" and so a free economy existed only when "associations of men and women who would work on the land, in the factories, in the mines, and so on, became themselves the managers of production" (Kropotkin 2014, 160, 187).

Collective decision making (democracy) must be contrasted to "the principle of *authority*, that is, the eminently theological, metaphysical, and political idea that the masses, *always* incapable of governing themselves, must at all times submit to the benevolent yoke of a wisdom and a justice imposed upon them, in some way or other, from above." Long before Rosa Luxemburg (1970, 119–120) made the same distinction, Bakunin contrasted two kinds of discipline: an "authoritarian conception" which "signifies despotism on the one hand and blind automatic submission to authority on the other" and another "not automatic but voluntary and intelligently understood" which is "necessary whenever a greater number of individuals undertake any kind of collective work or action." The latter was "simply the voluntary and considered co-ordination of all individual efforts for a common purpose" and did not preclude "a natural division of functions according to the aptitude of each, assessed and judged by the collective whole." However, "no function remains fixed and it will not remain permanently and irrevocably attached to any one person. Hierarchical order and promotion do not exist, so that the executive of yesterday can become the subordinate of tomorrow." In this way "power, properly speaking, no longer exists. Power is diffused to the collectivity and becomes the true expression of the liberty of everyone, the faithful and sincere realisation of the will of all" (Bakunin 1980, 408, 142, 414–415).

Yet while democratic, anarchist organisations have to be *egalitarian* for simply electing a few who govern the rest reintroduces hierarchies, albeit elected ones, and, lest we forget, government is the "delegation of power, that is, the abdication of the initiative and sovereignty of every one into the hands of the few" (Malatesta 2014, 136). As the "people does not govern itself" it meant that "free and equal citizens, not about to abdicate their rights to the care of the few, will seek some new form of organisation that allows them to manage their affairs for themselves." Kropotkin pointed to the sections of the French Revolution as popular institutions "not separated from the people" and "remained of the people, and this is what made the revolutionary power of these organisations." Rather than nominating representatives and disbanding, the sections "remained and organised themselves, on their own initiative, as permanent organs of the municipal administration" and "were practising what was described later on as Direct Self-Government." These were "the principles of anarchism" and they "had their origin, not in theoretic speculations, but in the *deeds* of the Great French Revolution" and "by acting in this way – and the libertarians would no doubt do the same today – the districts of Paris laid the foundations of a new, free, social organisation" for "the Commune of Paris was not to be a governed State, but a people governing itself directly – when possible – without intermediaries, without masters" (Kropotkin 2014, 225, 228, 419–425).

Anarchists tend to call this self-management, because democracy has, in practice, meant electing a government rather than a group of people governing themselves. Yet self-management does not preclude the need to "allocate a given task to others" in the shape of committees but it is a case of group members "not abdicating their own sovereignty" by "turning some into directors and chiefs" (Malatesta 2014, 214). Committees would be agents of the group rather than their masters for they would be "always under the direct control of the population" and express the "decisions taken at popular assemblies" (Malatesta 1993, 175, 129). How much an individual participates is up to each person but the option to take part is always there, for anarchist organisation is rooted in "the possibility of calling the general assembly whenever it was wanted by the members of the section and of discussing everything in the general assembly" (Kropotkin 2014, 426).

Just as individuals associate within groups, so groups will need to co-ordinate their activities by the same kind of horizontal links that exist within an association. In this *federalist* structure decisions are co-ordinated by elected, mandated and recallable delegates rather than representatives (Proudhon 2011, 377; Bakunin 1973, 170–172; Malatesta 2014, 63). This would, by definition, be a decentralised organisation for power remains at the base in the individuals who associate together into groups rather than at the top in the hands of a few representatives and the bureaucracies needed to support them. This would be in all areas of life: economic ("federations of Trade Unions"), social ("independent Communes") and personal ("free combines and societies") (Kropotkin 2014, 188). Federation is extensive:

> society will be composed of a multitude of associations, federated for all the purposes which require federation: trade federations for production of all sorts ... federations of communes among themselves, and federations of communes with trade organisations; and finally, wider groups covering all the country, or several countries, composed of men who collaborate for the satisfaction of such economic, intellectual, artistic, and moral needs as are not limited to a given territory. All these will combine directly, by means of free agreements between them ... for all sorts of work in common, for intellectual pursuits, or simply for pleasure.
>
> *(Kropotkin 2014, 105)*

The permanence of specific groups or agreements is very much dependent on the *functional* needs of the situation or the wishes of the participants and so cannot be formalised by a hard and fast rule. Some agreements will be fleeting (to provide specific goods or services) and others more-or-less permanent (to provide healthcare or railway networks). The key is that the federation lasts as long as is required, that association is produced by objective needs and does not exist for its own sake.

As Proudhon argues, the question of organisation is answered by "universal suffrage in its plenitude" for each "function, industrial or otherwise." Each functional group would elect its own delegates in its own separate bodies meaning "the country governs itself solely by means of its electoral initiative" and "it is no longer governed." Such popular assemblies are "a matter of the organisation of universal suffrage in all its forms, of the very structure of Democracy itself." Instead of centralising all issues into the hands of one assembly, there would be a multitude of assemblies each covering a specific social function for "a society of free men" is based on the "associating with different groups according to the nature of their industries or their interests and by whom neither collective nor individual sovereignty is ever abdicated or delegated" and so "the Government has ceased to exist as a result of universal suffrage". This "truly democratic regime, with its unity *at the bottom* and its separation *at the top*, [is] the reverse of what now exists" and co-ordination would "be effected from the bottom to the top, from the circumference to the centre, and that all functions be independent and govern themselves independently" (Proudhon 2011, 439–441, 461, 446–447).

While some suggest that anarchism inherently supports small-scale groups or industry this is not the case. It recognises that size is driven by the objective needs of a functional task. A workplace is as big as its output requires, while a commune can be a village, town or a city. While large organisations would – as is the case now – be sub-divided internally into functional groups, this does not change the fact that anarchists have *always* incorporated the fact of, and need for, large-scale organisation and industry. Indeed, federalism is advocated precisely to co-ordinate, plan and provide services judged by those who need them to be better done together.

What level a specific industry or service should be co-ordinated at will vary depending on what it is, so no hard and fast rule can be formulated, but the basic principle is that groups "unite with each other in a mutual and equal way, for one or more specific tasks, whose responsibility specially and exclusively falls to the delegates of the federation." For example, it is a case of "the initiative of communes and departments as to works that operate within their jurisdiction" plus "the initiative of the workers companies as to carrying the works out" for the "direct, sovereign initiative of localities, in arranging for public works that belong to them, is a consequence of the democratic principle and the free contract" (Proudhon 2011, 696, 594–595).

In short, *self-governing individuals join self-governing groups that, in turn, join self-governing federations.*

Individuals are free in-so-far as the associations they join are participatory and without hierarchy. Yet anarchists, like Kropotkin (2002, 143, original emphasis), do not think that there will be unanimity within each group for "*variety, conflict even, is life*" while "*uniformity is death*." In disagreements, the minority has a choice – agree to work with the majority, leave the association or practice civil disobedience to convince the majority of the errors of their way. Which option is best depends on the nature of the decision and the group. Similarly, the majority has the right to expel a minority (free association means the freedom *not* to associate).

Rather than being constantly governed by the few – whether that few is the elected of the majority matters little – individuals within an association will participate in decisions and will sometimes be in the majority, sometimes not, in numerous groups and federations. The "necessity of division and association of labour" means that there are fluid, evolving social relations specific to the task and generated to be as inclusive and anti-hierarchical as possible, as Bakunin (1953, 353–354) notes: "I take and I give – such is human life. Each is an authoritative leader and in turn is led by others. Accordingly there is no fixed and constant authority, but continual exchange of mutual, temporary, and, above all, voluntary authority and subordination." No one's permanent position would be one of subjection as under statism, capitalism, patriarchy or racism.

This self-managed society was termed by Proudhon (2011, 724) a "Labour Democracy" to clearly differentiate it from existing – bourgeois – forms of democracy:

> no longer do we have the abstraction of people's sovereignty as in the '93 Constitution and the others that followed it, and in Rousseau's *Social Contract*. Instead it becomes an effective sovereignty of the labouring masses

which rule and govern ... the labouring masses are actually, positively and effectively sovereign: how could they not be when the economic organism – labour, capital, property and assets – belongs to them entirely.

(Proudhon 2011, 760–761)

None of this assumes that the majority has the *right* to rule the minority just that, in general, members who join a group do so understanding the decision-making process within the association and can leave, as Malatesta (2014, 488–489) recognises, if they no longer agree with specific decisions of the majority. Thus we have majority decision making but not majority government for anarchists "have the special mission of being vigilant custodians of freedom, against all aspirants to power and against the possible tyranny of the majority" (Malatesta 1993, 161). The case for anarchy – self-management – is not that the majority is always right but that no minority can be trusted not to prefer its own advantage if given power.

Conclusion

Organisation is a fundamental aspect of any theory simply because it shows how it is applied. If an ideology places organisation to the periphery, then its adherents are not particularly bothered by their stated core principles for it expresses an indifference to whether they are achieved in practice. Anarchism is part of the reaction to liberalism and its, to use Kropotkin's (2002, 137) words, production of both "industrial servitude" and "obedient *subjects* to a central authority." Liberalism, as Pateman (1988, 39) attests, is a "theoretical strategy that justifies subjection by presenting it as freedom." It has "turned a subversive proposition" that we are born free and equal "into a defence of civil subjection" for "the employment contract (like the marriage contract) is not an exchange; both contracts create social relations that endure over time – social relations of subordination" (Pateman 1988, 148). Like democracy, anarchism saw its task as seeking a form of organisation within which freedom was protected.

In contrast to the stereotype of anarchism as an impractical dream without an understanding of the complexities of the modern world, anarchists have spent considerable time discussing how to organise to meet social needs in a world marked by large-scale industry and ever wider personal and social interactions while ensuring individual and social freedom. Anarchist critiques of Rousseau are driven not by a rejection of democracy but rather a desire to see a *genuine* one created. Woodcock (1986, 31) was wrong both logically and historically to proclaim that "the ideal of anarchism, far from being democracy carried to its logical end, is much nearer to aristocracy universalised and purified."

To "contract a relationship of voluntary servitude" was, as Bakunin (1973, 147, 68) concludes, inconsistent with anarchist principles as "the freedom of every individual is inalienable" and so associations could have no other footing "but the utmost equality and reciprocity." Anarchism values individual liberty but sees it as a product of social interaction and so embraces the necessity of equality within groups to ensure it remains meaningful. This, in turn, means embracing a critique of property to ensure that those who join a workplace are associates rather than master and servants. Finally, if self-management is applicable within the workplace then it is also applicable for all social and private associations.

Anarchism recognises that there are many types of organisation – those which are forced upon you and those you freely join, as well as those which are authoritarian (top-down) and those which are libertarian (bottom-up). Genuine liberty necessitates groups that are free to join *and* are free internally as voluntary *archy* is not *an-archy*. Anarchist organisational principles are core because they intersect with other core concepts by *expressing them*.

Notes

1 A longer, unedited, version of this chapter is available at http://anarchism.pageabode.com/anarcho/anarchist-organisation-practice-theory-actualised.
2 Cf. "Thus the grass my horse has bit; the Turfs my Servant has cut; and the Ore I have digg'd ... become my Property" (Locke 2013, 289, original emphasis).

References

Bakunin, Michael. 1953. *The Political Philosophy of Bakunin*. Edited by G.P. Maximov. New York: The Free Press.
Bakunin, Michael. 1973. *Michael Bakunin: Selected Writings*. Edited by Arthur Lehning. London: Jonathan Cape.
Bakunin, Michael. 1980. *Bakunin on Anarchism*, 2nd ed. Edited by Sam Dolgoff. Montréal: Black Rose Books.
Chomsky, Noam. 1993. *Letters from Lexington: Reflections on Propaganda*. Monroe/Edinburgh: Common Courage Press/AK Press.
Déjacque, Joseph. 2017 [1857]. "On the Male and Female Human-Being." *Anarcho-Syndicalist Review* 71 (Fall): 24–27.
Freeden, Michael. 2003. *Ideology: A Very Short Introduction*. Oxford: Oxford University Press.
Kropotkin, Peter. 1971. *The Great French Revolution, 1789–1793*. London: Orbach and Chambers Ltd.
Kropotkin, Peter. 1987. *The State: Its Historic Role*. London: Freedom Press.
Kropotkin, Peter. 2002. *Anarchism: A Collection of Revolutionary Writings*. Edited by Roger N. Baldwin. New York: Dover Press.
Kropotkin, Peter. 2014. *Direct Struggle Against Capital: A Peter Kropotkin Anthology*. Edited by Iain McKay. Edinburgh/Oakland/Baltimore: AK Press.
Locke, John. 2013. *Two Treatises of Government*. Edited by Peter Laslett. Cambridge: Cambridge University Press.
Luxemburg, Rosa. 1970. *Rosa Luxemburg Speaks*. Edited by Mary-Alice Waters. New York: Pathfinder Press.
Macpherson, C. B. 1964. *The Political Theory of Possessive Individualism: Hobbes to Locke*, Oxford: Oxford University Press.

Magraw, Roger. 1992. *A History of the French Working Class*, vol. 1. Oxford/Cambridge: Blackwell.

Malatesta, Errico. 1993. *Errico Malatesta: His Life and Ideas*. Edited by Vernon Richards. London: Freedom Press.

Malatesta, Errico. 2014. *The Method of Freedom: An Errico Malatesta Reader*. Edited by Davide Turcato. Edinburgh/Oakland: AK Press.

Marx, Karl, and Friedrich Engels. 1989. *Marx-Engels Collected Works*, vol. 44. London: Lawrence and Wishart.

McKay, Iain. 2012. *An Anarchist FAQ*, vol. 2. Edinburgh: AK Press.

Moss, Bernard H. 1980. *The Origins of the French Labour Movement 1830–1914: The Socialism of Skilled Workers*. Berkeley/Los Angeles/London: University of California Press.

Noland, Aaron. 1967. "Proudhon and Rousseau." *Journal of the History of Ideas* 28(1): 33–54.

Pateman, Carole. 1985. *The Problem of Political Obligation: A Critique of Liberal Theory*. Cambridge: Polity Press.

Pateman, Carole. 1988. *The Sexual Contract*. Cambridge: Polity.

Proudhon, Pierre-Joseph. 2011. *Property is Theft! A Pierre-Joseph Proudhon Anthology*. Edited by Iain McKay. Edinburgh/Oakland/Baltimore: AK Press.

Rousseau, Jean-Jacques. 1996. *The Social Contract and Discourses*. London: Everyman.

Turcato, Davide. 2015. *Making Sense of Anarchism: Errico Malatesta's Experiments with Revolution, 1889–1900*. Edinburgh/Oakland: AK Press.

Vincent, K. Steven. 1984. *Pierre-Joseph Proudhon and the Rise of French Republican Socialism*. Oxford: Oxford University Press.

Woodcock, George. 1986. *Anarchism: A History of Libertarian Ideas and Movements*. England: Penguin Books.

9

MICROPOLITICS

Laura Portwood-Stacer

> At the dances I was one of the most untiring and gayest. One evening a cousin of Sasha, a young boy, took me aside. With a grave face, as if he were about to announce the death of a dear comrade, he whispered to me that it did not behoove an agitator to dance. Certainly not with such reckless abandon, anyway. It was undignified for one who was on the way to become a force in the anarchist movement. My frivolity would only hurt the Cause.
>
> I grew furious at the impudent interference of the boy. I told him to mind his own business, I was tired of having the Cause constantly thrown into my face. I did not believe that a Cause which stood for a beautiful ideal, for anarchism, for release and freedom from conventions and prejudice, should demand the denial of life and joy. I insisted that our Cause could not expect me to became [sic] a nun and that the movement should not be turned into a cloister. If it meant that, I did not want it. "I want freedom, the right to self-expression, everybody's right to beautiful, radiant things." Anarchism meant that to me, and I would live it in spite of the whole world – prisons, persecution, everything. Yes, even in spite of the condemnation of my own closest comrades I would live my beautiful ideal.
>
> Emma Goldman (1970, 56)

Readers may be familiar with this episode from Emma Goldman's autobiography, *Living My Life*, which is a lively and lengthy account of her activisms and attachments while she lived in the United States. Yet this story has touched a much wider audience than those who have read the two-volume tome: it is the source of the much-repeated slogan, "If I can't dance, it's not my revolution," a phrase attributed to Goldman but never actually uttered by her. We often understand this brief phrase – reproduced on stickers and t-shirts *ad nauseam* – to suggest that if a movement isn't pleasurable for its members then it will fail to hold their allegiance. But encapsulated in the fuller text of the encounter reproduced above (an early account of leftist "mansplaining" [Solnit 2014] if there ever was one) is a deep idea about the sites where revolutionary politics can and should play out. Both Goldman and her comrade took it as given that the microscopic actions of individuals matter, politically, though they disagreed about what specific shape those actions should take.

Certainly, Goldman's political advocacy included the overthrow of the state and the reorganization of society into anti-hierarchical formations in which the working classes would no longer be subordinate to capitalist forces. But in her life and her attitudes we see something else, too: her insistence that the widespread freedom and joy that she expected to be brought about by an anarchist revolution must be prefigured in the experiences and interrelationships of individuals in the here and now. As it doesn't violate any of the core principles of anarchism, dancing at parties should be allowed in the revolution. Behavior-policing between comrades is not quite as aligned with Goldman's anarchistic ideals, and thus it is to be rejected. In this analysis of revolutionary politics' entry into the everyday experiences of a legendary anarchist over a century ago, we begin to get a glimpse of a phenomenon we now refer to by the term "micropolitics."

While the concept of micropolitics is often associated with poststructuralist thinkers such as Michel Foucault, Michel de Certeau, Gilles Deleuze, and Félix Guattari (more on them in a moment), it's clear from the much earlier writings of Goldman and others that anarchism has always been concerned with the individual's resistant relationship to power and domination.[1] Most anarchists[2] set their revolutionary sights not only on the macro-level institutions that re-inscribe domination in all its forms, but also on the more micro-level sites where ideologies of domination actually materialize in the immediate experiences of individuals. This means bringing the struggle against domination into each and every sphere of life, no matter how intimate. Anarchist ideology is not just for smashing the state; it's for building liberation within small organizations, households, interpersonal relationships, and even the minds and bodies of individuals themselves.

Practices and Theories of Micropolitical Power

In brief, micropolitics takes shared beliefs about the way power should be distributed at the society (macro) level and translates them to action at the personal (micro) level. This can take many forms. For example, an individual's work and the making of their livelihood can be pursued anarchistically; many who subscribe to anarchist political ideals try to earn their living in ways that are consistent with those principles. The ways in which individuals personally relate to the natural environment can also be guided by anarchist ethics; this too is micropolitical.

Even within what we might think of as "the micro level" there are sublevels. Micropolitics can manifest in small-scale institutions like activist organizations, community groups, and communal living situations. Take collective housing, for example.[3] For the last century at least, some anarchists have chosen to turn away from single-family households, where members tend to be related by blood or legal ties, to set up collective houses (sometimes called cooperative houses or co-ops) in which the residents are bound only by their shared commitment to a particular lifestyle ethos. By pooling resources and sharing domestic labor obligations, they provide mutual aid to one another and prefigure a "sharing economy" alternative to competitive individualism. Such arrangements also offer an emotional alternative to what many see as the oppressive privacy of the bourgeois nuclear family. Decisions affecting the household are usually made through consensus processes, and shared ethical principles are drawn upon in resolving conflicts that arise.

Moving downward in level from the small-scale institution, we can also see micropolitics at work in the way many anarchists approach relationships between individuals. Even things as intimately personal as romantic entanglements are inflected by political ideals for many anarchists. Dating back to their support of "free love" in the nineteenth century, some anarchists have challenged the compulsory nature of monogamous, heteronormative sexual arrangements.[4] In many anarchist circles today, for instance, polyamory exists alongside monogamy as an acceptable (perhaps even default) relationship formation. For its practitioners, the openness of polyamory represents a remedy for the interpersonal domination intrinsic to sexual exclusivity. When monogamous formations are maintained through the pressure of social norms and interpersonal attempts at controlling another's desire and bodily autonomy, some anarchists believe, they are not free associations and should thus be directly rejected. The high ethical value placed on consent within anarchist communities also speaks to a micropolitical commitment to anarchist principles of autonomy and non-domination.

At the most microlevel of all, an anarchist's relationship to oneself is shaped by one's political philosophy. Personal consumption habits, modes of bodily comportment and adornment, the language one uses, even the self-identifications one assumes, are frequently self-regulated on terms consistent with anarchist philosophies. Many anarchists feel, for example, that the ingestion of meat and dairy or the application of chemical hygiene products would be an act of acquiescence to corporate interests to the detriment of their own values and personal health. Some anarchists also assume wardrobes that mark them as standing outside the mainstream. The stakes of any given meal or outfit are demonstrably low, perhaps to the point of insignificance, but anarchist micropolitics holds that such gestures still matter. They matter because they prefigure the things that could be done universally in a just society. And, in the aggregate, micro practices adopted by individuals and communities who share a philosophy model that there are alternative ways of being in the world, outside of most people's present (oppressive) reality.

The above examples certainly don't exhaust the myriad ways anarchism is practiced micropolitically, but they give a sense of the ways in which a high-level political philosophy can filter down into the everyday practices of committed individuals. While there were anarchists viewing and practicing micropolitics in this way well before the work of Michel Foucault and other poststructuralists came into fashion, Foucault's theory of power helps to explain why anarchists concern themselves with the micro in addition to the macro. For Foucault, the power dynamics that animate social relations are made material at the level of the individual who feels and carries out the effects of power. Because the violence of power is directed at and felt by the individual, the individual is a key originary point of resistance to power.[5] Foucault's (1990, 139) concept of "anatomo-politics" describes the resistance to power at the very site on which it acts: the individual body. To put it in concrete terms, if someone beats you with a billy club, you might want to dismantle the conditions that put that person in the position to beat you and gave them the idea that they had the authority to do so, but you also might beat them back with your own hands. The beating back – that's micropolitics. Since anarchists oppose domination in all its forms and locales (most anarchists having long ago moved on from class reductionism), their resistance arises wherever they recognize domination.

Domination need not take the form of physical coercion. Norms, rules, and laws are all expressions of hierarchical power that anarchists question, intrinsically. Building on Foucault's work, Michel de Certeau's (1984, xv) study of "the clandestine, tactical, and makeshift creativity of groups or individuals already caught in the nets of 'discipline'" explains how resistant subjects use micro tactics to find spaces of empowerment within encompassing structures. For Certeau, everyday life is the terrain on which revolutionary "anti-discipline" naturally occurs. Micropolitics is also explicitly discussed in the work of two other poststructuralist theorists, Gilles Deleuze and Félix Guattari. In Todd May's (1994) philosophical examination of the relationship between poststructuralist theories and anarchist strategy, he quotes this passage from Deleuze and Guattari's (1980) *A Thousand Plateaus*:

> This is how it should be done: Lodge yourself on a stratum, experiment with the opportunities it offers, find an advantageous place on it, find potential movements of deterritorialization, possible lines of flight, experience them, produce flow conjunctions here and there, try out continuums of intensities segment by segment, have a small plot of land at all times.
>
> *(quoted in May 1994, 112–13)*

This is certainly reflective of the experimental, alternative practices adopted by many anarchists. The ideas that power acts at the level of everyday life, and that resistance can originate there as well, are clearly broadly in effect in anarchist circles, both historical and contemporary.

Well-known and oft-cited anarchist David Graeber (2002, 70) has observed that today's anarchism "aspires to reinvent daily life as a whole." Indeed, because so much of daily life in a society run by capitalism, patriarchy, white supremacy, and so on, is contoured by power hierarchies and domination, any attempt to live a life otherwise involves very conscious resistance to the default ways of doing things and the active adoption of alternatives in their place. This is why, as Cindy

Milstein (2010, 41) puts it, "Embracing anarchism is a process of reevaluating every assumption, everything one thinks about and does, and indeed who one is, and then basically turning one's life upside-down." This, again, is micropolitics, encapsulated.

Micropolitical Practice as Anarchist Praxis

A commitment to micropolitics is not unique to anarchism, but it plays out in particular ways in the context of anarchist ideology and praxis. The micropolitical practices of anarchists have specific philosophical underpinnings that root them in an anarchist tradition. These underpinnings include a rejection of institutionalized hierarchies and an embrace of direct action tactics and prefigurative ethics. Regardless of the particular project or target, these principles guide the way anarchists behave and how they approach problems to be solved. My point here is that, for many, these tenets form an ethical imperative for micropolitical practice: if individuals take the core principles of anarchism to their logical conclusions, then they *must* live their everyday lives in particular ways if they are to uphold the philosophy of anarchism.[6]

Perhaps the most central principle of anarchism is its opposition to hierarchical power structures. Just as the state and the economy can be organized hierarchically, so can relationships between individuals and between individuals and the institutions they find themselves interfacing with on a daily basis. For this reason, a philosophical opposition to hierarchy often manifests in individuals making personal choices and adopting personal practices that both minimize one's own exercise of hierarchical power and resist the exercise of hierarchical power over oneself by others. This might take the form of maintaining a vegan diet, for instance, on the basis of rejecting a hierarchy between human and non-human animals. Historically, it accounts for proto-feminist anarchists such as Emma Goldman (1969, 222) advocating for individual women "to stand firmly on [their] own ground and to insist upon [their] own unrestricted freedom," rejecting the social restrictions that would come at the hands of partners, families, and employers.

Acts of refusal – in the face of societal pressure to conform to hierarchical arrangements – are partly dictated by the principle of direct action, another core concept to anarchism. The idea is to bring about the reality one wishes to experience without appealing to a central or higher power to bring about a particular state of affairs first (de Cleyre, n.d.). While the concept is often used to refer to protest tactics aimed at higher-level forces emanating from the state, we can also take it down to the micro level. Micropolitical direct action can essentially be thought of as (relatively) low-stakes insurrection against any number of "laws" of social life. For example, if one of the moral laws of a capitalist consumer culture is that one should participate in the market in order to meet one's material needs, a direct-action approach would be to flout this law, act outside the market, and possibly DIY ("do it yourself") the object or service one would have paid for within the system. Contemporary anarchists DIY all sorts of things, from clothing to technology to education to medical procedures, and each time they do, they are bypassing capitalist social arrangements in microscopic ways. As another alternative to the market system, anarchists frequently enact mutual aid, freely giving away their possessions or labor to help others in need. The belief behind mutual aid is that solidarity is a resource more powerful than money or competition. It is a form of direct action because it affirms the ability of people who are horizontally networked to meet each other's needs outside the purview of institutional power. As anarchist Voltairine de Cleyre (n.d.) asserts in her definitive essay on the topic, "All co-operative experiments are essentially direct action."

In effecting transformations of their own lives, proponents of direct action also seek to do more than improve material conditions. They claim the legitimacy of their own *right* to do so autonomously, and they concurrently delegitimize the intermediary institutions to which people normally turn. In this they performatively establish their own authority to act, regardless of whether they are "permitted" to do so by the powers that be. These "powers" may be external or internal to the revolutionary movement; anarchists differ from other radicals in their rejection of a revolutionary vanguard that would prescribe strategy and tactics. As key individualist anarchist thinker Max Stirner put it, "The Revolution aimed at new arrangements; insurrection leads us no longer to let ourselves be arranged, but to arrange ourselves and sets no glittering hopes on 'institutions'" (quoted in Curran 2006, 25). Put another way by anarcha-feminist Carol Ehrlich (2012, 61), "anarchists insist that people must transform the conditions of their lives *themselves* – it cannot be done for them." For anarchists, then, direct action is about more than action alone; it has a representative dimension in its demonstrative commentary on the place where authority to act should and does reside. Individual insurrectionary actions thus prefigure the actions everyone would feel empowered to take in a radically democratic society.

This commitment to prefiguration is another foundational pillar of the anarchist tradition that helps to explain the place of micropolitics within anarchist praxis. Historically (and contemporarily) anarchists have stepped outside of repressive institutions and collaborated to create sustainable alternatives that would meet their needs. Cooperative houses, non-hierarchical relationship structures, anti-capitalist modes of consumption: these and other collectively adopted alternatives today make up what was once described by anarchist publisher Holley Cantine in 1942 as "a nucleus of the new society 'within the shell of the old,'" in reference to the mission of the Industrial Workers of the World (quoted in Cornell 2016, 160). For Cantine and those who shared his view that "the ideals of the revolution [must be] approximated as nearly as possible in daily life," experimenting directly with anarchist social arrangements was "a way of influencing the masses by example" (quoted in Cornell 2016, 160) through the prefiguration of what could be achieved on a broad scale if only masses of individuals would commit to it.

Within this framework, to embody anarchist values in one's daily life is to generate a kind of "propaganda by the deed" for the ways of life that would be possible for everyone in an anarchist society (Gordon 2008, 38). Many anarchists see the micropolitical performance of their values as a more effective communication tool than preaching anarchism to the unconverted (Portwood-Stacer 2013). This is partly because the very word "anarchism" can be off-putting to people due to the negative, and sometimes false, connotations heaped on it by hegemonic discourses. Prefiguration is also respectful of onlookers' autonomy to decide for themselves: rather than presenting a program that tells others how to behave, prefigurative practices "giv[e] away authority" by simply providing an example that others can follow if they so choose (Duncombe 2008, 36).

Representation and the Micro/Macro Relationship

To view the everyday practices of anarchists through the lens of prefiguration is to recognize that micro-level activities are not only important for what they are, but also for what they *represent*. It is in the mechanism of symbolic representation that we can detect an imagined relationship between micropolitical resistance and macropolitical change: micropolitical resistance to domination is said to incite macropolitical change by proving that resistance is possible and desirable at all, such proof in turn leading to widespread revolt and transformation. Yet it's possible this perceived potential is more a product of magical thinking than empirical evidence, since it's not always clear how prefigured alternatives would become socially dominant, a point made by Barbara Epstein (1991), a sociologist of direct action movements. Historian of leftist countercultures Doug Rossinow (1998, 292–293) argues that the ethos of prefigurative cultural politics assumes that people will automatically recognize the superiority of alternative cultural formations and voluntarily imitate them on a mass scale. This assumption becomes problematic for anarchists because they may not have what sociologist Pierre Bourdieu (1989) would call the "symbolic capital" to break through hegemonic ideologies to disrupt the dominant (often negative or indifferent) perception of their alternative practices. Further, as sociologist Wini Breines (1982, xi) cautions in her study of the New Left, although micropolitical practices can give people in radical social movements a sense of efficacy, shoring up their confidence in the ability to achieve real change, such confidence may be "disproportionate" to the structural obstacles that work against broad revolution.

Whether the micropolitical and the macropolitical can ever be directly linked in such a way is an unresolved (and perhaps unresolvable) question. Historian of US anarchism Andrew Cornell shows that over 100 years ago, anarchist educator Harry Kelly wondered "about whether social change demanded the concerted effort of 'masses' of people acting in unison, or whether it could be affected [sic] through the piecemeal efforts of individuals and small groups" (Cornell 2016, 50). Without an overhaul of capitalist class relations (i.e. macropolitics), Kelly thought, workers could not achieve the economic freedom truly necessary to live their lives autonomously on a micro scale. This is consistent with the social anarchist view that "individual flourishing can only occur in a communitarian society" (Curran 2006, 23). In more recent times, Cindy Milstein (2010) grappled with a similar paradox:

> the gap between what anarchists imagine to be fully ethical and the series of bad choices we all make under the present conditions illustrates that hierarchical social relationships will forever preclude our ability to be free. Anarchism's emphasis on the whole of life underscores that the current social order already frames the world for everyone down to the tiniest interactions; "choice" itself is already hobbled.
>
> *(42)*

Despite this quandary, Milstein and others embrace the effort of living otherwise in whatever small ways are possible, in order to at least have what Cornell (2016, 50) describes as "greater room for maneuvering within the current system." At best, anarchists can agree that both social and individual transformation are desirable ends, even if the precise relationship between the two remains undetermined.

In times of severe external repression, a "retreat" to the micro is indeed sometimes all that feels possible for activists. In the early twentieth-century United States, for example, the violent climate of red baiting and anti-immigrant sentiment led many anarchists to turn to "cooperative living, libertarian techniques for educating their children, and artistic expression as less confrontational means to promote their values" (Cornell 2011, 24). Small-scale social formations can serve as safe havens for the spirit of anarchism to stay aflame when a full, public conflagration is impractical or impossible. Micropolitical practices – even those that appear insignificant in their near-term effects – could thus serve as what feminist sociologist Verta Taylor (1989) terms "social movement abeyance structures." Social movement abeyance structures are activist efforts that provide a kind of underground continuity for movements in times of apparent inactivity and marginalization. Even if micropolitical actions do little more than help their practitioners maintain a personal sense of identification with the anarchist project, this might be a valuable and necessary contribution in itself.

Micropolitical practices of anarchism have the advantage of being adaptable to the conditions of the historical moment. But more than this, their micro nature makes them flexible enough to adapt to differing and changing contexts even at a single point in history. This is clearly a virtue within the context of anarchism, which is almost definitionally opposed to having a coherent ideological platform or program that would dictate the shape that political tactics must take (Graeber 2002). Anarchists do not need to agree on a singular set of final goals in order for individuals and small groups to implement anarchist ethics in their local situations. Rather than the lack of coherence being paralyzing for activists, micropolitics allows them to act in the here and now while they hammer out how they want to contribute to a broader project and even what they see that broader project as being.

Yet this virtuous flexibility can cause conflict, since a specific micropolitical practice that one person sees as crucial in the fight against domination another person will see as entirely irrelevant. Because each person's situation is different, each person's micropolitical response to their conditions will differ; this makes it a problem when *one* coherent assemblage of micropolitical practices becomes prescriptive. Some people will be guided by the sway of dominant power structures more strongly than others, and not all individuals have the wherewithal to adopt a micropolitical response in all aspects of their lives. An undocumented anarchist might choose not to organize in her workplace, for example, in the interest of not drawing scrutiny to her documentation status. This doesn't make her less authentic as an anarchist than those who can count more instances of active resistance in their everyday practices. And just as the capitalist market, the state, patriarchy, white supremacy, and so on, do not punish all individuals equally, specific tactics of resistance do not liberate all individuals equally.

Micro-level acts may be self-contradictory in their capacity to embody macropolitical principles – remember, they emerge in non-anarchistic conditions and will thus bear the imprint of domination – which is why no specific act can pass the anarchist purity test. Thus, no specific micropolitical intervention can be used as a litmus test of an individual's commitment to the anarchist project. I have described elsewhere how "politicking over lifestyle can fracture bonds of solidarity among activists who make different lifestyle choices" (Portwood-Stacer 2013, 10), making radical movements more exclusionary than they need be. Clearly, the specific contours of how micropolitics are enacted, and which enactments are privileged over others by the movement, are themselves political.

Micropolitics or Lifestylism?

While it may not be necessary for advocates of micropolitics to agree on their specific interventions or even their overall macropolitical aims, the one important precondition for micropolitical efficacy is that it have *some* analysis of power that connects the micro with the macro, at least conceptually, even if a direct line cannot be drawn between the two. Without a concept of how individual acts are dictated by and promote anarchist political philosophy, micro practices can amount to little more than a set of apolitical lifestyle choices. This porous boundary between micropolitics and lifestyle has seemingly always been a source of conflict within anarchist milieux. As early as the 1920s, controversy arose among American anarchists around the practice of building colonies where anarchist ways of life could be fully realized away from mainstream society. While proponents defended the propagandistic function of such experiments, others saw them as a distraction from the primary struggle of radical social transformation (Cornell 2016, 104). Half a century later, the punk movement of the late 1970s and 1980s brought anarchism to the daily lives of many disaffected youth in the United States and Europe, particularly via bands like Crass and the Dead Kennedys (Thompson 2004). This moment saw the flourishing of micropolitical practices such as collective living and anti-consumerism within anarcho-punk scenes. But again, the centrality of micropolitics became a source of conflict, because many of the youth who were attracted to the aesthetic and lifestyle habits of the punk scene were not deeply familiar with the broader political ideologies underlying these aspects. In the eyes of some critics this had an unfortunate effect of divorcing the micropolitics of anarchism from the larger political vision. The title of Murray Bookchin's (1995) screed on the topic – *Social Anarchism or Lifestyle Anarchism: An Unbridgeable Chasm* – sums up the divisiveness of the issue in anarchist movements. Such disagreements about the place of micropolitics within the larger anarchist project endure among today's anarchist activists (Portwood-Stacer 2013).

The slippage between micropolitics and apolitical lifestylism is all the more enabled by the conditions of postmodern media culture and a neoliberal political economic climate. The underlying politics of personal choices are easily divorced from the lifestyle practices themselves as these travel from person to person beyond the boundaries of their activist contexts. Think once more of Goldman's rich argument about "the Cause" in her thousand-page autobiography being condensed into an eight-word slogan and bandied about by well-meaning but less-than-informed supporters. Plenty of people like the idea of dancing in their revolution, but they may not understand exactly what Goldman's full vision of revolution actually was and why dancing had to be a part of it.

The trendiness of "ethical consumption" and the appropriation of radical signifiers by corporate brands further muddies the waters. Pretty much any aspect of daily life for which anarchists have developed alternatives is seemingly co-optable by corporate interests, a trend that was well documented twenty years ago by the likes of Thomas Frank (1997) and Naomi Klein (1999) and which has only intensified since. Think for example of the bastardized version of the "sharing economy" promoted by Silicon Valley in recent years, in which resources and costs are not so much communally shared as outsourced from corporations to individuals, who are made vulnerable by a lack of formal employment structure. A mobile app that lets you call a driver to your home instantly for a competitive price isn't at all the same thing as collectively owning a car with several other people (something anarchists who share a household may do). The superficial accommodation of alternative lifestyle practices only contributes to a tendency, described by Cornell (2016, 51), "for some purported anarchists to simply live their own lives in as free a fashion as their social status allowed for (as 'bohemians,' 'dropouts,' or 'punks') without investing themselves in struggles to create lasting structural transformations that would increase security and life options for the least well off."

Taking all this into account, the most effective anarchist micropolitics involves what de Certeau (1984, 56) calls a "strategic intention" that keeps focused on undoing oppressive power relations wherever they are found. Importantly, the capacity for individuals and small groups to "be the change they wish to see" (to paraphrase Gandhi's famous commandment of prefigurative politics, which has surpassed even Goldman's in its bumperstickerability) through micropolitics depends on the specific change in question. If the change one wants to see is fundamentally social (e.g. a revolutionary shift in social power relations), it's actually impossible to "be the change" as an individual, though one can try to live as much as possible *as if* that change has occurred. From a strategic perspective, then, micropolitics is most anarchistic when it goes beyond the lifestyle choices of isolated individuals and cultivates a community in which just social relations are reproduced at every level.

The fact that there are (and always have been) differences of opinion on the place of micropolitics within anarchism suggests that micropolitics is less than *core* to the anarchist tradition. However, there are ways in which many anarchists understand their core beliefs to dictate micropolitical critique and activism. This chapter has discussed these, in the interest of illuminating how micropolitical practices of anarchism on the ground give nuance and texture to the central tenets of anarchist philosophy. While anarch*ism* might theoretically exist as a philosophy or political system without a concept of micropolitics, empirical observation suggests that anarch*ists* do not. Where anarchist ideologies are made material – in the actions and experiences of the people who adhere to those ideologies – there we will find micropolitics. This means that while micropolitics are not at the essential *core* of anarchism as a political ideology, they are *adjacent* in that they nearly always emerge in the lived practice of anarchists, in all historical eras (Freeden 1996).

Micropolitical practices are useful to individual activists and to movements – they can make life more ethical and livable in the movement space – and so they can work in concert with other tactics aimed at radical political intervention. Micropolitics has its place in anarchist strategy, but it does not constitute an anarchist strategy in and of itself: dancing is not the be-all and end-all of revolution. Still, when deployed in thoughtful, critical ways, micropolitical resistance to domination can be both autonomous and collective, personal and truly powerful.

Notes

1 Indeed, Nathan Jun (2012) has also argued that classical anarchism anticipated many aspects of poststructuralist theory by over a century.
2 When used as a noun in this essay, the term "anarchist" should be understood to apply to those who subscribe to anarchist ideals, with recognition of the fact that some who fit into this category may be uncomfortable adopting it as a term of identity (Portwood-Stacer 2013, 75–104).
3 This example and those that follow are documented more thoroughly in *Lifestyle Politics and Radical Activism* (Portwood-Stacer 2013). Parts of the analysis presented in this essay

are also adapted from that text. It must be noted that anarchists as a group are not monolithic; none of the practices or beliefs mentioned in this article can accurately be attributed to *all* individuals who subscribe to anarchism as a philosophy or political identity. My own empirical research on anarchist activists focused on the contemporary North American context; the practices and beliefs of anarchists naturally vary across time and place.
4 For more extensive discussion of this history, see works by Goldman (1969; 1970), Greenway (2009), Heckert, Shannon, and Willis (2015), and Kissack (2008).
5 I mean violence here in a very literal sense, as the imposing of an external will, whether that will involves measurable harm or not.
6 This attitude is in keeping with "practical anarchism" or what anarchist historian Andrew Cornell (2016, 148) describes as "a conception of anarchism indebted to Henry David Thoreau and Leo Tolstoy that advocated individuals focus on living their own lives in a fashion that resembled their ideals as closely as possible."

References

Bookchin, Murray. 1995. *Social Anarchism or Lifestyle Anarchism: An Unbridgeable Chasm*. San Francisco, CA: AK Press.
Bourdieu, Pierre. 1989. "Social Space and Symbolic Power." *Sociological Theory* 71(1): 14–25.
Breines, Wini. 1982. *Community and Organization in the New Left, 1962–1968: The Great Refusal*. New York: Praeger.
Cornell, Andrew. 2011. "'For a World Without Oppressors': U.S. Anarchism from the Palmer Raids to the Sixties." PhD dissertation, New York University.
Cornell, Andrew. 2016. *Unruly Equality: U.S. Anarchism in the 20th Century*. Berkeley: University of California Press.
Curran, Giorel. 2006. *21st Century Dissent: Anarchism, Anti-Globalization and Environmentalism*. New York: Palgrave Macmillan.
de Certeau, Michel. 1984. *The Practice of Everyday Life*. Translated by Steven F. Rendall. Berkeley: The University of California Press.
de Cleyre, Voltairine. n.d. "Direct Action." Spunk Library: An Online Anarchist Library and Archive. www.spunk.org/texts/writers/decleyre/sp001334.html.
Deleuze, Gilles, and Félix Guattari. 1980. *A Thousand Plateaus*. Translated by Brian Massumi. Minneapolis: University of Minnesota Press.
Duncombe, Stephen. 2008. *Notes from the Underground: Zines and the Politics of Alternative Culture*. Bloomington, IN: Microcosm.
Ehrlich, Carol. 2012. "Socialism, Anarchism and Feminism." In *Quiet Rumours: An Anarcha-Feminist Reader*, 3rd ed., edited by Dark Star, 55–64. Oakland, CA: AK Press.
Epstein, Barbara. 1991. *Political Protest and Cultural Revolution: Nonviolent Direct Action in the 1970s and 1980s*. Berkeley: University of California Press.
Foucault, Michel. 1990. *The History of Sexuality*, vol. 1. Translated by Robert Hurley. New York: Vintage.
Frank, Thomas. 1997. "Why Johnny Can't Dissent." In *Commodify Your Dissent*, edited by Thomas Frank and Matt Weiland, 31–45. New York: Norton.
Freeden, Michael. 1996. *Ideologies and Political Theory*. Oxford, UK: Oxford University Press.
Goldman, Emma. 1969. "The Tragedy of Woman's Emancipation." In *Anarchism and Other Essays*, 213–225. Mineola, NY: Dover.
Goldman, Emma. 1970. *Living My Life*, vol. I. New York: Dover.

Gordon, Uri. 2008. *Anarchy Alive!: Anti-Authoritarian Politics from Practice to Theory*. Ann Arbor, MI: Pluto Press.

Graeber, David. 2002. "The New Anarchists." *New Left Review* 13 (January-February): 61–73.

Greenway, Judy. 2009. "Speaking Desire: Anarchism and Free Love as Utopian Performance in Fin de Siècle Britain." In *Anarchism and Utopianism*, edited by Laurence Davis and Ruth Kinna, 153–170. Manchester: Manchester University Press.

Heckert, Jamie, Deric Shannon, and Abbey Willis. 2015. "Queer Anarchism." In *International Encyclopedia of the Social & Behavioral Sciences*, 2nd ed., vol. 19, edited by James D. Wright, 747–751. Oxford: Elsevier.

Jun, Nathan. 2012. *Anarchism and Political Modernity*. New York: Continuum.

Kissack, Terence. 2008. *Free Comrades: Anarchism and Homosexuality in the United States, 1895–1917*. Oakland, CA: AK Press.

Klein, Naomi. 1999. *No Logo*. New York: Picador.

May, Todd. 1994. *The Political Philosophy of Poststructuralist Anarchism*. University Park, PA: The Pennsylvania State University Press.

Milstein, Cindy. 2010. *Anarchism and Its Aspirations*. Oakland, CA: AK Press.

Portwood-Stacer, Laura. 2013. *Lifestyle Politics and Radical Activism*. New York: Bloomsbury.

Rossinow, Doug. 1998. *The Politics of Authenticity: Liberalism, Christianity and the New Left in America*. New York: Columbia University Press.

Solnit, Rebecca. 2014. *Men Explain Things to Me*. Chicago: Haymarket Books.

Taylor, Verta. 1989. "Social Movement Continuity: The Women's Movement in Abeyance." *American Sociological Review* 54(5): 761–775.

Thompson, Stacy. 2004. *Punk Productions: Unfinished Business*. Albany: State University of New York Press.

10
ECONOMY[1]

Deric Shannon

> We are free, truly free, when we don't need to rent our arms to anybody in order to be able to lift a piece of bread to our mouths.
>
> *Ricardo Flores Magón*

Over a century ago, the great Russian prince-turned-anarchist, Peter Kropotkin (2002 [1892]), wrote an exposition of what he called "anarchist communism," with access to food central to his polemic. This was a work of analytical *political economy* – a piece of analysis that locates economics within larger relations of power, recognizing that economic processes cannot be coherently abstracted from the rest of social life, particularly for Kropotkin, the state. As Rudolf Rocker (2004 [1938], 11) succinctly put it, "the war against capitalism must be at the same time a war against all institutions of political power," recognizing that "exploitation has always gone hand in hand with political and social oppression." Like Karl Marx's (1977 [1859]) work before him, Kropotkin's theory was also a *critique* of political economy, which can be read as a suggestion that humanity might not be consigned to economy, that we might create a life of abundance where we are no longer governed by need, nor coerced to produce.

This makes introducing anarchist approaches to economy difficult. If one takes Kropotkin's view (among many others), we might say that at least some anarchists reject *economy*. The task, then, wouldn't be so much to outline an anarchist method to economy, but rather our rejection of it. But anarchism is a diverse anti-capitalist tradition, and Kropotkin's (version of) anarchist communism is one among a variety of perspectives within the anarchist tradition, some of which are *explicitly* advancing alternative political economic arrangements in opposition to capitalism, others who are (perhaps reluctantly) content to be subordinated to scarcity and/or the need to have some form of coercion to labor, provided those social relationships reflect a pattern that can be ethically judged as necessary, non-hierarchical (which advances larger questions around the organization of coercion), reciprocal, or some other set of values that reflect the anti-authoritarian spirit that gives life to anarchist ideas and practice.

Therefore, in this chapter, I attempt to give a broad outline of anarchist analyses of economy, or the way that we tend to define and critique capitalism. I also provide a sketch of anarchist positions on post-capitalism, which are tied to questions of how we define and critique capitalism and develop practices in opposition to it. I finish with my own argument about how we might create some tenuous agreements about economy, particularly if we focus on a human need like food. Along the way, I hope to be fair to the anarchist tendencies that I attempt to sketch here. But it might help readers contextualize this piece to mention that I'm largely sympathetic to Kropotkin's arguments and consider myself a part of the communist anarchist tradition, rooted as it is in a desire to abolish economy rather than create some liberatory version of it. Nonetheless, Kropotkin stood on the shoulders of giants and it is not clear that there is a developing line from earlier anarchist engagements with economy to his position.[2] Thus, this sketch, and any such attempt, will be incomplete. It also might make some sense to point out that anarchists reject representation, so this chapter is also not an effort to claim *the* anarchist position on economy, but rather an endeavor to give voice to some and, no doubt, miss some things along the way.

Defining and Critiquing Capitalism

Anarchists have a long and proud history opposing capitalism. One would be hard-pressed to make the case that anarchism could exist without an opposition to capitalism as *foundational* to it. As a practice, an ethic, and/or a theory developed in opposition to hierarchical society, the basic elements of capitalism, private ownership protected by states and the wage relation (i.e. being able to *rent* another person and extract value from her labor), fundamentally contravene anarchism's anti-authoritarianism. Mikhail Bakunin (n.d.) puts this concisely when he writes:

> What is property, what is capital in their present form? For the capitalist and the property owner they mean the power and the right, guaranteed by the State, to live without working. And since neither property nor capital produces anything when not fertilized by labor – that means the power and the right to live by exploiting the work of someone else, the right to exploit the work of those who possess neither property nor capital and who thus are forced to sell their productive power to the lucky owners of both … [P]roperty owners and capitalists, inasmuch as they live not by their own productive labor but by getting land rent, house rent, interest upon their capital, or by speculation on land, buildings, and capital, or by the commercial and

industrial exploitation of the manual labor of the proletariat, all live at the expense of the proletariat.

Indeed, a basic function of capitalism is to create and enforce the hierarchical arrangement of property through the organized violence of the state, existing alongside authoritarian "social dynamics which are generated, reproduced and enacted within *and* outside this apparatus" (Gordon 2007). Capitalism is, then, incompatible with anarchism, despite some misguided rhetorical attempts to fuse the two (predominantly in the United States under the banner of a historically disfigured "libertarianism"). But there is not shared agreement among anarchists on what exactly the defining features of capitalism are. To account for analyses and debates among anarchists, one might describe and analyze capitalism in terms of the following broad features (some of which may not be exclusive to capitalism, depending on how we define it): wage labor/exploitation, private property, markets, class society, and states.

Wage labor/exploitation is one of the basic constituent parts of capitalism. In order to access the social product, as illustrated by Bakunin above, workers must rent themselves out for a wage. The value produced under capitalism by workers, minus whatever wage the capitalist(s) pays, is then expropriated by capitalists in the form of surplus value – this process is exploitation. Some anarchists refer to this set of relationships as "wage slavery" to point out a historical continuity between *owning* another person and what is, essentially, *renting* another person. Not only do anarchists oppose wage labor and exploitation on the grounds that they are unfair, but these things are also against the material interests of working people and create a social relation of domination between the boss and the worker (which Bakunin so eloquently describes above). Many anarchists argue that the wage labor relation is *the* defining aspect of capitalism.[3]

This social relation (exploitation) is made possible by private property. Typically, anarchists define private property as property that allows for long-term absentee ownership. This is often juxtaposed with what is referred to as *personal property* or *possessions*, or forms of ownership that are defined by *occupancy* and *use*. This leaves plenty of room for disagreement about how we draw lines around use and occupancy, but it also visibilizes a social relation between persons and things that emerged from the historical context of the processes of accumulation that led to the development of capitalism. The notion that one can "own" a home, or better yet, a workplace, across the ocean, perhaps on another continent, without ever having to see it, occupy it, or use it, while charging rents or expropriating the value produced by workers within that location is not some eternal phenomenon. It is specific to capitalism and its development and those social relationships need not be permanent.

Another element of capitalist society as we know it is market relations. Generally, and likely because in dominant narratives Marxian economics are juxtaposed with capitalist models, we are told that for allocation we have a choice between central planning and markets. Anarchists, however, have often argued for decentralized forms of planning and some have suggested that we might have anti-capitalist, socialist markets.[4] This was a part of what was originally proposed by Pierre-Joseph Proudhon, among other workers who saw strategic advantages in cooperative enterprises – a market socialism in which self-managed worker-owned firms would exchange in a market regulated by an "agro-industrial federation" on the basis of reciprocity.

Anarchists point out that these economic arrangements led to the development of class society. While we are often told that we are all equals under the law or that we all have equal power through voting, anarchists point out that these claims (which serve to justify and naturalize capitalist society) are absurd. Rather, we do not live in a society of equals. We live in a society of *classes* – with different material interests. The ruling class in capitalist society has an interest in maintaining capitalism while the rest of us have an interest in smashing capitalism and ending our own exploitation. McKay (2008), like many anarchists, argues for a two-class analysis with the following taxonomy:

> *Working class* – those who have to work for a living but have no real control over that work or other major decisions that affect them, i.e. order-takers. This class also includes the unemployed, pensioners, etc., who have to survive on handouts from the state. They have little wealth and little (official) power. This class includes the growing service worker sector, most (if not the vast majority) of "white collar" workers as well as traditional "blue collar" workers. Most self-employed people would be included in this class, as would the bulk of peasants and artisans (where applicable). In a nutshell, the producing classes and those who either were producers or will be producers. This group makes up the vast majority of the population.
>
> *Ruling Class* – those who control investment decisions, determine high level policy, set the agenda for capital and state. This is the elite at the top, owners or top managers of large companies, multinationals and banks (i.e. the capitalists), owners of large amounts of land (i.e. landlords or the aristocracy, if applicable), top-level state officials, politicians, and so forth. They have real power within the economy and/or state, and so control society. In a nutshell, the owners of power (whether political, social or economic) or the master class.
>
> *(185)*

However, not everyone fits neatly into these broad categories. And some radicals, anarchists included, argue for the existence of a third class. Some refer to this as "the middle class," "the coordinator class," "the techno-managerial class," and so on. This is typically used to highlight the existence of people with a high degree of social power – often directly over working people – such as high-paid lawyers, tenured professors at elite institutions, and so on. This class is sometimes conceived as having their own sets of material interests, in opposition to the ruling class and the working class, and sometimes conceived as having similar interests as workers, but being placed above them in capitalist society due to their social power.

We might juxtapose this anarchist class analysis with sociological analyses of class that often split society into a lower (or "under") class, working class, lower middle class, upper middle class, and upper class. These popular sociological analyses are typically rooted in a Weberian analysis of power and one can certainly point to structural advantages that some workers have over others, cultural differences, and the like. However, in terms of *ruling* and *owning* society, this kind of broad-range sociological analysis of class can serve to mystify more than explain. Even a better-paid worker with more prestige than her counterparts, in some cases even in the same workplace, is still exploited and controlled by her boss at the end of the day.

Finally, anarchists point out that the social relations in capitalist society are protected and maintained by states. As the Italian anarchist Errico Malatesta (2005, 356) notes, we are taught that the state is "the representative ... of the general interest: it is the expression of the rights of all, construed as a limit upon the rights of each" and that states are "moral ... endowed with certain attributes of reason, justice." Anarchists point out that actually the state protects property relations, allowing for the existence of private property. A workplace can be owned and maintained and the workers exploited only through the organization of violence to stop them from simply taking the workplace and running it themselves. While in contemporary capitalism, ownership has become more convoluted and diffused throughout society than during Malatesta's time, it is still the state and its organized, legitimated violence that allows for buildings filled with shelves of food to exist largely untouched – except by consumers – with beggars directly outside asking for money to buy food!

Again, this is an attempt to break down capitalism to its basic and constituent elements: wage labor/exploitation, private property, markets, class society, and states. But this short descriptive analysis misses much. One might consider, for example, value production as central to capitalism, money or some other circulating medium of exchange, pricing mechanisms, and other possible essentials. Examining its fundamental constitution is important because capitalism is a resilient system, often changing forms in order to recuperate struggles against it. In what is perhaps one of its most insidious characteristics, capital's drive for accumulation has, at times, meant creating commodities out of rebellion, generating release valves for struggles against its inexorable search for growth and profit and its commodification of human life and desire, as well as the non-human world that we live with(in). Understanding these constitutive elements, then, is an absolute necessity for those who wish to undo capitalism.

Post-Capitalism

It is not easy to pen a section on anarchist ideas about what a post-capitalist society might look like for a number of reasons. For one, many anarchists reject visionary or generative thinking, preferring instead a politics of negation. This is particularly true of anarchist tendencies inspired by nihilism and individualism. The infamous nihilist anarchist, Renzo Novatore (1924) explains:

> Consequently, anarchy, which is the natural liberty of the individual freed from the odious yoke of spiritual and material rulers, is not the construction of a new and suffocating society. It is a decisive fight against all societies – christian, democratic, socialist, communist, etc., etc. Anarchism is the eternal struggle of a small minority of aristocratic outsiders against all societies which follow one another on the stage of history.
> *(quoted in Marcutti n.d.).*

Anarchy, conceived under these terms, is not so much about creating an anti-capitalist society, but resisting society as such, a line of tension that runs across a wide variety of anarchist egoist, nihilist, and individualist thinking, perhaps, in many ways, exemplified by Max Stirner (1845), who inspired Novatore, Emma Goldman, and many others.

Similarly, many anarchists are suspicious of visionary arguments and blueprints for the future, seeing anarchism as a conscious creation of the dispossessed and not a future that can be written within the context of the present. As Goldman (n.d.) put it:

> Anarchism is not, as some may suppose, a theory of the future to be realized through divine inspiration. It is a living force in the affairs of our life, constantly creating new conditions. The methods of Anarchism therefore do not comprise an iron-clad program to be carried out under all circumstances. Methods must grow out of the economic needs of each place and clime, and of the intellectual and temperamental requirements of the individual.

Following this, some anarchists would eschew labels and "hyphenations" like "anarchist-communism," tending to refer to their preference simply as "anarchy," or at times not to refer to a preference at all. Still others assume that visionary arguments are authoritarian, a method of conceiving a new society *without* the participation of those people who (will) compose it. In this way, the idea of a positive and visionary politics can be read as vanguardist and presumptive.

There is also a strong tradition of revolutionary pluralism in anarchism. In the past, some anarchists would advocate for an "anarchism-without-adjectives," perhaps most famously advanced by thinkers such as Voltairine de Cleyre, to indicate a tolerance for many visionary (and strategic) differences. Similarly, there have been (and are) anarchists who advocate for specific proposals, but see a need for a deep humility and commitment to pluralism in terms of vision. Malatesta (1984) provides one of the best examples of this, as he advocated for anarchist-communism, yet stated:

One may, therefore, prefer communism, or individualism, or collectivism, or any other system, and work by example and propaganda for the achievement of one's personal preferences, but one must beware, at the risk of certain disaster, of supposing that one's system is the only, and infallible, one, good for all men [sic], everywhere and for all times, and that its success must be assured at all costs, by means other than those which depend on persuasion, which spring from the evidence of facts.

(28–29, quoted in Price 2006)

Undoubtedly, this is also reflective of anarchist suspicion of visionary arguments and blueprints for a future society.

Nonetheless, one can identify strands of post-capitalist thinking by anarchists. These various positions can easily be found among contemporary anarchists, though often using different terms (and sometimes, advanced by thinkers who are not anarchists). This method of adoption might itself be reflective of anarchist pluralism, where contemporary anarchists often argue for any number of mixes of these arrangements or, at times, take on anti-state political economic ideas outside of the anarchist tradition. Typically, the three major proposals are referred to as mutualism, collectivism, and (anarchist) communism.

Mutualism

Proudhon was an advocate of a form of market socialism that many people refer to as "mutualism."[5] Mutualism, according to this view, is an anti-capitalist model that sees mutual banks and credit associations as a way to socialize productive property and allow for a form of dual power for workers, particularly through the use of low-interest loans, charging only the necessary interest to pay for administration. Proudhon argued for mutualism not only as a post-capitalist vision, but also as a strategic orientation stressing the need to build alternative economic relationships in the here-and-now that would eventually replace capitalism.

As Proudhon sketched it out, wage labor and landlordism would be abolished in a reciprocal arrangement of society. Ownership claims would be based on occupancy and use. Therefore, all workers would have access to their own means of production – most organizing into cooperative, non-hierarchical firms. These self-managed firms would exchange in a market, regulated by a grand agro-industrial federation. Many mutualists have argued that these firms would function in ways similar to worker cooperatives contemporarily, but without some of the pressures of operating in the context of a capitalist and statist society. Further, rather than capitalists expropriating surplus value from workers, workers would keep or trade those products that they produce. This would mean that distribution in a mutualist society would be "by work done, by *deed* rather than need. Workers would receive the full product of their labour, after paying for inputs from other co-operatives" (Anarcho 2009). This is an important distinction, particularly as anarchists who advocate for communism argue for forms of distribution by *need* and parts of the debates over anarchist ideas about post-capitalism are centered on the distribution of the things that we produce.

Perhaps some of the most visible contemporary proponents of mutualism are Kevin Carson, Shawn P. Wilbur, or groups like the Alliance of the Libertarian Left or Center for a Stateless Society.[6] Many of these modern mutualists, particularly those at the Center for a Stateless Society, have altered features of Proudhon's arguments in key ways, influenced by the American individualists like Benjamin Tucker and Josiah Warren. Some of the aforementioned groups see anti-statists working together across broad economic spectrums – some of whom are socialist, others who advocate for forms of capitalism and could not therefore properly be called "anarchists." And there seems to be a split among contemporary mutualists, with people like Wilbur[7] arguing for a return to original source materials by Proudhon (whose ideas are still being translated into English). Under this lens, mutualism is a social science rooted in reciprocity, rather than a set of prescriptive political economic ideas.

Collectivism

Collectivism is most often associated with Bakunin, who referred to himself as a "collectivist" to distinguish his theory from state-communists. While mutualism is often interpreted as a reformist and gradualist strategy that would try to *overgrow* capitalism over a long period of time, Bakunin saw a need for a revolutionary rupture with capitalism. Bakunin argued for a revolutionary movement that would expropriate property, socializing it.

Collectivism, then, begins with the assumption of social ownership of productive property. The product of labor, however, would be gathered into a communal market. Bakunin's friend, James Guillaume (1971 [1876]), when outlining Bakunin's vision called for a society where

> items ... produced by collective labor will belong to the community. And each member will receive remuneration for his [sic] labor either in the form of commodities ... or in currency. In some communities remuneration will be in proportion to hours worked; in others payment will be measured by both the hours of work and the kind of work performed; still other systems will be experimented with to see how they work out.
>
> *(361)*

Where communities used currency, it would be used to purchase items from the collective market.

And yet Sam Dolgoff (1971, 159) said of Guillaume that he "saw no difference in principle between collectivism and anti-state communism. The collectivists understood that full communism would not be immediately realizable. They were convinced that the workers themselves would gradually introduce communism as they overcame the obstacles, both psychological and economic." Thus, in this way, the idea of remuneration was not seen as an end in Bakunin's collectivism, but rather a transitional phase into a system of "full communism," presumably where norms of remuneration would be done away with. The term "collectivism" is still widely in use among anarchists, who often distinguish between collectivism and communist anarchism on the basis of debates over remuneration and distribution.

Contemporarily, there are few anarchists who advocate for collectivism, as such. But some of these concerns over remuneration can be seen as some anarchists advocate for participatory economics (or "parecon"), a non-market libertarian socialism developed by Michael Albert and Robin Hahnel (1991) and also advocated by Chris Spannos (2008) and the Organization for a Free Society. Albert (2012, 330) writes that "citizens should have a claim on society's economic product that increases if they do socially valued work longer or more intensely or under worse conditions." This is where we might see the descendants of collectivism in some ways. However, for advocates of parecon, it is typically not seen as a transitional phase into a full communism of free consumption, but an end unto itself, which differentiates it from Bakunin's theory.

Communist Anarchism

Communist forms of anarchism are the dominant tendency among anarchists (for those who identify with a particular economic tendency). Strategically, communist anarchists (sometimes referred to as anarcho-communists, anarchist-communists, or libertarian communists – with each of those terms, at times, connoting some strategic and theoretical differences) typically see a need for a revolutionary break with capitalism. Some envision, like Bakunin, this being a series of grand revolutionary events enacted by an organized working class. Others, however, see anarchism and communism more as processes than end goals, and often advocate for insurrectionary moments that would, perhaps, coalesce into revolutions.

Libertarian communists advocate for the social ownership of productive property (and, in some cases, its destruction) and distribution on the basis of need or, perhaps better stated, an end to ownership and property relations altogether (i.e. the abolition of property). This anarchist communism argues for economic visions organized around the principle "From each according to ability, to each according to need," though the details of how to realize this objective are certainly debatable. Added to this, "communism" is also a contested term with a variety of meanings, both historically and contemporarily. This makes for a category that is difficult to pin down with simple definitions, but much of the early communist anarchist theory was written in reaction to the collectivist wages system.

Communist anarchists typically argue against any form of currency or remuneration. In Kropotkin's (2008) view, this was a wrong-headed idea from the start and one that could possibly lead to the re-development of capitalism:

> In fact, in a society like ours, in which the more a man [sic] works the less he is remunerated, this principle, at first sight, may appear to be a yearning for justice. But it is really only the perpetuation of past injustice. It was by virtue of this principle that wagedom began, to end in the glaring inequalities and all the abominations of present society; because, from the moment work done was appraised in currency or in any other form of wage; the day it was agreed upon that man would only receive the wage he could secure to himself, the whole history of State-aided Capitalist Society was as good as written; it germinated in this principle.
>
> *(195)*

Kropotkin's (2008, 194–195) view presented a single way forward for a post-revolutionary society that has "taken possession of all social wealth, having boldly proclaimed the right of all to this wealth – whatever share they may have taken in producing it will be compelled to abandon any system of wages, whether in currency or labour-notes." Goldman (1908) also suggested a process of creating communism that precluded commercial processes:

> To make this a reality will, I believe, be possible only in a society based on voluntary co-operation of productive groups, communities and societies loosely federated together, eventually developing into a free communism, actuated by a solidarity of interests. There can be no freedom in the large sense of the word, no harmonious development, so long as mercenary and commercial considerations play an important part in the determination of personal conduct.

Kropotkin (2008, 195) was particularly adamant about this: "The Revolution will be communist; if not, it will be drowned in blood, and have to be begun over again."

Some contemporary inheritors of anarchist communism are the relatively small platformist federations, organized around the Anarkismo website, or the anarcho-syndicalist groups affiliated with the International Worker's Association, which includes the Spanish Confederación Nacional del Trabajo, famous for its historical role(s) during the Spanish Civil War. There are also insurrectionary communist anarchists who reject the formal organizations of platformists as well as the union form espoused by anarcho-syndicalists. The contemporary website, libcom.org, is a libertarian communist website, with engagements with both anarchist *and* Marxist writings with a large user base and huge repository of information hosted within its domain, as well as an active discussion forum. And there are contemporary egoist and individualist communists, some post-left anarchists, and an assortment of individuals and groups who are for the abolition of political economy, but would not refer to themselves as "communists" for a variety of reasons.

Bread

I opened this chapter with a quote by the Mexican revolutionary anarchist, Ricardo Flores Magón. Here he describes liberation as a practice tied to a basic human need: food. I want to close this chapter with an argument of my own. That is, I think that food ties us together in unique ways. For one, we require it. Secondly, food is an object that provides people with meaning and a sense of identity and community. Finally, food brings us together socially, perhaps best illustrated with the term "commensality."

Food, being a human *need*, is also central to any understanding of economy. That is, one reading of economy is that it "is needed for production, consumption, and allocation of the material means of life to serve both simple and complex human needs" (Spannos 2012, 43). Food is necessary for human life, even in its most basic form. It makes sense, then, to center food in any anarchist analysis of economic life.

Perhaps Kropotkin was on to something a bit more than just espousing anarchist communism in his *Conquest of Bread*. Like Magón, the anarchist-formerly-known-as-Prince centers food access in his polemic:

> Be it ours to see, from the first day of the Revolution to the last, in all the provinces fighting for freedom, that there is not a single man who lacks bread, not a single woman compelled to stand with the weariful crowd outside the bake-house-door, that haply a coarse loaf may be thrown to her in charity, not a single child pining for want of food.
>
> It has always been the middle-class idea to harangue about "great principles" – great lies rather!
>
> The idea of the people will be to provide bread for all. And while middle-class citizens, and workmen infested with middle-class ideas admire their own rhetoric in the "Talking Shops," and "practical people" are engaged in endless discussions on forms of government, we, the "Utopian dreamers" – we shall have to consider the question of daily bread.
>
> We have the temerity to declare that all have a right to bread, that there is bread enough for all, and that with this watchword of *Bread for All* the Revolution will triumph.
>
> (Kropotkin 2008, 97)

My suggestion is that we take Kropotkin seriously, that we center food access in our theory and our practice. This might be a way forward for many tendencies to find some commonality (and even, perhaps, commensality). Perhaps we can work toward the conquest of bread together and debate the particulars of economy along the way. In this, we might allow ourselves space for debates as well as cooperation while fulfilling a need that is fundamental to being human. The spirit of anti-authoritarianism, after all, no doubt rests more comfortably in a stomach that is not empty and in need.

Notes

1 Parts of this chapter are borrowed from past work (Shannon, Nocella, and Asimakopoulos 2012).
2 McKay (2012) offers an argument that *does* put forward the notion that anarchist communism was a part of the full development of earlier anarchist economic ideas.
3 See work by Shawn P. Wilbur (2015) for examples of interesting contemporary comments on Proudhon's theory of exploitation.
4 See http://mutualist.org/ for some modern examples of mutualist theory.
5 See work by Wilbur (2013) for a contrary read of Proudhon's mutualism, as an "anarchist encounter" rather than a set of political economic ideas.
6 See such websites as http://mutualist.blogspot.com/, http://libertarian-labyrinth.blogspot.com/, http://c4ss.org/, and http://all-left.net/.
7 See, for example, this series on Proudhon's ideas as a social science, www.mutualism.info/2015/08/29/new-series-proudhons-social-science/.

References

Albert, Michael. 2012. "Porous Borders of Anarchist Vision and Strategy." In *The Accumulation of Freedom: Writings on Anarchist Economics*, edited by Deric Shannon, Anthony J. Nocella II, and John Asimakopoulos, 327–343. Oakland, CA: AK Press.
Albert, Michael, and Robin Hahnel. 1991. *Looking Forward: Participatory Economics for the Twenty First Century*. New York: South End Press.
Anarcho. 2009. "The Economics of Anarchy." Anarchist Writers. Accessed October 2, 2015. http://anarchism.pageabode.com/anarcho/the-economics-of-anarchy.
Bakunin, Mikhail. n.d. "The Capitalist System." Anarchy Archives. Accessed September 9, 2015. http://dwardmac.pitzer.edu/anarchist_archives/bakunin/capstate.html.
Dolgoff, Sam. 1971. *Bakunin on Anarchy*. New York: Vintage.
Goldman, Emma. n.d. "Anarchism: What it Really Stands For." Anarchy Archives. Accessed October 3, 2015. http://dwardmac.pitzer.edu/Anarchist_Archives/goldman/aando/anarchism.html.
Goldman, Emma. 1908. "What I Believe." Anarchy Archives. Accessed October 3, 2015. http://dwardmac.pitzer.edu/Anarchist_Archives/goldman/whatibelieve.html.
Gordon, Uri. 2007. "Anarchism and Political Theory: Contemporary Problems." The Anarchist Library. Accessed September 11, 2015. http://theanarchistlibrary.org/HTML/Uri_Gordon__Anarchism_and_Political_Theory__Contemporary_Problems.html.
Guillaume, James. 1971 [1876]. "On Building the New Social Order." In *Bakunin on Anarchy*, edited by Sam Dolgoff, 356–379. New York: Vintage.
Kropotkin, Peter. 2002 [1892]. *The Conquest of Bread*. Oakland, CA: AK Press.
Malatesta, Errico. 1984. *Errico Malatesta: His Life and Ideas*. Edited by Vernon Richards. London: Freedom Press.
Malatesta, Errico. 2005. "Anarchy." In *No Gods No Masters: An Anthology of Anarchism*, edited by Daniel Guérin, 355–364. Oakland, CA: AK Press.

Marcutti, Enzo. n.d. "Renzo Novatore." Translated by Stephen Marietta. The Anarchist Library. Accessed October 1, 2015. https://theanarchistlibrary.org/library/renzo-novatore-toward-the-creative-nothing#toc5.
Marx, Karl. 1977 [1859]. *A Contribution to the Critique of Political Economy*. Moscow: Progress Publishers.
McKay, Iain. 2008. *An Anarchist FAQ*, vol. 1. Oakland, CA: AK Press.
McKay, Iain. 2012. "Laying the Foundations: Proudhon's Contribution to Anarchist Economics." In *The Accumulation of Freedom: Writings on Anarchist Economics*, edited by Deric Shannon, Anthony J. Nocella II, and John Asimakopoulos, 64–78. Oakland, CA: AK Press.
Novatore, Renzo. 1924. "Toward the Creative Nothing." The Anarchist Library. Accessed October 1, 2015. https://theanarchistlibrary.org/library/renzo-novatore-toward-the-creative-nothing.
Price, Wayne. 2006. "Malatesta's Anarchist Vision of Life After Capitalism." The Anarchist Library. Accessed October 2, 2015. https://theanarchistlibrary.org/HTML/Wayne_Price__Malatesta_s_Anarchist_Vision_of_Life_After_Capitalism.html.
Rocker, Rudolf. 2004 [1938]. *Anarcho-Syndicalism: Theory and Practice*. Oakland, CA: AK Press.
Shannon, Deric, Anthony J. Nocella II, and John Asimakopoulos. 2012. "Anarchist Economics: A Holistic View." In *The Accumulation of Freedom: Writings on Anarchist Economics*, edited by Deric Shannon, Anthony J. Nocella II, and John Asimakopoulos, 11–39. Oakland, CA: AK Press.
Spannos, Chris, ed. 2008. *Real Utopia: Participatory Society for the 21st Century*. Oakland, CA: AK Press.
Spannos, Chris. 2012. "Examining the History of Anarchist Economics to See the Future." In *The Accumulation of Freedom: Writings on Anarchist Economics*, edited by Deric Shannon, Anthony J. Nocella II, and John Asimakopoulos, 42–63. Oakland, CA: AK Press.
Stirner, Max. 1845. "The Ego and His Own." The Anarchist Library. Accessed October 2, 2015. https://theanarchistlibrary.org/library/max-stirner-the-ego-and-his-own.
Wilbur, Shawn P. 2013. "The Anatomy of the Encounter." Contr'un. Accessed October 3, 2015. http://libertarian-labyrinth.blogspot.com/2013/09/the-anatomy-of-encounter.html.
Wilbur, Shawn P. 2015. "Property and Theft: Proudhon's Theory of Exploitation." Accessed September 11, 2015. www.mutualism.info/2015/08/18/property-and-theft-proudhons-theory-of-exploitation/.

PART 3
Peripheral Concepts

11
INTERSECTIONALITY

Hillary Lazar

"Anarchism," comments Erich Mühsam (1932), "is the teaching of freedom as the foundation of human society. Anarchy (in English: without rule, without authority, without state) thereby denotes the condition of social order aspired to by the anarchists, namely the freedom of each individual through the general freedom." Being largely anti-doctrinaire, there is no single definition of what anarchism is. Rather, it is akin to "a broad river" with "a number of distinct currents" that have grown more or less pronounced in different historical and geographical contexts (Marshall 2009, 6). As Mühsam suggests, freedom from domination is one of these currents.

Given the fluid nature of anarchism, it is essential to contextualize its conceptual threads, to locate them in relation to other fronts of struggle and forms of radical thought. Michael Freeden's (2003) morphological approach provides a useful framework for doing so. Following this model, freedom from domination (rooted in hierarchical power relations) is identifiable as one of the "core" characteristics of anarchism. Implicit as it may be, it is critical to note that this specifically refers to *freedom for all* and *from all forms of domination* rather than more limited applications of eliminating certain top-down, dominant-subjugated relations or seeking liberty for select individuals or groups. For this reason, it is arguable that an "adjacent" or clarifying concept is that of the *universality* of anarchism's emancipatory aspirations. Yet, while contemporary anarchism continues to call for each person's individual liberation – and even perceives this to be a necessary pre-condition for any degree of social emancipation – it has moved away from this concept of universality.

Freeden's schema helps elucidate why this has occurred and what the implications are by asking – *how has anarchism's understanding of "freedom for all" been influenced by other ideas or altered in different contexts?* Addressing this question points to how, for recent anarchist thinkers, "freedom" has taken on new meanings, and how perceptions of how power operates, who constitutes oppressed subjects, shape what steps are necessary to liberate all peoples. It also suggests that there has been an important shift from conceptualizations of freedom in terms of "universality" to that of an interlocking understanding of oppression – i.e., the idea that anarchism must better account for the diverse instantiations of oppression, while still recognizing the interdependence of systems of domination such as white supremacy, heteropatriarchy, ableism, colonialism, and capitalism. This change has critical ramifications for current anarchist praxis, particularly in terms of engagement with other liberatory struggles.

As will be explored in this chapter, the conceptual shift is largely due to the influence of post-structuralist rejection of universals on anarchism and, in turn, the resonance this has had with Black feminist intersectionality as well as other radical currents, including queer theory and decolonial thought. In short, to use Freeden's terminology, "proximity" to and "permeability" with these theories and their corresponding political efforts have led to a more nuanced and deepened approach to the "priority" of freedom for all – one that reflects a more inclusive, interdependent anarchist vision of a free society and a greater spirit of solidarity in collective struggle.

Universal Freedom in Classical Anarchism

In order to understand why freedom from domination has featured as one of the key facets of anarchism, it is necessary to trace it back to the roots of classical anarchism.[1] In so many words, classical anarchism – tied to Western philosophical traditions coupled with a smattering of insurrectionary action and revolutionary trade unionism – emerged through a confluence of the rise of Industrial capitalism and the Enlightenment. Informed by the Enlightenment's concern for individual liberty and freedom, nineteenth-century anarchist thinkers such as Mikhail Bakunin, Pierre-Joseph Proudhon, Max Stirner, and Peter Kropotkin sought to make sense of the rapidly changed social landscape in the wake of industrialization. More specifically, they endeavored to resolve how to respond to new forms of inequality and coercion that now derived less from feudal or manorial rule than from an increasingly centralized State and the conditions of labor under capitalism (Marshall 2009; Runkle 1972; Woodcock 1962).

Unlike their Marxist contemporaries (for whom the primary concern was exploitation of the newly emergent working class), anarchists thought that the real goal was ensuring freedom from domination in all its forms. Long before Mühsam's comments on anarchism and freedom, Proudhon (2005, 79) expressed this succinctly by noting that: "We seek unbounded freedom for man and the citizen, as long as he respects the liberty of his neighbor: Freedom of association. Freedom of assembly. Freedom of religion. Freedom of the press. Freedom of thought and of speech. Freedom of labor, trade and industry. Freedom of education. In short, absolute freedom." Echoing this, Lucy Parsons (2004) explained that "anarchism has one infallible, unchangeable motto, 'Freedom': Freedom to discover any truth, freedom to develop, to live naturally and fully." Perhaps one of the best summaries of this is by Alexander Berkman (1977 [1929], 2):

> Anarchism means that you should be free; that no one should enslave you, boss you, rob you, or impose upon you. It means that you should be free to do the things you want to do; and that you should not be compelled to do what you don't want to do. It means that you should have a chance to choose the kind of a life you want to live, and live it without anybody interfering. It means that the next fellow should have the same freedom as you, that every one should have the same rights and liberties. ... In short, Anarchism means a condition or society where all men and women are free, and where all enjoy equally the benefits of an ordered and sensible life.

Furthermore, it was not simply that the early anarchists sought to attain universal emancipation, but that, by extension, every individual's liberty was dependent on that of the others. In other words, all forms of oppression were inextricably bound together (Bakunin 1867). Yet, like the other facets of anarchism, this idea of the universality of freedom is not static. It has changed in response to anarchism's contact with other political currents and historical contexts. While classical anarchists were concerned with eliminating all hierarchies and coercive relations, for the most part, their attention focused on State-citizen dynamics. To be sure, if to a lesser degree, they also addressed equality among the sexes. Consider, for example, another of Bakunin's (2005, 151) remarks: "I am truly free only when all human beings around me, men and women alike, are equally free." And, certainly, there is also a long tradition of feminist-informed anarchist thought dating back to the late nineteenth century. Emma Goldman, Voltairine de Cleyre, Parsons, Mother Jones, Helen Keller, Louise Michel, and "thousands of other historical figures and contemporary feminist anarchists" helped to advance the critical perspective that "true equality can never be achieved within the capitalist system ... [and] we need to be clear that when feminist gains are won, it is in the name of true equality for all people" (Dunbar-Ortiz 2012, 11; Revolutionary Anarcha-Feminist Group Dublin 2012, 14).

Furthermore, as Uri Gordon (2015) has shown in his essay on anarchism and multiculturalism, "anarchists were early and consistent opponents of racism and imperialism, both in advanced capitalist countries and in the colonial and post-colonial world ..." Some anarchists including Joseph Déjacque, James F. Morton, Henry Lloyd Garrison, and even Kropotkin were vocal opponents of segregation and slavery. Others supported anti-colonial, national liberation efforts, including actively engaging in struggles such as the Algerian resistance to French colonialism. Even so, as Gordon (2015, 68) points out, this solidarity with struggles for racial and sexual emancipation was largely "grounded in a universalist ethics of humanism and rationalism."

This is where much of contemporary anarchism diverges from classical anarchist thought. Although current anarchism remains committed to supporting these movements and acting in solidarity with other struggles, it speaks less to humanitarian concern with universal freedom and more to an inclusive, interlocking framework as the vital starting point for revolutionary struggle. This change is attributable to the complementary overlap between post-structuralist anarchist theory and other influential radical currents such as Black feminist intersectionality, queer theory, and decolonial thought.

Beyond Universals: Post-Anarchism

Post-anarchism – a blend of post-modernism and post-structuralism with more traditional anarchist principles – first emerged in the last decades of the twentieth century. Coined by Hakim Bey (1987), the term was meant to denote a call for a move beyond classical philosophical anarchism towards more practicable, grounded forms of anarchist theory. Along with being centered on the idea that transformative radical change necessitates an epistemological move away from State-centric conceptions of power, it also calls into question essentialist notions of human nature and society. Both conceptual shifts were critical for helping to move anarchism away from the "universal" perception of freedom.

Informed by the post-structuralist repudiation of essentialism, post-anarchists challenge the Enlightenment thinking of many classical anarchists. Saul Newman (2007, 13), for instance, explains that classical thinkers such as Bakunin and Kropotkin based their understandings of liberation in a "rational logic" that was only "intelligible through" science. Kropotkin employed a kind of anti-Darwinian analysis to argue for a mutual aid-based society based on his observations of cooperation in the natural world. Bakunin, meanwhile, appealed to the concept of "progress" and belief in an "immutable" natural law regarding revolutionary processes and possibilities. Post-anarchists, however, abjure any "natural" rationale for revolutionary resistance. Instead, they subscribe to the position that "the socio-political field does not bear some objective, rational truth that science can reveal; rather it is characterized by multiple layers of articulation, antagonism and ideological dissimulation" (Newman 2007, 14).

Related to this, post-anarchists reject the viewpoint that human nature is inherently "benign or cooperative" or that there is a teleological march towards "the social revolution and the creation of a free society [which] would allow man's immanent humanity and rationality to finally be realized" (Newman 2007, 13). As Todd May comments, "one does not solve the ethical problem by positing a good human nature and then saying that it should be allowed to flourish. There is too much evidence against the idea of an essentially good (or essentially bad) human nature for that claim to be made" (Perspectives Editorial Collective 2000, 6). In lieu of appealing to *a priori* universals about humanity, post-anarchists instead perceive reality to be the result of socially constructed meanings.

Given this, post-anarchist ethics depends on careful interrogation of how social structures and systems of power are co-created and maintained. Based on this analysis, political power is diverse, complex, and subtle. Mounting any substantive challenge to power requires equally diverse, complex, and subtle tactics and analysis. For this reason, the core underpinning of post-anarchism "should be seen as a critique of domination, rather than as a critique of the state" (May 2007, 21). Viewing anarchism this way dovetails with (or to use Freeden's terms, reflects permeability across) post-structuralist – Foucauldian – notions of power as diffused throughout the capillaries of society.

Already, then, it is possible to see how these perspectives contributed to expanding the anarchist project from simply focusing on the State to multiple locations. In so doing, by encouraging anarchist thinkers to shift away from essentialist and totalizing worldviews, it created space for a better fit with other schools of thought, including Black feminist, queer theorist, and indigenous critiques of the idea of universal experience. Moreover, post-anarchists (and contemporary anarchists more broadly) understand that universalism cannot "provide adequate grounding for political action in a situation where dominant values masquerade as everyone's values and where opposing identities (and the values and practices associated with them) are necessarily multiple, fragmented, and at best provisional" (Ackelsberg 1996, 93).

Necessarily, this more nuanced analysis of power is a critical step for anarchist understanding of – and participation in – solidarity efforts. Yet, it is also important to note, that contemporary anarchism's overlap with other radical currents is not simply a result of proximity between anarchist and poststructuralist thought. The relationship is more complicated than that. Hakim Bey's original essay, in fact, was in part a response to the observation that anarchism neither appealed to nor supported communities of color and other marginalized people. In it, Bey (1987) commented:

> The anarchist "movement" today contains virtually no Blacks, Hispanics, Native Americans or children ... even tho in theory such genuinely oppressed groups stand to gain the most from any anti-authoritarian revolt. Might it be that anarchism offers no concrete program whereby the truly deprived might fulfill (or at least struggle realistically to fulfill) real needs & desires?

Furthermore, May and others have argued that post-anarchism was itself informed by "the lessons of the struggles against racism, misogyny, prejudice against gays and lesbians, etc." – "that power and oppression are not reducible to a single site or a single operation" and that anarchists "need to understand power as it operates not only at the level of the state and capitalism, but in the practices through which we conduct our lives" (Perspectives Editorial Collective 2000, 6). Consequently, the interactions across these theories and struggles must be understood as both dynamic and multi-directional.

Black Feminism and Intersectionality in Contemporary Anarchism

Of contemporary radical currents, it is arguable that Black feminism has had the greatest overlap with anarchism. In part, this reflects the prominence of Black feminism – and specifically, intersectional theory – in contemporary American and Western activist thought. Hence, there have been greater opportunities for linkages. This relationship also speaks to an obvious permeability between the anarchist aspiration towards freedom and a theory of interlocking oppressions – a more nuanced form of Black feminist intersectional analysis – which underscores interdependent connections across all systems of domination. Related to this, Black feminism has also sparked important debates among anarchist thinkers about how to understand the relationship between identity and power, what solidarity looks like, and how anarchists should participate in other struggles.

Black feminism, or third wave feminism, developed in response to the color-blind perspectives of second wave feminism. Challenging notions of a universal womanhood, these theorists sought to highlight previously ignored power dynamics within the women's movement and feminist discourse that better captured the messiness and conceptual complexity of the overlapping, interactive nature of differing forms of oppression. One of the earliest and most influential articulations of this was Black feminist legal scholar Kimberlé Crenshaw's (1991) concept of "intersectionality."

Based on her experience as a legal scholar, Crenshaw argues that there has been a systematic erasure of the experiences of women of color, poor, and other oppressed groups under the law. This erasure reflects a broader social tendency to only think along "singular axes of identity," which misses how someone may experience multiple forms of discriminatory oppression at once. To illustrate this, she suggests that domination should instead be thought of as analogous to a four-way traffic intersection in which injury can come from any direction. Although clearly an important intervention into second wave white feminist thought, Crenshaw's intersectionality (along with identity politics and privilege theory, for which it serves as a conceptual underpinning) has been heavily critiqued for having an "additive" quality – i.e., the more marginal categories under which an individual may fall, the greater their experience of oppression. Necessarily, this flattens otherwise more complex dynamics of power, including the ways in which an individual may be in a position of privilege in some instances and oppressed in others.

Along with other critics, this has led many anarchists to question its merit as a theoretical tool. For example, Jen Rogue and Abbey Volcano (2012) highlight the importance of adopting an intersectional lens while warning against its potential reductionist framework. For them, we must avoid "simply listing [race, class, gender, sexuality, etc.] as though they all operate in similar fashions" and instead understand them "as mutually-constituting processes … categories [that] do not exist independently from one another … overlapping, complex, interacting, intersecting, and often contradictory" (Rogue and Volcano 2012, 45–46). Similarly, in his critique of identity politics, Lupus Dragonowl (2015) argues that while intersectionality and "the recognition of multiple forms or axes of oppression, with complex interacting effects" should be considered "an effective theoretical response to the problems of Identity Politics," there are difficulties putting them into practice as some people "who claim to be intersectional end up treating one or two oppressions as primary."

Certainly, intersectional analysis is not the only theory that endeavors to explain the dynamic relationship between categories of oppression. There have been numerous other metaphors or concepts used to illustrate the complex nature of multiple oppressions, each of which offers a slightly different perspective on how to disentangle these relationships. Of them, however, interlocking theory resonates most with anarchism as it suggests that the interconnectedness of oppressions necessitates elimination of all systems of domination.[2] Above all, this is because unlike Crenshaw's intersectionality (at least as it is interpreted by contemporary activists and scholars), given its interdependent perspective, interlocking oppression theory avoids the problematic additive approach.

The notion of interlocking oppressions was first expressed by the Combahee River Collective – primarily a Black lesbian group – more than a decade prior to Crenshaw's coining of the term "intersectionality." Writing in 1977, they asserted that:

> the most general statement of our politics at the present time would be that we are actively committed to struggling against racial, sexual, heterosexual, and class oppression, and see as our particular task the development of integrated analysis and practice based upon the fact that the major systems of oppression are interlocking. The synthesis of these oppressions creates the conditions of our lives. As Black women we see Black feminism as the logical political movement to combat the manifold and simultaneous oppressions that all women of color face.
>
> *(Combahee River Collective 1983, 210)*

As they argue, it would be impossible to address only a single issue at a time – true liberation required addressing the simultaneously occurring and inseparable experiences of oppression. Hence, their insistence that "we are not just trying to fight oppression on one front or even two, but instead to address a whole range of oppressions …. If Black women were free, it would mean that everyone else would have to be free since our freedom would necessitate the destruction of all the systems of oppression" (Combahee River Collective 1983, 214–215).

Since the Combahee first issued their Statement, Black feminists and other activists have taken on this language of interlocking oppression. Patricia Hill Collins (1990; 2000), for instance, underscores interlocking notions of oppression in her concept of the "matrix of domination." According to her, "By embracing a paradigm of race, class, and gender as interlocking systems of oppression, Black feminist thought re-conceptualizes the social relations of domination and resistance" (Collins 2000, 273). As she explains, looking at the multiple axes of oppression such as race, class, and gender and their situational relationships elucidates the ways in which they share "ideological ground." This common ground is "a belief in domination, and a belief in the notions of superior and inferior, which are components of all of those systems …. [It]'s like a house, they share the foundation, but the foundation is the ideological beliefs around which notions of domination are constructed" (Collins 1990). As bell hooks (1984) elucidates:

> Feminism is a struggle to end sexist oppression. Therefore, it is necessarily a struggle to eradicate the ideology of domination that permeates Western culture on various levels as well as a commitment to reorganizing society so that the self- development of people can take precedence over imperialism, economic expansion, and material desires.
>
> *(24)*

Given these principles, it is easy enough to see the complementarity of interlocking oppression theory and anarchism's core emphasis on freedom from domination. Importantly, the rejection of universal womanhood dovetails with a rejection of essentialism and post-anarchism's understanding of oppressive power. The concept of interdependence implicit in this framework also fits well with other anarchist concepts. For example, mutual aid – i.e., collaboration as the basis for human relations – can be considered a kind of interdependence. Interlocking theory also resonates with Murray Bookchin's (1964) social ecological perspective of "unity in diversity" – the idea that social harmony would flow from allowing the diversity of humanity to flourish and from recognizing the interconnectivity between humans and the natural world. It is no surprise that, as anarchists came into contact with Black feminist thought, they embraced a more inclusive and nuanced analysis of interactions between systems of oppression.

Chris Crass, founder of the Catalyst Project,[3] speaks directly to this including the historical context that helped to encourage these influential links. According to him, "the anarchism taken up and developed in the 1990s was a product of the movement experiences of the preceding four decades," during which the "Black Freedom movement, the women's liberation movement, and other liberation movements … [were] challenging multiple forms of oppression" (Crass 2013, 3). In fact, Crass (2013, 5) notes that anarchists in the 1990s increasingly employed the "integrated analysis" of oppression originated by the Combahee River Collective – an analysis which "suggests that systems of racism, capitalism, heteropatriarchy, and ableism operate with and through each other" in interconnected ways.

No doubt this greater attentiveness to an interlocking politics is also due to critical interventions from within the anarchist movement including a collection of essays put out by the Anarchist People of Color (2004). This dialogue remains ongoing as anarchists of color continue to call for a more nuanced and inclusive approach to contesting hierarchical domination. As explained in a zine written by Oakland-based Anarchist People of Color (2015):

> Racism, classism, and this gendered system are overlapping social systems of oppression constructed to serve the elite white men that divided and conquered the population ... If we are serious about fighting white supremacy, patriarchy needs to be fought with the same energy, at the same time.

In other words, while discrimination and prejudice have far from been eliminated within contemporary anarchist spaces, this more inclusive and interdependent approach has at the very least encouraged a greater priority on an interlocking politics and attention to developing an analysis of solidarity with those marginalized groups who have traditionally received less attention in anarchist theory and practice.

The anarchist understanding of solidarity, in fact, has shifted in recent years to better reflect this perspective. The concept of allyship, for example, has come under heavy critique both for being too liberal and meaningless in practice. In recent years, there has been a discursive shift from the term "ally" to "accomplice" as a way to suggest a more active, collaborative, and mutually dependent emancipation. As explained in a zine offering "an Indigenous perspective & provocation" (Indigenous Action Media 2015, 88), "the risks of an ally who provides support or solidarity (usually on a temporary basis) in a fight are much different than that of an accomplice. When we fight back or forward, together, becoming complicit in a struggle toward liberation, we are accomplices." Or as the popular activist saying goes, "If you have come here to help me, you are wasting your time. But if you have come because your liberation is bound up with mine, then let us work together" (Watson n.d.).

Queer Theory, Anti-Colonialism, and Contemporary Anarchism

Without offering an exhaustive account of connections between contemporary anarchism and queer theory and anti-colonialism, a brief look at each may be helpful for understanding the overlapping relationship between interlocking theory and important radical currents within anarchist thought. Indeed, it is partly *because* of the influence of Black feminist interlocking theory – and, by extension, increased attention to solidarity efforts – that contemporary anarchism has significant linkages with both these movements. To be clear, both have their own historical relationship with anarchism, which includes important theoretical contributions by queer, trans, and indigenous activists. Nor are these the only examples of other political trends that are helping to re-shape the anarchist meaning of universal freedom.[4] Yet, like Black feminism, queer theory and anti-colonialism have had an especially high degree of proximity to and permeability with current anarchist theory.

Queer theory emerged in the 1990s out of a confluence of post-structuralism, critical theory, feminism, and gay studies. Building off feminist and post-structuralist critiques of biological essentialism, it suggests that one must consider the ways in which all facets of sex and gender or related normative categorizations are merely constructs to be done away with. In particular, queer theory challenges the notion of binaries and instead posits that sex, gender, and sexuality must all be understood as functioning along a continuum. Additionally, that which is defined as queer (i.e., not normal) must be understood as positional – i.e., based on the fluidity of what is deemed the social norm and what can be construed as deviant (Butler 1990; Halberstam 1998; Halperin 1997; Foucault 1978–86). Queer can be thought of as "whatever is at odds with the normal, the legitimate, the dominant" – it "demarcates not a positivity but a positionality vis-à-vis the normative" (Halperin 1997, 62).

Popularized by theorists such as Judith Butler and Michel Foucault, these ideas have made their way into anarchist theory and practice. They also reflect a longer historical relationship between anarchism and queer liberation. As Terrence Kissack (2007) shows, queer liberation was salient to some of the prominent early anarchists. There is also, of course, a tradition of anarcha-feminist attention to gender and sexual equality going back to Emma Goldman's (1911) work on marriage and the turn of the century movement for free love. Given this history, it makes sense that, with the increased visibility of the mainstream LGBT rights movement and more radical queer and trans struggles, anarchist theorists have been calling for a "queering" of anarchist thought.

Anarchist adoption of queer theory has been encouraged by on-the-ground activism. ACT UP and Outrage!, two radical gay activist networks working in the 1980s and 1990s, for example, used the term "queer" as a way to distinguish themselves and their politics from more mainstream, "assimilationist" LGBT movement organizations. Meanwhile, Bash Back (an explicitly anarchist group known for taking direct action to counter homophobia) and the Pink Bloc (a queer counterpoint to the black bloc tactic) are other instances of this. Consequently, calls to "queer" anarchism must be considered an extension of radical queerness that pushes the boundaries of liberal support for gay rights. As Ryan Conrad (2012, 23) puts it: "How do we as radical queer and trans folks, push back against the emerging hegemony of rainbow flavored neoliberalism and the funneling of our energy into narrow campaigns that only reinforce hierarchical systems and institutions we fundamentally oppose?"

Along with Black feminism, queer theory encourages a more nuanced and inclusive articulation of what freedom should mean for anarchists. Rejecting binaries, queer theory helps to expose the complexity of sex, gender, or sexuality by placing identity "under a destabilizing lens." In so doing, it helps to make visible all who are being defined as deviants within a system of heteropatriarchy.

In terms of anarchist theory and politics, along with "adding a needed critical analysis of sex, sexuality, and gender" (Daring et al. 2012, 14), this means "tearing down the normative assumptions that are used to uphold status quo that puts some of us above others in the social order as a result of our sexual and/or gender practices" (Volcano 2012, 33).

In short, queer theory's repudiation of binary identities resonates with and helps to expand anarchist conceptualizations of freedom. It also suggests that experiences of oppression are interdependent – reinforcing the interlocking (mutual aid-based) framework within anarchism. In her essay on queering heterosexuality, Sandra Jeppesen (2012, 157) writes that "[t]he liberation of one person is predicated upon the liberation of those around them." For her, this means putting anarchist principles of mutual aid into practice so as to create more caring, sustainable queer communities and networks. It also means doing so with "an anti-statist and anti-capitalist perspective, and bringing anti-racism, anti-colonialism and other intersectional movements and ideas" as a way of "anarchizing queer movements" and "queering anarchist movements" (Jeppesen 2012, 158). Liat Ben-Moshe, Anthony Nocella, and A.J. Withers (2012, 216) similarly emphasize that a core tenet for queer-crips is interdependence, which they define as akin to mutual aid, the "macro-socio-political system to build communities and relationships" that rejects individualist competition in favor of cooperative collaboration. Implicitly, this includes adopting an interlocking approach to solidarity in struggle.

Anti-colonialism has similarly contributed to the shift in anarchist perspectives of freedom. There are several related expressions of decolonial thought and politics – from anti-globalization efforts to indigenous sovereignty. While each of these has their own unique set of problematics to be solved, decolonial theory can be broadly summarized as "a 'political and epistemic de-linking' from western dominance and the ways of thinking it imposes – not in order to compete with it in the geopolitical and neoliberal arena, but to assert an ethic of respect for all life and for oppressed peoples' struggles" (Gordon 2015, 73). For anarchists engaged in anti-colonial resistance, there is also a stress on understanding how neo-imperial projects forge a connection across migrant, colonized, and indigenous peoples while being tied to other hegemonic systems of oppression.

Recognizing "[t]he connections between the rights of immigrants and indigenous peoples both forcibly displaced by the demands of the global economy and militarization of borders" enables us to "recognize, unweave, and replace persistent racism, sexism, and all other related patterns of oppression by which colonial dominion has been justified" (Ramnath 2012, 14–15). In practice, adoption of a decolonial stance has led many anarchists to participate in solidarity work with the occupied territory of Palestine as well as efforts to end to all borders and State-based control of populations (Ramnath 2013; Gordon 2010). Notably, these activists conceive of these struggles as based on interlocking systems of domination. In fact, in her prefigurative account of decolonization, Harsha Walia (2013, 16) explicitly draws on "critical race theory, feminist studies, Marxist analysis, and poststructuralism" for the ways in which it "theorizes and evaluates border imperialism from within intersectional pedagogy." For her, not only is border imperialism "the nexus of most systems of oppression," but "[w]e are all … simultaneously separated by and bound together by the violences of border imperialism" as all people are impacted in some way by global capitalism and by processes of border control, displacement, military occupation, and commodification of migrant labor (16). Meanwhile, according to Gordon (2010, 429) in his study of anarchist participation in anti-Apartheid wall efforts, while the focus for activists was on Palestinian liberation, there was also a commitment to "equality for all" implicit in their politics.

In addition, there has been an important "de-centering" that has led to weaving an anti-colonial framework into anarchism, while expanding understandings of anarchism in practice. Rather than accepting the "diffusionist line" that anarchism originated in Europe and spread to the Global South, a "de-centered" approach to anarchism redefines it as "a form of 'strategic positioning' and 'deliberate statelessness' going back at least two millennia. This is an anarchism … that both preceded and arose out of capitalism, industrialization, and the modern nation-state" (Craib 2015, 4). This extends anarchism beyond the Western thinkers traditionally thought of as foundational anarchists. Instead, there is a much longer and deeper tradition of anarchist thought and sensibility, found outside the boundaries of the west, that dates back as far as many ancient Eastern philosophies (Marshall 2009; Ramnath 2013; Maxwell and Craib 2015).

Beyond granting agency to these actors, de-centering is critical for the creation of a more expansive understanding of anarchism and its importance throughout history. As Silvia Federici (2015) comments:

> [A]narchism "as we have known it" is a principle that is present in every age and country, expressing an irrepressible desire for individual and collective self-determination, of which European anarchism is only *one embodiment* shaped by specific historical conditions …. Once we leave Europe, in fact, we discover that statelessness and the desire for self-government are not eternally receding utopias, but are principles that for millennia have structured communities in every part of the world.
>
> *(350–351, original emphasis)*

Put otherwise, "the idea and practice of anarchy are not exclusive to self-conscious anarchists" (Bamyeh 2010, 24). Following this logic, it is arguable that anarchist tendencies are traceable to early Eastern philosophies such as Confucianism and Daoism (Marshall 2009, 53–142) or even the nomadic peoples of Zomia described by James C. Scott (2010). And, certainly, Zapatismo – critical for inspiring the resurgence of interest in anarchism during the Global Justice Movement – is reflective of an amalgamation of indigenous cosmology, Catholicism, and peasant praxis rather than "classical," a.k.a. Western, anarchism (Klein 2015; Reitan 2007; Martinez and Garcia 2004).

In addition, Indigeneity – another element of anti-colonialism that grew out of the Red Power movement and is a core element of movements such as Idle No More in Canada – is helping to cement the notion of interlocking oppression through its own emphasis on interdependent struggle. To be sure, just as there is no single indigenous worldview, there is no single definition of "Indigeneity." As a base line, it can be thought of as opposing "colonial ways of thinking and acting" by demanding an "Indigenous starting point and an articulation of what decolonization means for Indigenous peoples around the globe" and a shared desire for "Indigenous sovereignty over land and sea, as well as over ideas and epistemologies" (Sium, Desai, and Ritskes 2012, II).

In terms of its connections with anarchism, interdependence of struggle and eliminating domination are core characteristics of indigenous-centered decolonial thought. As one Idle No More activist explains it, as part of its challenge to colonial-capitalist oppression, Indigeneity seeks "an alternative relationship – to the earth, to its resources, and to each other – a relationship based not on domination but on reciprocity." Furthermore, this perspective advances the idea that "any movement that seeks to create deep, lasting social change – to address not only climate change but endemic racism and social inequality – must confront our colonial identity and, by extension, this broken relationship" (Klein 2013). For indigenous anarchists, there is also an explicit appeal to an interlocking approach. Decolonization is seen as "a gendered and ecological undoing of settler colonial society and the colonial state" with addressing heteropatriarchy as central to this work (Hall 2016, 82).

Conclusion: Towards a More Inclusive, Interlocking Anarchist Vision of Freedom

In some ways, the notion of freedom has gained even greater priority in recent anarchist theory. This is in part due to anarchism's increased prominence in contemporary movements and its corresponding proximity with other complementary political currents. No doubt, anarchism has served as the guiding praxis for numerous movements throughout history and, consequently, has been influenced by the other strains of radical thought it encountered, such as the fusing of Quaker consensus process, anarchism, feminism, and even pagan spiritualism in American anti-nuclear efforts in the 1970s and more recent anti-globalization organizing (Epstein 1991; Cornell 2011). Yet, perhaps even more so than in the past, late twentieth-century and early twenty-first-century social movements bear the stamp of anarchism.

Since this time, we have witnessed "the full-blown revival of a global anarchist movement, possessing a coherent core political practice, on a scale and scope of activity unseen since the 1930s … [as] anarchist forms of resistance and organizing have effectively replaced Marxism as the chief point of reference for radical politics in advanced capitalist countries" (Gordon 2010, 414). Of course, throughout this period, anarchists have not been operating in a vacuum. As anarchism moved from a marginal role to a central one during the Global Justice Movement, it came into contact with other radical political traditions, including Black feminist, indigenous, and queer activism. Within this context, anarchism has had the opportunity to intersect with these struggles and radical schools of thought, which in turn, has impacted its current theory and praxis – including its conceptualization of freedom and how mechanisms of domination operate in society.

In sum, to use Freeden's terminology, contemporary anarchism's proximity with complementary, radical currents – which has accelerated since the "anarchist turn" – has led to a more inclusive, interlocking framework for understanding one of its core concepts – freedom. As we have explored, this change is largely due to post-anarchist rejection of universals and the high degree of permeability with the Black feminist concept of interlocking oppression. Moreover, it has deepened the importance that contemporary anarchism places on solidarity and mutuality of struggle in attaining a free society.

Other currents such as anti-colonialism and queer theory, meanwhile, are also contributing to a broadened meaning of what socio-political emancipation looks like, while underscoring the impact of an interlocking framework on anarchism. Queer theory has been critical for drawing relief to the particularities of oppression based on gender and sexuality while contesting binary understandings of power and domination within anarchist thought. And decolonial thought has helped to "de-center" anarchism from its Eurocentric roots – both by giving voice to non-Western anarchists and histories and by infusing anarchist theory with a more nuanced understanding of how colonialism undermines individual and collective autonomy. Indigeneity also advances its own perspective on the interdependence of struggles.

Despite these shifts, if greater priority were given to addressing the simultaneity of various oppressions – white supremacy, heteropatriarchy, ableism, colonialism, capitalism, for starters – it may help to cultivate an even more emancipatory anarchist politics. Furthermore, a more intentional leveraging of the permeability across these currents might encourage deeper, multi-directional intersections across them (Hall 2016). Even so, the understanding of socio-political liberation in twenty-first-century anarchism is, indisputably, far more nuanced, inclusive, and predicated on interconnected struggle than was classical anarchism's call for universal freedom.

Notes

1 An important caveat is that anarchism is not merely a western ideological creation and that many traditions have called for an end to hierarchy as an essential condition for socio-political emancipation.

2 In some cases, intersectionality refers to identifying the "interlocking" nature of oppression, so that the two terms are used synonymously. Yet, for theoretical clarity, it is critical to distinguish interlocking theory from other intersectional analytical frameworks. It should be noted that there is also a strong post-structuralist critique of any form of intersectional analysis – a viewpoint known as post-intersectional theory. The basic argument is that all identity categories are social constructs and, thereby, inherently essentialist. Yet, while many anarchist streams informed by post-structuralism (such as post-anarchists, anarcha-feminists, queer anarchist theorists, etc.), reject universals and are critical of identity politics, they still support interdependent/interlocking frameworks.
3 The Catalyst Project is an activist training organization that focuses on racial justice and workers' rights.
4 Social ecology and green anarchist perspectives, for instance, maintain that it is essential to end human domination and exploitation of the earth if we are to eliminate all forms of hierarchy. Similarly, animal liberationists – many of whom are anarchists – consider veganism as vital for ending the enslavement of sentient beings. For them, disregard for animal life merely reifies violent hierarchical relations.

References

Ackelsberg, M.A. 1996. "Identity Politics, Political Identities: Thoughts Toward a Multicultural Politics." *Frontiers: A Journal of Women Studies* 16(1): 87–100.
Anarchist People of Color, ed. 2004. "Our Culture, Our Resistance: People of Color Speak Out on Anarchism, Race, Class and Gender." http://tucsonabc.org/wp-content/uploads/2016/04/ocor_book_1.pdf.
Anarchist People of Color in Oakland. 2015. "Anarchy in the Town: An Intro for People of Color." The Anarchist Library. https://theanarchistlibrary.org/library/anarchist-people-of-color-anarchy-in-the-town?v=1466192603.
Bakunin, Mikhail. 1867. "Solidarity in Liberty: The Workers' Path to Freedom." Anarchy Archives. http://dwardmac.pitzer.edu/Anarchist_Archives/bakunin/writings/Bakliberty.html.
Bakunin, Mikhail. 2005. "God and the State." In *No Gods, No Masters*, edited by Daniel Guérin, 150–152. Oakland, CA: AK Press.
Bamyeh, Mohammed. 2010. *Anarchy as Order: The History and Future of Civic Humanity*. Lanham, MD: Rowman and Littlefield.
Ben-Moshe, Liat, Anthony J. Nocella, II, and A.J. Withers. 2012. "Queer-Cripping Anarchism: Intersections and Reflections on Anarchism, Queerness, and Dis-ability." In *Queering Anarchism: Addressing and Undressing Power and Desire*, edited by C.B. Daring, J. Rogue, Deric Shannon, and Abbey Volcano, 207–220. Oakland, CA: AK Press.
Berkman, Alexander. 1977 [1929]. *ABC of Anarchism*. New York: Freedom Press. https://libcom.org/files/AlexanderBerkman-ABCofAnarchism.pdf.
Bey, Hakim. 1987. "Post-Anarchy Anarchism." The Anarchist Library. http://theanarchistlibrary.org/library/hakim-bey-post-anarchism-anarchy.
Bookchin, Murray. 1964. "Ecology and Revolutionary Thought." The Anarchist Library. https://theanarchistlibrary.org/library/lewis-herber-murray-bookchin-ecology-and-revolutionary-thought.
Butler, Judith. 1990. *Gender Trouble: Feminism and the Subversion of Identity*. London: Routledge.
Collins, Patricia Hill. 1990. "Black Feminist Thought in the Matrix of Domination." In *Black Feminist Thought: Knowledge, Consciousness, and the Politics of Empowerment*, 221–238. Boston: Unwin Hyman. www.hartford-hwp.com/archives/45a/252.html.

Collins, Patricia Hill. 2000. *Black Feminist Thought: Knowledge, Consciousness, and the Politics of Empowerment*, 2nd edition. New York: Routledge.

Combahee River Collective. 1983. "A Black Feminist Statement." In *This Bridge Called My Back: Writings by Radical Women of Color*, edited by Cherríe Moraga and Gloria Anzaldúa, 210–218. New York: Kitchen Table / Women of Color Press.

Conrad, Ryan. 2012. "Gay Marriage and Queer Love." In *Queering Anarchism: Addressing and Undressing Power and Desire*, edited by C.B. Daring, J. Rogue, Deric Shannon, and Abbey Volcano, 19–24. Oakland, CA: AK Press.

Cornell, Andrew. 2011. "A New Anarchism Emerges, 1940–1954." *Journal for the Study of Radicalism* 5(1): 105–131.

Craib, Raymond. 2015. "A Foreword." In *No Gods, No Masters, No Peripheries: Global Anarchisms*, edited by Barry Maxwell and Raymond Craib, 1–8. Oakland, CA: PM Press.

Crass, Chris. 2013. *Towards Collective Liberation: Anti-Racist Organizing, Feminist Praxis, and Movement Building Strategy*. Oakland, CA: PM Press.

Crenshaw, Kimberlé. 1991. "Mapping the Margins: Intersectionality, Identity Politics, and Violence Against Women of Color." *Stanford Law Review* 43(6): 1241–1299.

Daring, C.B., J. Rogue, Abbey Volcano, and Deric Shannon. 2012. "Introduction: Queer Meet Anarchism, Anarchism Meet Queer." In *Queering Anarchism: Addressing and Undressing Power and Desire*, edited by C.B. Daring, J. Rogue, Deric Shannon, and Abbey Volcano, 5–18. Oakland, CA: AK Press.

Dragonowl, Lupus. 2015. "Against Identity Politics." *Anarchy – A Journal of Desire Armed* 76: 29–51.

Dunbar-Ortiz, Roxanne. 2012. "Quiet Rumours: An Introduction." In *Quiet Rumors: An Anarcha-Feminist Reader*, edited by Dark Star Collective, 11. Oakland, CA: AK Press.

Epstein, Barbara. 1991. *Political Protest & Cultural Revolution: Nonviolent Direct Action in the 1970s and 1980s*. Berkeley: University of California Press.

Federici, Silvia. 2015. "Global Anarchism: Provocations." In *No Gods, No Masters, No Peripheries: Global Anarchisms*, edited by Barry Maxwell and Raymond Craib, 349–358. Oakland, CA: PM Press.

Foucault, Michel. 1978–86. *The History of Sexuality*, 3 vols. Translated by Robert Hurley. New York: Pantheon.

Freeden, Michael. 2003. *Ideology: A Very Short Introduction*. Oxford: Oxford University Press.

Goldman, Emma. 1911. "Marriage and Love." In *Anarchism and Other Essays*, Second Revised Edition, 233–245. New York and London: Mother Earth Publishing Association. http://dwardmac.pitzer.edu/Anarchist_Archives/goldman/aando/marriageandlove.html.

Gordon, Uri. 2010. "Anarchists Against the Wall: Anarchist Mobilization in the Israeli–Palestinian Conflict." *Peace & Change* 35(3): 412–433.

Gordon, Uri. 2015. "Anarchism and Multiculturalism." In *Philosophies of Multiculturalism: Beyond Liberalism*, edited by Luís Cordeiro-Rodrigues and Marko Simendić, 63–79. London: Routledge.

Halberstam, Jack. 1998. *Female Masculinity*. Durham, NC: Duke University Press.

Hall, Lauren. 2016. "Indigenist Intersectionality: Decolonizing and Reweaving an Indigenous Eco-Queer Feminism and Anarchism." *Perspectives in Anarchist Theory* 29: 81–93.

Halperin, David. 1997. *Saint Foucault: Towards a Gay Hagiography*. Oxford: Oxford University Press.

hooks, bell. 1984. *Feminist Theory: From Margin to Center*. Cambridge, MA: South End Press.

Indigenous Action Media. 2015. "Accomplices Not Allies: Abolishing the Ally Industrial Complex." In *Taking Sides: Revolutionary Solidarity and the Poverty of Liberalism*, edited by Cindy Milstein, 85–96. Oakland, CA: AK Press.
Jeppesen, Sandra. 2012. "Queering Heterosexuality." In *Queering Anarchism: Addressing and Undressing Power and Desire*, edited by C.B. Daring, J. Rogue, Deric Shannon, and Abbey Volcano, 147–164. Oakland, CA: AK Press.
Kissack, Terrence. 2007. *Free Comrades: Anarchism and Homosexuality in the United States, 1895–1917*. Oakland, CA: AK Press.
Klein, Hilary. 2015. "The Zapatista Movement: Blending Indigenous Traditions with Revolutionary Praxis." In *No Gods, No Masters, No Peripheries: Global Anarchisms*, edited by Barry Maxwell and Raymond Craib, 22–43. Oakland, CA: PM Press.
Klein, Naomi. 2013. "Dancing the World into Being: A Conversation with Idle No More's Leanne Simpson." *Yes! Magazine* March 5.
Marshall, Peter. 2009. *Demanding the Impossible: A History of Anarchism*. Oakland, CA: PM Press.
Martinez, Elizabeth (Betita), and Arnoldo Garcia. 2004. "Zapatismo – What is Zapatismo? A Brief Definition for Activists." In *Globalize Liberation: How to Uproot the System and Build a Better World*, edited by David Solnit, 213–216. San Francisco: City Lights Books.
Maxwell, Barry, and Raymond Craib, eds. 2015. *No Gods, No Masters, No Peripheries: Global Anarchisms*. Oakland, CA: PM Press.
May, Todd. 2007. "Jacques Rancière and the Ethics of Equality." *SubStance* 36(2): 20–36.
Mühsam, Erich. 1932. "The Liberation of Society from the State: What is Communist Anarchism?" Translated by C.R. Edmonston. The Anarchist Library. http://theanarchistlibrary.org/library/erich-muhsam-the-liberation-of-society-from-the-state-what-is-communist-anarchism.
Newman, Saul. 2007. "Anarchism, Poststructuralism and the Future of Radical Politics." *SubStance* 36(2): 3–19.
Parsons, Lucy. 2004. *Freedom, Equality & Solidarity: Writings & Speeches, 1878–1937*. Edited by Gale Ahrens. Chicago: Charles H. Kerr.
Perspectives Editorial Collective. 2000. "Poststructuralist Anarchism: An Interview with Todd May." *Perspectives on Anarchist Theory* 4(2): 1, 6–7, 12.
Proudhon, Pierre-Joseph. 2005. "Peoples' Election Manifesto." In *No Gods, No Masters*, edited by Daniel Guérin, 71–80. Oakland, CA: AK Press.
Ramnath, Maia. 2012. "Colonialism." Institute for Anarchist Studies, Lexicon Series. www.revolutionbythebook.akpress.org/wp-content/uploads/2012/03/lex_colonialism_master.pdf.
Ramnath, Maia. 2013. *Decolonizing Anarchism: An Antiauthoritarian History of India's Liberation Struggle*. Oakland, CA: AK Press.
Reitan, Ruth. 2007. *Global Activism*. London: Routledge.
Revolutionary Anarcha-Feminist Group Dublin. 2012. "Why Anarcha-Feminism?" In *Quiet Rumors: An Anarcha-Feminist Reader*, edited by Dark Star Collective, 13–14. Oakland, CA: AK Press.
Rogue, J., and Abbey Volcano. 2012. "Insurrection at the Intersection: Feminism, Intersectionality, and Anarchism." In *Quiet Rumors: An Anarcha-Feminist Reader*, edited by Dark Star Collective, 43–46. Oakland, CA: AK Press.
Runkle, Gerald. 1972. *Anarchism: Old and New*. New York: Delacorte Press.
Scott, James C. 2010. *The Art of Not Being Governed: An Anarchist History of Upland Southeast Asia*. Princeton, NJ: Princeton University Press.

Sium, Anna, Chandni Desai, and Eric Ritskes. 2012. "Towards the 'Tangible Unknown': Decolonization and the Indigenous Future." *Decolonization* 1(1): I-XIII.

Volcano, Abbey. 2012. "Police at the Borders." In *Queering Anarchism: Addressing and Undressing Power and Desire*, edited by C.B. Daring, J. Rogue, Deric Shannon, and Abbey Volcano, 33–42. Oakland, CA: AK Press.

Walia, Harsha. 2013. *Undoing Border Imperialism*. Oakland, CA: AK Press.

Watson, Lilla. n.d. *Lilla: International Women's Network*. https://lillanetwork.wordpress.com/about/.

Woodcock, George. 1962. *Anarchism: A History of Libertarian Ideas and Movements*. Cleveland: World Publishing.

12

REFORM

Leonard Williams

In Michael Freeden's morphological approach to understanding ideologies, most of the attention is given to the core concepts that constitute the very identity of an ideological tradition (Freeden 2013). Relatively little attention, however, has been paid to the peripheral concepts that enable an ideology to adapt to a range of social and political contexts. In the evolution of an ideological stance, such concepts typically change more frequently than do core or adjacent ones. They also appear at the "interface between the conceptual arrangement of an ideology and the social practices, events, and contingencies that occur in its environment" (Freeden 2013, 125–126).

In thinking about the anarchist tradition, I would argue that *reform* falls into the domain of a peripheral concept. This may seem an odd stance to take, given anarchism's revolutionary and insurrectionist heritage. Indeed, for most people, the prevailing image of an anarchist is either that of the bearded, bomb-in-hand practitioner of *l'attentat* or that of the balaclava-clad brick-thrower smashing a plate-glass window (Thompson 2010). Sometimes it seems as if no one is more anarchist than the street-fighting youth opposing everything, feeding on riot porn, and battling the cops at a moment's notice. Yet those standard pictures are hard to square with the range of other (dis)guises that anarchists may adopt – for instance, art critics and philosophers, infoshop clerks and vegan restaurateurs, or radical lawyers and community organizers. In such (dis)guises, anarchist activists can blend in, reach out, and spread the word to new audiences; they can build affinities, influence movements, and find new contexts in which to challenge structures of domination. These anarchists focus their energies on building networks of activists, participating in movements embracing a diversity of tactics, and/or constructing alternative institutions (Ehrlich 1996).

Framing our thinking about radical politics as a choice between reform and revolution has a long history within the socialist tradition (Luxemburg 1999

[1900]). Activists and thinkers in contemporary anarchist circles wrestle with similar issues (Olson 2009). In the sections that follow, I will briefly explore anarchist views about the concept of reform. The story to be told is largely one of ambivalent identities and practices – a perpetual tension between revolutionary ambitions and pragmatic accommodations. Given limited time and space, though, my telling of that story cannot hope to be comprehensive in scope or rich in detail. Instead, I will present selected highlights and illustrative examples.

Identities

The most pervasive understanding of anarchist identity is a simple one: an anarchist *is* a revolutionary. Certainly, that is how such luminaries as Mikhail Bakunin (1866) and Errico Malatesta (2014) spoke about things. Works of anarchist theory and practice repeatedly focus on revolutionary spirit, insurrection, and a ruthless opposition to everything existing. As noted above, the image of the anarchist in popular culture remains that of the revolutionary activist, poised to throw the brick or bomb that would draw the battle lines and call the masses to action.

All the same, there are suggestions in the anarchist tradition that not everything can be or should be cast aside. Pierre-Joseph Proudhon (2011), for example, identified quite a few economic and social practices (economic co-operatives, for example) that could be maintained and still benefit ordinary people. Gustav Landauer (2010) suggested that the focus should be on inventing new forms of social relationships, not blowing them up or otherwise abandoning them altogether. More recently, James C. Scott (2012) has suggested that anarchists should embrace politics instead of pressing for an anti-political theory and practice; indeed, he asserted that our practice should be one of "anarchist calisthenics," of preparing for the great refusal, all the while giving anarchism two cheers. In a more spiritual vein, Jamie Heckert (2012, 112) has called for an "anarchy without opposition" – one through which its advocates can genuinely listen "across lines of identity and ideology."

No matter how it has been conceived, the idea of revolution has always held out the hope of radical change. It pursues major social, political, and economic transformations from a standpoint of total opposition to the established order, seeking rapid demolition of the bedrock institutions supporting the status quo. By contrast, advocates of reform have suggested that revolution – on the off chance it succeeds – inevitably brings such deleterious consequences as violence and tyranny. If the aim is for people to welcome and accept change (rather than have it imposed upon them), then one needs to take a more democratic, evolutionary approach. Reforms obtained in this fashion are deemed to be longer lasting and more palatable than those brought by revolution.

The tension between reform and revolution is a longstanding one within the anarchist tradition – just as it has been in other radical political arenas. In the context of anarchism's revolutionary standpoint, the path of gradual reform – when understood as a political strategy – has been continually challenged. As Malatesta (n.d.) observed:

> It is not true to say therefore, that revolutionaries are systematically opposed to improvements, to reforms. They oppose the reformists on the one hand because their methods are less effective for securing reforms from governments and employers, who only give in through fear, and on the other hand because very often the reforms they prefer are those which not only bring doubtful immediate benefits, but also serve to consolidate the existing regime and to give the workers a vested interest in its continued existence.

The trope of reform-or-revolution thus forms the boundary along which people are deemed to be either bourgeois poseurs or authentic anarchists. Indeed, the reform-versus-revolution binary underlies the reception given to two prominent anarchist thinkers – Noam Chomsky and Murray Bookchin. Their views, and the labels attached to them, help illustrate how the concept of reform has operated within the anarchist tradition.

In 1988, Noam Chomsky (2004, 630) told an interviewer this: "I don't think most political terms mean much, to tell you the truth. If you wanted a term, I'm some kind of anarchist. But the terms don't mean much." Often an influential anarchist, Chomsky (2005, 135) initially identified as little more than a "derivative fellow traveler." Best known for his critiques of foreign policy and the mass media, Chomsky (2005, 191) eventually proclaimed that his "personal visions are fairly traditional anarchist ones, with origins in the Enlightenment and classical liberalism." Yet, the question of whether Chomsky really is an anarchist has often been asked.

For Chomsky, anarchism is "just the point of view that says that people have the right to be free, and if there are constraints on that freedom then you've got to justify them" (Mitchell and Schoeffel 2002, 202). As a libertarian socialism, anarchism aims "to seek out and identify structures of authority, hierarchy, and domination in every aspect of life, and to challenge them" (Chomsky 2005, 178). While even revolutionary anarchists would agree with this characterization, Chomsky's views have been criticized for relying upon more reformist notions of workers' control, self-management, and a radically democratic society. He has also run into trouble for suggesting that anarchists may need to defend, rather than simply attack, certain state institutions – while nevertheless seeking to democratize them (Chomsky 2005, 194, 212–215). In short, one widespread claim is that Chomsky cannot be an anarchist because he advocates a politics of reform. Commenting on a book of interviews with Chomsky, John Zerzan (2009) once noted that it "supposedly provides the answers to such questions as 'Why, as a supporter of anarchist ideals, he is in favor of strengthening the federal government.' The real answer, painfully obvious, is that he is not an anarchist at all."

To be sure, Chomsky does say that, in the face of neoliberal attacks on the welfare state, "the immediate goal of even committed anarchists should be to defend some state institutions, while helping to pry them open to more meaningful public participation, and ultimately to dismantle them in a much more free society" (Mitchell and Schoeffel 2002, 344). Hostile to much that passes for revolutionary theory, Chomsky's (2012, 91) politics encourages people to work within a range of opportunities "from electoral politics to demonstrations, resistance and organizing public pressure." Why? Simply because people must be persuaded that institutional change is necessary, that it is worth the risk and the effort. He (Chomsky 2007, 121) writes: "That's why every serious revolutionary is a reformist. If you are a serious revolutionary, you don't want a coup. You want changes to come from below, from the organized population, but why should people be willing to undertake what's involved unless they think that the institutions don't permit them to achieve just and proper goals?" In this context, the question remains: Is Chomsky an *anarchist*? Although rooted in conventional notions of reform, Chomsky's values, principles, and persistent critiques of power seem to make him *anarchist enough* for most activists and thinkers.

What about Bookchin? Although he was an important voice for anarchist and ecological concerns for decades, Bookchin came to notoriety with the 1971 publication of *Post-Scarcity Anarchism* (Bookchin 2004). Since then, he has long been a central, if paradoxical, figure in the anarchist pantheon. At times hailed as the most significant anarchist theorist of the twentieth century, he has been criticized for being a statist masquerading as an anarchist (Marshall 2010).

A long-time radical thinker, Bookchin continually aimed to create a libertarian socialist movement that would restructure society on the bases of self-sufficiency and self-management (Bookchin and Foreman 1991, 80–81). Neither the student activists of the Sixties nor the deep ecologists that followed could create that sort of movement, however. He quarreled with both the counterculture's narcissism and the anti-technological stance of the ecologists. Bookchin eventually turned from using relatively concrete political terms such as social ecology and anarchism, and began describing his positions in a more abstract and philosophical vocabulary – dialectical naturalism, libertarian municipalism, and communalism.

Was Bookchin an anarchist? Certainly, critics such as Bob Black (1997) never thought so. Indeed, whether Bookchin was discussing the Athenian *polis* or describing libertarian municipalism, Black saw his views as a form of statism, because it ultimately rested upon a belief in government – albeit a democratic one. Bookchin's ultimate break with the anarchist movement can be attributed to a number of factors – bitter quarrels with a host of activists, perpetual reevaluations of his core ideas, and a general acceptance of political institutions (White 2008, 185–186). While the political break with anarchism could be dated to the 1990s, the intellectual break may well have come with the publication of *The Ecology of Freedom* (Bookchin 1982). Whether he wrote as a thinking activist or as a comprehensive theorist, and no matter how reformist his actions, Bookchin's ideas share enough family resemblances with those of other anarchists for him to be counted among their number. Toward the end of his career, his central theme remained that we should reopen "a public sphere in flat opposition to statism, one that allows for maximum democracy in the literal sense of the term, and to create in embryonic form the institutions that can give power to a people generally" (Biehl 1997, 175).

Our thinking about the question of political identity, about who is and who is not an *anarchist*, has thus been shaped by the binary of reform-versus-revolution. For activists and theorists alike, it seems that assessments of others' authenticity, purity, or ideological correctness have always been present. Such assessments have not appeared only with the emergence of a "lifestyle anarchism," for they can be found in the debates and struggles within the workers' movement that coalesced into the First International (Bookchin 1995; Graham 2015). The contrast between revolutionary commitments and reformist compromises belongs not just to the past of conspiracies and communes, but also to the present of insurrections and infoshops. People have long used this contrast to distinguish true comrades from false ones, correct actions from wrong ones.

Practices

The long-sought social and political changes that anarchists have desired likely cannot be brought about simply by choosing one's theorists and comrades carefully. Changing the world is not only about the saying or the being; it must also be about the doing. If anarchism rests on "an ethical duty to question and resist domination in all its forms," if it embraces an "ethics of commitment and politics of resistance," then it should appeal to poststructuralist thinkers and anti-authoritarian activists alike (Newman 2001, 166; Critchley 2007, 3). In accepting that duty and meeting its demands, anarchists continually challenge the state and question authority. Operating as a tactical theory (focused on social and political practice) rather than a strategic one (focused on the ultimate goal), anarchism embodies a pervasive and compelling spirit of revolt (May 1994). As such, anarchism should be understood as a practical doctrine, as a fighting creed formed in the context of action, as a form of thinking through doing.

Focusing on either seizing state power or pursuing a reformist program would simply reinstitute oppression. As John Holloway (2005, 17) reminds us, "You cannot build a society of non-power relations by conquering power. Once the logic of power is adopted, the struggle against power is already lost." Rather, the point of political activity is to act as if one were already free. Anarchist practice is thus built upon a preference for self-directed action, for cooperation without hierarchy or domination, for a prefigurative politics. More so than most ideological traditions, it encourages people to take matters into their own hands, to engage in direct action, to advance the cause through various forms of "propaganda of the deed." In recent years, as anarchist politics again revived, debates over the direction of the movement reappeared. In those debates, the trope of insurrection took root and the meme of insurrectionary anarchism created "new forms of activism, forms that discard older logics of protest, visibility and organization and embrace instead spontaneity and invisibility" (Cooper 2009; The Invisible Committee 2009). Amid the numbing spectacle that is modern life, insurrection throws off the ideological masks of the old society, and lays the groundwork for the new one.

The radical breaks associated with insurrection do not exhaust anarchist possibilities, however. As Landauer (2010, 214) famously noted, "The State is a social relationship; a certain way of people relating to one another. It can be destroyed only by creating new social relationships; i.e., by people relating to one another differently." On that view, anarchist practice must also be focused on creating institutions, resources, skills, and experiences that delegitimize authority and induce people to change their perspectives. Building the new society in the shell of the old lets activists demonstrate that there is indeed an alternative to the present order, lets them support reforms without embracing a reformist orientation. Realizing that anarchist aspirations cannot be achieved all in one go, no less a revolutionary spirit than Malatesta (2014, 849; Turcato 2015, 213–238) concluded that "anarchism is of necessity gradualist."

The binary of revolution-versus-reform has thus infused anarchist practice just as much as it has shaped anarchist identity. Activists and theorists alike have sought to disrupt the binary or take sides. For some, the proper practical response is one of thoroughgoing revolutionism. The recent popularity of insurrectionist ideas represents one important manifestation of this approach, as has the emergence of the trope of ferality, becoming wild (Feral Faun 2005; de Acosta 2010; Green Anarchy and Wild Roots Collective 2004). One may recognize, though, that a lifetime of feral expression can be enervating and that insurrections are infrequent and often short-lived. A rational anarchist needs both tactical orientation and strategic guidance, if one's actions are to be fruitful, let alone meaningful. One must weigh the pros and cons of momentary expressions of rage against those associated with longer-term efforts to build organizations and culture. Whenever it seeks to disrupt the binary by preferring its revolutionary side, the anarchist tradition must still consider the question of reform (Price 2006).

Perhaps we should note a few cases in which anarchist thinkers and activists have wrestled with questions of reform and reformism. The specific questions on which these issues have emerged in the anarchist tradition are legion. We could point to economic matters such as labor disputes over the eight-hour day and the minimum wage or to government legislation that might benefit producer and consumer cooperatives. Alternatively, our discussion could focus on local issues of gentrification or more universal goals such as women's liberation, on continuing issues facing movement politics (e.g., diversity of tactics) or event-focused concerns of the moment (e.g., Occupy Wall Street). Though the possibilities are many, I would like to consider the tensions between reform and revolution in the context of two recent debates within the North American anarchist community.

Marriage Equality

Let me focus first on marriage equality. An issue that taps into sometimes overlooked considerations of sexuality and gender, it also raises matters in which public policy figures front and center. State and local policymakers repeatedly have confronted the issue; decades of popular referendums have produced varying levels of support for both sides of the question; interest groups and movement activists have aimed to influence both government officials and the public at large. Certainly, on no other issue has the United States seen such a dramatic shift in public opinion, even prior to the Supreme Court decision in *Obergefell v. Hodges* (2015).

No discussion of anarchist views in this area should neglect the decades of anarcha-feminist efforts to oppose sexism, the state, and capitalism (Dark Star Collective 2012). Nor should we neglect the more recent framework of intersectionality that has shaped both liberal and radical feminist thinking on these matters, with the anarchist conception of intersectionality resting not only on an anti-state and anti-capitalist perspective, but also on "a revolutionary stance regarding white supremacy and heteropatriarchy" (Rogue and Volcano 2012, 45). When one thinks about gender and revolution from the perspective of queer theory, as well as feminism, it reinforces the idea that being an anarchist requires struggling against all forms of domination (Milstein 2010). Acting as an anarchist thus means "fighting against and in some instances unlearning relations of domination including, but not limited to, racism, ableism, sexism, heterosexism, and so on" (Daring et al. 2012, 16). Individual efforts to unlearn those relations, to understand patterns of domination in an intersectional fashion, may not yet be enough to get one past reformism. Indeed, some activists promote a structural analysis of oppression, yet immerse themselves in practices that reduce multiple, diverse "freedom struggles to current campaigns for increased electoral representation or symbolic inclusion" (Tipu's Tiger 2015, 52).

In this context, Ryan Conrad (2012, 34) offers a critique of mainstream approaches to marriage equality by asking an important question: "Do we really want full inclusion in the institution of marriage, a social contract that explicitly limits the ways in which we can organize our erotic and emotional lives?" If the state sanctions some relations but not others, should the goal be to have it sanction all? The marriage equality movement certainly has argued as if it should – for both principled and utilitarian reasons (Shantz 2013; Spade and Willse 2013). Conrad (2012, 34–40) attributes that reformist approach to the reliance of mainstream gay and lesbian organizations on both a discourse of individual rights (including a right to love one's chosen partner) and a discourse of equality. Regardless of the discursive framework employed, however, mainstream efforts to seek marriage equality are fundamentally limited. By accepting the state's role in regulating human relationships at all, one has already lost much of value. Such pragmatic, reformist impulses do not permit the kind of radical queer future that Conrad and other anarchists might envision. Only a world in which no state exists, in which no authority can sanction any kind of relationship, would be able to meet the entire range of material and affective needs that people have.

Incarceration

Another issue that raises questions of reform and revolution is that of incarceration. As it has played out in the United States, incarceration not only has been addressed by a host of mainstream figures (elected officials, candidates for office, and academics, for example), but also has engaged the attention and energies of participants in a variety of movements (prison reform, prison abolition, and more recently, Black Lives Matter). Another reason for focusing on incarceration is that prisons have been a longstanding focus of anarchist political work. Interestingly, Alexander Berkman (1929) linked a discussion of crime and prison to his critique of reformers and politicians. It makes sense, then, for us to explore challenges to the system of incarceration as a means for understanding anarchist views about reform.

Today, prison abolition seems to be an important concern for any movement dedicated to radical social and political change. Layne Mullett (2015, 27) notes that while "reform efforts might cause the structures of mass incarceration to shift, and lead to decreases in the prison population …, a more fundamental transformation is necessary if we hope to see an actual rather than cosmetic shift in the meaning and practice of 'justice.'" While highlighting and removing the many factors that produce mass incarceration is an important task, one must recognize that the prison system could not operate, let alone exist, without also reflecting the racism, sexism, heterosexism, and class structure characteristic of the broader society. In short, programs of reform – no matter how helpful – are just never enough; they can never get around to addressing the structural roots of any social problem. Where the reformer wants to improve conditions by passing laws, the revolutionary believes in abolishing social and political evils altogether (Berkman 2008, 1).

Should anarchists and other radicals ignore or refuse to participate in reform efforts, though? Far from it. Just as advocates of abolition often work with or demonstrate alongside advocates of reform, so the most diehard abolitionist would not reject hard-won reforms that have reshaped sentencing and parole practices. Despite their limitations, struggles to enact reforms that alter the prison-industrial complex can provide opportunities to build new alliances and to mobilize activists for struggles against existing systems of oppression. Indeed, Mullett (2015, 33) suggests that anarchists pursue a strategy of *decarceration*, which "involves chipping away at the policies and practices that build up the criminal legal system." Agitation for new sentencing policies or for the decriminalization of drug use, say, cannot be left to the mainstream political actors alone. "At their best, decarceration strategies win real victories that bring people home from prison or keep people from going to prison, while building a bigger and more powerful movement that can mount larger challenges to the prison system itself" (Mullett 2015, 33). In other words, reform efforts are fine enough in the short run, but they are no substitute for building an authentically radical, even revolutionary movement.

Militant Reformism?

These considerations once again highlight the tension between reform and revolution. In the aftermath of Occupy Wall Street, there was an online discussion about the possibilities of reform featuring Juan Conatz (2011) and Nate Hawthorne (2011). They seemed to agree that reforms are possible, if unlikely, but even so, Hawthorne was careful to note that reform largely works to support the interests of capitalism and capitalists. Social, economic, and political reforms that further entrench capital and the State have long been antagonistic to revolution-minded socialists and anarchists alike (Gorz 1968; Price 2007).

Yet, as Robin Hahnel (2005) notes: "Campaigns to reform capitalism and building alternative institutions within capitalism are both integral parts of a successful strategy to accomplish in this century what we failed to accomplish in the past century – namely, making this century capitalism's last!" Recognizing the need to pursue both short-term and long-term goals, André Gorz (1968, 111–112, original emphasis) recommended a socialist practice "which *starts* with the gradual application of a coherent programme of reforms, but which can only proceed by way of a succession of more or less violent, sometimes successful, sometimes unsuccessful, trials of strength" – in other words, modern socialist politics required efforts toward yielding what he later called "non-reformist reforms" or "structural reforms" that could simultaneously attack the system and lay the foundation for future, more radical changes (Rooksby 2015).

The neoliberal era of the last forty years has not only threatened the economic and political gains made since the 1930s, it has also yielded significant challenges for any number of movements seeking to create an alternative future (Foucault 2004; Brown 2015). In that context, a question naturally arises: "namely, how radicals can and should relate to militant reformist groupings" and struggles (Hawthorne 2015). Such a question both supports and follows the identification of reform as a peripheral concept for anarchism and other radical ideologies. Its answer, of course, will depend on the species of reform being pursued. For anarchists, reform efforts that co-opt activists or channel otherwise revolutionary politics – ones that limit action to the politics of demand (Day 2005) – doubtless would be rejected. Proposals that would remedy problems in ways that could achieve ready victories for social movements, build alliances among radical political agents, or promote direct action and mutual aid would be embraced just as readily. Efforts to ameliorate or mitigate harms, but do not clearly and directly promote future revolutionary action, are precisely the ones that would produce extended debates about anarchist identity and practice.

Conclusions

The tension between reform and revolution within the anarchist tradition remains. Indeed, the poles of that binary have shaped discussions of both anarchist identity and anarchist practice. With anarchism being revolutionary at its core, the prevalent attitude towards reform is an ambivalent one. Because of this decidedly ambivalent approach, the very idea of reform quite naturally appears as a peripheral concept within the anarchist framework.

When prominent reform proposals are front and center, they clearly should be considered by mainstream activists and anarchists alike. What stance should anarchists take toward such reforms when they are proposed or even enacted? Most commonly, anarchists will certainly engage with reform proposals on a case-by-case basis. They will have to weigh and balance the ethical and political implications of engaging in this sort of struggle or joining with that sort of movement. Faced with an inherent ambivalence, rooted in a sort of revolutionary gradualism, the most likely response to the question of endorsing any given reform is "yes, but ..." In such a reply, the *yes* acknowledges that reforms could make life better for people, move us a bit closer to a society of genuine mutual aid, while the *but* recognizes the obvious limitations that reforms have amid the twin evils of capitalism and domination.

Rather than focus on fostering cataclysm or rupture, to the exclusion of capitulation or acceptance, perhaps we should instead be attending to such anarchist ideas as gradualism or even broader concepts such as punctuated equilibrium. Micropolitics, not macro; the spirit of revolt, rather than fealty to the Revolution. With an emphasis on struggle and community, the focus of radical theory and practice might not be upon achieving a certain outcome, but upon carrying forward with a process. It is not about the thinking or the saying of the revolution; it is about the doing of rebellion every day. *La lutte continue* ... the struggle continues.

In the end, an anarchist stance toward resolving the question of revolution or reform might come to echo that of Stuart White (2007, 24), who asserted that "the practical role of the anarchist is not to build this unattainable dream, but to push the messy complexity of society in a more anarchist direction." Such a faith in the value of small acts of resistance, in the here and now rather than in the years to come, may well be the only thing to sustain us in the continuing struggle.

References

Bakunin, Mikhail. 1866. "Revolutionary Catechism." The Anarchist Library. Last modified 23 February 2009. Accessed 5 July 2017. https://theanarchistlibrary.org/library/michail-bakunin-revolutionary-catechism.

Berkman, Alexander. 1929. "What Is Communist Anarchism?" The Anarchist Library. Last modified 12 March 2009. Accessed 5 July 2017. http://theanarchistlibrary.org/library/alexander-berkman-what-is-communist-anarchism.

Berkman, Alexander. 2008. *Reformers, Socialists, and Communists: An Anarchist Critique.* Edmonton, Alberta: thoughtcrime ink.

Biehl, Janet, ed. 1997. *The Murray Bookchin Reader.* London: Cassell.

Black, Bob. 1997. *Anarchy after Leftism.* Columbia, MO: Columbia Alternative Library.

Bookchin, Murray. 1982. *The Ecology of Freedom: The Emergence and Dissolution of Hierarchy.* Palo Alto, CA: Cheshire Books.

Bookchin, Murray. 1995. *Social Anarchism or Lifestyle Anarchism: An Unbridgeable Chasm.* Oakland, CA: AK Press.

Bookchin, Murray. 2004. *Post-Scarcity Anarchism.* 3rd ed. Oakland, CA: AK Press. Original edition, 1971.

Bookchin, Murray, and Dave Foreman. 1991. *Defending the Earth: A Dialogue Between Murray Bookchin and Dave Foreman.* Montréal: Black Rose Books.

Brown, Wendy. 2015. *Undoing the Demos: Neoliberalism's Stealth Revolution.* Brooklyn, NY: Zone Books.

Chomsky, Noam. 2004. *Language and Politics.* Edited by C. P. Otero. 2nd ed. Oakland, CA: AK Press.

Chomsky, Noam. 2005. *Chomsky on Anarchism.* Edited by Barry Pateman. Oakland, CA: AK Press.

Chomsky, Noam. 2007. *What We Say Goes: Conversations on U.S. Power in a Changing World.* New York: Metropolitan Books.

Chomsky, Noam. 2012. *Occupy.* Occupied Media Pamphlet Series. Brooklyn, NY: Zuccotti Park Press.

Conatz, Juan. 2011. "Is Reform Possible?" libcom.org. Accessed 28 February 2016. https://libcom.org/blog/reform-possible-22122011.

Conrad, Ryan. 2012. "Gay Marriage and Queer Love." In *Queering Anarchism: Addressing and Undressing Power and Desire,* edited by C. B. Daring, J. Rogue, Deric Shannon and Abbey Volcano, 33–42. Oakland, CA: AK Press.

Cooper, Sam. 2009. "The Coming Insurrection: Nothing Will Change Without a Revolution." Adbusters. Accessed 5 July 2017. www.adbusters.org/article/the-coming-insurrection-3/.

Critchley, Simon. 2007. *Infinitely Demanding: Ethics of Commitment, Politics of Resistance.* London: Verso.

Daring, C. B., J. Rogue, Abbey Volcano, and Deric Shannon. 2012. "Queer Meet Anarchism, Anarchism Meet Queer." In *Queering Anarchism: Addressing and Undressing Power and Desire,* edited by C. B. Daring, J. Rogue, Deric Shannon and Abbey Volcano, 11–32. Oakland, CA: AK Press.

Dark Star Collective, ed. 2012. *Quiet Rumours: An Anarcha-Feminist Reader.* 3rd ed. Oakland, CA: AK Press.

Day, Richard J. F. 2005. *Gramsci Is Dead: Anarchist Currents in the Newest Social Movements.* London: Pluto Press.

de Acosta, Alejandro. 2010. "Anarchist Meditations, or: Three Wild Interstices of Anarchism and Philosophy." *Anarchist Developments in Cultural Studies* (1): 117–138.

Ehrlich, Howard J. 1996. "How to Get from Here to There: Building Revolutionary Transfer Culture." In *Reinventing Anarchy, Again,* edited by Howard J. Ehrlich, 331–349. Edinburgh: AK Press.

Feral Faun. 2005. "'Feral Revolution'." In *Against Civilization: Readings and Reflections*, edited by John Zerzan, 227–230. Los Angeles: Feral House.

Foucault, Michel. 2004. *The Birth of Biopolitics: Lectures at the Collège de France, 1978–1979*. Translated by Graham Burchell. New York: Picador.

Freeden, Michael. 2013. "The Morphological Analysis of Ideology." In *The Oxford Handbook of Political Ideologies*, edited by Michael Freeden, Lyman Tower Sargent and Marc Stears, 115–137. Oxford: Oxford University Press.

Gorz, André. 1968. "Reform and Revolution." *Socialist Register* 5: 111–143.

Graham, Robert. 2015. *We Do Not Fear Anarchy, We Invoke It: The First International and the Origins of the Anarchist Movement*. Oakland, CA: AK Press.

Green Anarchy and Wild Roots Collective. 2004. "Rewilding: A Primer for a Balanced Existence Amid the Ruins of Civilization." *Green Anarchy* 16 (Spring). Accessed 19 June 2013. www.archive.org/details/GreenAnarchy16.

Hahnel, Robin. 2005. "Fighting For Reforms Without Becoming Reformist." ZNet. Accessed 17 May 2016. https://zcomm.org/znetarticle/fighting-for-reforms-without-becoming-reformist-by-robin-hahnel/.

Hawthorne, Nate. 2011. "Reform Is Possible and Reformism Is Guaranteed." libcom.org. Accessed 28 February 2016. https://libcom.org/blog/reform-possible-reformism-guaranteed-22122011.

Hawthorne, Nate. 2015. "Militant Reformism and the Prospects for Reforming Capitalism." libcom.org. Accessed 6 July 2017. http://libcom.org/blog/militant-reformism-prospects-reforming-capitalism-17032015.

Heckert, Jamie. 2012. "Anarchy without Opposition." In *Queering Anarchism: Addressing and Undressing Power and Desire*, edited by C. B. Daring, J. Rogue, Deric Shannon and Abbey Volcano, 105–125. Oakland, CA: AK Press.

Holloway, John. 2005. *Change the World Without Taking Power: The Meaning of Revolution Today*. London: Pluto Press.

Landauer, Gustav. 2010. *Revolution and Other Writings: A Political Reader*. Edited by Gabriel Kuhn. Oakland, CA: PM Press.

Luxemburg, Rosa. 1999 [1900]. "Reform or Revolution." Rosa Luxemburg Internet Archive. www.marxists.org/archive/luxemburg/1900/reform-revolution/index.htm.

Malatesta, Errico. 2014. *The Method of Freedom: An Errico Malatesta Reader*. Oakland, CA: AK Press.

Malatesta, Errico. n.d. "Reformism." The Anarchist Library. Last modified 4 March 2009. Accessed 5 July 2017. https://theanarchistlibrary.org/library/errico-malatesta-reformism.

Marshall, Peter. 2010. *Demanding the Impossible: A History of Anarchism*. London: PM Press.

May, Todd. 1994. *The Political Philosophy of Poststructuralist Anarchism*. University Park, PA: Pennsylvania State University Press.

Milstein, Cindy. 2010. *Anarchism and Its Aspirations*. Oakland, CA: AK Press.

Mitchell, Peter R., and John Schoeffel, eds. 2002. *Understanding Power: The Indispensable Chomsky*. New York: The New Press.

Mullett, Layne. 2015. "Brick by Brick: Creating a World Without Prisons." *Perspectives on Anarchist Theory* (28): 27–47.

Newman, Saul. 2001. *From Bakunin to Lacan: Anti-Authoritarianism and the Dislocation of Power*. Lanham, MD: Lexington Books.

Olson, Joel. 2009. "The Problem with Infoshops and Insurrection: U.S. Anarchism, Movement Building, and the Racial Order." In *Contemporary Anarchist Studies: An*

Introductory Anthology of Anarchy in the Academy, edited by Randall Amster, Abraham DeLeon, Luis A. Fernandez, Anthony J. Nocella and Deric Shannon, 35–45. London: Routledge.

Price, Wayne. 2006. "Our Program is the Anarchist Revolution!" The Anarchist Library. Last modified 13 May 2009. Accessed 9 April 2016. http://theanarchistlibrary.org/library/wayne-price-our-program-is-the-anarchist-revolution.

Price, Wayne. 2007. "Fragments of a Reformist Anarchism." The Anarchist Library. Last modified 12 May 2009. Accessed 3 April 2016. https://theanarchistlibrary.org/library/wayne-price-fragments-of-a-reformist-anarchism.

Proudhon, Pierre-Joseph. 2011. *Property Is Theft! A Pierre-Joseph Proudhon Anthology*. Edited by Iain McKay. Oakland, CA: AK Press.

Rogue, J., and Abbey Volcano. 2012. "Insurrection at the Intersections: Feminism, Intersectionality, and Anarchism." In *Quiet Rumours: An Anarcha-Feminist Reader*, edited by Dark Star Collective, 43–46. Oakland, CA: AK Press.

Rooksby, Ed. 2015. "Andre Gorz, Nicos Poulantzas and the Question of 'Structural Reform'." https://edrooksby.wordpress.com/2015/12/31/andre-gorz-nicos-poulantzas-and-the-question-of-structural-reform/.

Scott, James C. 2012. *Two Cheers for Anarchism: Six Easy Pieces on Autonomy, Dignity, and Meaningful Work and Play*. Princeton, NJ: Princeton University Press.

Shantz, Jeff. 2013. "An Anarchist View of the Marriage Debate." *Fifth Estate* (389). www.fifthestate.org/archive/389-summer-2013/anarchist-view-marriage-debate/.

Spade, Dean, and Craig Willse. 2013. "Marriage Will Never Set Us Free." Organizing Upgrade. Accessed 6 July 2017. www.organizingupgrade.com/index.php/modules-menu/beyond-capitalism/item/1002-marriage-will-never-set-us-free.

The Invisible Committee. 2009. *The Coming Insurrection*. Los Angeles: Semiotext(e).

Thompson, A. K. 2010. *Black Bloc, White Riot: Anti-Globalization and the Genealogy of Dissent*. Oakland, CA: AK Press.

Tipu's Tiger. 2015. "Dangerous Allies." In *Taking Sides: Revolutionary Solidarity and the Poverty of Liberalism*, edited by Cindy Milstein, 48–63. Oakland, CA: AK Press.

Turcato, Davide. 2015. *Making Sense of Anarchism: Errico Malatesta's Experiments with Revolution, 1889–1900*. Oakland, CA: AK Press.

White, Damian. 2008. *Bookchin: A Critical Appraisal*. London: Pluto Press.

White, Stuart. 2007. "Making Anarchism Respectable? The Social Philosophy of Colin Ward." *Journal of Political Ideologies* 12(1): 11–28.

Zerzan, John. 2009. "Who Is Chomsky?" The Anarchist Library. Last modified 6 February 2012. Accessed 5 July 2017. http://theanarchistlibrary.org/HTML/John_Zerzan__Who_is_Chomsky_.html.

13

WORK

Ekaterina Chertkovskaya and Konstantin Stoborod

Introduction

In this chapter, we are going to talk about work, a notion which is as familiar to most of us as it is alien(ating). This chapter will not try to absolve work from its negative aura, nor is it going to condemn it. It will focus on work as a concept, its place in anarchist tradition, and the ramifications of the analysis of its ideological status.

Before attempting any sensible discussion on the subject, it is worth trying to introduce a more or less acceptable definition of *work*. The easiest option would be to resort to a definition of such kind: "work is defined as the act by which an employee contracts out her or his labour power as property in the person to an employer for fair monetary compensation" (Brown 1995). This rather simple definition is, however, already problematic and is far from being considered rigorous.[1] Intuitively and experientially we might know that the notion of "work" cannot be exhausted by a strictly economic definition. There are various meanings (sometimes conflicting) that people attach to work – a calling, a chore, a duty, a necessity, a curse, a salvation, and this list could go on almost indefinitely. Consequently, for various theorists as well as for practising anarchists, the subject of work is a matter of ongoing contestation. That is why we find it reasonable not to strive for the rigour of definitions, and thereby, avoid the fallacious quest of analytic philosophy for universal and ahistorical conceptual invariants (Franks 2012, 52).

Instead, we adopt Michael Freeden's (1994; 1996; 2003) conceptual approach to the analysis of ideologies. Informed by this approach, the concept of work has been classified as *peripheral* in this present volume. In this chapter, we will focus on the discussion of work in anarchist thought and suggest the extent to which this categorisation may be considered accurate.

Freeden's analysis centres around identification of the morphology of ideology, which exhibits interdependence between the concepts that vary in their significance for the semantic understanding of ideology. In this sense, the concept of work is "not essential to the comprehension of the core or the survival of the ideology" of anarchism (Freeden 1994, 158). Understood this way, work will be peripherally related to such core anarchist concepts as egalitarianism, non-hierarchy, and autonomy, and will encompass a set of views on how work should be perceived and executed when egalitarianism and autonomy are instituted as paramount in the society. At the same time, it seems clear that the concept of work is a more universal and integral concept for political philosophy, than, say, "pro-choice stance" or "gun control policies," which could be legitimately considered as peripheral concepts of the different versions of contemporary liberalism. We believe that the ideas associated with work should not be considered on par with mere policy proposals, as they not only permeate a considerable amount of writing in anarchist philosophy, but also work is a concept in its own right that "may be found situated closer to the core of *other* ideological configurations" (Freeden 1994, 157). When analysed in the context of what anarchism is up against – namely the hegemony of capitalism and neoliberalism – it is vital to heed the traction that the concept of work has in increasingly economistically stipulated times.

In examining the concept of work in anarchist tradition, this chapter will unfold as follows. First, the landscape of critical theorising of work will be explored, to suggest that it could be misguiding to surmise that work lacks "the generalisation and sophistication associated with a concept" (Freeden 1994, 157). Second, we will make the case for the continued relevance of the anarchist critique of work. Third, we will discuss the possibility of an anarchist work ethic, limiting our search to a set of principles that can be directly derived from anarchist tradition. Finally, as anarchism could and should also be considered as a theory of organisation (Ward 1966; Bookchin 1969; Stoborod and Swann 2014), not least of productive practices, the last section will be devoted to the discussion of some practical aspects of organising work and how they relate to anarchist principles.

Context for the Critical Investigation of the Concept of "Work"

There is no shortage of the critical analysis of work in our society. Since the full-fledged advent of industrial revolution in Western Europe in the nineteenth century, the concept of work has received attention from various theoretical camps, including social theory, Marxism, and anarchism.[2] With either Marx's insights on alienation or Weber's illuminating account of the Protestant work ethic, work within rapidly industrialised settings was problematised at the time. In classic anarchist thought, there would be an agreement that the majority of work done in industrial capitalist societies is degrading, dehumanising, and alienating, which reproduces and sediments hierarchy, authority, and injustice, thereby serving the interests of the more privileged while squeezing out all the vitality from the lives of most people.[3] Industrial settings were also the focus of Harry Braverman's (1998) classical analysis of work in the twentieth century, dominated by Taylorist and Fordist principles in production.

Today, a lot of work is still conducted in industrial settings, fuelling the so-called immaterial, digital and knowledge economies, as well as heating and polluting our planet (Roos, Kostakis, and Giotitsas 2016). Sweatshop labour is not uncommon, but even if health and safety regulations are in place, work itself is still standardised, monotonous, conducted at an enormous pace and over long hours. The largest portion of this work falls on the shoulders of people in the global South, but is not limited to it. Post-Fordist production gave rise to the amount of work conducted in offices and other non-industrial spaces, but oppressive conditions and Tayloristic work principles are also part and parcel of service, digital, and knowledge economies, as well as the almost invisible domestic sphere (Jiang and Korczynski 2016; Costas and Kärreman 2016).

Even those of us occupying more privileged positions suffer from the problems described above. Burnouts and mental stress are also very common facets of the often accelerated and noncreative work that capitalism keeps churning out, so that a "burnout society" seems to be a suitable label for modern, though predominantly western, life (Han 2015). Modern anarchist writings on work, too, provide severe critiques of work or even call for abolishing it the way we know it (Black 1995; Bonnano 1987–1995; Graeber 2013; Krisis-Group 1999; Shantz 2003). At the same time, in the face of rising precarity of work and employment, our societies can still be characterised as work-centric, where our relation to work, employment, and employability define our worth as human beings (Chertkovskaya et al. 2013; Standing 2011). Being expected to be "entrepreneurs of ourselves," our very subjectivities are governed by the demands of work, with negative consequences for employability in case of failing to align our "selves" with what is required by the market (Chertkovskaya et al. 2013).

Notably, some aspects of work evolved tremendously throughout the twentieth century, and at the turn of the twenty-first century. Instead of exercising strict control over the work process, "soft" methods of organising work became common (Burawoy 1979; Sennett 1998). They may involve putting emphasis on teamwork and co-operation between employees, downplaying hierarchy and having flatter organisational structures, allowing workers to engage in self-management, encouraging them to "be themselves" or even to play at work (Butler et al. 2011; Lopdrup-Hjorth et al. 2011; Murtola and Fleming 2011). At the same time, new meanings of work – often connected to consumption, self-actualisation, or new forms of the Protestant work ethic – challenge the boundaries between work and other areas of life.[4] These new aspects of work result in people becoming immersed in work and identifying themselves with it, sometimes losing sight of its problematic aspects. Having received substantial attention in critical management studies and the sociology of work, these themes are arguably missing from contemporary anarchist discussion. This may result in confusing practices that bring principles compatible with anarchism into work – such as non-hierarchy, play, and creativity – with fundamental changes in work or society (Barrington-Bush 2013).[5]

Anarchist critique of work, however, helps to lay bare the problems with work, which are often concealed by contemporary work ethic, as well as by the somewhat "sterile" and toned down way of writing in academia itself. For example, David Graeber (2013) unequivocally brands a lot of work done today as "bullshit jobs." A broader argument put forward in anarchist discussion, but often avoided elsewhere, is that some kinds of work and professions, being there to reproduce capitalism or simply to create more work, would not be needed if our societies were organised along anarchist principles (Black 1995). Overall, anarchist writings on work draw our attention not only to the political critique of predominant forms of work and its organisation, but also help to bring ethical issues – such as necessity of (certain kinds of) work, as well as questions of human flourishing and ecological sustainability – into the picture.

From this, it follows that the tradition of anarchist political philosophy does not stand alone when it comes to identifying the drudgery of contemporary work. There are certain theoretical strands that can supplement it with a more nuanced conceptual framework for the analysis of work carried out within the neoliberal regime. Yet, we can appreciate how anarchism retains insightful sobriety when it comes to identifying foundational ailments of the dominant economic system. In the next section, we shall demonstrate that the bulk of classical anarchist writings remain as pertinent to the critique of relations of exploitation and inequality as ever.

Anarchist Critique of Work

At the heart of anarchist positions against work, we can identify three important avenues for critique – wage labour, division of labour (including specialisation), and dehumanising aspects of work.

We begin with wage labour for, as Pyotr Kropotkin (1906) argued, the wage system is one of the two key institutions of capitalism (the other being representative government). As such, the socioeconomic relationships reified in wage labour play a crucial role in perpetuating the dominant political system. They institutionalise servility, born out of the history of inequality and result in what Kant would have called heteronomy. Thus, in anarchist thought, wage labour is often referred to as "wage-slavery," and is in most direct breach of the core anarchist principle of autonomy (Bakunin 1973; Goldman 1911a; Kropotkin 1906; Proudhon 1840). Caught up in this system, people are left only with pseudo-autonomy, whose sole purpose is to reproduce political order and ensuing inequality.[6]

Furthermore, compensation in the form of wages is always incomplete.[7] According to Pierre-Joseph Proudhon (1840, ch. III, §5), "[t]he laborer retains, even after he has received his wages, a natural right of property in the thing which he has produced." He saw the solution to this problem of wages to be changing the structure of property ownership and compensating labour according to time spent in production.[8] This solution, though in different forms, holds for collectivists and broader socialist thought of the time, and is often exercised in anti-capitalist organisations of today, where work is organised on the principle of wage labour (Kokkinidis 2015). However, Kropotkin saw wage labour and similar forms of compensation as problematic, whichever form of property they were exercised in.[9] Most importantly, he finds the very idea of valuing the contribution to society in monetary terms impossible.[10] All in all, Kropotkin uncompromisingly finds absurd all ways to execute the labour theory of value – whether based on time, complexity or unpleasantness of work – because they simply reproduce the capitalist order.

Fundamental inequalities inherent in a wage labour system, characteristic of capitalism, are formalised and further exacerbated through the division of labour. Division of labour is seen as problematic in anarchist thought, whether within a society, across societies, or within specific work/activity; so, too, is the positioning of existing divisions of labour as natural in science and in public common sense (Kropotkin 1906; Tolstoy 1942 [1886]). Notably, Kropotkin also brings attention to the division of labour in the domestic sphere, which is always treated as the specialisation of women and not accounted for in discussions of work. Division of labour creates hierarchies between different types of work and different roles within the working process. Hence, it contributes to the inequality of people.[11]

The critiques of the division of labour do not necessarily imply it should be rejected completely. For example, for Leo Tolstoy (1942 [1886], 125) a "division of labour always has existed and does exist, but it is only justified when man's conscience and reason decide what it should be, and not when man merely observes that it does exist." The key problem is that division of labour is framed by power relations within a concrete society with its injustices, and globally too. The distinctions between manual work and brain work, or between complex and simple work, are often artificial and political – justified, for example, by one's privileged access to education in the first place (Kropotkin 1906; 1998 [1898]). As a result, when assessing our understanding of work and its future within a system based on the division of labour, we should be wary of the fact that a new society cannot be built whilst keeping old divisions of labour, for they inevitably reproduce old hierarchies (Kropotkin 1906).

Specialisation and instrumentalisation of the human potential, normalised through the division of labour, have gained unprecedented momentum under the auspices of progress, the development of technologies, and an orientation toward economic growth (Bookchin 1993). Seen as a necessary element in the progressivist project that was heralded in the nineteenth century, the division of labour instead had adverse effects on working men and women – cementing societal divisions and widening the chasm between the privileged few and the rest of the humanity.[12] Technological breakthroughs that to this day hold a promise of liberation, enslaved people even further and aggravated inequality,[13] as well as contributed to ecological degradation.

Corollary to both "wage-slavery" and the division of labour is the dehumanising effect that work casts on people. The division of labour within quantity-oriented work processes has become inextricable from severe dehumanising consequences. It positions the potential interest in work and human well-being secondary to productivity, which makes it normal that workers become easily replaceable "cogs" of production, uninterested in their work (Goldman 1911a; Kropotkin 1906; Tolstoy 1942). The emphasis on production results not only in standardisation of production processes, but also in an enormous pace with which dull and monotonous work has to be conducted, abusing the very bodies and minds of those who labour (Kropotkin 1998 [1898]).[14] Notably, growth-centric capitalism and neoliberalism, with their constant strive for optimising costs and cutting public spending, have brought dehumanising elements way beyond the industrial work setting. The service and "knowledge" economies (including previously privileged spheres such as teaching, research, and medicine) suffer from increased fragmentation, administration, dissipation of autonomy, and the need to comply with "excellence" criteria externally foisted upon them by the state or by the bosses.

Tolstoy (1954, 173–201) takes the critique of the morally degrading effects of work even further, by countering orientation on productivity and panegyrics for the virtuousness of work with the ethics of "nonaction."[15] He refuses to see any virtue in labour for he, first of all, through the style of defamiliarisation characteristic to his social writings, wonders how we can celebrate working indiscriminately. Brokers, military men and industrialists are all working hard, but we should rather be abhorred by the fruits of their labour. Crucially, Tolstoy posits that labour is not just lacking any virtue, but is a stumbling block on the path of social progress because of its "morally stupefying" effects.[16]

In light of the discussion thus far, it can be resolutely concluded that work has been treated by the anarchist tradition with nothing but hostility, ranging from suggestions for radical improvements in working conditions to pleas for the abolition of work. Yet it is worth noting that anarchism is predominantly focused on the critique of the *ways that work is organised*, and not work per se. Even Tolstoy (1954), who vehemently attacked the Protestant work ethic, proposing instead a Taoist alternative of nonaction, stipulates a physiological need for work, which when unmet, often leads to suffering. Thus, we should ask: is it possible to engage in work – or whatever will come to substitute it – as world-making,[17] creating a society which is not built on oppression and injustice, supported by consumerism, (neo)colonialism, and neoliberalism? The next section will try to answer this question, by looking at the possibility of an anarchist work ethic.

Anarchist Vision of Work

To begin with, we should recall that there are plenty of tasks we should perform daily just to survive and to socially reproduce. Even if we envisage a better organised society, plenty of dreary activity will persist. That is what is needed for basic survival.[18] Kropotkin, who recognised that a lot of work needed for basic survival rests on the shoulders of women in a household, put his faith in technology to relieve women from "kitchen-slavery." Alas, technology failed to deliver on this expectation. That is why we tend to agree with arguments that regard the abolition of work thesis as somewhat solipsistic and as undermining an ethic of care. Not all members of the society are fortunate enough to be able to care and provide for themselves for various reasons. As Neala Schleuning (1995) argues, "as human beings, we have the obligation to contribute, at minimum, to collective survival work. No one should have the luxury of refusing to work." Insofar as we accept collective anarchist ethos, there is an a priori associative obligation to provide a minimal level of working input.

Meanwhile, the forebears of anarchism have never been against work in principle. Vis-à-vis the anarchist critiques of work organised on capitalist grounds, they set general ethical principles for organisation of work, as well as organisational forms it takes place in.[19] Perhaps, the main defining feature of the anarchist work ethic is that it is comprehensive. It is impossible to proselytise virtuousness of work that co-exists with inequality and oppression. Therefore, work organised according to anarchist principles will provide a setting which makes work ethically acceptable.

The organisation of work in line with anarchism would, following Emma Goldman (1911b), aspire to "strip labor of its deadening, dulling aspect, of its gloom and compulsion" and aim "to make work an instrument of joy, of strength, of color, of real harmony." Run by voluntary collectives, associations or organised in commons, work will cater for the essential needs of the society, as well as recognise "the right of the individual, or numbers of individuals, to arrange at all times for other forms of work, in harmony with their tastes and desires" (Goldman 1911b). Recognising individual preferences for work as their right also suggests that not all work has to be done in collectives. We can see two ideal types of work emerging, by no means clear-cut – work that is necessary and work that is more playful, catering for individual preferences (Goldman 1911a; Albert 2000; Goodman and Goodman 1960). The former acknowledges that certain work will never be pleasant and certain things will need to be done, but sharing them in society and making them complement the kind of work people find meaningful should be possible. Furthermore, engaging even in this necessary work within a society organised in line with anarchist principles may bring additional meanings and subjectivities to it.

Division of labour and specialisation would still be possible, but happening by choice, individual and/or collective, and not rooted in injustice.[20] It is the integrity and wholeness of work, however, that is likely to bring joy and harmony. Anarchism would allow for a plethora of ways in which this can be achieved – by combining "manual" and "brain" work, artisanal work, DIY ethos or simply producing enough for oneself to live on (Kropotkin 1998 [1898]; Bookchin 1986; Tolstoy 2012; Thoreau 1854). Non-hierarchical and self-managed organisation of work will be a guarantor of the perpetuation of the anarchist work ethic. This does not eliminate certain "leadership" or coordination positions within organisations, but they would be temporary and not attached to particular people or "leaders" (Sutherland, Land, and Böhm 2014).

More broadly, an anarchist organisation of work by all means implies an anarchist organisation of our entangled societies and their economies. The right to live, human flourishing, and ecological sustainability would be at the heart of such societies, instead of relentless productivism, consumerism, and the growth imperative (Bookchin 1986; Goldman 1911a; Kropotkin 1906).[21] Collective forms of organising would be most common in such a society, whilst leaving space for individual freedoms. Crucially, while work does not have to be abolished and societal needs are to be accommodated, the very ability to live in such a society would not be tied to work. Organising the society along these lines is likely to change dramatically what is produced and consumed, eliminating many of the "bullshit" or even harmful jobs and professions, and hence change the purposes and outcomes of work.

Conclusively, it seems evident that the concept of work, despite some misapprehensions, has been rather central to a lot of debate within anarchist political philosophy. One possible explanation for that is the fact that the anarchist stance on work is part of a wider set of practices and ethical considerations about the fairer organisation of society. In any case, it seems feasible to conclude that an anarchist work ethic is possible, with a proviso that work settings follow the principles outlined above. Classical anarchist writers did not eschew work, perhaps because they had a strong conviction that a different world was possible. We should work for this as well. Additionally, the task of basic survival does not permit any form of escapism. In order to go beyond theoretical considerations, we explore in the last section of the chapter the potential of particular initiatives (policy suggestions) on work to move us closer to engendering the anarchist work ethic in practice.

The Future of Work

Though we are far from realizing an anarchist vision of work, discussion of the problems with work has been on the rise, with several initiatives around work being actively discussed. We are aware that these initiatives may have only a limited potential for changing the way we work and live, and might also be not in complete alignment with some core anarchist values. However, not engaging with them, or calling for abolition of work, would be signs of naivety, withdrawal, and defeatism (Schleuning 1995). Instead, serious discussion and scrutiny of the proposals around work can inform the direction of action and struggle in ways that might help move work and society closer to an anarchist ideal (Franks 2012, 62–63). In what follows, we will open this discussion by reviewing the following common propositions in relation to work: job guarantee, work-sharing, shorter working week, and basic income (see D'Alisa, Demaria, and Kallis 2015).

Job guarantee is a policy proposal that would make the state guarantee a paid job to any qualifying person in search of one and support it financially, thus ensuring full employment. Decentralised ways of managing it are often suggested, involving, for example, local governments, not-for-profit, and other organisations. Work-sharing is a proposal where work is shared and more time is released for other activities or other work. The same holds for a shorter working week, which would reduce the number of hours one spends in paid work. Finally, basic income is a proposal for a minimum level of income that a person would receive independently of their work status.

The immediate problem with a job guarantee is that it still confines us to work-centric societies and risks imposing employment as compulsory, being too focused on the economic goal of fighting unemployment, with the assumption that having a job always has positive social effects. Both job guarantees and work-sharing are initiatives that are tied to work that is already there, i.e., which the guarantor gives or which one is doing already. Thus, they may offer some ways out in concrete situations within unemployment-stricken contexts or precarious labour markets. However, even if generously compensated, they do not change the organisation of work itself or the organisational settings where work takes place, keeping intact the same divisions of labour and inherent inequalities. They do not prevent people from having to do "bullshit" jobs or having to engage in dehumanising work.

The very possibility of work-sharing is less likely to apply to work that brings joy, harmony, and integrity, but more so to standardised and easily replaceable kinds of work. At the same time, work-sharing, if not undermining one's right to live (e.g. coming with no loss of social security), may have a side effect of releasing one's time and energy for other kinds of work and activities. Some form of work-sharing – more likely for work that has to be done – might be present in an anarchist society and has been integrated into anarchist visions of work. However, work-sharing does not offer much potential as a way forward if implemented to work and societies the way they are now.

Similarly, a shorter working week does not change the work we do or the way we do it. Nevertheless, it has a different logic from job guarantees and work-sharing as it releases the time and is not confined to a particular job. Historically, reduction of working time went hand in hand with improvements in work and living conditions. Today, such reduction can be liberating, especially when one has a chance to do less of work they do not like. Hence if all other conditions stay the same and this time does not come with a decrease in one's living standards, a shorter working week releases time for one to engage in other activities – whether this is care, leisure, other work, pure contemplation, collective feasts or something else – and for them to be organised in a different way. It may thus help to prepare the soil for a non-work-centric society.

Out of these four initiatives engaging with the question of work, basic income has probably gained most attention lately, having been supported by social movements, research, and real-life experiments, as well as having received some discussion in policy-making. If set at a level that allows one to live well and have access to a generous social security system, basic income is as close as it gets to a non-work-centric idea of a society. With such an income, one would be freer to decide which work to engage in and potentially have more influence on organising it. However, the discourses that surround a system reliant on basic income can head in numerous directions, from reproducing unsustainable capitalist productivism and entrepreneurialism to radical re-organisation of society on grounds that would go in hand with anarchist visions. Hence when supporting it, it is important to promote articulations of basic income in terms of the latter. Furthermore, we still live in a world of nation states and all sorts of borders (re-)erected by them. It is at this level that the question of incorporating basic income into policies has been discussed so far, for example, in Finland and Switzerland. If a particular country establishes basic income of the kind we mentioned above, who will be able to get it and how will this reflect this country's migration policy? These are the crucial questions to address, particularly in light of present and future migrations of people. This brings us back to the concept of the state that is so central to anarchist thought.

To conclude, we believe that work deserves more attention in anarchist thought precisely because it is at the core of reproducing the capitalist order. Even if not promoted to the status of a core concept, it needs to be thoroughly engaged with by anarchists. A society organised on anarchist principles would challenge productivism and economic growth as ends in themselves and be centred around human flourishing and ecological sustainability. Work-centrism would go, but work would stay and be(come) part of an anarchist world-making. The initiatives on work that we discussed also need to be engaged with and the contexts within which they are implemented need to be analysed. Though all these initiatives are subject to critique, and we are not ready to universally promote any of them, a basic income and a shorter working week are more likely to be stepping stones towards the kind of society and organisation of work that anarchism might find worth supporting. Not being connected to work itself, and/or releasing our time, they might help us transcend a productivist obsession and overworking as well as the human and ecological degradation that come with these, and hence prefigure a better world.

Notes

1 Even if we were to assume that there is a significant number of people who buy into the idea of "fairness" involved, further complications await: "This way of describing

work, of understanding it as a fair exchange between two equals, hides the real relationship between employer and employee: that of domination and subordination. For if the truth behind the employment contract were widely known, workers in our society would refuse to work, because they would see that it is impossible for human individuals to truly separate out labour power from themselves" (Brown 1995).

2 Indeed, even Bertrand Russell (1932), the founder of the analytic tradition in philosophy, claims that "I think that there is far too much work done in the world, that immense harm is caused by the belief that work is virtuous, and that what needs to be preached in modern industrial countries is quite different from what always has been preached."

3 For example, Emma Goldman (1940) writes: "The average worker has no inner point of contact with the industry he is employed in, and he is a stranger to the process of production of which he is a mechanical part. Like any other cog of the machine, he is replaceable at any time by other similar depersonalized human beings." See also work by Peter Kropotkin (1906; 1998 [1898]) and Pierre-Joseph Proudhon (1840).

4 A variety of work ethics has been discussed in the sociology of work and in critical management studies: see work by Richard Sennett (1998), Paul Heelas (2002), and Emma Bell and Scott Taylor (2003). Although these meanings are often constructed in line with certain ideologies of work (Anthony 1977), work as craft, work as a way to contribute to or even change the society, or work as a pleasurable activity in itself, are also among meanings that can be associated with work.

5 In our view, Barrington-Bush buys into the fancy practices introduced in modern workplaces, not sufficiently addressing the hierarchies and power relations that are still inherent to them.

6 Goldman (1940): "The masses plod on, partly because their senses have been dulled by the deadly routine of work and because they must eke out an existence. This applies with even greater force to the political fabric of today. There is no place in its texture for free choice of independent thought and activity. There is a place only for voting and tax-paying puppets."

7 Proudhon (1840, ch. III, §5): "The money with which you pay the wages of the laborers remunerates them for only a few years of the perpetual possession which they have abandoned to you. Wages is the cost of the daily maintenance and refreshment of the laborer. You are wrong in calling it the price of a sale. The workingman has sold nothing; he knows neither his right, nor the extent of the concession which he has made to you, nor the meaning of the contract which you pretend to have made with him. On his side, utter ignorance; on yours, error and surprise, not to say deceit and fraud."

8 Kropotkin (1906, ch. XIII, §1): "It is also easily understood why Proudhon took up the idea later on. In his Mutualist system he tried to make Capital less offensive, notwithstanding the retaining of private property, which he detested from the bottom of his heart, but which he believed to be necessary to guarantee individuals against the State."

9 Kropotkin (1906, ch. XIII, §4): "... after having proclaimed the abolition of private property, and the possession in common of all means of production, how can they [collectivists] uphold the wages system in any form? It is, nevertheless, what collectivists are doing when they recommend *labour-cheques*."

10 Kropotkin (1906, ch. XIII, §4): "No distinction can be drawn between the work of each man. Measuring the work by its results leads us to absurdity; dividing and measuring them by hours spent on the work also leads us to absurdity. One thing remains: put the *needs* above the *works*, and first of all recognize the right to live, and later on, to the comforts of life, for all those who take their share in production."

11 Proudhon (1847, ch. III, §1): "I insist upon this precious datum of psychology, the necessary consequence of which is that the hierarchy of capacities henceforth cannot

be allowed as a principle and law of organization: equality alone is our rule, as it is also our ideal."
12 Proudhon (1847, ch. III, §1): "But, at this solemn hour of the division of labor, tempestuous winds begin to blow upon humanity. Progress does not improve the condition of all equally and uniformly, although in the end it must include and transfigure every intelligent and industrious being. It commences by taking possession of a small number of privileged persons, who thus compose the elite of nations, while the mass continues, or even buries itself deeper, in barbarism."
13 Proudhon (1847, ch. III, §1): "Division, in the absence of which there is no progress, no wealth, no equality, subordinates the workingman, and renders intelligence useless, wealth harmful, and equality impossible."
14 Cf. J.B. Say: "A man who during his whole life performs but one operation, certainly acquires the power to execute it better and more readily than another; but at the same time he becomes less capable of any other occupation, whether physical or moral; his other faculties become extinct, and there results a degeneracy in the individual man" (quoted in Proudhon 1847, ch. III, §1).
15 Quotes from this essay are translated into English by us.
16 Tolstoy (1954): "Labour is not just lacking virtue, but in our falsely organised society it is mostly a moral anaesthetic akin to smoking or liquor, which conceals wrongness and wickedness of one's own life."
17 See the distinction between *animal laborans* (the subject of labour) and *homo faber* (the subject of work) in Hannah Arendt (1998 [1958]). *Homo faber* is the subject involved in world-making (i.e. transforming and creating the world), but, according to Arendt, we are all *animal laborans*.
18 Neala Schleuning (1995): "Basic survival is, of course, a given when we think about the necessity for work ... 'Someone' must do all this work – co-operatively, individually, by lot, by coercion – the work must be done."
19 Kropotkin (1898, §VI): "We do not wish to have the fruits of our labor stolen from us. And by that very fact, do we not declare that we respect the fruits of others' labor?" See also Bakunin (1947 [1867]): "The true, human liberty of a single individual implies the emancipation of all: because, thanks to the law of solidarity, which is the natural basis of all human society, I cannot be, feel, and know myself really, completely free, if I am not surrounded by men as free as myself. The slavery of each is my slavery."
20 Even Tolstoy (1942 [1886], ch. XIII), a severe critic of the division of labour, would have such a stance towards it: "A division of labour always has existed and does exist, but it is only justified when man's conscience and reason decide what it should be, and not when man merely observes that it does exist. And the conscience and reason of all men decide this question very simply, indubitably, and unanimously."
21 See also Jeppesen in this volume. Notably, these goals are very similar to those articulated by other strands of academia and social movements of today, such as degrowth, feminist economics, and ecological Marxism. Hence, this is where anarchism can build alliances.

References

Albert, Michael. 2000. *Moving Forward: Programme for a Participatory Economy*. London: AK Press.
Anthony, P.D. 1977. *The Ideology of Work*. London: Tavistock Publications.
Arendt, Hannah. 1998 [1958]. *The Human Condition*. Chicago: University of Chicago Press.
Bakunin, Michael. 1947 [1867]. "Solidarity in Liberty: The Workers Path to Freedom." In *Bakunin's Writings*, edited by Guy A. Alfred. New York: Modern Publishers. Anarchist Archives. http://dwardmac.pitzer.edu/anarchist_archives/bakunin/writings/Bakliberty.html.

Bakunin, Michael. 1973. *Selected Writings*. Edited by Arthur Lehning. Worcester and London: Trinity Press. https://libcom.org/files/Michael%20Bakunin%20-%20Selected%20Writings.pdf.

Costas, Jana, and Dan Kärreman. 2016. "The Bored Self in Knowledge Work." *Human Relations* 69(1): 61–83.

Barrington-Bush, Liam. 2013. *Anarchists in the Boardroom*. London: More Like People.

Bell, Emma, and Scott Taylor. 2003. "The Elevation of Work: Pastoral Power and the New Age Work Ethic." *Organization* 10(2): 329–349.

Black, Bob. 1995. *The Abolition of Work and Other Essays*. Port Townshend: Loompanics Unlimited.

Bonnano, Alfredo M. 1987–1995. "Let's Destroy Work, Let's Destroy the Economy." The Anarchist Library. https://theanarchistlibrary.org/library/alfredo-m-bonanno-let-s-destroy-work-let-s-destroy-the-economy.

Bookchin, Murray. 1969. "Anarchy and Organization: A Letter to the Left." *New Left Notes*, 15 January. Anarchy Archives. http://dwardmac.pitzer.edu/Anarchist_Archives/bookchin/leftletter.html.

Bookchin, Murray. 1986. "Municipalization: Community Ownership of the Economy." *Green Perspectives: Newsletter of the Green Program Project*. February. Anarchist Archives. http://dwardmac.pitzer.edu/Anarchist_Archives/bookchin/gp/perspectives2.html.

Bookchin, Murray. 1993. "What is Social Ecology?" In *Environmental Philosophy: From Animal Rights to Radical Ecology*, edited by Michael E. Zimmerman, J. Baird Callicott, George Sessions, Karen J. Warren, and John Clark, 354–373. Englewood Cliffs, NJ: Prentice-Hall.

Braverman, Harry. 1998. *Labor and Monopoly Capital: The Degradation of Work in the Twentieth Century*, 25th Anniversary Edition. New York: Monthly Review Press.

Brown, L. Susan. 1995. "Does Work Really Work?" *Kick It Over*, 35. The Anarchist Library. https://theanarchistlibrary.org/library/l-susan-brown-does-work-really-work.

Burawoy, Michael. 1979. *Manufacturing Consent: Changes in the Labor Process under Monopoly Capitalism*. Chicago and London: University of Chicago Press.

Butler, Nick, Lena Olaison, Martyna Sliwa, Brent Meier Sørensen, and Sverre Spoelstra, eds. 2011. "Work, Play and Boredom." Special issue, *ephemera: theory & politics in organization* 11(4).

Chertkovskaya, Ekaterina, Peter Watt, Stefan Tramer, and Sverre Spoelstra, eds. 2013. "Giving Notice to Employability." Special issue, *ephemera: theory & politics in organization* 13(4).

D'Alisa, Giacomo, Federico Demaria, and Giorgos Kallis, eds. 2015. *Degrowth: A Vocabulary for a New Era*. London: Routledge.

Franks, Benjamin. 2012. "Anarchism and Analytic Philosophy." In *The Continuum Companion to Anarchism*, edited by Ruth Kinna, 50–71. London: Continuum.

Freeden, Michael. 1994. "Political Concepts and Ideological Morphology." *Journal of Political Philosophy* 2(2): 140–164.

Freeden, Michael. 1996. *Ideologies and Political Theory: A Conceptual Approach*. Oxford: Clarendon.

Freeden, Michael. 2003. *Ideology: A Very Short Introduction*. Oxford: Oxford University Press.

Goldman, Emma. 1911a. *Anarchism and Other Essays*. Second Revised Edition. New York: Mother Earth Publishing Association. Anarchist Archives. http://dwardmac.pitzer.edu/anarchist_archives/goldman/GoldmanCW.html.

Goldman, Emma. 1911b. "Anarchism: What It Really Stands For." Anarchy Archives. http://dwardmac.pitzer.edu/anarchist_archives/goldman/aando/anarchism.html.

Goldman, Emma. 1940. *The Place of the Individual in Society*. Chicago: Free Society Forum. Anarchist Archives. http://dwardmac.pitzer.edu/anarchist_archives/goldman/goldmanindiv.html.

Goodman, Percival, and Paul Goodman. 1960. *Communitas: Means of Livelihood and Ways of Life*. New York: Vintage Books. 1960.

Graeber, David. 2013. "On the Phenomenon of Bullshit Jobs." *Strike! Magazine* 17 August: 10–11. http://strikemag.org/bullshit-jobs/.

Han, Byung-Chul. 2015. *The Burnout Society*. Stanford, CA: Stanford University Press.

Heelas, Paul. 2002. "Work Ethics, Soft Capitalism and the Turn to Life." In *Cultural Economy: Cultural Analysis and Commercial Life*, edited by Paul du Gay and Michael Pryke, 78–96. London: Sage.

Jiang, Zhe, and Marek Korczynski. 2016. "When the 'Unorganizable' Organize: The Collective Mobilization of Migrant Domestic Workers in London." *Human Relations* 69(3): 813–838.

Kokkinidis, George. 2015. "Spaces of Possibilities: Workers' Self-Management in Greece." *Organization* 22(6): 847–871.

Krisis-Group. 1999. "Manifesto Against Labour." www.krisis.org/1999/manifesto-against-labour/.

Kropotkin, Pyotr. 1898. *Anarchist Morality*. San Francisco: Free Society. Anarchist Archives. http://dwardmac.pitzer.edu/Anarchist_Archives/kropotkin/AM/anarchist_moralitytc.html.

Kropotkin, Pyotr. 1906. *The Conquest of Bread*. New York and London: G.P. Putnam's Sons. Anarchist Archives. http://dwardmac.pitzer.edu/anarchist_archives/kropotkin/conquest/toc.html.

Kropotkin, Pyotr. 1998 [1898]. *Fields, Factories and Workshops Tomorrow*. Edited by Colin Ward. London: Freedom Press.

Lopdrup-Hjorth, Thomas, Marius Gudmand-Høyer, Pia Bramming, and Michael Pedersen, eds. 2011. "Governing Work Through Self-Management." Special issue, *ephemera: theory & politics in organization* 11(2).

Murtola, Anna-Maria, and Peter Fleming, eds. 2011. "Authenticity." Special issue, *ephemera: theory & politics in organization*, 11(1).

Proudhon, Pierre-Joseph. 1840. *What is Property? An Inquiry into the Principle of Right and Government*. The Anarchist Library. https://theanarchistlibrary.org/library/pierre-joseph-proudhon-what-is-property-an-inquiry-into-the-principle-of-right-and-of-governmen.

Proudhon, Pierre-Joseph 1847. *System of Economical Contradictions: Or, The Philosophy of Poverty*. The Anarchist Library. https://theanarchistlibrary.org/library/pierre-joseph-proudhon-system-of-economical-contradictions-or-the-philosophy-of-poverty.

Roos, Andreas, Vasilis Kostakis, and Christos Giotitsas, eds. 2016. "The Materiality of the Immaterial: ICTs and the Digital Commons." Special issue, *tripleC: Communication, Capitalism & Critique* 14(1).

Russell, Bertrand. 1932. "In Praise of Idleness." The Anarchist Library. https://theanarchistlibrary.org/library/bertrand-russell-in-praise-of-idleness-11-02-05-22-00-46.

Schleuning, Neala. 1995. "The Abolition of Work and Other Myths." *Kick it Over* 35 (Summer). Libcom.org. http://libcom.org/library/AbolitionWorkMythNealaScleuning.

Sennett, Richard. 1998. *The Corrosion of Character*. New York: W.W. Norton & Company.

Shantz, Jeff. 2003. "Reflections on the End of Work." *Green Anarchy* 12: 22–23. http://greenanarchy.anarchyplanet.org/files/2012/05/greenanarchy12.pdf.

Standing, Guy. 2011. *The Precariat: The New Dangerous Class.* London: Bloomsbury Academic.
Stoborod, Konstantin, and Thomas Swann, eds. 2014. "Management, Business, Anarchism." Special issue, *ephemera: theory & politics in organization* 14(4).
Sutherland, Neil, Christopher Land, and Steffen Böhm. 2014. "Anti-Leaders(hip) in Social Movement Organizations: The Case of Autonomous Grassroots Groups." *Organization* 21(6): 759–781.
Thoreau, Henry David. 1854. *Walden: Or, Life in the Woods.* http://thoreau.eserver.org/walden00.html#toc.
Tolstoy, Leo N. 1942 [1886]. *What Then Must We Do?* Translated by Aylmer Maude. www.arvindguptatoys.com/arvindgupta/whatthenmustwedo.pdf.
Tolstoy, Leo N. 1954. *Polnoe Sobranije Sochinenij v 90 Tomah, tom 29.* Moskva: Hudojestvennaya Literatura.
Tolstoy, Leo N. 2012. *Russkiy Mir.* Moskva: Labirint.
Ward, Colin. 1966. "Anarchism as a Theory of Organisation." Panarchy. www.panarchy.org/ward/organization.1966.html.

14
DIY

Sandra Jeppesen

DIY or *Do It Yourself* is a key practice that involves doing things ourselves rather than expecting the state or corporations to serve us. It is an anarchist ethos or set of principles for translating the anarchist concepts discussed in this book into practice. Moreover, it is arguably the quintessential practice of anarchist politics, bringing together other anarchist concepts such as prefiguration, anti-capitalism and horizontalism that are foundational to anarchist organizing and cultural practices. However, DIY maintains a peripheral placement in anarchism because it is a fairly recent addition to the anarchist lexicon, as the brief history below elucidates. Nevertheless, a DIY ethos has been crucial to anarchism since its inception, arising as it did in the anarchist counter-publics of the nineteenth century (Cohn 2014).

DIY means Do It Yourself: rather than looking to capitalism and the state to produce products, culture, and services, anarchists get together and generate these by and for ourselves; moreover, we do so in a way that keeps the production, distribution, and consumption processes as separate from capitalism as possible. A DIY approach is therefore a way to seize power by creating counterhegemonic cultural forms and practices consistent with anarchist anti-authoritarian values. Stephen Duncombe (1997) draws attention to the double force of DIY anarchism, in which critiques are offered of mainstream culture and image systems and, simultaneously, new media and image systems are produced. It is this active creation of anarchist culture that is at stake in DIY politics.

Not all DIY practices are anarchist, due to an ongoing process of capitalist co-optation; therefore, the terms *DIY anarchism* or *DIY anarchy* will be used to distinguish specifically anarchist contexts or characteristics.

This chapter is organized into two main sections. The first consists of an episodic history of the usage of the term DIY, exploring the various cultural forms in which it has emerged, while also deepening our understanding of the specific definition and practices of DIY anarchism. In the second, seven key characteristics of DIY anarchist culture are mapped, explaining their importance to anarchism, exploring some challenges and contradictions, and analyzing their relationship to other anarchist concepts. Some conclusions follow, providing direction for further investigation.

An Episodic History of DIY Anarchist Cultural Forms

The term DIY was first used in 1952 to signify doing home repairs without professional help,[1] but it soon became appropriated by a series of countercultural music movements. It was used in the jazz scene in the 1950s, according to George McKay (1998, 1), who argues that 1950s jazz musicians created "skiffle," a kind of "do-it-yourself music, primitive jazz played on home-made or improvised rhythm instruments as an accompaniment to the singing of folk-blues." Holtzman, Hughes, and van Meter (2007) situate the roots of DIY within the 1960s and 1970s counterculture. They suggest that, "even as the political climate during the 1970s worsened, a means of circumventing the powers-that-be emerged through the Do It Yourself (DIY) ethic. DIY is the idea that you can do for yourself the activities normally reserved for the realm of capitalist production …. Thus, anything from music and magazines to education and protest can be created in a nonalienating, self-organized, and purposely anticapitalist manner" (Holtzman, Hughes, and van Meter 2007, 44).

1970s: The Emergence of DIY Punk Music

DIY emerged in the punk scene of the 1970s, sharing the hippie rejection of consumer culture. In the UK, "British punks apparently appropriated the notion of 'DIY' from British hardware stores, which are often designated as 'DIY' or 'Do It Yourself' stores" (Ferrell 1996, 198). Punk musicians rejected corporate record labels, and they produced and distributed their music autonomously on their own labels, organizing shows at underground venues. Therefore, "punks in the U.S. and Great Britain … resurrected this sense of direct anarchy with their notion of 'D.I.Y.' – that is, a 'do it yourself' approach to musical and cultural production" (Ferrell 1996, 164).

Alan O'Connor (2008, 27) explains that in the 1970s–1990s there was a growing tension between commercial punk record labels and DIY labels: "The DIY sector … is often operated from a musician's house (the basement, a spare room, even a closet) and often shares the same phone line. The label is usually done by one or two people. The bands are friends and there is no question of legal contracts." Record pressings would be small, for example, under 2000 records or CDs, and profits were shared 50/50 with bands. Operating a DIY label is a labour of love rather than a profit-making venture: "Everyone who runs a

DIY punk label also says they love the music. Some also mention the importance of a social network, friends they have made, just being part of the scene" (O'Connor 2008, 27). These principles set the foundation for the DIY anarchist movement: anti-profit, small scale, creative, community oriented. Punk soon branched out to include Riot Grrrl, Queercore, and Afropunk as subgenres producing their own music (e.g., the mixtape *Revolution grrrl style now!*), films (e.g., *Afro-punk*), and more.

1970s: The Emergence of DIY Zines

Zines are self-produced magazines, sometimes called "fanzines," that emerged out of the science fiction and punk scenes, often produced by fans. They are small-scale publications produced with little money, whose creators have no interest in profit. *Punk* was the first zine produced by the punk subculture in the US in 1976, selling "3,000 issues locally and eventually 25,000 worldwide" over four years (Duncombe 1997, 124). *Sniffin' Glue* was the first punk fanzine in Britain, produced just seven months after *Punk* (Triggs 2006, 69). The "initial photocopier run was 50 but by the end of *Sniffin' Glue* in 1977 up to 10,000 were in circulation" (Triggs 2006, 72). The Riot Grrrl movement gained momentum through the publication of zines such as the Riot Grrrl Newsletters and *Bikini Kill*, which was both a zine title and the name of a band.

1960s and Beyond: DIY Comics

Underground comix grew out of the counterculture of the 1960s and 1970s, and many were explicitly anarchist (see *World War 3 Illustrated, AnarComics*). Counterculture participants such as comic artists Robert Crumb and Art Spiegelman produced and distributed their work through underground networks as early as the 1960s. There were "definite links between the Do-It-Yourself attitude of punk and the rise of the DIY or 'small press' comic. A similar DIY approach had produced the Underground comics," though punk subject matter and aesthetics were not necessarily evident (Lawley 1999, 100–111). Today we see anarchist comic artists such as Fly (*PEOPs*), Seth Tobocman (*You Don't Have to Fuck People Over to Survive*), Clifford Harper (*Anarchy: A Graphic Guide*), and Gord Hill (*The 500 Years of Resistance Comic Book*).

1990s: DIY Autonomous News Media

"The sorry state of the media system in most countries has inspired people the world over to challenge dominant media institutions ... and to begin the work of building their own democratic media" (Uzelman 2005, 20). Anarchists produce their own news reports because their campaigns are often misrepresented or ignored by mainstream media (Atton 2002, 19). In addition, DIY anarchists produce "artistic expression such as culture jamming or adbusting, billboard liberation, political graffiti and murals, street theatre and other forms of performance art" (Uzelman 2005, 24). Examples of DIY anarchist news media include SchNEWS, the Indymedia network, and Green Anarchist (Atton 2002).

Contemporary DIY Book Publishing

DIY publishing is crucial in "representing challenges to hegemony, whether on an explicitly political platform, or employing the kinds of indirect challenges through experimentation and the transformation of existing roles, routines, emblems and signs" (Atton 2002, 19). In DIY publishing, "for many the content as well as the process of DIY production expresses a confrontation with the cultural codes of everyday life" (Shantz 2010, 164). These codes are subverted or appropriated for alternative ends in a kind of guerrilla semiotics, narrating alternative values and lifestyles. Anarchist publishers such as AK Press, PM Press, Black Rose, and CrimethInc. produce books with content critical of dominant culture and proposing anarchist alternatives (Jeppesen 2011).

1990s: DIY Video Emerges

When video emerged as a portable technology, DIY "video activists had to become more adept in the use of secret camerawork and sneaking into difficult places with cameras" (Harding 1998, 94). DIY video is used to record protests to support legal defences, produce outreach materials for activist campaigns, and create anarchist YouTube videos and political documentaries on a shoestring budget, often through crowdfunding. Examples of DIY video programmes that feature news and analysis include Undercurrent, which produced VHS tapes in the 1990s, and subMedia TV which produces online video commentary (https://sub.media/).

1990s: Tech Activism

Early adoption of new technologies led to the creation of Indymedia in 1999, and anarchists play a role in white hat hacker communities known for using "hacktivist" technologies for positive social transformation. Online activism or alternative computing "involves the material infrastructure of information technologies and media" (Lievrouw 2011, 98). Tech activists "reconfigure systems with the purpose of resisting political, commercial and state restraints on open access to information and the use of information technologies" (Lievrouw 2011, 98). The activism itself is embedded in the architecture of the technologies. In the 1990s, the Electronic Disturbance Theater developed an application called FloodNet that was used by the Zapatistas in Mexico and allies globally to take down government websites through DDoS (Direct Denial of Service) attacks (Lievrouw 2011, 98, 173–174).

Similar electronic civil disobedience groups include the Critical Art Ensemble and the Institute for Applied Autonomy. They engage in the Internet as a site of struggle in and of itself. Anarchist DIY tech activists also create collectively self-owned platforms such as Indymedia, resist, riseup, nomadology and others.

1990s: DIY Lifestyles and Spaces

In the 1990s, the DIY movement expanded to include "squat culture, the traveller movement and later Acid House parties," as well as other forms of participatory underground culture such as dumpster diving, freight hopping, gleaning or wildcrafting, guerrilla gardening, guerrilla stencilling, graffiti, and more (McKay 1998, 2). Everyday lifestyles become so engaged in DIY that the boundaries between art, politics, and everyday life are blurred: "Inspired by and following in the footsteps of the protest movements and countercultures of the sixties, seventies, and eighties, the DiY protest movement is finally breaking down the barriers between art and protest" (Jordan 1998, 129). These communities of DIY practice create DIY or "affinity" spaces such as punk record shops and venues, infoshops, free skools, community arts spaces, and pirate radio (Lankshear and Knobel 2010, 2), such as the well-known network of social centres in Spain.

Key Characteristics of DIY Anarchism

We will now map seven key characteristics of DIY anarchism that emerge from this episodic history: (1) oppositional content, (2) aesthetic experiments, (3) communities of practice, (4) anti-hierarchical organizational structures, (5) prefigurative processes, (6) anti-capitalist economics, and (7) direct action. As you will note, many of these characteristics are connected to core anarchist concepts, as DIY anarchism is the practice emerging out of and contributing to these theories.

DIY Representation: Oppositional Content

"DIY activities suggest a striving for what an earlier era might have called control over the means of production and what has now come to include control over the means of representation" (Shantz 2010, 164). DIY anarchists have long been committed to "defining who they were and what they believed in. You did-it-yourself because no one else out there was doing it. Or because when they did it, they got it horribly wrong. Doing-it-yourself was also a reaction against how the mass media was doing you" (Duncombe 1997, 126). For women, queers, people of colour, trans, and other marginalized groups, producing their own media allowed them to overcome forms of oppression, alienation, isolation, misrepresentation, and silencing. For example, for Riot Grrrls, producing zines "helped to disassemble the feelings of relative powerlessness that had been inflicted upon grrrls" (Holtzman, Hughes, and van Meter 2007, 49).

Autonomous media also created a forum for anarchist news and analysis. Independent Media Centers (IMCs) created spaces for alternative media activists to report on protests directly from the streets, providing counter-analysis to the dominant messages of mainstream media. Since then, "IMCs have emerged not only as a source of information and analysis, but also as a forum in which participants can voice their own experiences, opinions, stories, and criticisms" (Holtzman, Hughes, and van Meter 2007, 53). In the UK, DIY journalists produced a series of DIY tapes called *Undercurrents*, and a newspaper called *SchNEWS*.

DIY media allow practitioners to produce DIY non-expert knowledge as legitimate, valuing marginalized experiences, lived experience of oppression, and knowledge generated through the process of community organizing. In doing so, they challenge what it means to be an "expert" as well as the mainstream processes requiring economic, social, cultural, and institutional capital to produce knowledge and culture – for example, journalist accreditation, graduate school, or a corporate record label. Oppositional knowledge producers do not submit to censorship, control, and top-down hierarchies of capitalist or state-funded cultural institutions, rather they produce knowledge using DIY practices.

Thus, producing DIY anarchism from the margins becomes itself a space of empowerment, not just through production of oppositional content, but also with experiments in style.

DIY Style: Anarchist Aesthetic Experiments

Anarchists create agitation-oriented art using the "graphic language of resistance" (Triggs 2006, 69). This visual semiotic subversion is an anti-aesthetic: it supports oppositional content by embracing underground image systems; it values aesthetics that counter mainstream norms; and it questions the need for aesthetic norms at all.

Triggs (2006, 69) argues, for example, that the "stapled and photocopied fanzines of the late 1970s fostered the 'do-it-yourself' (DIY) production techniques of cut-n-paste letterforms, photocopied and collaged images, hand-scrawled and typewritten texts, to create a recognizable graphic design aesthetic." This aesthetic drew from visual imagery that had been negatively associated with deviance and crime, such as the "cut-n-paste letterforms" of kidnapping letters used in Jamie Reid's Sex Pistols album covers. Triggs argues that "The Sex Pistols single release of 'Anarchy in the UK' (1976) summed up punk's radical position" as McLaren is cited by Triggs (2006, 70) saying, they embodied "'a statement of self-rule, or ultimate independence, of do-it-yourself.'" The images of broken windows and ironic subversions of the Queen and the British flag were created in an edgy style that emerged from and spawned punk subcultural style (Hebdige 1979).

In anarchist art, spontaneity, innovation, and political aesthetics occur through the integration of artistic practices into everyday life. As John Jordan (1998, 130) suggests, DIY anarchy "calls for a society where the personal and the political, the passionate and the pragmatic, art and everyday life, become one." Art transgresses boundaries when it is mobilized at protests: protest becomes art, reporting becomes protest, galleries include political action, and art departs from galleries to be displayed on overpasses, brick walls, subways and train cars.

Instead of searching for a correctly anarchist representation, DIY anarchist art calls into question the very notion of correctness: "In the same way that anarchism moves beyond 'truth' to an ongoing process of inquiry, then, it disavows 'correct' social models and methodologies in favour of an emergent process of challenge and change" (Ferrell 1996, 165). Change happens through emergent practices of participatory artistic engagement: "Since the beginning of this [twentieth] century, avant-garde agitational artists have tried to demolish the divisions between art and life and introduce creativity, imagination, play and pleasure into the revolutionary project. ... [T]he DiY protest movement has taken these 'utopian' demands and made them real" (Jordan 1998, 129).

Alternative content and experimental aesthetics, when engaged in by individuals, create a sense of autonomy and empowerment, but they do not create the collective autonomy crucial to DIY anarchy. In order for that to occur, production of DIY content and style must take place in and establish radical communities of anti-authoritarian collaborative practice.

DIY Collaboration: Communities of Practice

DIY anarchism is not, contrary to what the expression implies, about doing it all by yourself: "Part of the mission of the early punk fanzines, besides spreading news about and interviews with punk bands, was to convince their readers to go out and do it themselves" (Duncombe 1997, 124–125). In other words, the goal is to form communities of practice where people are engaged in autonomous cultural production together. Anarchist creative producers struggle to reproduce ourselves in like-minded communities in order to subvert the capitalist social and creative reproduction of our multiple subjectivities as a target market or audience-commodity. As Holtzman, Hughes, and van Meter (2007, 45–46) assert, "DIY is the struggle of the collective individual against the production of its subjectivity, against its reproduction as a commodity of capitalism."

In creative collaborations, anarchist values such as resource sharing, mutual aid, skill sharing, and cooperation construct a shared political-artistic project. For example, zines "played a fundamental role in the construction of punk identity and a political community" (Triggs 2006, 70). Moreover, collective production offers the opportunity to find "substantive ways of abandoning capitalist institutions and building alternative networks and communities" (Holtzman, Hughes, and van Meter 2007, 47). DIY thus creates "a system of horizontal linkages that bind one into a web of interconnected political aims and aspirations," linkages constructed through relationships that create connected communities of political-artistic practice (Ruiz 2005, 198).

Communities also allow for a fluid conception of DIY anarchist identities. As Laura Portwood-Stacer (2013, 42) argues, "In the case of anarchist anti-consumers, practices of refusal, DIY, and the like, are material expressions of what it means to be an anarchist. Constructing such an identity narrative is both an individual and a collective process. That is, performances of self are both intrasubjective and intersubjective: the performance is done for oneself and also for others." DIY identity production is thus not an individual but a collective project, as Henry Jenkins (2010) argues:

> "Do It Yourself" is too easy to assimilate into some vague and comfortable notion of "personal expression" or "individual voice" that Americans can incorporate into long-standing beliefs in "rugged individualism" and "self-reliance." Yet, what may be radical about the DIY ethos is that learning relies on these mutual support networks, creativity is understood as a trait of communities, and expression occurs through collaboration. Given these circumstances, phrases like "Do It Ourselves" or "Do It Together" better capture collective enterprises within networked publics.
>
> *(233)*

DIY anarchist culture is therefore based on an implicit shared understanding of interdependency, mutual aid, and reciprocity.

Interdependency lends itself to a rejection of top-down single authorship in favour of collective authoring. For example, Indonesia punk fashion designers Unkl347 use "a method of critical appropriation, a variety of commercial satire, even a defiant assertion of the social nature of production over the individual rights of 'the author'" (Luvaas 2013). In DIY, there is an explicit recognition that all creativity is social, taking place in dialogue with others, and therefore to assert authorial rights is to claim ownership over creative culture without acknowledging the socius. In contrast, "frequent use of anonymity and pseudonymity in new social movement media suggests an aversion to the professionalization of intellectual activists based on personality and reputation" (Atton 2002, 120). Using collective pseudonyms further challenges the Western notion of the lone artistic or poetic genius, acknowledging instead the dialogic role of community. Triggs (2006, 70) suggests that DIY punk movements "fostered an active dialogue with a community of like-minded individuals." For these artists, the antiprofessional aesthetic "stressed the immediacy of its production and of the information, but also the transparency of the design and journalistic process itself" (Triggs 2006, 72).

The concept of community, however, is multifaceted – communities can also be authoritarian, hierarchical, and oppressive. DIY anarchists address this by prioritizing self-reflection, process, and structure in horizontalism.

DIY Structure: Horizontal Organizing

Atton (2002, 30) sees DIY and alternative "media as reflexive instruments of communication practices in social networks: there is a focus on process and relation." Uzelman (2005, 23) argues that "autonomous media often are much more open to democratic decision making, popular participation in the creation of content, and dialogue between participants." For Holtzman, Hughes, and van Meter (2007, 47), DIY anarchy is grounded in "explicit forms of resistance, such as cultural networks organized on principles antithetical to the conservative, individualistic, and pro-corporate environment" in mainstream arts production. In DIY anarchism, therefore, artistic-political structures are organized to be horizontal and prefigurative.

DIY anarchists organize cultural production as they organize everything else – in horizontal participatory collectives:

> DIY reoriented power often fosters a newly found awareness of individual and collective ability to produce and further social change. The emphasis DIY placed on direct participation advanced the practices and ideals of the movement. One punk described his early involvement as the "realization that people like us all over the world were creating their own culture. A democratic culture was ours for the taking, but as a true democracy implies, we had to participate."
>
> *(Holtzman, Hughes, and van Meter 2007, 48)*

For DIY anarchist culture to be participatory and directly democratic, it is often horizontally organized. Decisions in horizontal groups are often made by consensus with open participation of whoever shows up. Chris Atton (2002, 18) argues that in DIY publishing, processes such as distributive use, horizontal networks of communication, and transformed social relations of equality are key. As Pollyanna Ruiz notes, "autonomous media activists are distinguished by their commitment to an egalitarian, do-it-yourself, anti-authoritarian ethic in the struggle for democratic media" and culture (quoted in Uzelman 2005, 23).

In addition to horizontalism within DIY anarchist production, horizontal relationships are cultivated between producers and consumers so that the audience is also empowered (Holtzman, Hughes, and van Meter 2007, 52). Horizontal structures are important as they attempt to prefigure a desired world in the present.

DIY Process: Prefigurative Practices

In other words, "individuals are not asking power to address their needs and concerns through processes of representation – they are carrying out actions on their own behalf in which the means are also the ends" (Holtzman, Hughes, and van Meter 2007, 53). This is prefigurative politics. Prefiguration is defined as a kind of direct action with a consistency of means and ends, an attempt to put the principles and values of anarchism into practice in the present. In creating horizontal, prefigurative practices and processes, the process of organizing is as important as the end product (Atton 2002, 27). For example, anti-racist media and cultural producers may use anti-oppression practices to prefigure anti-racist communities, paying attention to power dynamics within a community of practice.

Within DIY genres, therefore, specific challenges to dominant culture occur via experimental forms and anti-authoritarian content, as well as the integration of these politics into creative practices. A DIY group might be anti-racist, pro-immigrant rights, and against borders; take an intersectional feminist approach; or be focused on indigenous sovereigntist organizing, environmental organizing, queer and trans rights, mobilizing against police brutality and war, and/or foregrounding gender and sexual diversity or reproductive justice. These forms of oppositional content will often be reflected in the composition of the group and the processes they use to prefigure a world they want to see in the here and now.

In other words, "DIY production methods reflected the promotion of politics" through practice, not just theory or content (Triggs 2006, 69). For DIY anarchists, "the forms of these campaigns are as significant as their content in so far as they illustrate the possibility of thinking, and therefore doing, things differently" (Ruiz 2005, 204–205). Whereas one small group of anarchist DIY makers can only have a minimal impact, the combined force of many DIY campaigns creating media, arts, and culture have the potential to "impact forcefully on the mainstream" (Ruiz 2005, 205). The demonstration in the here and now of thinking and organizing differently is powerful in making change, not only at the personal and interpersonal levels but also at the infrastructural and institutional levels.

This includes online spaces. While the Internet has often been hailed as radically open and democratizing, Curran, Fenton, and Freedman (2012, 179) have found that "the internet did not promote global understanding in the way that had been anticipated because the internet came to reflect the inequalities, linguistic division, conflicting values and interests of the real world." Nor did it rejuvenate democracy, transform the economy to be more equitable, or promote citizen journalism; instead, those corporations and social groups that already held power continued to exercise and strengthen that power using online tools, because "the internet's influence is filtered through the structures and processes of society" (Curran, Fenton, and Freedman 2012, 179). Kate Milberry (2014, 59) also emphasizes the danger in assuming the Internet is "inherently democratic" when it has grown out of the military industrial complex and extends "capitalist social relations from the material to the immaterial realm." For online spaces to be part of a model of DIY anarchism, they must challenge these hierarchical structures.

Hackers, hacktivists, and Free/Libre Open Source Software (FLOSS) advocates develop and reconfigure online structures to be more consistent with DIY anarchism, including the use of horizontalism and prefiguration. They organize in horizontal collectives, and the technologies they produce provide opportunities for horizontal participation, explicitly exploiting and amplifying the potentials of the Internet for equality, democracy, and cooperative content production. To these ends, they produce open source software or freeware, open editorial platforms such as the Indymedia network and its legacies, and net neutrality avenues. As

Kate Milberry (2014, 56) argues, "tech activists have heeded the call for a politics of technological transformation in building technologies of resistance intended to support grassroots struggle online, remaking the Internet as a more democratic and humane communication medium in the process."

In addition to using tech skills in creative projects, "technologies of resistance are imbued with a prefigurative politics of emancipation. They seek to assist activists in their social justice work by providing secure communications and enhancing privacy and anonymity online" (Milberry 2014, 57). Text message and email encryption software such as PGP, CryptoSMS, TextSecure, and RedPhone have been developed by activist and anarchist coders for digital communications in the era of pervasive state surveillance of activists. Milberry (2014, 60) suggests that hackers are able to carve out spaces for "joyful, creative, collective and subversive [immaterial] labour" that is based not on capitalist exploitation and authoritarian work relationships but rather in "voluntaristic cooperation, self-determination, and the fulfillment of species-being," all of which prefigure a utopian future both on- and offline.

DIY anarchist projects embody anti-authoritarian, horizontal, prefigurative processes and structures that make space for the equal participation of all in creative making. However, this participation might be limited under neoliberal capitalism, so DIY anarchist culture must add anti-capitalism to its list of characteristics.

DIY Economics: Anti-Capitalist Culture

DIY anti-capitalism replaces the profit motive expected by capitalism with alternative approaches to economics – based on the presumption that we live in a culture of plenty and generosity rather than of scarcity and selfishness – including gift economies, mutual aid, bartering, dumpstering, and gleaning. As anti-capitalists, DIY anarchists disavow the economic profit imperative inherent in the culture industry "through explicitly anti-capitalist modes of cultural production, for example: lo-fi inexpensive productions such as zines, resource and skill sharing, trading or giving away texts, selling texts at cost, anti-copyrighting, free downloadable PDFs, and pirating. Using these specific tactics, anarchists put anti-capitalist values into practice" (Jeppesen 2010, 475).

Anti-capitalist economic practices can range from the informal economy to formalized organization of DIY production such as worker cooperatives, critical maker collectives, and the punk record labels and hacker groups mentioned earlier. Processes of media and arts production are geared toward generating not income but output through simultaneous production of lived social relations of equality and empowerment. As Holtzman, Hughes, and van Meter (2007, 44) put it, "DIY has been effective in empowering marginalized sectors of society, while simultaneously providing a means to subvert and transcend capitalism."

Rather than money, in other words, people invest passion and creative ideas to reap collective empowerment. As Indonesia punk fashion designer Dendy suggests, "The only thing necessary is passion and intent. Design for [him] means 'doing what's in [his] heart without worrying about what will sell,' or even whether it's any good" (Luvaas 2013). Like DIY punks, DIY fashion designers are concerned not with sales but with expressing themselves through DIY style. The emphasis on heart, passion, self-expression, and positive relationships supplants the exploitative business relationships of bosses over workers, instead creating positive affective experiences.

Ultimately, "DIY is not simply a means of spreading alternative forms of social organizing or a symbolic example of a better society; it is the active construction of counter-relationships and the organization against and beyond capitalism" (Holtzman, Hughes, and van Meter 2007, 45). The value of cultural products is determined not by the capitalist marketplace but rather by its personal meaning for people. DIY is perhaps better "understood as a two-step process, first addressing value and then social relationships. It undermines exchange-value while simultaneously creating use-value outside of capitalism" (Holtzman, Hughes, and van Meter 2007, 45). The inherent tension in this process is that, "while DIY still takes place in a monetary economy, and all the vestigial elements of capital have not left its processes, commodities produced in DIY fashion have expanded their use-values in relation to their exchange-value. Exchange-value is no longer the predominant attribute of the commodity, and use-value – 'worth,' to its participants – is primary" (Holtzman, Hughes, and van Meter 2007, 44). This worth is defined not in monetary terms but in terms of community and positive affective relationships.

DIY communities also redistribute both economic wealth and social power at the grassroots. For example, Food Not Bombs uses a DIY approach to food sharing and redistribution of wealth through producing meals from dumpstered or donated ingredients and serving them in the community (Holtzman, Hughes, and van Meter 2007, 49–50). Participants also redistribute social power by providing a space for people to coproduce and share food without any intervening institution that might require ID and an explanation of one's poverty or need, as we might see in food banks. Similarly community gardens provide both a social space for shared production of food and a direct action DIY space for the community to feed itself, cutting out corporate or state intervention. As "a distinct form of anti-capitalist struggle, DIY culture has provided a means of circumventing the power of capitalist structures, while at the same time creating substantive alternatives" (Holtzman, Hughes, and van Meter 2007, 54).

These alternatives effectively integrate political objectives into content, aesthetics, organizational forms, and anti-capitalist practices: "In a strategic sense, the DIY elements found in the current movements against capitalism are among the most successful. They are highly participatory, practical, positive, constructive, non-ideologically based, and often go beyond simplistic oppositional politics and critique" (Holtzman, Hughes, and van Meter 2007, 54). DIY culture creates oppositional spaces for anarchist production and lifestyles, and thereby "reconstructs power relationships differently than those found under capital, by abandoning the institutions of capital and the state, and constructing counter-institutions based upon fundamentally different principles and structures" (Holtzman, Hughes, and van Meter 2007, 45). These differentiated and equalized power relationships form a key element of prefiguration and horizontalism explicitly from an anti-capitalist anarchist perspective.

Zines provide a good example of how power is redistributed. Kirsten Kozolanka, Patricia Mazepa, and David Skinner (2012, 21) note that "zines have a high social value within anarchist culture, largely because they disavow the economic and are seen as inherently anti-capitalist" when produced within DIY anarchist spaces and practices. This redistribution of power is also based on a reconceptualization of what it means to be successful. Similar to the notions expressed by DIY fashion designer Denny, "The anarchist ethos of success is that one person's success makes space for the success of others, in contrast to mainstream [capitalist] ideologies in which one person's success is seen as a marker of other people's failures. Success in zine production fosters more zine production, which both supports and reflects a healthy cultural community" (Jeppesen 2012, 272). Success for DIY anarchists is based on the generation of projects in which culture can be produced and shared among equals, not just outside of capitalism but in direct opposition to it.

DIY Events: Direct Action Protest

Similarly, direct action events or "protestivals" (St. John 2008), which integrate protest with cultural elements in a festival-like atmosphere, such as Reclaim the Streets (RTS), snake marches, dance parties, and Critical Mass bike rides, engage a DIY anti-authoritarian and anti-capitalist ethos. Without asking for permission, these actions "reclaim power from the state [and capital] in taking action, thus helping to create new avenues for participation in politics and everyday life" (Holtzman, Hughes, and van Meter 2007, 51). They provide free cultural spaces for participation, challenging the assumption that entertainment must be paid for and consumed in a spectacle-like passive consumer experience. Moreover, this model of DIY protestival redistributes power as people do not look to hierarchically-elevated others – such as actors, event producers, or art galleries – to provide entertainment, but rather discover the infinite possibilities of participating in the despectacularized "politics of everyday life" with others. For Jordan (1998, 131), "What makes DiY protest powerful is that ... [b]y making the art completely invisible, DiY protest gives art back its original socially transformative power."

These cultural productions are forms of direct action. DIY cultural production can be a key component of direct action protest, and vice versa. In this sense, DIY involves the integration of direct-action politics into cultural and media production. "There can be no text without action, and neither text nor action can exist without discussion before, during, and after the action – thus there can be no action without texts" (Jeppesen 2012, 269). DIY events, like direct action campaigns, do not make demands. Instead, the action itself creates change. For example, protest road blockades directly prevent traffic, blocking out car culture and in its place creating festivals, bike culture, and other forms of active transportation and pleasure. Logging road blockades, similarly, directly prevent loggers from working, thus protecting old-growth forests from being clear-cut. Guerrilla gardens directly provide participants with resources and skills for growing food themselves. As such we can see that DIY direct action is used to organize community cultural spaces for "protest, pleasure and living" such as temporary or permanent autonomous zones, occupations, squats, community art spaces, free skools, autonomous houses, protest camps, and infoshops (McKay 1998, 3).

As we have seen, the connection between political cultural production and distribution, protest organizing, and the creation and maintenance of collective anarchist DIY spaces is their consistent use of the set of characteristics set out here, many of which are closely tied to other anarchist concepts explored in this volume: oppositional content, experimental aesthetics, action in community, horizontal organizing, prefigurative horizontal processes, anti-capitalism, and direct action.

Conclusion

The term DIY, appropriated from the hardware industry by punks, has grown to include a wide range of practices, to which this chapter has provided a brief introduction. We have also mapped key characteristics of DIY anarchism that can help us to better understand DIY projects and practices.

Today, a quick Internet search turns up books and websites on DIY everything, from coffee to projects for luxurious living, media in the classroom to netporn. Clearly, some of these DIY projects are distant from the DIY anarchist content and practices mapped out here. From its appropriation by punks and anarchists, DIY has been co-opted by capitalism in a cycle of cross-appropriation. DIY entrepreneurs who start businesses in order to do what they love and make profits are essentially start-up protocapitalists and thus perhaps eventually unlink with DIY anarchism. Similarly, educators who incorporate DIY media into the classroom are not engaged in the prefigurative and horizontal processes of grassroots DIY anarchism, as they are incorporating DIY into a top-down model of instruction within the neoliberal education system. While introducing skill-sharing, self-exploration, and other values of DIY production, these types of protocapitalism and pedagogy are not DIY anarchism, which seeks to destroy the hierarchies imposed by formal education, reject neoliberal capitalism, and engage in direct action controlled by those participating in collaborative communities of practice.

However, some value-practices of anarchism do get taken up in more mainstream institutionalized practices. For example, the loosely defined "copyleft" or anti-copyright used in the 1960s and 1970s by anarchist writers, publishers, and pirates has been codified into the Creative Commons licensing system for widespread use by musicians, writers, and other cultural producers. Holtzman, Hughes, and van Meter (2007, 54) argue DIY is "a political concept, but one based on composition rather than ideology. This concept is flexible, has the potential of being utilized across a broad area of activities and struggles, and is not simply applicable only to those of a particular counterculture or music-oriented youth culture. Ultimately, however, the direction of DIY is up to the participants themselves."

This flexibility is in fact a defining feature evident in many of the characteristics mapped out in this chapter. The direction of DIY anarchism comes from and is decided upon by participants in cooperation with others. As such, "though DIY is most prominent in the realm of cultural production, it is continually being expanded to reclaim more complex forms of labor, production, and resistance" (Holtzman, Hughes, and van Meter 2007, 44). DIY anarchism, as it continues to be practised, defined, and rethought, has thus become a widespread practice of social, political, and cultural transformation.

Note

1 *Merriam-Webster OnLine*, s.v. "DIY," accessed December 11, 2015, www.merriam-webster.com/dictionary/DIY.

References

Atton, Chris. 2002. *Alternative Media*. Thousand Oaks: SAGE.
Cohn, Jesse. 2014. *underground passages: anarchist resistance culture 1848–2011*. Oakland: AK Press.
Curran, James, Natalie Fenton, and Des Freedman. 2012. *Misunderstanding the Internet*. London: Routledge.
Duncombe, Stephen. 1997. *Notes from Underground: Zines and the Politics of Alternative Culture*. New York: Verso.
Ferrell, Jeff. 1996. *Crimes of Style: Urban Graffiti and the Politics of Criminality*. Lebanon, NH: Northeastern University Press.
Harding, Thomas. 1998. "Viva Camcordistas! Video Activism and the Protest Movement." In *DiY Culture: Party and Protest in Nineties Britain*, edited by George McKay, 79–99. New York: Verso.
Hebdige, Dick. 1979. *Subculture: The Meaning of Style*. London: Methuen.
Holtzman, Ben, Craig Hughes, and Kevin van Meter. 2007. "Do It Yourself and the Movement Beyond Capitalism." In *Constituent Imagination: Militant Investigation//Collective Theorization*, edited by Stevphen Shukaitis and David Graeber, 44–61. Oakland, CA: AK.
Jenkins, Henry. 2010. "Afterword: Communities of Readers, Clusters of Practices." In *DIY Media: Creating, Sharing and Learning with New Technologies*, edited by Colin Lankshear and Michele Knobel, 231–252. New York: Peter Lang.
Jeppesen, Sandra. 2010. "Creating Guerilla Texts in Rhizomatic Value-Practices on the Sliding Scale of Autonomy: Toward an Anti-Authoritarian Cultural Logic." In *New

Perspectives on Anarchism, edited by Nathan J. Jun and Shane Wahl, 473–496. Lanham: Lexington Books.

Jeppesen, Sandra. 2011. "The DIY Post-Punk Post-Situationist Politics of CrimethInc." *Anarchist Studies* 19(1): 23–55.

Jeppesen, Sandra. 2012. "DIY Zines and Direct-Action Activism." In *Alternative Media in Canada*, edited by Kirsten Kozolanka, Patricia Mazepa, and David Skinner, 264–281. Vancouver: UBC Press.

Jordan, John. 1998. "The Art of Necessity: The Subversive Imagination of Anti-road Protest and Reclaim the Streets." In *DiY Culture: Party and Protest in Nineties Britain*, edited by George McKay, 129–151. New York: Verso.

Kozolanka, Kirsten, Patricia Mazepa, and David Skinner. 2012. "Considering Alternative Media in Canada: Structure, Participation, Activism." In *Alternative Media in Canada*, edited by Kirsten Kozolanka, Patricia Mazepa, and David Skinner, 1–22. Vancouver: UBC Press.

Lankshear, Colin, and Michele Knobel. 2010. "DIY Media: A Contextual Background and Some Contemporary Themes." In *DIY Media: Creating, Sharing and Learning with New Technologies*, edited by Colin Lankshear and Michele Knobel, 1–26. New York: Peter Lang.

Lawley, Guy. 1999. "I Like Hate and I Hate Everything Else: The Influence of Punk on Comics." In *Punk Rock: So What?: The Cultural Legacy of Punk*, 1st edition, edited by Roger Sabin, 100–119. London: Routledge.

Lievrouw, Leah A. 2011. *Alternative and Activist New Media*. Cambridge: Polity.

Luvaas, Brent. 2013. *DIY Style: Fashion, Music and Global Digital Cultures*. London: BERG.

McKay, George. 1998. "DiY Culture: Notes Towards an Intro." In *DiY Culture: Party and Protest in Nineties Britain*, edited by George McKay, 1–53. New York: Verso.

Milberry, Kate. 2014. "(Re)making the Internet: Free Software and the Social Factory Hack." In *DIY Citizenship: Critical Making and Social Media*, edited by Matt Ratto and Megan Boler, 53–64. Cambridge: MIT Press.

O'Connor, Allan. 2008. *Punk Record Labels and the Struggle for Autonomy: The Emergence of DIY*. Lanham: Lexington Books.

Portwood-Stacer, Laura. 2013. *Lifestyle Politics and Radical Activism*. New York: Bloomsbury.

Ruiz, Pollyanna. 2005. "Bridging the Gap: From the Margins to the Mainstream." In *Global Activism, Global Media*, edited by Wilma De Jong, Martin Shaw, Neil Stammers, 194–207. London: Pluto Press.

Shantz, Jeffrey. 2010. *Constructive Anarchy: Building Infrastructures of Resistance*. Farnham: Ashgate.

St. John, Graham. 2008. "Protestival: Global Days of Action and Carnivalized Politics in the Present." *Social Movement Studies* 7(2): 167–190.

Triggs, Teal. 2006. "Scissors and Glue: Punk Fanzines and the Creation of a DIY Aesthetic." *Journal of Design History* 19(1): 69–83.

Uzelman, Scott. 2005. "Hard at Work in the Bamboo Garden: Media Activists and Social Movements." In *Autonomous Media: Activating Resistance and Dissent*, edited by Andrea Langlois and Frédéric Dubois, 17–28. Montreal: Cumulus.

15

ECOCENTRISM

Sean Parson

To date, the year 2016 was the warmest year on record. This will likely be a shortly held record, as we can well expect that, with each successive year, a newer record will be set. There is now little doubt that the future of this planet will be warmer. We will see increased droughts and, paradoxically, yearly 100-year floods; the expansion of infectious diseases like malaria and dengue fever; and the relocation of people living in coastal cities and islands as rising seas turn their homes into the new Atlantis. At this point, there is very little that can reasonably be done to stop climate change, and with it, the potential extinction of 95% of all species on this planet. No matter how much we like to believe that a solar- and wind-based power grid will solve our energy needs, while saving the earth's atmosphere, there is little to no evidence that this is the case (Zehner 2012). Not surprisingly, there is also no evidence that capitalist economic relations can be marshaled to fix the climate crisis (Rodgers 2013). With no prospect of solving our ecological crises via renewable energies, what is the solution? Anarchism, much more than other radical ideologies, has focused on ecological issues – from the proto-anarchism of Henry David Thoreau to the ecologically minded work of Peter Kropotkin and Elisée Reclus to the contemporary work of Murray Bookchin. Because of this, an ecocentric anarchism or *eco-anarchism* provides a unique lens for understanding and exploring a radical response to our ecological crises. In this chapter, I contend that anti-civilizational anarchism – one of the more recent and more controversial branches of ecologism – is linked intellectually to these earlier strands of anarchist thought, and that it provides unique insights that are essential for humanity to understand as we face the prospect of catastrophic climate change.

In what follows, I will provide a basic intellectual overview of ecological anarchism, and then use Michael Freeden's understanding of ideology to create a basic mapping of it. This will be followed by a deeper examination of the anti-civilizational thread of contemporary American anarchism, a variety of ecocentric thought that is often excluded from anarchist discussions. Examining this strand of thought will help identify important critiques and ideas that can be used to expand the ecological discussion within the anarchist milieu. Anti-civilization anarchism is a branch of anarchist politics and theory that has received little attention by academics and anarchist scholars (Bookchin 1995; Kahn 2005; Smith 2007; Parson 2008), even though the radical activist community has intensely debated primitivism for years. The final section will provide a series of concepts, questions, and ideas that anti-civilizational anarchism offers for other strands of radical and anarchist thought, in hopes that this creates a larger dialogue around ecological sustainability, technological systems, and modern industrialism.

Eco-Anarchism: A Brief Introduction

Prior to the capitalist revolution in production, ecological crises tended to be localized and related to local over-production, natural disaster, or war. Under feudalism, the productive system was not nearly efficient enough, nor did it have the desire, to increase production to the level that we began to see with the industrial revolution. As the commons became enclosed, factories emerged as a means of channeling the labor of the newly landless classes into expanding economic production. The revolutionary changes that happened during the rise of capitalism altered nearly every aspect of life, and radical thinkers and activists began to notice and act. While most Marxist thinkers during the nineteenth century focused on the workers – paying only partial attention to the ecological impacts of capitalism – most anarchists tended to be more aware of the broader damage that capitalism was causing.

Peter Kropotkin (2009) was one of the first to link the changing production system to ecological changes as well. According to Kropotkin (2017), urbanization had a deleterious effect on the soil and land, as well as on the soul and mind of the worker. Instead of calling for a radical expansion of industrial production – as many Marxists did – Kropotkin called for a turn to the local, a reimagining of economic systems so that production, consumption, and distribution can be linked to local concerns. This approach would allow for a stronger link between people and the land. It would also greatly weaken the impact of industrial production to the natural environment. According to Graham Purchase (1996), we should actively think of Kropotkin (along with Thoreau and John Muir) as one of the founders of contemporary environmentalism, though he never really made ecological concerns central to his work. His primary concern was with the violence that capitalism and the state enacted on human populations.

In addition to Kropotkin, Elisée Reclus, the anarchist French geographer, provided one of the first examples of a "total liberation" approach to politics – linking human, ecological and animal liberation (Colling et al. 2014). Reclus (2013) strongly argued for animal rights, correctly saw old growth logging as moral and ethical violence, and understood that the exploitation of workers by capitalists is analogous to our own domination of animals and the natural world. Reclus provided a complex analysis that linked important concepts together, but he focused almost entirely on educating people about vegetarianism and environmentalism.

In the twentieth century, Murray Bookchin, a well-known anarchist theorist, was at the forefront of environmentalism. He published *Our Synthetic Environment* initially in 1962, a few months before the appearance of Rachel Carson's own groundbreaking book, *Silent Spring* (Carson 2002). In it, Bookchin (1974) provided one of the first critiques of the modern usage of pesticides, warning of ecological dangers similar to those Carson describes in her book. For the next four decades, he developed and expanded his theory of "social ecology" (Bookchin 2005), which combined anarchist values and commitments with ecological and humanitarian visions. Bookchin's social ecology argued that the devastation to the natural world is inherently linked to human oppression of other humans. In making this argument, he provides a powerful argument against the politics of domination – seeing the development of domination starting with the developing of large-scale sedentary societies and the religious and warrior cultures they need to thrive. It is this larger system of domination that destroys the environment and oppresses people which needs to be confronted by anarchist and environmental activists. By focusing on human-human relationships – politically, economically, and socially – we can work not only to combat capitalism but also to address ecocide.

More recently, thinkers such as Jeff Shantz (2012) are working to develop a "green syndicalism." Syndicalism, an anarchist political project that focuses on radical workplace democracy, is most commonly associated – in the English-speaking world – with the Industrial Workers of the World (IWW). Shantz sees the legacy of IWW workplace organizing as a model that can link workers' struggles with ecological struggles. He writes:

> For their part theorists of green syndicalism envision the association of workers [moving] toward the dismantling of the factory system, its work, hierarchies, regimentation. This may involve a literal destruction, as factories may be dismantled or perhaps converted to "soft" forms of localized production. Likewise, productive activity can be conceived in terms of restoration, including research into a region's natural history.
>
> *(Shantz 2012, 169)*

In effect, green syndicalism looks to radicalize workers against the destructive aspects of capitalist production, which would inherently include the environmental impacts of industrial production that affect the health of their families. By pushing for workplace agitation, sabotage, and worker democracy councils, green syndicalism seeks to address the ecological issue by empowering workers at the site of production.

Regardless of which thinker discussed above might inspire us, we should understand ecological anarchism as a form of ideological thought. In this light, we should note that Michael Freeden (2006) has revolutionized the study of ideology by moving the field away from the analytic and ahistoric approach developed by liberal scholars and from the pejorative usage of the term commonly deployed by Marxist scholars. What Freeden has developed is a complex and fluid understanding of ideology that focuses on the semantic and practical ways in which ideologies function. He writes:

> First, by politics we understand any human interaction that involves power transactions, the ranking and distribution of significant goods, the mobilization of support, the organization of stability as well as instability, and decision-making for collectivities that includes the construction of – or resistance to – political plans and visions. Second, such views of the world have a fluid morphology that may be grouped together in broad family resemblances, but is concurrently in constant flux over space and time. Third, while the particulars of any such view are elective, the existence of ideology is inevitable. We can only access the political world through decontesting the contested conceptual arrangements that enable us to make sense of that world, and we do so – deliberately or unconsciously – by imposing specific meanings onto the indeterminate range of meanings that our conceptual clusters can hold.
>
> *(Freeden 2006, 19)*

As the above quotation indicates, Freeden understands ideologies as always existing, meaning that there is no political engagement with the world that is post-ideological. He also views ideologies as complex constellations of differing values and beliefs that are structured by the gravity of shared intellectual values and concepts, which create a "family resemblance." When it comes to ecological anarchism there are a handful of overlapping values that keep the disparate views connected. Most notable is the linking of human oppression to ecological domination. While Bookchin clearly laid out this position, even the work of Kropotkin and Reclus supports the idea that the dehumanization of individuals is predicated on the ability to destroy and exploit the natural world. Likewise, Shantz argues that workers, exploited on the job, are also the primary victims of environmental injustices. As such, the hierarchies and dominations inherent in capitalism poison the natural world while actively exploiting the worker. These thinkers all promote a politics that seeks to embed people within the larger ecological system, effectively showing that the despoiling of the environment affects humans as well because we are interconnected with the broader ecological world.

Another primary concept that links together different versions of ecological anarchism is a critique of industrialism. In *Fields, Factories, and Workshops*, Kropotkin (2017) argues against the division of labor that exists within factory production between physical and mental labor and between urban and rural communities.

Reclus (1896) goes further, arguing that industrialism as an economic system is devastating the planet and he sees the clear-cut logging of the forests in the Pacific Northwest as an example of capitalist hubris and the "barbarity" of supposedly "civilized" peoples. To Reclus, the violent ways in which industrial society has devastated the natural world mirrored the violent way it objectifies people as tools to generate accumulation. Similarly, Bookchin critiques the "workerism" of Marxism and most anarchisms, arguing that their focus on labor and production ignores the complex ways in which the capitalist economy constructs domination and hierarchy throughout society. Instead of a politics focusing on the workplace and workers, Bookchin calls for a democratic municipalism in which production and distribution are democratically run by the community. This decentralized and democratic space would be a different way of organizing social and economic life, a drastic shift from industrial capitalism. Finally, Shantz promotes an anti-industrial eco-anarchist politics while directly opposing Bookchin's stance on labor and workplace democracy. Shantz (2012) writes:

> ... Green syndicalism, as opposed to Marxism or even anarcho-syndicalism, opposes large-scale, centralized, mass production. Green syndicalism does not hold to a socialist optimism of the liberatory potential of industrialism.
> Ecological calls for a complete, immediate break with industrialism, however, contradict radical eco-philosophical emphases upon interconnectedness, mutualism, and continuity.
> *(168)*

All the ecocentric anarchist political ideologies, while disagreeing on how best to accomplish this radical political project, share this opposition to industrialism.

Overall, eco-anarchism can be seen as a coherent political ideology in which different strategic and philosophical perspectives coexist within a broader political project that centralizes the link between human and ecological violence and that seeks to undermine and replace industrial capitalism. Next, we turn to anti-civilization anarchism, a newer variant of ecocentric anarchism that has been relatively marginalized among anarchist thinkers.

Introduction to Green Anarchism

Anti-civilizational anarchism, which is also called green anarchism or anarcho-primitivism, is a branch of anarchist thought that contends that civilization, along with domestication, is responsible for environmental destruction and human subjugation. Over the last few decades the tenets of anti-civilizational anarchism have been regularly debated amongst the English-speaking anarchist movement. Well-known anarchist public intellectuals, like Noam Chomsky and Michael Albert, have actively critiqued this tendency. Chomsky (2005, 434) has argued that primitivism would lead to "the mass genocide of millions," and Michael

Albert (2010) has said that "the most visible advocate and exemplar of what I called 'not so desirable anarchism' is John Zerzan." While some anarchist academics have been critical of anti-civilizational anarchism, Bron Taylor (2006, 2) has argued that primitivism had a significant influence on Earth First! and led to a "decreasing importance of Deep Ecology" in the radical environmental movement. Similarly, anti-civilizational thought has had a large impact on several groups – like the Earth Liberation Front, the Animal Liberation Front, and Mexico's *Individualidades Tendiendo a lo Salvaje* (ITS) – and ideological tendencies, such as post-left anarchism. In addition, anti-civilizational anarchism fits clearly within an ecocentric standpoint, understood as an important eco-anarchist strand of thought and sharing the same values as the ideologies discussed in the last section.

It is important to note that anti-civilizational thought is complex and diffuse. Much like sexuality, per Deleuze and Guattari, there are as many types of anti-civilizational anarchism as there are anti-civilizational anarchists. The point of this chapter, though, is not to pull apart the different strands of anti-civilizational anarchism but instead to highlight the commonalities among them. Following Freeden, anti-civilizational anarchism is not only part of the "common family" of ecocentric anarchism, but it is also a nuanced ideological position centered around four main concepts: civilization, technology, domestication, and collapse.

Civilization

All anti-civilizational anarchists contend that civilization is devouring the natural world and suppressing human desires.[1] Derrick Jensen (2006) defines civilization as

> a culture – that is, a complex of stories, institutions, and artifacts – that both leads to and emerges from the growth of cities …, with cities being defined – so as to distinguish from camps, villages and so on – as people living more or less permanently in one place in densities high enough to require the routine importation of food and other necessities of life.
>
> *(17)*

In this definition, one of the defining characteristics of a civilization is that it requires the importation of resources (food, oil, etc.) in order to continue its existence. This definition of civilization is taken from the academic analysis of the rise of cities and the mega-machine put forward by Lewis Mumford (1971). Mumford's work has been influential on radical environmental and neo-Luddite movements. For example, the deep ecologists and neo-Luddites Chellis Glendinning (1994) and Kirkpatrick Sale (1996) both use Mumford's work as a foundation for their analyses. Overall, this need for external resources is why anti-civilizational anarchists argue that "civilization originates in conquest abroad and repression at home" (Diamond 1974, 1).

Central to this account of civilization is the work of anthropologists during the 1960s and 1970s, most notably Marshall Sahlins (1974), Richard Lee (1979; Lee and Daly 1999), Stanley Diamond (1974), Pierre Clastres (1989), and Harold Barclay (1996). These social scientists revolutionized the understanding of gatherer-hunter societies, and posited an analysis of these societies as being both egalitarian and libertarian. In addition, Diamond, Clastres, and Barclay not only critiqued civilization, but each identified as anarchist. These anthropologists thus provided the foundation for an anti-civilizational conception of the primitive and provided an anarchist base for anti-civilizational thinkers to use.

In this regard, the critique of civilization is something much more complex and broad than the general anti-statism traditionally associated with anarchism. Civilization, in this context, includes more than the state and capitalism, and it even goes beyond anti-industrialism. What is included in civilization is all of those institutions, but also the division of labor, capital accumulation, institutional and social hierarchies, as well as agriculture and animal husbandry. Of course, what counts as a civilization is very difficult to define and is a central debate amongst anti-civilizational theorists. Some, such as Zerzan (2012), argue that most indigenous people in the Americas were civilized, because they engaged in agriculture and reared animals for use as tools or food. By contrast, Jesús Sepúlveda (2005) argues for an indigenist[2] and communalist life, centered on communal festivals, nature myths, and primitive skills/folk-science to serve as a blueprint for a post-civilizational world. In his mind, agriculture and animal husbandry are not antithetical to the primitive, as the village, and not the social band, defines the ideal primitive social arrangement. In all cases, though, anti-civilizational anarchism is opposed to civilization understood as a larger social system rooted in the need to move resources from one area to sustain cities.

At its core, the concept of civilization here is colonial, as cities tend to colonize smaller rural areas. This colonization leads not only to the destruction and depletion of rural areas that are feeders to cities, but also to urban pollution, social hierarchies, and increased military power. From an anti-civilizational perspective, an urban anarchism that requires the importation of resources from outside will inevitably be maintaining a hierarchical and colonial relationship in which certain groups of people are seeing their land base destroyed (for instance to produce coal or oil) for the technological and economic advantage, for the resource and luxury needs, of those in urban spaces.

Technology

In Mumford's (1971) work, technology can be defined as the techniques and tools that require and enforce a division of labor. Interestingly, though critical of modern technology and civilization, Mumford was not absolutely opposed to either. In his work, he saw the culture that civilization creates – especially art, music, and theatre – and certain technologies, such as those that promote travel and communication, as benefiting humankind more than it harms us. Expanding on Mumford's work on technique and technology, Jacques Ellul (1964) argues that modern technology and technique undermine human freedom and liberty. To Ellul, the technological society promotes automaton-ism, economic rationalism, and a rigid division of labor. Because of this, the technological system undermines human freedom, liberty, and autonomy. Anti-civilizational anarchists latch onto Ellul's argument and universally oppose technological systems, viewing them as non-neutral enforcers of state and capitalist power.

There is a difference between the two strands of anti-civilizational thought in how absolutist they are in their opposition to technology. Zerzan (1999) not only rejects technology but also symbolic logic, numbers, and language. David Watson (1996) and Fredy Perlman (1983), on the other hand, do not reject agriculture or any non-industrial technology absolutely, but reject a technological system that requires massive social inequalities. They instead promote a certain "folk" technology and knowledge that is simple, uses little to no electricity, and does not radically alter human social relationships.

Both strands of anti-civilizational thought, though, do share a radical critique of modern technological systems. This critique argues that technology is not value neutral, and therefore, helps to produce the social hierarchies that anarchists regularly challenge – so long as the social and economic relationships in society are not altered. This Luddite critique is essential for any contemporary radical thinker trying to think through solutions to climate change. Instead of just looking to engineering solutions, it is worth asking what social arrangements are needed and supported by this technological system. Does solar energy actually promote decentralization and the development of sustainable communities, or does it require a more complex social hierarchy in which some people are needed to extract resources from their land base, where technological expertise will be rewarded with either increased wealth or social and political power, etc.? If the goal of anarchism is the end of domination, illegitimate hierarchies, and the expansion of personal and communal liberty, understanding the negative implications of technological systems is essential for moving forward.

Domestication

Flowing from the need to ensure and impose order for its survival, civilization must homogenize and domesticate life, both human and non-human, on the planet. This attempt to control the wild is a central characteristic of civilization; all that is wild and feral is a threat to the civilizational order. This control is required to ensure the flow of natural resources needed to keep civilization afloat and is commonly achieved through the use of military/economic force or by the process of domestication. Domestication is the process through which animals (human and non-human) and plants are controlled for societal benefit. Human domestication, according to Feral Faun (2013), takes many forms, some of which are difficult to recognize. Government, capital and religion are some of the more obvious faces of authority. But technology, work, language with its conceptual limits, the ingrained habits of etiquette and propriety – these too are domesticating authorities which transform us from wild, playful, unruly animals into tamed, bored, unhappy producers and consumers.

(28)

In other words, our social system – morality, work, and education – domesticate and placate humanity for the benefit of the social order. This domestication removes from life spontaneity, passion, freedom, and liberty. Domestication, according to Zerzan (1999, 77), requires "initiation of production, vastly increased divisions of labor, and the completed foundations of social stratification." Due to this, Zerzan, much like Friedrich Engels, claims that domestication is the root cause of sexism, racism, war, and capitalism. To confront the totality of civilization and return us to our natural ways of life, green anarchists support undermining social institutions that domesticate and turn us docile. For instance, Ivan Illich (1971; 1973; 1976), an influential thinker for both Watson and Perlman, argues against contemporary social institutions such as schools and medical centers, because he sees them as molding people for the benefit of society. For instance, in *Medical Nemesis*, Illich (1976) argues that industrialized medicine does not heal illness but instead creates a level of dependence between people and civilization. In many instances, the actions of societies cause illness, rather than cure it – consider how, with many types of cancer, people seeking to survive become dependent on the same system that made them ill in the first place.

Collapse

The final component of anti-civilizational anarchist theory is a belief in an imminent collapse of industrial civilization. This collapse will be the result of civilization's unsustainable quest for resources and the resulting environmental damage. Authors such as Zerzan, Jensen, and Watson all argue that if we do not abolish civilization soon then the collapse will only be made worse. This desire is expressed by David Watson (1996, 45) who argues that "industrial civilization [is] one vast, stinking extermination camp. We all live in Bhopal, some closer to the gas chambers and to the mass graves, but all of us close enough to be victims." To Watson, the destruction of civilization must occur abruptly. If not, he wonders what will happen when "we all live in Bhopal and Bhopal is everywhere?" This is the worst-case scenario for him – an environment too ravaged for human life to survive. Watson, Zerzan, and Jensen all believe that ending civilization now, and not waiting for the planet to do it for us, is a more sympathetic and compassionate approach than any technological or humanist venture. The current knowledge regarding climate change, peak oil, species die-off, etc. might be providing additional empirical proof that ecological systems are overly strained and that industrial society is far from sustainable. This concept of collapse, and the possibly reactionary politics that might emerge from it, have been wonderfully critiqued in the book, *Catastrophism: The Apocalyptic Politics of Collapse and Rebirth* (Lilley et al. 2012). In this book, the authors argue that a reactionary and not liberatory politics emerges from a fixation on collapse; collapse does not promote the needed social movement building that is required for liberatory futures. They also argue that the fixation on collapse emerges because of the political impotence of the modern left – its inability to confront capitalism. Because we feel that we cannot organize against capitalism, we hang our revolutionary future not on our actions, but on a *deus ex machina*, in which the environment solves our failure to bring about the revolution by doing it for us. While there is definitely more than a kernel of truth in these critiques – concerning the political limitations of this frame and the dangers of putting our hopes on collapse – they miss the primary question that comes out of anti-civilizational thought: which is not whether collapse is useful for organizing a political opposition, but whether it is an economic and ecological necessity. Can we avoid collapse while maintaining industrial forms of production? If not, then the critique put forward by the anti-civilizational thinkers needs to be more adequately addressed. If industrialism is not sustainable, what vision would be sustainable?

Complicating Anarchism: Questions about Technology, Industrialism, and Sustainability Moving Forward

This chapter started with a reminder about the scary futures that we, as a planet, are facing. Over the last few hundred years, the natural world has been ravaged to the point in which many of the ecological thresholds needed to maintain life on this planet are being passed. While it now seems nearly impossible to fully mitigate our actions and stop a coming ecological crisis, there is a lively debate about the ways in which we can make our communities and ecosystems more resilient and possibly adapt to a much more hostile future. In effect, while we are all increasingly admitting that the future will be much worse than we might have imagined even a few decades ago, there is a chance we can avoid a *Mad Max* type post-apocalyptic political environment. To do so, though, we need to start asking incredibly uncomfortable questions – questions about the causes of ecological crisis, about what aspects of our lives are and are not sustainable, and about the tactics, strategies, and long-term goals and visions that we need to survive (as a species) in the coming centuries. The ideas and theoretical positions of the anti-civilizational anarchists need to be front and center for all radicals, all anarchists, and all individuals looking to build and develop a sustainable future. So, what are the primary questions that an open-minded engagement with anti-civilizational anarchism forces anarchism to engage with?

Question 1: Can Industrialism be Made Ecologically Sustainable?

One of the core assumptions of anti-civilizational anarchist theory is that any system is unsustainable if is not able to maintain itself via its own land base. This requires a radically diminished economy, one based on the logic of autarky and not on global systems of trade. The argument made by the anti-civilizational thinkers is that any large economic system, one requiring the transportation of goods and services to maintain itself, will cause two things to happen: 1) the depletion of a land base, where resources are removed, and 2) the dumping of additional waste and the creation of urban pollution. In both cases, the result is a system that is not ecologically sustainable. This argument is a radicalized version of what Brett Clark, John Bellamy Foster, and Richard York (Foster et al. 2011) call the "ecological rift" – a rift that is rooted in the capitalist mode of production. They argue that prior to capitalist economics the rift was maintained, largely, by the more localized nature of the economy. The anti-civilizational question here concerns whether or not that timeline is accurate. Was it only after the development of capitalist economic relationships that the rift was formed and the system became unsustainable? Does the story of Gilgamesh and the cutting down of the cedars of Lebanon, the ecological collapse of multiple ancient civilizations, not show that the ecological rift began further back in time?

This question, and the debate above, matters for a handful of important reasons. Most importantly, as we move forward and try to imagine a sustainable future, we need to have a sense of what our economic system might look like. If industrialism is not sustainable, then we need to envision what is. From that position, we must begin to think about what sort of tactics and strategies will move us closer to what we need. What does an anti-industrial labor politics look like? Can we fight for economic justice and economic democracy while promoting a de-growth and anti-industrial project?

Question 2: Is There a Way to Have Industrialism Without Systems of Domination?

One of Zerzan's favorite hypothetical questions to ask at talks is: In the anarchist future who will go into the mines? At first glance, this question might seem overly simple in that it asks an essential question about industrialism. Imagine, for a second, that we are living in a free world, one without domination and hierarchy. Now let's say that our community lives above an important natural resource. While this resource might help the world in a utilitarian sense, mining for it would most likely devastate my community's land base, polluting the soil, poisoning the water, and putting at risk the workers who are going into the mine. As a local community, we would be sacrificing our land and health for the benefit of others. How do you get people to do this without force? Is altruism enough and could it ever be?

This question gets to the core of the complex relationship between technology and society that underscores anti-civilizational thought: complex technological systems have webs of relationships and these relationships are not always equal or fair. If we try to imagine a world free of domination, coercion, and hierarchy, we need to think through the entire web of relationships that our complex technological and social systems require. Can we have computers and maintain our anarchist visions? If so, who will mine the materials needed to make it? Who will house its decaying and polluting corpse after it must be disposed of? What incentives do people and communities have to do so? If the answers to such questions are unpalatable, then we need to reimagine our world radically, to think of a world that is free of extractive industries – from mining to logging.

Question 3: If Industrialism Is Not Sustainable, How Can We Transition to a Sustainable Future?

One of the most often employed critiques of anti-civilizational thought is that the transition primitivists are envisioning would mean the deaths of billions of people. If we push for a collapse of industrial civilization, let alone civilization more broadly, the decreased production and distribution would lead to a massive decrease in human population. To flip Chomsky's contention on its head: if anti-civilizational thinkers are correct about the unsustainable nature of our current system, how can we transition to a sustainable future without falling into a misanthropic politics that acquiesces in the deaths of countless human beings? Is there a way to maintain the anarchist commitment to freedom and autonomy while moving toward a sustainable future?

Most of the conversations that we are having around the transition are shallow, focusing primarily on creating more resilient and more sustainable versions of what we already have. People are not discussing, nor moving towards, a radically different world than the one we currently inhabit. But if we want to think about a radical transition, then we need to do so – and soon. We need to imagine what kinds of radical shifts can happen and how can we do them in a way that is humane, caring, and democratic.

Concluding Remarks

The ecological crisis we are facing has sadly not led to massive changes in the economic, social, or political institutions of the US or Europe. The longer this crisis goes unaddressed, the more likely it is that what will emerge is a discourse of "emergency" in which states and militaries will use their power in ways that attempt to benefit from the crisis. This is a vision of fascistic future, one centered around a corporate feudalism; this is a world in which power and inequalities are maintained through force, even in the face of the inevitable. This is a vision that I do not want to come true, and as such, we need to start thinking unreasonably and start asking questions that get to the core of our current crisis. We need not worry about being called fanatics, radical extremists, or ecological zealots – if anything we need to start embracing these names. When confronting an unacceptable future, one where most of the species on this planet might go extinct and where billions of people throughout the planet will either die or be forced to relocate, we need to respond in kind. If our demands for a healthy planet are unreasonable to those in power, then we need to realize that there is a war for the future of this planet going on and those in power are our enemies. In this case, much like the class war, we are currently losing but, to be fair, we have yet to really start fighting.

Notes

1 In noting that civilization both *devours* and *suppresses*, it is important to remember that one influential force within the *Fifth Estate* school of anti-civilizational anarchism, Fredy Perlman (1983), frequently uses "Leviathan" as a synonym for civilization.
2 Sepúlveda in this regard seems similar to Ward Churchill, who refers to himself as an indigenist, rather than a Marxist or an anarchist.

References

Albert, Michael. 2010. "Anarchism = Zerzan?" The Anarchist Library. Accessed June 27, 2017, from https://theanarchistlibrary.org/library/michael-albert-anarchism-zerzan.
Barclay, Harold. 1996. *People Without Government: An Anthropology of Anarchy*. London: Kahn & Averill Publishers.
Bookchin, Murray. 1974. *Our Synthetic Environment*. Revised edition. New York: Harper & Row.
Bookchin, Murray. 1995. *Re-Enchanting Humanity: A Defense of the Human Spirit Against Antihumanism, Misanthropy, Mysticism, and Primitivism*. London and New York: Cassell.
Bookchin, Murray. 2005. *The Ecology of Freedom: The Emergence and Dissolution of Hierarchy*. Oakland, CA: AK Press.
Carson, Rachel. 2002. *Silent Spring*. 40th anniversary edition. Boston: Houghton Mifflin.
Chomsky, Noam. 2005. *Chomsky on Anarchism*. Edited by Barry Pateman. Oakland, CA: AK Press.
Clastres, Pierre. 1989. *Society Against the State: Essays on Political Anthropology*. Cambridge, MA: Zone Books
Colling, Sarat, Sean Parson, and Alessandro Arrigoni. 2014. "Until All are Free: Total Liberation Through Revolutionary Decolonization, Groundless Solidarity, and a Relational Framework." In *Defining Critical Animal Studies: An Intersectional Social Justice Approach for Liberation*, edited by Anthony J. Nocella II, John Sorenson, Kim Socha, and Atsuko Matsuoka, 51–73. New York: Peter Lang Books.
Diamond, Stanley. 1974. *In Search of the Primitive: A Critique of Civilization*. New Brunswick, NJ: Transaction Books.
Ellul, Jacques. 1964. *The Technological Society*. New York: Vintage Books.
Faun, Feral. 2013. *Feral Revolution*. Asheville, NC: Elephant Editions.

Foster, John Bellamy, Richard York, and Brett Clark. 2011. *Ecological Rift: Capitalism's War on the Earth*. New York: Monthly Review Press.
Freeden, Michael. 2006. "Ideology and Political Theory." *Journal of Political Ideologies* 11(1): 3–22. https://doi.org/10.1080/13569310500395834.
Glendinning, Chellis. 1994. *My Name is Chellis and I'm in Recovery from Western Civilization*. Berkeley, CA: Shambhala Publications.
Illich, Ivan. 1971. *Deschooling Society*. New York: Harper & Row.
Illich, Ivan. 1973. *Tools for Conviviality*. New York: Harper & Row.
Illich, Ivan. 1976. *Medical Nemesis: The Expropriation of Health*. New York: Pantheon Books.
Jensen, Derrick. 2006. *Endgame*. Vol. 1: *The Problem with Civilization*. New York: Seven Stories Press.
Kahn, Richard. 2005. "From Herbert Marcuse to the Earth Liberation Front: Considerations for Revolutionary Ecopedagogy." *Green Theory and Praxis: The Journal of Ecopedagogy* 1(1).
Kropotkin, Peter. 2009. *Mutual Aid: A Factor in Evolution*. London: Freedom Press.
Kropotkin, Peter. 2017. *Fields, Factories, and Workshops: Or Industry Combined with Agriculture*. London: Forgotten Books.
Lee, Richard B. 1979. *The !Kung San: Men, Women and Work in a Foraging Society*. Cambridge: Cambridge University Press.
Lee, Richard, and Richard Daly, eds. 1999. *The Cambridge Encyclopedia of Hunters and Gatherers*. Cambridge: Cambridge University Press.
Lilley, Sasha, David McNally, Eddie Yuen, and James Davis. 2012. *Catastrophism: The Apocalyptic Politics of Collapse and Rebirth*. Oakland, CA: PM Press.
Mumford, Lewis. 1971. *Myth of the Machine: Technics and Human Development*. San Diego, CA: Harvest Books.
Parson, Sean. 2008. "Understanding the Ideology of the ELF." *Green Theory and Praxis: The Journal of Ecopedagogy* 4(2): 50–66.
Perlman, Fredy. 1983. *Against His-Story, Against Leviathan!* Detroit: Black and Red.
Purchase, Graham. 1996. *Anarchism and Ecology*. Portland, OR: Black Rose Books.
Reclus, Elisée. 1896. "The Progress of Mankind." *The Contemporary Review* 70 (December): 761–783. https://books.google.com/books/about/The_Contemporary_Review.html?id=h5PQAAAAMAAJ.
Reclus, Elisée. 2013. *Anarchy, Geography, Modernity: Selected Writings of Elisée Reclus*. Edited and translated by John Clark and Camille Martin. Oakland, CA: PM Press.
Rodgers, Heather. 2013. *Green Gone Wrong: Dispatches from the Front Line of Eco-Capitalism*. London: Verso Press.
Sahlins, Marshall. 1974. *Stone Age Economics*. Piscataway, NJ: Transaction Publishers.
Sale, Kirkpatrick. 1996. *Rebels Against the Future: The Luddites and their War on the Industrial Revolution: Lessons for the Computer Age*. New York: Basic Books.
Sepúlveda, Jesús. 2005. *The Garden of Peculiarities*. Los Angeles: Feral House.
Shantz, Jeff. 2012. *Green Syndicalism: An Alternative Red/Green Vision*. Syracuse, NY: Syracuse University Press.
Smith, Mick. 2007. "Wild-Life: Anarchy, Ecology, and Ethics." *Environmental Politics* 16(3): 470–487.
Taylor, Bron. 2006. "Experimenting with Truth." In *Igniting a Revolution: Voices in Defense of the Earth*, edited by Steven Best and Anthony J. Nocella II, 1–7. San Francisco: AK Press.

Watson, David. 1996. *Against the Megamachine: Essays on Empire and its Enemies*. New York: Autonomedia.
Zehner, Ozzie. 2012. *Green Illusions: The Dirty Secret of Clean Energy and the Future of Environmentalism*. Lincoln, NE: University of Nebraska Press.
Zerzan, John. 1999. *Elements of Refusal*. Columbia, MO: Columbia Alternative Library.
Zerzan, John. 2012. *Future Primitive Revisited*. New York: Feral House Press.

INDEX

15M 101, 104, 108–9
17N (Revolutionary Organization 17 November) 75

ABC No Rio 26
Acid House 207
ACT UP 104, 166
Action Directe Non Violente 76
activists: anarchist 8, 41n1, 138, 140n3, 175; media 208, 211; queer and trans 185; tech 206–08 *see also* hacktivism
adjacent concepts *see* concepts, adjacent
aesthetics *see* art
affinity groups 24, 76, 78, 83n3, 93, 104, 115
Afro-Punk (film) 205
Afropunk (genre) 205
agency, 7–8, 56, 60–72, 88, 168
AK Press 206
Albert, Michael 150, 223–4
Alliance for the Libertarian Left 149
analytic political philosophy 2, 10n1, 188, 198n2, 222
anarcha-feminism 10, 16, 75, 104, 134, 166, 171n2, 181,
anarchism, anti-civilization *see* anarchism, green
anarchism, classical 29, 61, 66–8, 71, 107, 139n1, 158–60, 169–70, 189, 191, 195
anarchism, communist 30, 92, 107, 131, 142, 147–8, 150–2, 153n2

anarchism, eco- 10, 219–24; *see also* anarchism, green
anarchism, green 7, 75, 94, 220, 223; *see also* anarchism, eco-
anarchism, individualist 51–2, 54–6, 134, 147, 149, 151
anarchism, insurrectionary 7, 10, 93–4, 151, 158, 176, 179–80
anarchism, lifestyle 179, *see too* lifestylism
anarchism, philosophical 2, 160
anarchism, post- 10, 28–9, 39–40, 64, 66, 68, 70–1, 160–1, 164, 170, 171n2
anarchism, post-left 36, 151, 224
anarchism, social, 7, 31, 35, 51–6, 136
anarchism 'without adjectives' 147
Anarchist Black Cross (ABC) 24
Anarchist FAQ, An 17
Anarchist People of Color 164–5
anarcho-capitalism *see* propertarianism
anarcho-feminism *see* anarcha-feminism
anarcho-primitivism *see* anarchism, green *and* primitivism
anarcho-syndicalism 10, 17, 79–80, 102, 107, 151, 223
AnarComics 205
Anderson, Benedict 30
animal liberation 81, 171n4, 220
Animal Liberation Front 81, 224
anthropocentrism 15
anti-authoritarianism 8, 18, 31, 33, 101–2, 106–7, 143, 153, 161, 179, 203, 209, 211–3, 215

Index

anti-capitalism 8, 22, 31, 40, 101, 134, 142, 145, 147–8, 167, 181, 192, 203–4, 207, 213–6
anti-civilization 219–220, 223–230, 231n1
anti-colonial 165–6, 169–70 *see too* de-colonial *and* post-colonial
anti-copyright 213, 217
anti-hierarchy 7–8, 15–26, 31, 33, 35, 40, 75, 77, 83, 125, 130, 207; see also non-hierarchy
anti-monarchy 39, 117, 208
anti-political 8, 29–30, 32, 75–7, 81, 83n3, 176
anti-politics 28, 35–6, 39, 75
anti-racism 167, 211–2
anti-semitism 63, 71
anti-statism 4, 8, 15, 31, 45, 130, 148–9, 157, 167, 181, 225
Arab Spring 104
archē 29, 36, 39; *an-* 39, 41n5
art 62, 82, 87, 136, 175, 205–18, 225
artisan, journal de la class ouvrière, L' 118
Atton, Chris 210–1
autogestión see self-management
authoritarian Marxism *see* Marxism, orthodox
authority 2, 15–18, 20–1, 23–6, 50, 74, 77, 89, 106, 115, 121–3, 126, 132, 134–5, 157, 177, 179–80, 182, 189, 227
autonomist Marxism *see* Marxism, autonomist
autonomous media *see* media, autonomous
autonomous zone 76, 95, 216
autonomy 8, 15–7, 22, 24–5, 34, 40, 45, 47, 49, 54–5, 60–1, 70, 77–8, 80, 95, 101–2, 104, 106, 109, 112, 120, 131, 134–6, 139, 168, 170, 189, 191, 193, 204, 209, 213, 226, 230

Bakunin, Michael (Mikhail), 4, 18, 30, 41n6, 45, 61, 63–4, 66–7, 71, 78, 83n2, 89, 91, 106, 11–2, 125–6, 143–4, 149–50, 158–60, 176, 199n19
Barcelona en Comú (Barcelona in Common) 109
Barclay, Harold 225
Bash Back 166
Baudelaire, Charles 81–2
Bellegarrigue, Anselme 89
Ben-Moshe, Liat 167
Berkman, Alexander (Sasha) 53, 89–90, 129, 159, 182
Berlin, Isaiah 47, 49, 54

Berlin Wall 101
Bey, Hakim 36, 160–1
Bhopal disaster 227
Bikini Kill (band) 205
Bikini Kill (zine) 205
Biopolitics 67–8, 70
black bloc 166, 175
Black, Bob 178
Black Lives Matter 101, 182
Black Rose 206
Blackledge, Paul 35–6
Blanc, Louis 118
Boggs, Carl 29–30, 33–4
Bonanno, Alfredo 93
Bonaparte, Louis-Napoléon (Napoleon III) 111
Bookchin, Murray 138, 164, 177–9, 219, 221–23
Bottomore, Tom 2
Bourdieu, Pierre 34, 135
Bourne, Randolph 20
Braverman, Harry 190
Breines, Wini 29–30, 135
Butler, Judith 69, 166

Caballero, Mónica 109
Cantine, Holley 134
capital *see* capitalism
capitalism 16–8, 21–2, 28–9, 31, 33, 35, 38, 52, 67, 70, 75, 81, 89, 93, 111, 116–8, 125, 132, 142–6, 148–51, 158, 161, 164, 168–70, 181, 183–4, 189–94, 197, 203, 208–9, 212–6, 219–23, 225–9
Carson, Kevin 149
Carson, Rachel 221
Catalyst Project 164, 171n3
Catastrophism: The Apocalyptic Politics of Collapse and Rebirth 228
Catholicism 168
Center for a Stateless Society 149
CGT (General Labour Federation) 80, 102
Chomsky, Noam 177–8, 223, 230
Christiania (Copenhagen) 26
Clamshell Alliance 104
Clark, Brett 229
Clark, John P. 35, 37
class conflict 60, 65, 79–80, 87, 107, 231
class struggle *see* class conflict
class war *see* class conflict
Classical Marxism *see* Marxism, orthodox
Clastres, Pierre 225
climate change 9, 169, 219, 226–7 *see also* Ecology, threats to

CNT (*Confederación Nacional del Trabajo*) (National Federation of Labour) 78, 80, 102, 151 *see also Federación Anarquista Ibérica*
Colectivo Situaciones 103
Collins, Patricia Hill 163–4
colonialism 16, 158–9, 167, 169–70, 225
Combahee River Collective 163–4
comics and comic strips 205
Commissiones Obreras (Workers Commissions) (CCOO) 78
communism, anti-state 149, *see also* anarchism, social
communism, libertarian 75, 80, 93, 150–1 *see also* anarchism, social
Communist Party 78
Conatz, Juan 183
concepts, adjacent 1, 5–9, 40, 86–7, 139, 157, 175; contested 4, 86, 222; core 1, 5, 6–9, 15–7, 21, 23, 26, 28–31, 39–40, 44–7, 49, 60, 75, 86–8, 90, 95, 115, 122, 126–7, 130, 133, 139, 157, 161, 164, 167, 169–70, 175, 184, 189, 191, 195, 197, 207, 225, 229; peripheral 1, 5–7, 9, 30–1, 40, 60–1, 86–7, 175, 183–4, 188–9, 203
conceptual approach 1–10, 23, 26, 31–2, 35, 40, 46–7, 49, 56, 76, 86–7, 157–8, 160, 162, 164, 170, 175, 188–9, 191, 222
Confucianism 168
Conquest of Bread 152
Conrad, Ryan 166, 181–2
consensus decision making 35, 101–7, 111, 116, 131, 169, 211
consequentialism 31, *see also* utilitarianism
conservatism 3, 86, 105, 211
Contra la democracia 108–9
cooperation, 22, 33, 52–3, 69, 71n3, 88, 95, 121, 134, 136, 151, 153, 160, 167, 179–80, 190, 199n18, 209, 213, 217
cooperative enterprises, 93, 118, 145, 148, 151, 176, 213
cooperative housing 131, 134, 136
cooperatives, workers *see* cooperative enterprises
core concepts, *see* concepts, core
Cornell, Andrew 103, 135–6, 138, 140n6
Crass 138
Crass, Chris 164
Crenshaw, Kimberlé 162–3
CrimethInc. 22, 206
Critchley, Simon 76

Critical Art Ensemble 207
Crowder, George 29
Crumb, Robert 205
Cuban Revolution 87
cultural production *see* art
Curran, James 212

Daoism 168
de Certeau, Michel 130, 132, 139
de Cleyre, Voltairine 18, 134, 147, 159,
Dead Kennedys 138
de-colonial 159–60, 167, 169–70 *see too* anti-colonial *and* post-colonial
decontesation 1, 3–7, 47, 56, 86–8, 90–2, 222; and macro-decontesation 5–6; and micro-decontesation 5–6
Deep Ecology 178, 224
Déjacque, Joseph 121, 159
Deleuze, Gilles 66–7, 104, 130, 132, 224
democracy, direct 24, 102–3, 105, 108–12
Democracy Now! 206
Democratic Party 111
Devrimci Anars ist Faaliyet (Revolutionary Anarchist Action, DAF) 110
dialectics 38, 76, 178; anti- 66–7; Bakunin 63, 66, 71n2; Hegel 37; Marx 62, 66, 71n2; Proudhon 62–3, 71n2
Diamond, Stanley 225
Dictionary of Marxist Thought 2–3
direct action 8, 25, 32, 35, 74–83, 86, 89–90, 93–5, 101–2, 104, 111–2, 133–5, 166, 179, 183, 207, 211, 215–6
Dirlik, Arif 30
Do It Yourself (DIY) 9, 32, 76, 134, 195, 203–17
Dolgoff, Sam 149
domination 8–9, 16, 22–3, 29, 33, 50, 87, 91–2, 94, 96, 105, 112, 130–2, 135, 137, 139, 144, 157–8, 161–5, 167, 169–70, 171n4, 175, 177, 179, 181, 184, 198n1, 221–3, 226, 229–30
Don't Look Now 40
Dragonowl, Lupus 163

Earth First! 104, 224
Earth Liberation Army 81
Earth Liberation Front 81, 224
ecocentrism 8, 219–31
ecologism 22, 39, 75, 80–1, 93, 169, 178, 191, 193, 195, 197, 219–220
Ecology of Freedom, The 178
Ecology, Deep *see* Deep Ecology
Ecology, threats to 75, 81, 219, 230–1

egalitarianism 20–4, 54, 103, 108, 123, 189, 211, 225
egoism 17, 55, 94, 147,151
Ehrlich, Carol 16, 134
Electronic Disturbance Theater 206
Ellul, Jacques 226
Empire 67–8, 70, 94
encryption 213
Engels, Friedrich 121, 227
epistemology 28, 31–2, 34, 39–40, 160, 169, 208
Epstein, Barbara 135
equality 4, 29, 51, 53, 55, 62, 68–8, 117–9, 121–2, 127, 158–9, 166, 168–9, 181–2, 191, 199n11, 199n13, 211–3, 215, 220; *see also* inequalities, contestation of
essentialism 68–9, 71, 94, 160–1, 164, 166, 171n2
ethics 3, 9, 22, 30–4, 36–40,76, 83, 83n3, 89, 94–5, 101, 130–1, 133, 136–9, 143, 159–61, 167, 179, 184, 189–91, 193–5, 198n4; *see also* utilitarianism *and* virtues
exploitation 7, 17, 67–70, 79, 92, 118–9, 121, 142, 144–6, 153n3, 158, 171n4, 191, 213, 221 *see also* capitalism
expropriation 78, 80, 90, 144, 149

fanzines *see* zines
fascism 31, 40, 75, 86, 92, 122, 122, 230
fashion, DiY 210, 214–5
Faun, Feral 226
Federación Anarquista Ibérica (FAI) 112 *see also* CNT
Federici, Silvia 168
feminism 10, 68, 86, 104, 107,136, 159,162–7 169–70, 181. 199n21; 212; anarcha- *see* anarcha-feminism; Black, 158, 160–6, 170; liberal 181, proto- 133, radical 10, 181
Fenton, Natalie 212
Flood, Andrew 111
Fly 205
Food Not Bombs 24, 104, 214
Fordism 190; post- 21, 190
Foster, John Bellamy 229
Foucault, Michael 34, 67, 130–2, 166
Fourier, Charles 118
Fowler, R.B. 50
Franco, Francisco 80
Frank, Thomas 138
Freeden, Michael 1–5, 7–10, 30–1, 44–6, 51, 60, 63, 112, 115, 157–8, 161, 170, 175, 188–9, 219, 222, 224

Freedman, Des 212
freedom 4–6, 8,15, 18, 22, 36, 44–57, 60–1, 65, 70, 75, 77–8, 83n2, 86, 109–10, 116–7, 119–23, 125–7, 129–30, 133, 136, 147, 151–2, 157–60, 162–7, 169–70, 177, 181, 195, 199n19, 226–7, 230; positive (freedom to) 47–9, 52, 54–5; negative (freedom from) 47–52, 54–5
French Revolution 87, 106, 116–8, 123
Fry, Douglas 20

Gandhi, Mahatma 139
Ganemos Madrid (Let's win Madrid) 109
GARI (International Revolutionary Action Groups) 78–9
Garrison, Henry Lloyd 159
Gautney, Heather 31, 33
Gezi Park 101, 104, 110
Ghiraldo, Alberto 82
Glendinning, Chellis 224
Global Justice Movement 101, 104, 168, 170
Godwin, William 45
Goldman, Emma 4, 18, 29–30, 32, 38–9, 53, 71, 129–30, 133, 138–9, 140n4, 147, 151, 159, 166, 194, 198n3
Gordon, Uri 22–3, 28, 31, 40n1, 159, 168
Gorz, André 183
gradualism 149, 180, 184
Graeber, David 24, 33, 106–7, 132, 191
GRAPO (*Grupos de Resistencia Antifascista Primero de Octubre*) 75
green syndicalism *see* syndicalism, green
Grubačić, Andrej 28, 33
Grupos Anarquistas Coordinados (Coordinated Anarchist Groups) 108–9
Guattari, Félix 67, 104, 130, 132, 224
guerrilla gardening 207, 216
Guillaume, James 29–30, 149

hacktivism 206, 212
Hahnel, Robin 150, 183
Hammond, John 29
Hardt, Michael 60, 64, 66–71
Harman, Chris 35
Harper, Clifford 205
Hawthorne, Nate 183
Heckert, Jamie 140n4, 176
Hegel, G.W.F. 37, 41n4, 66, 82–3n2
heterosexism 16, 181–2
Hill, Gord 205
Hodgson, Torrance 95

Holloway, John 179
Holtzman, Ben 204, 209, 211, 213, 217
hooks, bell 164
horizontalism 7–8, 23, 26, 31, 40, 75, 101–12, 123, 134, 209–13, 215–6
Horizontalism: Voices of Power in Argentina 103
Hughes, Craig 204, 209, 211, 213, 217

identity 1, 4, 9, 32, 34, 46, 60, 89, 104, 139n2, 140n3, 152, 162–63, 166, 169, 171n2, 175–6, 179–80, 184, 209–10
identities, queer and trans, 166, 207
Idle No More 169
Iglesias, Pablo 110
Illich, Ivan 227
Independent Media Centers (IMCs) 208
Indigeneity 11, 165, 167–70, 212, 225, 231n2
Individualidades Tendiendo a lo Salvaje (ITS) 224, 227
individualism 4, 6, 17, 50, 52–3, 94, 131, 147–9, 167, 210–1 *see also* anarchism, individualist
Industrial Workers of the World (IWW) 32, 134, 221
Indymedia 22, 206–7, 212
inequalities, contestation of 22, 23, 77, 151, 156, 191–4, 212
Infoshop and infoshops 22, 175, 179, 207
Institute for Applied Autonomy 207
insurrection 90, 94, 133–4, 150, 158, 176, 179–80 *see also* anarchism, insurrectionary
International Workingmen's Association (First international) 63, 81, 151, 179
intersectionality 4, 9, 23, 62, 88, 94, 169–171, 181, 212
Invisible Committee, The 76, 93
Iranian revolution 87
Irish Workers Solidarity Movement 111

Jacobins 106, 117–8, 120; neo- 118
jazz music 82, 204
Jenkins, Henry 210
Jensen, Derrick 224
Jeppesen, Sandra 167, 199n21
Jordan, John 208, 215
Journal of Political ideologies 7
journalism 208; citizen 212; DiY 208, 210
Juris, Jeffrey 21–2

Keller, Helen 159
Kelly, Harry 135–6

Keywords 3
Klein, Naomi 138
Knowles, Dudley 2
Kozolanka, Kirsten 215
Kropotkin, Peter (Pyotr) 30, 65–6, 68, 71, 72n3, 78, 82, 88–91, 123, 125–6, 142–3, 151–2, 158–60, 191–4, 198n3, n8–n10, 199n19, 219–20, 222
Kukathas, Chandran 47

labor 7, 25, 52, 55, 61–2, 64, 68–9, 71, 88, 116–9, 125–6, 148, 188, 190–3, 198n1, 199n16, n19, n20; 134, 142–4, 148–9, 158, 168, 191–2, 194, 199n12, 199n17, 217, 220, 222–3, 229 , abstract 37; affective 69; disputes, 180; division of 37, 191–6, 199n20, 222, 225–7; immaterial 123, organization 116, 125, 131
Laclau, Ernesto 66, 68
Lakey, George 105
Lamb, Dave 37
Landauer, Gustav 19–21, 23, 81–2, 95, 176, 180
Lawson, James 104
Lee, Richard 225
Lenin, Vladimir Illich 35, 64–6, 71
Leninism *see* Marxism, orthodox
liberalism 3, 10n2, 31, 40, 44–51, 53, 56, 66, 105, 108, 116–7, 121, 126, 165–6, 189, 222; classical, 50–1, 54, 116–7, 177, 181; neo- 40, 67, 70, 101, 138, 166–7, 178, 183, 189, 191, 193, 213, 216
libertarian, left- 8, 28, 37, 110, 121, 123, 127, 136, 225; Marxism 10, 31 *see too* anarchism, social; right *see* propertarianism; socialism 150, 177–8 *see also* anarchism, social and libertarian, left-
liberty *see* freedom
lifestyle 131, 137–9, 139n3, 179, 206–7, 215
lifestylism 137–8
Linebaugh, Peter 30
Locke, John 116–7, 119
Luddite 227 *see also* neo-Luddite
lumpenproletariat 63–4, 67, 71
Luxemburg, Rosa 122

MacIntyre, Alasdair 34, 37
macropolitics 70, 130, 135–7
Mad Max 228
Maeckelbergh, Marianne 28, 32–4
Magón, Ricardo Flores 142, 152
Magonistas 101

Mahkno, Nestor 93, 112
Malatesta, Errico 53, 89, 92–3, 112, 115, 126, 146–7, 176–7,180
Mansplaining 129
Marcuse, Herbert 28, 36–8,
market forces *see* capitalism
marriage, criticism of 4, 121, 126, 166
marriage equality 181–2
Marshall, Peter 78
Marx, Karl 3, 41n4, 61–4, 71n2, 142
Marxism 2–3, 10 60–1, 63, 65–6, 68, 70, 86, 106, 151, 158, 167, 170, 189, 220, 222–3, 231n2; autonomist 30, 38, 60, 64; orthodox 28–31, 35, 36, 63–4, 67–8, 71, 75, 94–5, 106; libertarian *see* libertarian Marxism; post- *see* post-Marxism,
Marxist-Leninism *see* Marxism, orthodox
May, Todd 23, 66–9, 132, 160–1
Mazepa, Patricia 215
McKay, George 204
McKay, Iain 145, 153n2
McLaughlin, Paul 2
Media, autonomous 205–6, 208, 210–1
Medical Nemesis 227
Meltzer, Albert 22
Michel, Louise 159
micropolitics 6, 70, 94, 129–39, 184
MIL-GAC (Iberian Liberation movement – Autonomous Combat Group) 78
militarism 21, 167, 230
Milberry, Kate 212–3
Milstein, Cindy 23, 133, 136
minimum income, guaranteed 195–7
minimum wage 79, 180
Molyneux, John 35
morphological approach; *see* conceptual approach
Morton, James F. 159
Mother Jones 159
Mouffe, Chantal 66, 68
Movement for a New Society (MNS) 104–5
Mueller, Tadzio 94
Mühsam, Erich 157–8
Muir, John, 220
Mullett, Lynne 182–3
multitude 67–9, 71, 124
Mumford, Lewis 224–6
music 82, 204–5, 217, 225
mutual aid 24, 53, 68, 77, 79, 87, 93, 95, 103, 112, 131, 134, 160, 164, 167, 183–4, 209–10, 213
mutualism 120, 148–9, 153n5, 198n8 223

Napoleon III *see* Bonaparte, Louis-Napoléon
Negri, Antonio 60, 64, 66–71
neoliberalism *see* liberalism, neo-
neo-Luddite 224 *see also* Luddite
New Right 22 *see also* propertarianism
Newman, Saul 36, 39–40, 66–9, 160
nihilism 147
Nocella, Anthony 167
non-hierarchy 24–5, 71, 95, 102, 104–8, 111–2, 134, 143, 148, 189, 191, 195
non-violence 64–5, 76–7, 104
Nôson Seinan Sha 30
Novatore, Renzo 147
Nuit Debout 104

Occupy 33, 101, 104, 108, 110; the Party 110–1; Wall Street, 105, 107, 110, 112, 180, 183
October Revolution *see* Russian Revolution
Olson, Joel 25, 76, 95
Ontology 34, 36, 39–40, 44, 47, 49, 66
organization 7–9, 15–6, 18, 20–5, 28–36, 40, 51, 56, 75, 78–80, 82, 88, 90–3, 95, 101–12, 115–27, 130, 133, 137, 143, 146, 148, 150–1, 164, 166, 169, 171n3, 175, 178, 180–1, 189–97, 199n16, 203–4, 207–8, 210–4, 216, 221–3, 228 *see also* labour unions *and* syndicalism
Organization for a Free Society 150
Organisational Platform of the Libertarian Communists 93 *see also* Platformists
Ostergaard, Geoffrey 2–3
Our Synthetic Environment 221
Outrage! 166
Oxford Handbook of Political Ideologies 7

pacifism *see* non-violence
Palestinians, solidarity with 167–8
Paris Commune 91, 123
Parsons, Lucy 158–9
party, political anti-; 111; political democratic 101, 106, 110–1; political revolutionary 36–7, 106; workers' 111
patriarchy 16, 69, 75, 94, 112, 121, 125, 132, 137, 158, 164–7, 169–70; heteropatriarchy, 170, 181
Peacemakers 104
performativity 69
Perlman, Fredy 226–7, 231n1
permeability, morphological 1–2, 10, 158, 161, 166, 169–70

Phenomenology of Spirit 37
philosophy 2, 38, 51, 60–2, 74, 86, 131, 133, 139; analytic 2, 188, 198n2; anarchist, 51, 60, 71n2, 131, 133, 137, 139, 140n3, 189, 195; Eastern 167; eco- 223; German 62, 83n2; Hegelian 83n2; Marxist 61; moral *see* ethics; political 2, 131, 137, 189, 195, 198n2; post-anarchist 132; propertarian 22; Western 158
philosophical anarchism *see* anarchism, philosophical
Philosophy of Poverty, The 61
Pilar Basilica bombing 109
Pink Bloc 166
Platformists 93, 151
PM Press 206
Podemos (We can) 109–110
poetry 81–2, 83n5
polyamory 131
Portwood-Stacer, Laura 137, 209
postanarchism *see* anarchism, post-
post-colonialism 68–9, 159 *see too* anti-colonial; colonial; and de-colonial
post-Fordism 21, 190
post-Marxism 66–8, 71
Post-Scarcity Anarchism 178
post-structuralism 66, 69–70. 88, 94, 132, 158, 160–1, 166, 171n2
Pouget, Émile 35, 76
Poverty of Philosophy, The 61
practices, social 8, 10, 21, 29, 33–6, 38–40, 76, 80, 102–6, 111–2, 115, 130–3, 135–9, 143, 161, 175–6, 179–81, 189, 191, 195, 204, 210–2, 213, 215–6 and cultural, 203–4, 208–12, 215–6
praxis 16, 25, 75–6, 83n3, 94, 133–4, 158, 169–70,
prefiguration 7–8, 26, 28–41, 75–6, 86, 89–90, 93–4, 103, 106, 130–1, 133–5, 139, 167, 179, 197, 203, 207, 211–3, 215–6
primitivism 220, 223–5, 230
priority, morphological, 1–2, 7, 31, 40, 158, 165, 169–70, 210
prison abolition 20, 182–3
prisoner support 24, 182–3
proletariat *see* working class
propaganda of the deed 25, 76, 82, 135, 138, 179 *see also* direct action *and* terrorism
propertarianism 17, 22, 45, 144

property 62, 81, 117–21, 127, 143–4, 146, 148–50, 192; private 18, 52, 116, 119, 127n2, 144, 146, 151, 198n8–9
proportionality, morphological 1–2, 5–7, 49, 51
Protestant work ethic 189–90, 193
Proudhon, Pierre-Joseph 29, 46, 61–3, 67, 71, 91, 106, 111, 118–21, 123–6, 145, 148–9, 153n3, 158, 176, 191, 198n3, n7–8, n11, 199n12–4
proximity, morphological, 1–3, 31, 40, 65, 102, 158, 161, 166, 169–70
publishers, anarchist 22, 83n4,206, 211, 217
Punk (zine) 205
punk 138, 204–5, 207–11, 213–4, 216; *see also* Afropunk, Crass, Dead Kennedys, Queercore, Riot Grrrl *and* Sex Pistols
Purchase, Graham 220

Quakers 104, 169
queer; analysis and theory 88, 94, 158, 160–1, 165–70, 171n2, 181; communities 167; futures 182; rights *see* rights, LGBTQ+
Queercore 205

racism 16, 63, 75, 125, 159, 161, 164, 167, 169, 181–2, 227
Rancière, Jacques 36, 39
Read, Herbert 82
Reaktion in Deutschland: Ein Fragment von Einen Franzosen, Der 78
Reckwitz, Andreas 34
Red Army Faction 75
Red Emma's Bookstore Coffeehouse 26
Red Power 169
reform 9, 38, 86, 88–90, 107–11, 117, 149, 175–84
Reid, Jamie 208
revolution 8–9, 21, 28, 30, 33, 35–9, 50, 56, 61, 63–7, 75–6, 78–82, 86–96, 105, 111, 120, 129–30, 132, 134–5, 138, 147, 149–52, 158, 160, 175–84, 209, 228; capitalist, 220; industrial 118, 189, 220
Revolution grrrl style now! 205
rhizomes 68, 104
rights 52, 65, 79, 117, 119, 123, 146, 159, 181; animal 81, 221 *see also* animal liberation; immigrant, 167; civil 104; economic 119; immigrant 212; individual 181, 210; LGBTQ+ 166, 181 212; political 119; workers 171n3

Rimbaud, Arthur 81
Riot Grrrl 205, 207
Rogue, Jen 162
Rossinow, Doug 135
Rousseau, Jean-Jacques 62, 71n1, 116–7, 119–20, 125–26
Ruiz, Pollyanna 211
Russian Revolution 29, 71n3, 87, 92

Sahlins, Marshall 225
Saint-Simon, Claude Henri de 118
Sale, Kirkpatrick 224
Sanders, Bernie 110
Schleuning, Neala 194, 199n18
SchNews 206, 208
Scott, James C. 168
self-consciousness 54, 104, 107
self-determination *see* autonomy
self-management, workers 102–3, 109, 121, 125, 127, 145, 150, 177, 221, 223
  see also organisation, workers
Sepúlveda, Jesús 225, 231n2
Sex Pistols 208–9
sexuality 69–70, 131, 159, 162–3, 166–7, 170, 181, 212, 224
Shantz, Jeff 221–3
Sheehan, Seán 20
Silent Spring 221
Simmons, A. John 2
Sitrin, Marina 103
Skinner, David 215
Skinner, Quentin 60
Sniffin' Glue 205
Social Anarchism or Lifestyle Anarchism: An Unbridgeable Chasm 138
Social Ecology 164, 171n4, 178, 221
social movements 93, 95, 101, 103, 135–6, 169, 184, 197, 199n21, 228; new 24, 210
socialism, 33, 36 52, 66, 90–1, 105–6, 111, 116, 147, 149, 175, 178, 183, 192, 223; libertarian *see* libertarian socialism; market 145, 148; state 87–8; utopian 118
Solar, Francisco Javier 109
solidarity 33, 36–7, 40, 53, 55, 95, 103, 134, 137, 151, 158–62, 165, 167, 170, 199n19,
Spanish Civil War 26, 83n4, 151
Spannos, Chris 150
Spiegelman, Art 205
Springer, Simon 94
Starhawk 23, 25

state, the 2, 8, 19–23, 25, 30–1, 33, 35–6, 45, 50, 56, 61–2, 70, 74, 78–9, 82, 87–9, 91–3, 106, 116–7. 119–23, 130, 133, 137, 142–6, 151, 157–61, 163, 167–9, 177–83, 193, 196–7, 198n8, 203, 206, 208, 213–5, 220, 225–6, 230
statelessness 94, 168
State and Employers' Association 79
Stirner, Max 20, 134, 147, 158
streaming, anarchist 206
struggle; class *see* class conflict; queer and trans, 166
Students for a Democratic Society (SDS) 104
Student Nonviolent Coordinating Committee (SNCC) 104
Sturgeon, Nöel 32
subMedia TV 206
surveillance 20–1, 213
sustainability 15, 22, 25–6, 39, 134, 167, 197, 226, 230; ecological, 21, 191, 195, 220, 227–30
syndicalism 17, 35, 76, 93, 115, 151, 221; anarcho- *see* anarcho-syndicalism; green, 221, 223

Taylor, Bron 224
Taylor, Verta 136
Taylorism 190
Tech activism, see activism, tech
technology 21, 34, 36–8, 94, 104, 117, 134, 192–4, 206, 212, 220, 224–8, 230; anti- 81, 178, 226; communication 21, 206; folk 226; hyper- 93; information 206
teleology 39–40, 54, 56, 66, 160
terrorism, 22, 75, 106, 109, 175 *see also* violence, terrorist
Thoreau, Henry David 140n6, 219, 220
Thousand Plateaus, A 132
Tiqqun 76–7, 94
Tobocman, Seth 205
Tolstoy, Leo (Lev) 64–5, 71, 76, 140n6, 192–5, 199n16, 199n20
traditional Marxism *see* Marxism, orthodox
transphobia 112
Translating Anarchy: The Anarchism of Occupy Wall Street 107
Triggs 208, 210
Tucker, Benjamin 51, 149

Umanità Nova 92
Undercurrent 206

Unkl347 210
Unruly Equality: U. S. Anarchism in the 20th Century 103
utilitarianism 181, 229 *see also* consequentialism
utopianism 35, 37, 152, 168, 209, 213; anti- 93
Uzelman, Scott 210

van der Walt, Lucien, 30, 57n3
van Meter, Kevin 204, 209, 211, 213, 217
veganism 133, 171n4, 175
video, anarchist 206
violence 19, 52, 63–4, 80, 87, 90–1, 136, 140n5, 171n4, 176, 183, 220, 223; biopolitical, 132; ecological, 223; ethical, 221; liberatory, 38–9, 65, 76–8, 91; state,15, 21, 78, 87, 91, 144, 146, 168, 220; structural 26, 132; terrorist, 78–9
virtues 34, 40, 193–4, 198n2, 198n16
Volcano, Abbey 162

Walter, Nicholas 24
Ward, Colin 19, 95
Warren, Josiah 149
Watson, David 226–7
Weber, Max 146, 189
"What is to be Done?" (Tolstoy) 65
What is to be Done? (Lenin) 65
What is Property? 118
Weathermen, The 76

White, Stuart 184
Wilbur, Shawn P. 149, 153n3
Williams, Raymond 3, 10n2
Withers, A.J. 167
Wolff, Robert P. 2
Woodcock, George 115, 126
work 9, 53, 62, 116, 118, 122, 124–5, 145, 148–51, 188–98, 205, 213, 221, 227
workerism 223
workers *see* working class
workers' councils 79–80, 121, 221 *see also* self-management, workers
workers' organisation, 118, 221; see also cooperative enterprises 148
workers' parties *see* party, workers'
working class 26, 31, 33, 36, 61–5, 67–71, 78–80, 83, 90–1, 93, 102, 106, 111, 116, 118–9, 121–2, 130, 136, 144–6, 148, 150–2, 158, 171n3, 177, 179, 198n1 & n3, 199n13, 213–4, 220–2, 229
workplace 32, 80, 101, 103, 117–9, 121–2, 124, 127, 137, 144–6, 221, 223
World War 3 Illustrated 205

Yates, Luke 28, 31, 33–4
York, Richard 229

Zapatistas 101–2, 168, 206
Zerzan, John 177, 224–7, 229
zines 205, 207, 209, 213, 215
Zomia, nomadic peoples of 168